The Untold Story of the Talking Book

Matthew Rubery

The Untold Story
of the Talking Book

 Harvard University Press

Cambridge, Massachusetts, and London, England

2016

First printing

Frontispiece: A group listening to a recording of *Reader's Digest*, ca. 1940. Photo © by the estate of Wendell S. MacRae. Reproduced by permission of the estate and the Witkin Gallery, New York, NY.

Epigraph: Oscar Wilde, "The Critic as Artist," in *Criticism: Historical Criticism, Inventions, the Soul of Man*, ed. Josephine M. Guy, *The Complete Works of Oscar Wilde* (Oxford: Oxford University Press, 2007), 4:138.

Library of Congress Cataloging-in-Publication Data

Names: Rubery, Matthew, author.
Title: The untold story of the talking book / Matthew Rubery.
Description: Cambridge, Massachusetts : Harvard University Press, 2016. |
    Includes bibliographical references and index.
Identifiers: LCCN 2016005605 | ISBN 9780674545441 (cloth)
Subjects: LCSH: Audiobooks—History. | Literature and technology—History. |
    Talking books—History.
Classification: LCC Z286.A83 R83 2016 | DDC 002.09—dc23
    LC record available at http://lccn.loc.gov/2016005605

Yes: writing has done much to harm writers.
We must return to the voice.

—Oscar Wilde, "The Critic as Artist"

Contents

The Untold Story of the Talking Book

Introduction

WHAT IS THE HISTORY OF AUDIOBOOKS?

What difference does it make whether we read a book or listen to it? *The Untold Story of the Talking Book* sets out to resolve this question by tracing the history of recorded books since Thomas Edison's invention of the phonograph in 1877. Edison anticipated using sound-recording technology to make books, even if it would take several decades before his prediction came true. A fledgling trade in discs holding a few minutes of verse eventually grew into a billion-dollar industry accounting for a substantial percentage of annual book sales today.[1] Audiobooks have long been publishers' main source of non-print income; as late as 2010, they still generated more revenue than electronic books.[2] And yet, despite the audiobook's prominence (it stands out as one of the only types of reading to have grown in popularity), we still lack a vocabulary for discussing its relationship to conventional books, not to mention its uncertain standing in the world of letters.[3] Consider the following pages an intervention into awkward conversations about recorded books.

This project began when a friend mentioned reading a book, then suddenly backtracked to confess that he had not actually *read* the book—he had *listened* to it. Listening to books is one of the few forms of reading for which people apologize. His apology differed so much from the usual way of discussing books as a personal achievement and sign of distinction that I felt compelled to look into the roots of this shame. My investigation led me to a sector of the publishing world that I had hardly noticed despite a lifelong interest in books. Soon I discovered that audiobooks have a longer history than is generally thought, one extending all the way back to Edison's recitation of "Mary Had a Little Lamb" on a sheet of tinfoil. Hence, my account follows the tradition from phonographic books made on wax cylinders to talking

1

books made for blinded soldiers returning from the First World War and, much later, the commercial audiobooks heard on car stereos and headphones today.

Before going any further, let me explain exactly what is meant by a talking book. Booksellers often use the phrases "talking book" and "audiobook" interchangeably to describe any narrative recorded onto a record, cassette tape, compact disc, MP3 digital file, or other audio format. My book's title uses the term in this expansive way to cover all recorded books. Historically, though, no single term has been available to describe all of the different types of spoken word recordings. People talked about "phonographic books" for nearly fifty years after Edison's invention. Government agencies and charities spoke of "talking books" when describing the shellac and vinylite records made in the 1930s for people who were blind. The Caedmon label referred to "spoken word records" in the 1950s. Two audio publishers of the 1970s, Books on Tape and Recorded Books, protested against the generic use of their names to describe all taped books. (You can still find a "books on tape" shelf at many bookstores even though it will be full of compact discs.)

There was no consensus over the phrase "audiobook" until the early 1990s, when publishers sought to eliminate confusion over the many different terms used by the industry. It was not until 1994 that the Audio Publishers Association confirmed "audio book" (note the space) as the industry standard.[4] Using the phrase for spoken word recordings made before that date is anachronistic. Even so, it's the most useful one we've got. As much as my chronicle tries to respect an era's vocabulary, it will occasionally use the term "audiobook" more broadly for the sake of clarity and coherence.

Of course, the idea of a talking book captured the popular imagination long before the technology came along to record the human voice. The literary conceit in which a physical book speaks directly to readers can be found in Greek, Roman, and Anglo-Saxon literature.[5] This rhetorical stratagem preserved the illusion of oral speech within a written text; in fact, the concept of a book with a voice would have made little sense in an oral culture in which all narratives were spoken. The conceit persisted after the transition from manuscript to print culture. Cyrano de Bergerac fantasized about mechanical talking books worn dangling from one's ears, and Washington Irving portrayed a talking book—a yawning one, no less—complaining about its long confinement in Westminster Abbey.[6] The trope has often been applied in cases in which illiterate African Americans heard the Bible speak to them.[7] In one slave memoir from 1775, James Albert Ukawsaw Gronniosaw recalls pressing his ear against a prayer book; as Henry Louis Gates, Jr., points out, the encounter depicts an "un-Talking Book" familiar to slaves excluded from the privileges of literacy enjoyed by free men and women.[8]

We should note discrepancies even within this elastic category. At one end of the spectrum, talking books made for blind people stick as closely as possible to the printed source, reading verbatim everything from acknowledgments to appendices, sometimes even preserving the original's typos; at the spectrum's other end we find commercial audiobooks featuring sound effects, full casts, and, in some cases, ruthless cuts to the narrative. We are hardly talking about equivalent items when comparing Linda Stephens's forty-nine-hour recording of *Gone with the Wind* with that same title's rendition on *10 Classics in 10 Minutes* by a narrator known as "Mighty Mouth."[9]

Nor is there a clear line separating audiobooks from closely related formats such as radio drama.[10] When the *Guardian* newspaper published a list of the best audiobooks, the overall vote winner was not, strictly speaking, an audiobook at all; *The Hitchhiker's Guide to the Galaxy* had originated as a BBC radio series before being adapted into a novel (and not the other way around).[11] I am interested in the audiobook's permutations, not least the postmodern phenomenon of "born-audio" books with no print original that tie people in knots figuring out what to call them: Are they still *books?* Unless otherwise noted, however, the term "audiobook" will be used here to mean a single speaker's word-for-word recording of a book originally published in print. The questions taken up by my study can best be answered by comparing books to their closest kin rather than to distant cousins that may have more in common with audiovisual adaptations.

The audiobook's identity has always been defined in relation to print. My account takes us back to the origins of sound-recording technology in order to understand how recorded books have evolved in relation to printed ones. It seeks to establish a precise affiliation between the two media. This study's main contention is that the talking book developed both as a way of reproducing the printed book and as a way of overcoming its limitations. Publishers have responded to this tension either by adhering as closely as possible to the printed book despite adapting it for a different medium or, conversely, by capitalizing on the affordances of sound recording (voices, music, sound effects) to do things that printed books are unable to do. The emphasis can be on "talking" or "book." Surveying over a century of spoken word recordings reveals the same dynamic to be at work: emulation of the printed book versus exploitation of sound recording. These twin impulses help to explain why we find it so difficult to decide whether audiobooks should be considered books or something else altogether.

Of course, not everyone agrees that audiobooks, the name notwithstanding, should be treated as books.[12] My historicist approach takes its cues from audio publishers who nearly always conceive of themselves in relation to conventional books. Despite the audiobook's subliterary reputation, most audio publishers consider themselves to be champions of the book who have found a way to help people read even more of them. In their eyes, they make books accessible to people with busy schedules, long commutes, and print disabilities who would not otherwise be able to read them. There is no doubt in their minds that audiobooks are first and foremost books, and their editing decisions often reflect this philosophy. Publishers seeking to untether audiobooks from other books are a recent development. Only in the last few years have publishers begun to experiment in earnest with alternative forms of storytelling that treat the audiobook as an independent art form in its own right or as one that no longer needs a printed source to justify its existence.

The story of the talking book has yet to be told. Various attempts to do so can best be described as stories of the talking book machine, not the book itself. Such accounts overwhelmingly privilege the medium's technological, legislative, and economic backgrounds over its cultivation of the spoken word. As valuable as these studies may be to our understanding of the history of recorded sound, I came away from them wanting to know more about how spoken word recordings forged a distinctive identity. The questions in which I was interested as both a book historian and a reader of books were left unanswered or never raised in the first place.

As is the case with many people, my initial decision to listen to audiobooks was a practical one. I am an avid reader who could not find enough hours in the day to read everything I wanted, and I wished to make the most of time squandered on chores, commuting, and keeping fit. Audiobooks are ideal companions when one's hands are occupied but not one's mind. The timing was fortunate since audiobooks were becoming increasingly easy to obtain by downloading digital files—no more flipping 119 records to hear *War and Peace*. At first I enjoyed the sheer pleasure of storytelling, reminiscent of children being read aloud to by their parents. It was much later that I began to formulate the aesthetic concerns animating this study: What exactly is the relationship between spoken and printed texts? How does the experience of listening to books compare to that of reading them? What influence does a book's narrator have over its reception? What methods of close listening are appropriate to such narratives? What new formal possibilities are opened up by sound technology?

My intention at the outset of this project was to listen to as many literary recordings as possible, starting with Edison's inaugural nursery rhyme. While I have logged countless hours doing just that, my interests moved from textual analysis of spoken word recordings to understanding their cultural contexts—who recorded them, how they related to the source, and what impact they had on audiences. Charting the audiobook's reception history turned out to be especially challenging since its readers were even less likely than those of other books to leave behind traces; at least we occasionally find notes scribbled in a page's margins. No such luck with records. The lesson: new media themselves are not always the best guides to their own history. Consequently, my history of audiobooks has been pieced together primarily from good old-fashioned print media (correspondence, manuals, memoirs, newspapers, album sleeves, and other material mined from archives and private collections). The book's notes will serve as a map for anyone interested in navigating for themselves the extensive resources available on the history of spoken word recordings, especially bibliophiles venturing beyond the printed page for the first time.

A number of recordings cited by this study are complex works of art worthy of sustained critical attention in their own right. Nothing would give me greater pleasure than writing an entire chapter on Derek Jacobi's *Iliad*. However, the goal here is to piece together the broader story encompassing various phases of the recorded book's development—from phonographic books to talking books, audiobooks, and whatever comes next. Doing so should make it easier for others to tell the captivating stories behind the individual titles mentioned here (as scholars have already been doing in their respective fields and time periods). These episodes can then be viewed as part of a coherent tradition of spoken word recordings instead of exceptional or idiosyncratic events. Such a framework should lead to common ground between episodes of sound recording that are usually discussed in isolation; for example, there is no reason that the impassioned debates over how to read a talking book that took place among blind people in the 1930s should be cordoned off from a nearly identical set of debates over the audiobook's legitimacy in the 1990s.

The audiobook industry needs to know its own history in order to avoid repeating it. As we will see, nearly every audio publisher seems to think that they were the first to come up with an idea that's as old as the tinfoil phonograph.

Audiobooks are both a new form of storytelling and a very old one. Fans often justify their listening habit by pointing out that stories were recited in ancient times. The Greeks listened to heroic tales sung by bards; Homer is the best-known author to have been heard instead of read.[13] From this perspective, sound technology returns us to literature's roots, letting us once again hear tales read out loud. If only it were so simple. There are crucial differences between listening to a performer in Homer's time and listening to Derek Jacobi on earbuds in the twenty-first century.

Historians have written extensively about the centuries-long transition from oral to print culture. "A goose quill put an end to talk," as Marshall McLuhan summed it up.[14] Writing profoundly influenced how people read. In the fourth century, Saint Augustine memorably recalled his astonishment upon finding his teacher Saint Ambrose reading silently to himself.[15] This episode marks a symbolic turning point from the noisy, communal performances of antiquity toward the silent, solitary behavior associated with reading today.[16] From the mid-fifteenth century, the printing press accelerated this transition by making books ever more accessible.[17] McLuhan credited its invention with ushering in a visual culture that had a profound impact on human consciousness, including a split between eye and ear.[18] It is hardly surprising that McLuhan, a former English professor as well as the son of an elocutionist, would discern the implications of this shift. If the break between orality and print was not nearly as decisive as McLuhan suggests, it is nevertheless true that reading aloud plays a far less prominent role in modern times than in ancient ones.

Consider its disappearance from universities. Oratory pervaded the curriculum for much of the nineteenth century, when eloquence in speaking was thought to be a prerequisite for civic life. As Gerald Graff notes, a number of English professors believed reading aloud to be essential to the appreciation of literature; the most charismatic ones regularly read aloud from the Bible, Shakespeare, and other works of literature.[19] We should recall that it was a member of Harvard's faculty who established the first series of recorded poetry, beginning with T. S. Eliot, and well into the twentieth century, reading aloud continued to play a role in the pedagogy of I. A. Richards and F. R. Leavis, two figures associated with the techniques of close reading often blamed for recitation's demise.[20]

Elocution went out of fashion only to be replaced by "expressive reading," "interpretive reading," or "oral reading," which favored a less dramatic, artificial style and permitted orators to read from the page instead of from memory. Combining recitation with literary appreciation, oral interpretation—as elocution's successor came to be known in the curriculum—straddled the border between English and drama departments, where it unsuccessfully fended off suspicions that "reading aloud is an inferior kind of silent reading."[21] Reading aloud is but a quaint memory now that hushed, solitary reading is the default in today's classrooms.[22]

Nevertheless, converging media have done away with misleading narratives of historical supersession. The telephone, phonograph, radio, cinema, television, and other modern communications technologies to a large extent have displaced print's privileged spot in our lives and turned society back into an acoustic or at least audiovisual one. We are no longer dealing with a world untouched by print, of course, but rather with what Walter Ong called the "secondary orality" of a culture saturated with media of all kinds—in this case, audiobooks instead of rhapsodes.[23] Notably, audiobooks replicate manuscripts, not impromptu performances marked by declamatory styles and mnemonic formulae. They rely on scripts whose typography and language— even when dictated—have been designed for the page, not the studio.[24] This is hardly Homer. The audiobook's remediation of the printed book into an audible format makes it a distinctly modern form of entertainment despite the affinities with traditional storytelling. Today, no one knows what to do with a book that speaks for itself.

We are not even sure what to call this voice. The terms "reader" and "narrator" generate needless confusion when used to describe a book's speaker. In the former case, "reader" might refer to someone telling the tale out loud, scanning the page in silence, or even listening to the story; in the latter case, "narrator" could mean a fictional character or a real person. Other terms such as "speaker" and "performer" have their own baggage. "Speaker" can refer to figures inside or outside the narrative, and "performer" gestures toward an entertainment industry that many publishers are anxious to avoid. As we will see, voice actors are sharply divided when it comes to reading in a theatrical way or in an understated manner that distances them from radio.

The speaker's voice is the audiobook's greatest virtue and liability. All books strive for a distinctive voice in a metaphorical sense—David Foster Wallace called it the "brain voice."[25] But audiobooks have actual voices. No matter whether authors, actors, amateurs, or synthetic voices are speaking, the result is the same: someone other than the book's audience determines how it sounds. This is no trivial detail. Vocalizing or giving voice to a text may be essential to reading literature.[26] This mental effort supposedly sets reading apart from the passive consumption of entertainment associated with television.[27] (For Colm Tóibín, listening to books instead of reading them is "like the difference between running a marathon and watching a marathon on TV."[28]) Philosopher Peter Kivy observes that reading books requires our imaginations to supply the sensory content provided for us by other audiovisual media; on these grounds, Kivy distinguishes between actress Julie Harris's tape recording of *Jane Eyre* (an act of reading, for her at least) and the audience, who are merely attending someone else's performance.[29] What's left for the audience to do if someone else has already done all of the hard work?

Yet the speaker's voice is precisely what readers cherish most about audiobooks. *Seinfeld*'s George Costanza spoke for many when complaining, "I can't read books anymore. Books on tape have ruined me . . . I need that nice voice."[30] Audio recordings enhance the illusion of an author speaking directly to us and establish an intimacy felt to be lacking from print. Nowhere is this more apparent than in genres such as autobiographies or memoirs that presuppose familiarity with the speaker's voice. We might as well have the real thing. It is now commonplace for celebrities and politicians to record their books. All recent presidents have done so. These speakers recognize and exploit the fact that many readers want the authentic voice, not an imagined one. Ghostwriters, yes; ghostreaders, no. You can hear the difference immediately when listening to the distinctive voices of Sherman Alexie, Woody Allen, Maya Angelou, James Baldwin, Jennifer Finney Boylan, Bill Bryson, Michael Caine, Ellen DeGeneres, Junot Díaz, Tina Fey, Eddie Huang, John le Carré, Garrison Keillor, Frank McCourt, Toni Morrison, Barack Obama, Sidney Poitier, David Sedaris, Zadie Smith, Amy Tan, Studs Terkel, Barbara Walters, Elie Wiesel, Oprah Winfrey, and others who write about class, ethnicity, gender, race, sexuality, or national identity. There are limits to how much of these voices we're able to imagine.

Listening to books makes it clear that some readings are better than others—as any child will tell you. Edison's phonograph gave people a chance to hear trained experts. Audiences would benefit, in his words, from "the greater enjoyment to be had from a book when read by an elocutionist than when read by the average reader."[31] Who wouldn't prefer to hear a professional? Audiences in Edison's time already paid to hear actors like Sarah Siddons or authors such as Dickens read aloud.[32] Spoken word recordings promised to make celebrated voices available outside the theater.

Yet this idea has been slow to gain traction in a DIY reading culture that values individual acts of reading as an end in themselves. The strong imperative to read for oneself implies that the best reading is one's own reading. Few would condone the idea that anyone should forego the experience of reading in order to listen to someone else do it, at any rate, no matter how eloquent the speaker may be. Our investment in reading as a solitary, salvific pursuit sits uneasily alongside the fact that some readings are superior to others—before disagreeing, listen to Jeremy Irons's *Lolita* or Meryl Streep's *The Testament of Mary*. This notion would hardly raise an eyebrow if applied to other media, such as music or film, that we expect to be performed by professionals. Reading is exceptional among the arts in favoring the amateur.

That my own reading might be found wanting never occurred to me when growing up. Only in retrospect have I realized how much was missing from my first encounters with great literature. A few examples: the Yorkshire dialect in *Wuthering Heights* came across as gibberish to me, the French in *Vanity Fair* was opaque, and I had no idea what the Mozart aria hummed by Leopold Bloom throughout *Ulysses* actually sounded like. These are books that I have since gotten to know intimately. But my initial encounters would have benefited from outside help in pronunciation. For readers like me, all three examples—dialects, foreign languages, and song lyrics—might be better heard than read. The voices in our head are simply not up to the job. (As a test case, read David Sedaris's account of singing "Away in a Manger" in the style of Billie Holiday, then listen to him do it.[33])

I have grudgingly come to accept that some people are simply better readers than me—at least out loud. Whereas my favorite books were first read in silence, other titles I did not care for in print have been redeemed by audiobooks. There is a reason that so many celebrities, from Charles Laughton and Gregory Peck to Johnny Cash and James Earl Jones, have recorded the Bible. These speakers enable us to grasp the narrative differently than we could on our own. I'd read Charlotte Brontë's *Jane Eyre* a dozen times, too, only to feel as if I was hearing it anew when narrated by British actress Juliet Stevenson.

Voice actors bring out as much from the page as they do from a script. There is no question that my internal monologue is impoverished when compared to the virtuoso performances of Ruby Dee, Frank Muller, Barbara Rosenblat, and other acclaimed narrators. Professionals are nearly always superior readers to the book's author and—I'm reluctant to admit—to me. Presumably I am not alone in wanting to hear books that I have read before because I want to hear them read well. Or at least differently. Some of our attention might be spent identifying exactly what distinguishes readings by Mitzi Friedlander (who recorded over 2,000 titles for the American Printing House for the Blind) or the comparative virtues of, say, Jim Dale versus Stephen Fry in their rival readings of the Harry Potter series.

Casting is the single most important decision made by an audio publisher. It is a truism that narrators can make or break a story. For me, Lenny Henry's bravura performance does something magical to Neil Gaiman's *Anansi Boys* and its cast of elderly Jamaican matriarchs. A good narrator resembles a good actor: we are simultaneously aware and unaware of their presence, immersed in the persona and the plot. By contrast, impostors disrupt fiction's spell, making us too aware of their voices or of a mismatch between speaker and subject matter. Pity the audience listening to Gilbert Gottfried read *Fifty Shades of Gray.*

Authors who are mediocre readers can be especially disillusioning. *The Hitchhiker's Guide to the Galaxy* is beloved by many but not when read by Douglas Adams. In fact, Friedrich Kittler described the invention of sound recording as a trap since the author's actual voice was bound to be a disappointment after the printed one's deification.[34] The risk persists in the twenty-first century: the contrast is jarring between Bryan Cranston's assured narration of *The Things They Carried* and the author's own puny voice heard at the end of that recording.

Narrators influence a story's reception at a formal level through accent, cadence, emphasis, inflection, pitch, pronunciation, resonance, tempo, tone, and any eccentricities that stand out. These sonic details matter since, as literary critics never tire of pointing out, reading aloud is itself an act of interpretation. Consider the following exchange: F. R. Leavis read aloud Dickens's *The Uncommercial Traveller* to Ludwig Wittgenstein only to be told, "Don't interpret."[35] Leavis replied that there's no such thing as reading neutrally. But more important, the human voice affects us at a gut level. Audiences develop passionate attachments to the voices of audiobook narrators even when they know nothing else about them. "The voice is like a fingerprint," explains Mladen Dolar.[36] It is a powerful form of intimacy nostalgically associated with the early days of radio.[37] People may no longer find the disembodied voice uncanny, but it casts a spell over us nonetheless.[38]

The following account of the audiobook industry evaluates how publishers have handled the combustible issue of casting narrators over the past century as well as the industry's ongoing campaign to persuade a skeptical public of the benefits of listening to them. It sketches a gradual shift away from velvet-voiced radio broadcasters toward "fit" between speaker and subject matter appropriate to scripts as different as, say, *Their Eyes Were Watching God* and *Twilight*. Voices have grown more diverse while at the same time more famous; publishers have intensified the use of celebrities familiar to the public from other media such as film and television. This tradition runs from Eleanor Roosevelt lending her voice to talking books in the 1930s up through Audible's A-List Collection of classic fiction read by Hollywood actors. Authors no longer worry about the stigma, either; Nobel Prize winner Toni Morrison has recorded nearly every one of her novels. (Morrison decided to make the recordings after hearing actresses use different rhythms and inflections than she heard in her own mind.[39]) Whether marquee names or anonymous talent, narrators wield tremendous influence over a book's reception as well as its sales figures. To put it another way: a talking book's success depends largely on who's doing the talking.

Can a book talk? The term "talking book" implies as much, even if there is little agreement as to whether it counts as a book at all. Turning a book into something other than print risks forfeiting the very qualities that make it a book. Audiobooks are unique in preserving a book's contents while at the same time discarding much of its tangible material, from binding to paper and ink, or what Jerome McGann calls "bibliographical codes."[40] And yet the audiobook is not strictly an adaptation either—at least, not in the sense of a TV show, film, or game—because it reproduces the book's words verbatim. In sum, an audiobook both is and isn't a book. This ambiguity has drawn hostility and defensiveness in equal measures from book lovers. The audiobook presents a compelling test case for literary criticism in particular since it forces us to make explicit and even to rethink our understanding of what it means to read a book.

Book historians have spent the past several decades enumerating all the different kinds of books beyond hardcovers and paperbacks. The word "book" is used by them in its widest sense. A central tenet of the discipline is that there is no such thing as "the book" since historically books have come in so many different shapes and forms, from clay tablets to computer screens, that are constantly changing in response to technological developments, fluctuating resources, and competition from other media. A few examples: *Reading in America* begins with the term's dictionary definition in order to underscore its manifold meanings as material object, symbolic text, and cultural phenomenon.[41] The book's contours grow fuzzier with each volume of the *History of the Book in America* as it moves forward in time from ancient codex to today's virtual software.[42] The *Oxford Companion to the Book* pragmatically uses the term as "shorthand for any recorded text," thereby justifying an entry for audiobooks.[43] What these resources share is an impulse to establish boundaries for historical inquiry while at the same time unsettling preconceptions of what constitutes a book. Their "Gutenberg Galaxy" usually draws the line at print (a sleight of hand to include newspapers, magazines, and even maps) while at the same time acknowledging the crucial role played historically by reading aloud in the centuries leading up to what might be called the "Edison Galaxy."[44]

The book's elasticity has long been recognized. D. F. McKenzie's celebrated Panizzi Lectures of 1985, for example, urged bibliographers to embrace the new media now sharing the book's role of textual transmission (while at the same time noting that nonverbal elements have always played a crucial role in books).[45] If audiobooks have to this point been neglected by McKenzie's heirs, our current moment of rapid media change is an opportune time to investigate their dubious status. Digital media have made us acutely aware of the book's distinctive qualities as well as its complexity and sophistication as a media artifact in its own right.[46] After all, old media were once themselves new media. We now have a better understanding of how books shape and are shaped by the complex media ecology in which they once played the starring role. "Our understanding of the book has undergone a tremendous narrowing over time," observes Andrew Piper, making it all the more critical that we recall the extent to which other media have shaped people's interactions with books.[47] Such admonitions reflect the discipline's transition from the study of books in isolation from other media to the book as a key vector in media history.

My account aims to restore the centrality of sound technology, not screens, to the book's development. It establishes how such devices gave rise to recorded literature while simultaneously asking why this transformation has so frequently been left out of conventional histories of the book. These accounts tend to move in an unbroken line from codex to electronic book without so much as a glance at the impact sound technology has had on the book's identity.[48] It is no accident that my introduction's title invokes Robert Darnton's seminal essay "What Is the History of Books?"[49]

The simplest explanation for the audiobook's neglect may be bibliophilia. Changing the book's form inevitably changes our relationship to it. Theologian John Hull explains how losing his sight affected his connection to books: "Has the love of books transferred to the love of tapes? Hardly! Nobody loves cassettes the way people love books."[50] One consequence of sound technology is the reduction of an intimate physical relationship with books to a single sensory dimension; gone is the comfort taken in a book's rustling pages. The talking book is a tangible object just like any other book—whether it be shellac records, cassette tapes, compact discs, digital files, or some other delivery mechanism—albeit one with which we have minimal, and hardly intimate, interaction.

Some book lovers argue that touch is vital to a book's reception.[51] Reminiscences about physical contact with books can be poignant as well as pertinent to conversations about what aspects of reading should be preserved by emerging media. But touch is no more essential than other senses to reading. There is even a countertradition of people longing for less tactile alternatives to print. A strand of utopian literature from the late nineteenth century (as we will see in Chapter 1) envisioned post-Edisonian readers freed from the labor of holding cumbersome tomes after a hard day's work. Book stands advertised in newspapers at the turn of the century promised to relieve readers of "arm-ache" and "cramped fingers."[52] Many braille readers welcomed spoken word recordings as a chance to give their fingers a break and to free their hands for knitting or smoking. The American Foundation for the Blind's president found braille so "arduous" that he avoided recreational reading until after graduating from college.[53] Literary critics swayed by the findings of cognitive psychologists have suggested that we are oblivious to our physical environment anyway when absorbed in a story.[54] The audiobook has some advantages in this respect: we cannot read a book through tears, but we can still listen to it. The key point here is that books engage an array of senses—whether touch, sight, or hearing—any one of which should not be idealized at the expense of another.

A more formidable explanation for the audiobook's neglect has to do with the enduring controversy over its legitimacy. The long debate continues over what to call listening to books: reading or something else? It's a curious thing—the mere mention of an audiobook is often taken as an invitation to debate the very nature of reading. Audiobooks bring out the Saint Augustine in us all.

My interlocutors have urged me to appeal to neuroscience in order to determine what counts as reading. It is true that reading with the eyes uses a different part of the brain (the visual cortex) than does reading with the ears (the auditory cortex). Brain-imaging methods have identified an area of the brain devoted specifically to word processing; one neuroscientist has described a part of the visual cortex equipped to recognize print as "the brain's letterbox."[55] From a neuroscientist's perspective, reading entails decoding graphic symbols into language using a specific region of the brain associated with vision; stroke victims who suffer injuries to this area will lose the ability to read even if they have been competent readers for their entire lives. Therefore, reading is neurologically and cognitively different from what takes place when a person hears a book.

Matters are hardly straightforward, however. Neuroscientists warn against trying to map complex activities like reading to a precise location in the brain.[56] In fact, there is no single, straightforward neurological activity that might be described as reading. Rather, decoding letters makes use of multiple visual and auditory networks, as well as different regions of the brain. Paul Armstrong describes reading as a "neurological hybrid" that uses an array of brain functions, which evolved for purposes other than reading, to comprehend written words.[57] The brain carries out a complex series of cerebral operations—some of which involve decomposing words into their constituent letters and sounds before recomposing them again—even though these processes feel automatic and effortless to most of us.[58]

Reading is not even a purely visual task; instead, word recognition relies on both vision and audition. Mapping sounds to letters is an essential step in literacy. Impoverished access to spoken language is a key reason why deaf children struggle to learn to read.[59] Problems with processing speech sounds also underlie reading disorders; for example, people with dyslexia (sometimes called "word blindness") are often incapable of deciphering words and in many cases are eligible for the National Library Service for the Blind and Physically Handicapped's talking book service. Adult reading involves a balance between sounding out words and soundlessly translating them into meaning. There are at least two pathways in the brain, one of which translates printed words phonologically before determining their meaning, the other of which trans-lates print directly into meaning.

We might also note that reading aloud to oneself activates both the brain's visual and its auditory cortexes. Certainly both parts of the brain were in use when, as a student, I listened to Shakespeare recordings while simultaneously following the script with my eyes. For one of Gertrude Stein's psychological experiments at Radcliffe, she even read aloud to herself while at the same time hearing a story read aloud by another person.[60] The distinction between reading with the eyes and with the ears is hardly an absolute one. Oliver Sacks describes the case of a blind woman who imagined speech as lines of print displayed on a book; her eyes ached after hearing books read aloud.[61]

We should be cautious about narrowly defining reading in terms of a single sense since recent experiments prove that it's possible to read without using one's eyes at all—as Dr. Seuss's *I Can Read with My Eyes Shut!* told us long ago.[62] Vision is not the only conduit to the brain area responsible for processing text. Brain-imaging studies measuring neural activity in congeni-tally blind adults confirm that reading braille uses the same area of the visual cortex as sighted readers do, not the region dedicated to tactile information.[63] In other words, the brain activity of sighted and blind readers is practically indistinguishable.

Such findings confirm the suspicions of braille readers—many of whom are vocal opponents of talking books—that tactile reading is equivalent to visual reading since both activities entail the translation of abstract codes for speech.[64] Hence, even a neurological definition of reading must be elastic enough to accommodate such findings. Susanna Millar, who worked with vi-sually impaired readers at Oxford's Department of Experimental Psychology, defines reading as a means "to understand heard language through another sense modality," thereby leaving room for senses other than vision.[65] A subse-quent study, titled "Reading with Sounds," has shown that blind people like-wise activate the visual cortex when using sight-to-sound sensory substitution devices to identify letters.[66] The area of the brain associated with reading can process words using multiple senses (vision, hearing, touch), it seems, even if our anatomies are poorly equipped to do so.

Even silent reading isn't entirely silent. Many readers imagine a speaker's voice—sometimes his or her own, sometimes another's—pronouncing the words on a page. "Inner voice" is the term used to describe the reader's covert pronunciation of written text during an otherwise silent transaction.[67] But our heads are filled with more than just imaginary voices.[68] We talk to ourselves while we read, using our actual voices—or at least the same parts of the body used for speech. In a process called "subvocalization," tiny movements in the larynx, tongue, lips, and other muscles involved in speech accompany the mental activity of reading.[69] In a sense, we're reading aloud to ourselves even when reading silently.

Humanities scholars have long understood reading to be more than just neurological decoding. Instead, their interests lie in strategies of interpretation and the behavior of actual readers. At least one historian has concluded that there is no definitive answer to the question "What is reading?"[70] Others note the numerous ways in which "reading" has been used since antiquity, offering salient reminders that the term's meaning varies according to time and place. Historians value case studies precisely for their capacity to illuminate, not flatten, differences among individual readers, whether it be a priest reading aloud the liturgy, a housewife absorbed in a novel, or a teenager scanning the Internet. These episodes seek to delineate the full range of activities corresponding with behavior thought of today as silent and solitary.[71] In short, people read in remarkably different ways.

Far from reducing reading to an abstract set of mental operations, historians endeavor to preserve ways of reading that have disappeared from view. Roger Chartier has led the way in valuing methods of reading that differ from our own: "A history of reading must not limit itself to the genealogy of our own contemporary manner of reading, in silence and using only our eyes."[72] Reading aloud and being read to appear high on the list of those practices threatened with obsolescence. Modern usage has narrowed the term's meaning substantially since earlier eras in which it was by no means clear whether a text was to be taken in through the eye or the ear. In doing so, we risk an impoverished understanding of the degree to which written texts (the Bible, most notably) have for centuries been pitched to the ear. Audiobooks hardly seem unusual when we recall that people have been listening to stories for far longer than they have been reading them silently.

Literary critics likewise seek to multiply, not limit, the term's meanings. As early as 1940, Mortimer Adler's *How to Read a Book* began by noting that the *Oxford English Dictionary* listed twenty-one meanings for "read."[73] Countless others have focused on reading as an act of interpretation, not a physiological set of responses. These critics show more interest in distinguishing among various kinds of reading (close, distant, slow, hyper, symptomatic, surface, and so forth) than in formulating what the activity itself consists of. The objects of their scrutiny stray well beyond print to television, film, and practically anything else that can be interpreted as a text.

Guidance might be sought from media historians who have tried to accommodate the kinds of storytelling associated with today's digital environment. Foremost among them, N. Katherine Hayles makes the case for redefining reading in response to the blend of words, images, and sounds streaming at us from electronic devices. A pair of National Endowment for the Arts reports documenting a long-term decline in print reading lead her to conclude, "Now it is time to rethink what reading is."[74] She highlights the damage caused by a narrow definition that treats any deviations from print as impostors. Instead, her approach would have us build bridges between traditional literacies associated with print and the kinds of reading used to navigate electronic media.

Writing a history of recorded books has helped to debunk, for me, at least, the book's privileged standing. It is easy to forget that readers have yearned for alternatives to printed books—from braille to sound recordings and electronic facsimiles—practically since they first came off the press. Technology has made it possible to remake the book for reasons of taste, access, or convenience. Historically, alternative formats have been especially important to people excluded from access to books. As Mara Mills observes in "What Should We Call Reading?" the difficulties we face in formulating a definition of reading adequate to the digital media environment have been addressed for over a century by people with disabilities.[75] An ingenious array of formats designed to make print accessible through vision, hearing, touch, and even smell raises questions about whether such activities still qualify as reading or whether the problem lies with our restrictive understanding of it.

Blind people have debated the validity of multimodal reading ever since talking books were invented in the 1930s. Their very identities as readers are at stake; whereas sighted readers can choose between formats, many others have no choice. Spoken word recordings represent their only means of access to literature. Disagreements over the legitimacy of various kinds of reading (visual, aural, tactile) are at the same time disputes over blind people's capacity to define themselves as readers or to be defined by others as nonreaders.

The *Journal of Visual Impairment and Blindness* represented both sides of the dispute in its 1996 forum "Is Listening Literacy?" On one side, Philip Hatlen, superintendent of the Texas School for the Blind, advocated braille (even before brain scans) as the only adequate system of reading since, similar to letterpress, it involves deciphering an abstract code for speech. Audio formats might supplement braille but were not thought to be sufficient in themselves. Nor could someone who uses talking books be considered literate without changing that term's meaning; put in reverse, sighted people who listen to audiobooks but cannot read print, much less write it, would still be considered illiterate.[76] It is the difference between what some historians call *reading* and *accessing* a book's contents.

On the other side, D. W. Tuttle, professor emeritus at the University of Northern Colorado, favored redefining the term "literacy" to accommodate disabilities. His proposal goes beyond processing visual symbols or a specific medium: "Reading could be defined better as the recognition, interpretation, and assimilation of the ideas represented by symbolic material, whether it is displayed visually, tactilely, or aurally."[77] By shifting the focus from letters to ideas, Tuttle's formulation controversially includes listening alongside other forms of reading. Nevertheless, it calls attention to people with print disabilities for whom the existing terminology is inadequate.[78] Even Hatlen seemed uncomfortable with the fact that a lifelong reader could be rendered "illiterate" by sight loss late in life.

The divide is to some extent misleading since most blind and partially sighted people read in more than one way. In other words, they use a combination of print, braille, and recorded material. (On that point, the majority of audiobook consumers are avid readers of print.) Testimonials from blind readers make a powerful case for the benefits of multimodal reading. Their voices should be heard in debates over recorded books since people with disabilities are seldom accused of listening to books as a shortcut or way of "cheating."[79] As we'll see in Part II, the terminology used to describe reading has a political dimension for people with vision impairments.

Memoirs by blind writers share their diverse personal experiences of books with audiences who may have little understanding of what it is like to be a blind reader (a group that includes most people, if my experience is anything to go by). In *Sight Unseen,* Georgina Kleege describes her reliance on technology to access printed information; she rejects the "But is it really reading?" question as a prejudice of sighted people.[80] John Hull takes a similar line in describing reading as a way of transmitting information to the brain regardless of the sense organ through which it travels. "I do not regard myself as listening to a spoken book any more than a sighted person thinks that he or she is looking at a book," he told me. "Looking, feeling and hearing are the means of access; reading is of the mind."[81] He should know. Hull read books in the conventional way until losing his sight at the age of forty-eight.

Reading can be done well or badly in any medium. My own experiences of listening to books, combined with those I have learned about from other people, blind and sighted alike, have convinced me that storytelling can be every bit as engaging with the ears as with the eyes. When making comparisons, we should resist the tendency to idealize reading print, which can be sloppy, distracted, and downright lazy; let's not forget that, according to legend, the philosopher Democritus blinded himself in order to devote his full attention to ideas. Criticisms of audiobooks as a passive or "semi-attentive" form of reading, done while driving, jogging, or cleaning the house, should likewise acknowledge the possibility of concentrated listening.[82] Stephen Kuusisto could still quote books from his childhood thirty years later, for example, aligning him with the blind people of ancient Israel known as "baskets of books" for memorizing entire narratives.[83] They make the custodians of literature in Ray Bradbury's *Fahrenheit 451* look like amateurs.

Nor should we valorize listening either, which has its own problems, energetically documented by skeptics since even before the phonograph's invention. Florence Nightingale dreaded listening to books as the Victorian equivalent to waterboarding; for her, being read to felt "like lying on one's back, with one's hands tied and having liquid poured down one's throat."[84] Modern critics from Jonathan Kozol to Harold Bloom and Sven Birkerts have been less graphic but no less blunt.[85] The latest evidence even points to a higher rate of mind wandering than with print.[86] One man who lost his sight late in life told me that the biggest problem he has with listening to books is staying awake.

Distinctions between "reading" and "being read to" have serious implications in the context of disability. Nevertheless, the testimonials of braille readers who denigrate listening must be given equal weight as those who defend listening. Historically, blind people have been among the most vocal champions *and* skeptics of recorded books; braille readers in particular have expressed doubts about talking books as a viable form of reading. It may be the case that blind auditors have equally rich, if not richer, encounters with books as other readers. But this does not necessarily mean that they are having the *same* contact with literature. This is why talking books pose such a dilemma: listening to books both resembles and deviates from conventional habits of reading in a way that makes the question of "real" reading impossible to resolve satisfactorily.

This book tells the story of the talking book's evolution over more than a century. One of its abiding concerns will be how publishers have handled the fraught relationship between printed and talking books. My account undoes this conventional opposition by emphasizing their co-development. Attending to the poetics and politics of recorded literature, it continues to push scholarship away from literary representations of sound toward actual recordings of literature. The approach taken here pays close attention to the historical context of literary recordings while at the same time respecting their formal and aesthetic properties. Three concerns find their way into nearly every chapter: the audiobook's standing as a "book," its reception by a bemused public, and controversies over whether listening to books qualifies as a form of reading. Questions thought to be of recent origin, it turns out, have preoccupied publishers ever since the phonograph spoke its first words.

My focus is on fiction despite the audiobook's long-standing ties to other genres, namely self-help—a commuter staple mocked by the title of Ben Stiller and Janeane Garofalo's *Feel This Audiobook: Instant Therapy Only a Crazy Person Would Ignore*. Fiction is the genre for which most is at stake when it comes to questions about voice. To put it another way, people care whether you read Hemingway in print or hear Charlton Heston read him to you; no one cares how you read *The Seven Habits of Highly Effective People* (the first audiobook to sell more than a million copies in bookstores).

Poetry plays a minor role in my story, and there are good reasons for this. The main one is that poetry recitations have not suffered the same critical neglect as prose ones.[87] The lyric's traditional ties to music and the platform's importance as a means of disseminating poetry make the boundary between writing and speech less of an issue for poets than for novelists. The history of poetry performances has been affectionately traced and key milestones singled out for scholarly attention.[88] In addition, the establishment of digital repositories have lain the groundwork for the kinds of close and distant listening being done with print. As an audiobook historian, I have watched with envy. There is a less enviable reason for verse's omission, however. Poetry sales have always been marginal to the audio publishing industry (with notable exceptions such as Caedmon). Regrettably, commercial publishers accepted that there was little interest or profit in verse—claims to be inspected in the chapters to come.

This book's three parts correspond to the major phases of recorded books: experimental phonographic books, talking books made for people with vision impairments, and commercially oriented audiobooks. Part I takes us all the way back to the phonograph's invention, where my story begins with Edison's ambition to record a Dickens novel on wax cylinders. One of the first questions asked about the new sound technology was how it would affect print: "Are we to have a new kind of books?"[89] Spectators were captivated by the possibility of recorded literature and the upending of our reading habits. The fact that wax cylinders could hold only a few minutes of speech did little to dampen the public's enthusiasm. Barely audible recitations of poets and tragedians invited speculation about a future in which an entire novel could be heard on a miniature phonograph tucked inside one's hat. Historians have generally treated the nineteenth century's brief scraps of poetry and prose as having little to do with books since full-length narratives were not recorded until the next century. My account shows instead how the very possibility of sound recording led writers to rethink the book's capabilities and constraints. Efforts to disrupt the publishing industry began long before the digital revolution.

Part II documents the establishment of talking book libraries for war-blinded soldiers in America and Britain in the 1930s. Talking books represented the biggest advance in literacy among blind people since the invention of braille. Disabled veterans and civilians who were unable to read braille could still hear books read aloud on phonograph records. The American Foundation for the Blind and the Library of Congress began making full-length recordings of novels and other books in 1934, when technological advances in the music industry made it possible for the first time to record more than a few minutes of speech.

The program's success led to an ambitious, transatlantic partnership with Britain's Royal National Institute of Blind People to establish an international talking book library. Its initial recordings included the Bible; plays by Shakespeare; and fiction by Gladys Hasty Carroll, Agatha Christie, Joseph Conrad, Rudyard Kipling, and P. G. Wodehouse. These recordings made literature accessible to new audiences while at the same time raising a vexing set of questions about the nature of reading. My account investigates how the talking book's development challenged conventional notions of the book as a print resource and of reading as an activity performed exclusively with the eyes instead of a multitude of senses.

The few existing accounts of the talking book chronicle the format in terms of its technological or legislative history. My account pays attention instead to its social impact, drawing on archival sources in order to reconstruct how the first generation to hear books mechanically read aloud responded to and shaped the medium in crucial ways. The aim here has been to recover the voices of people who heard talking books. Working among archives has enabled me to locate testimonials in correspondence, memoirs, pamphlets, periodicals, reports, and sound recordings preserved by charities for blind people in Britain and the United States. Such findings permit readers with visual disabilities to speak for themselves when possible and provide us with a better understanding of the relationship among literacy, disability, and technology.

The section on talking books takes up the questions I'm most frequently asked about my research: Who decided which books to record? Which ones did they choose? How were the books read aloud? And what did people think of them? Chapters 2 and 5 describe the talking book's development after the First World War as well as its impact on the lives of people who had no other way of reading books and, in many cases, had given up hope of ever being able to read for themselves. Chapters 3, 4, and 6 address a series of controversies over the legitimacy of recorded books, book selection policies, appropriate reading styles, the handling of obscenity, and accusations of censorship. As we'll see, talking books encountered formidable opposition from Helen Keller and other braille readers when the service was first announced.

Another group of blind people protested against being treated differently from other readers and demanded access to Hemingway's *A Farewell to Arms,* James Joyce's *A Portrait of the Artist as a Young Man,* Willa Cather's *My Ántonia,* Margaret Mitchell's *Gone with the Wind,* and other titles excluded from talking book library catalogs for reasons having to do with taste or copyright. One of the most protracted disputes among blind people concerned the best way to read books aloud: plainly or theatrically? Such controversies should be brought into dialogue with a similar set of debates over agency, authenticity, and pleasure taking place in relation to audiobooks.

It should be apparent by now that talking books rarely stay still. Decades before audiobooks made their way onto America's highways, talking book records traveled the globe along more conventional routes. The initial rivalry between Britain and the United States evolved into a transatlantic partnership enabling the two countries to develop equipment and accumulate inventory at a faster pace than would otherwise have been possible. Blindness knows no borders: meetings between representatives from both countries in August 1934 led to an agreement to do everything possible to share resources and swap records.

The potential benefits for the world's blind population were obvious from the start. Shortly after the talking book's debut in America and Britain, soldiers carried machines back home to Australia, Canada, New Zealand, South Africa, and India in order to establish libraries there too. The National Institute for the Blind expressed optimism about the technology's proliferation and even its wish that talking books combined with braille would one day serve as "the link that connects the blind throughout the world."[90] Although recorded books are generally perceived to be an anglophone phenomenon (an impression reinforced to some extent by this book's scope), the technology could be used anywhere. It was not long before France, Germany, and other European countries set up their own libraries.[91] By 1965, the equipment had reached Libya, Jordan, Saudi Arabia, and other parts of the Arab world. Today, recorded books (including both audiobooks and talking books made for people with disabilities) are a global phenomenon with distinctive histories—their own untold stories—in different parts of the world. It is my hope that other scholars with the appropriate linguistic expertise will take it upon themselves to tell these stories after this book's publication.

Part III switches our attention to spoken word recordings made for the commercial market beginning in the 1950s. It starts with Caedmon Records, whose inaugural album featured Dylan Thomas reciting "A Child's Christmas in Wales." Caedmon was the first to specialize in spoken word recordings of literature after long-playing (LP) records went on the market in 1948. Bear in mind that literary recordings were not yet widely known. Many readers heard the voices of Joyce, Stein, William Faulkner, Sylvia Plath, Eudora Welty, and other writers for the first time through its albums.

Chapter 8 takes us forward to Books on Tape, a pioneer of taped books aimed at the country's growing number of commuters in the 1970s. Americans who wished to read books but lacked the time to do so could now hear stories read aloud to them while driving, exercising, or ironing shirts. The company set itself apart by offering unabridged recordings of *The Thorn Birds* and other bestselling titles in its mail-order catalog instead of the abridgments and excerpts favored by its predecessors. Books on Tape was one of several audio publishers to seek legitimacy by sticking closely to the printed book instead of trying to compete with radio or television.

Audio publishers faced a formidable challenge: persuading book lovers to start buying records and tapes. Marketing campaigns sought to convince potential customers of the compatibility between serious literature and sound technology. They insisted that spoken word recordings not only reproduced great works of literature verbatim but also held advantages over print. Namely, audiences could hear their favorite authors read aloud while at home, stuck in traffic, or jogging through the park. Caedmon, Books on Tape, and countless others strove to change the recorded book's reputation as a medium used exclusively by blind people—a stigma that persists in some circles. Once derided as the lazy man's way to read, recorded books would gradually become associated in the popular imagination with hardworking professionals who had little time to read the old-fashioned way.

Yet the question will not go away: Are these people actually reading? The industry has struggled to overcome suspicions that listening to books is not equal to reading them. Questions persist about a form of reading that can be done behind a steering wheel. The industry's growth has only made the problem worse. Customers continue to put up with insinuations that recorded books are some kind of shortcut, cheat, or what some have called "Kentucky Fried literature."[92] For the audiobook's critics, listening means always having to say you're sorry.

Chapter 9 addresses the ongoing shift to digital recordings available from Audible and other publishers. Making audiobooks accessible online has opened up the market to new customers while at the same time bringing these recordings into closer contact with other media including television, film, and games. This closing chapter considers how Audible's online platform (now owned by Amazon) benefits publishers everywhere by making their products easy to acquire while at the same time acknowledging their concerns about the company's growing clout.

The book's final pages turn our attention away from the format's legitimacy and toward a different question: What can audiobooks do that printed books cannot? Whereas charities entrusted to record books for people with impaired vision worry that deviations from the original book will lead to them being treated as inferior, commercial publishers fret less about fidelity. They make the most of audio formats by embellishing the printed page with sound effects and other tools unavailable to print. When it suits them, commercial publishers blithely disregard fidelity to the printed text by abridging, adapting, or enhancing the script with celebrity narrators, sound effects, and a full cast. They turn books into a form of entertainment designed to compete with television, film, and computers. In taking up such experiments, this chapter makes a case for understanding audiobooks not as derivative versions of printed books but rather as an emerging form of entertainment willing to sever its ties to the book altogether.

One last confession before the story begins. I started this project as an audiobook agnostic, someone who neither believed nor disbelieved in its standing as a book. No strong feelings guided me one way or the other. Audiobooks were what I listened to when I didn't have time to read books in any other way. While I would not describe myself as a true convert in that I continue to read printed books, I came away from this project feeling that audiobooks deserve to be taken seriously. For too long audiobooks have been the Rodney Dangerfield of literature: they don't get no respect. Conversations involving raised eyebrows, rolled eyes, or outright smirks have left little doubt in my mind that the hostility to audiobooks is about something deeper than a preference for the printed word. The dispute seems to touch on the fundamental experience of what it means to read a book and, therefore, to be a reader of books. It has as much to do with our identities as readers as with the vanishing line between books and other forms of entertainment.

A reader's stance toward audiobooks is nearly always a moral one, not an aesthetic one. This helps to explain the anxiety hovering in the background during conversations about audiobooks—especially for those of us in the awkward position of having to explain that we have not read a book but listened to it. Jon Stewart's greeting to the "nonreaders" listening to his book nods to the discomfort felt by anyone caught in this position.[93] How audiobook publishers, narrators, and audiences have confronted this dilemma over the past century is a tale worth telling and, I hope you'll agree, worth reading. Whether you do so with your eyes or your ears, I'll leave up to you.

PART I

The Phonographic Library

1

Canned Literature

The history of recorded sound begins in verse. Thomas Edison announced his plans to mechanically reproduce the human voice in a letter to *Scientific American* published on November 17, 1877.[1] Three weeks later, Edison's associates assembled a simple device on which Edison recorded "Mary Had a Little Lamb." Whatever disagreements exist among historians as to the exact events of that day, there is no disputing that the words of this nursery rhyme were among the first spoken by the phonograph.[2] Their fame makes it all the more surprising that histories of the phonograph have had so little to say about the prominence of the spoken word at its initial demonstrations in America and Europe.[3]

No recordings were made of the exhibitions, unfortunately, but press reports enable us to reconstruct the sequence of events at many of them.[4] A typical demonstration began with an explanation of how the machine worked, followed by displays of recording and playback (Figure 1.1). The program opened with a greeting from the phonograph ("The phonograph presents its compliments to the audience") before moving on to some combination of recitations, songs, music, and random noises. Members of the audience were then invited to speak their own effusions into the phonograph, and the exhibitor usually brought the evening to a close by handing out torn-off slips of tinfoil as souvenirs. At nearly all of the demonstrations, the spoken word played a prominent role in showcasing recorded sound to audiences who had never before heard speech mechanically reproduced. Historians are only telling half the story when they describe the talking machine as if it were a singing machine.[5]

A witness to one of the initial phonograph demonstrations posed the question on every reader's mind: Was it possible to record a novel "so that books can

29

Figure 1.1. "New Jersey.—Professor Edison exhibiting the phonograph to visitors, at his laboratory, Menlo Park." From *Frank Leslie's Illustrated Newspaper,* March 30, 1878, 68.

be procured in this form and by being placed on the Phonograph the entire story be told to the listening ear?"[6] Unfortunately, the wish was years ahead of the technology. There was little hope of recording an entire novel in 1878 since tinfoil cylinders could only play for a few minutes and were extremely difficult to reproduce.[7] The first recordings that might be thought of as literary were not made until a decade later, when Edison's improved phonograph made it possible to record the poets Alfred Tennyson and Robert Browning; recordings of full-length books had to wait until philanthropic initiatives for blind people in the 1930s.[8] However, it would be a mistake to think that the phonograph's limitations in its own time constrained speculation about its future. Even if the inaugural recordings consisted of nursery rhymes and snippets of verse, the advent of sound-recording technology made it possible to conceive of a recorded book fifty years in advance of its actual completion.

This chapter takes up the question asked by Edison's contemporaries about the impact of sound-recording technology on print: "Are we to have a new kind of books?"[9] From the phonograph's first utterance, observers were powerfully drawn to the notion of a new kind of book existing in recorded form, to be heard rather than read. It has been said that the brief excerpts of verse and prose initially recorded on the phonograph had little to do with the concept of "the book" since recordings of full-length novels were not made until the next century.[10] My findings tell a different story. They show instead how the very possibility of sound recording led audiences to reevaluate what the book was capable of doing in the first place. The pattern is a familiar one to media historians. The introduction of a new technology leads to renewed awareness of established technologies at the moment when their roles have been called into question, and the ensuing competition makes the advantages and limitations of both media stand out.[11] In this case, the possibility of sound recording provoked a debate about the future of the book.

The deliberations over the book's future call into question whether the book has ever held a privileged position in relation to other media. Instead of accepting the printed book's superiority, a vocal group of readers valued spoken word recordings both as a return to literature's roots in the ancient Homeric tradition and as the next stage in the book's evolution. The preference for the spoken word suggests a different way of thinking about the influential narrative according to which the printing press marked a decisive turn away from orality and toward stable, introspective, and formally complex forms of print. For the first time, the phonograph confronted readers with a choice between two different forms of mechanical reproduction for their literature. The readers who stood to benefit ranged from those who were simply curious about alternative formats for literature to those who had been left behind because of disabilities, illiteracy, or limited access to print.

The book would compete with other media in the coming century—namely, film, radio, television, and, most recently, digital media—but the phonograph was the first to challenge its monopoly on the word. Friedrich Kittler credited the phonograph with "the death of the author" for bringing audiences into contact with the writer's actual voice at the expense of the imagined one invoked by the page.[12] Yet Kittler's devaluing of the voice in the wake of sound-recording technology underestimated the spoken word's aura. As the demand for recorded literature attests, the death of the author was the birth of the listener. Edison anticipated reaching a new audience through "Phonographic Books," for instance, each consisting of roughly 40,000 words recorded on a single ten-inch-square metal plate. According to Edison, "The advantages of such books over those printed are too readily seen to need mention. Such books would be listened to where now none are read."[13]

Edison's proposal brings into focus how sound-recording technology altered conceptions of the book in the closing decades of the nineteenth century. What has yet to be explained is why so many of Edison's contemporaries assumed that the phonograph would lead to the demise of the printed book altogether. The following investigation accounts for the book's premature obituary through its attention to, first, the initial responses to the phonograph as a potential rival to the printed book, and, second, a series of hypothetical reading machines proposed by Edward Bellamy, Octave Uzanne, Albert Robida, and others writing at the end of the nineteenth century. As we'll see, the questions about the book's future raised by these writers in response to the new media of their time have once again become pressing questions in our own time.

Bottled Authors

The press began to speculate about the impact sound recording would have on the book even before the phonograph's completion. The *New York Times* used an unlikely analogy to explain the invention a month before its trial at Menlo Park. The preservation of speech on tinfoil, the paper advised, was comparable to that of wine by the bottle; when it comes to sound, the phonograph "bottles it up" for future use. Audiences would be able to purchase "bottled orations" sold in quart bottles for fifty cents apiece, and the man of taste would have a "well-stocked oratorical cellar" to entertain guests with a "dry 'Mark Twain.'"[14] The speed with which "bottled speech" became a stock phrase in subsequent reporting about Edison indicates how reassuring audiences found it to have a new technology explained in terms of an old one. *Punch* responded to the conceit with a cartoon showing a cellar full of bottled opera to be uncorked on special occasions (Figure 1.2).

Humorous as it may be, the oratorical cellar represents one of the earliest forecasts of a commercial market for recorded speech. Before even hearing the phonograph, the *New York Times* made the following tongue-in-cheek prediction about its impact on the novel:

> There is good reason to believe that if the phonograph proves to be what its inventor claims that it is, both book-making and reading will fall into disuse. Why should we print a speech when it can be bottled, and why should we learn to read when, if some skillful elocutionist merely repeats one of "George Eliot's" novels aloud in the presence of a phonograph, we

Figure 1.2. Cellar full of bottled music. From *Punch's Almanack for 1878,* December 14, 1877, 3.

can subsequently listen to it without taking the slightest trouble? We shall be able to buy Dickens and Thackeray by the single bottle or by the dozen, and rural families can lay in a hogshead of "Timothy Titcomb" every Fall for consumption during the Winter. Instead of libraries filled with combustible books, we shall have vast storehouses of bottled authors, and though students in college may be required to learn the use of books, just as they now learn the dead languages, they will not be expected to make any practical use of the study.[15]

Books to bottles: an audacious claim to make about an invention that had yet to utter a word. The facetious report nevertheless formulated ideas that were taken seriously in the upcoming battle of the books. First, the report identifies a potential market for recorded literature through its image of a storehouse of bottled authors made up of Eliot, Dickens, Thackeray, and Josiah Gilbert Holland. Second, it calls into question the future of bookmaking by insisting that the recorded book would supersede, not supplement, the printed book. Third, the report establishes a link between recorded literature and the professional reader. Only someone trained in the discipline of elocution could read a book to maximal effect while asking from the reader minimal effort ("without taking the slightest trouble"). Use of the passive term "consumption" here invokes a long tradition of denigrating novels as overly commercial commodities with little aesthetic value that would later be revived by twentieth-century critics to dismiss audiobooks along the same lines.[16] While the newspaper's exaggerated claims may be easy to disregard, the press took its other themes increasingly seriously.

The *New York Times* was not alone in anticipating the swift obsolescence of print. Talk of the book's future had begun with a letter to *Scientific American* from Edison's representative, Edward H. Johnson, announcing the possibility of sound recording. In response to Johnson's announcement, an editor posed the question, "Are we to have a new kind of books? There is no reason why the orations of our modern Ciceros should not be recorded and detachably bound so that we can run the indented slips through the machine, and in the quiet of our own apartments listen again, and as often as we will, to the eloquent words."[17] The answer was yes for those who tolerated the printed page only because there weren't any other options. Prior to the phonograph, reading aloud had been a communal activity; there was no precedent for the experience of listening to a stranger read aloud in the privacy of one's home. The passage's emphasis on solitary listening ("the quiet of our own apartments") and repeated playback ("as often as we will") suggests that readers discerned new possibilities for close listening which would have been impossible amid the hubbub of a public recitation. For such listeners, phonographic books represented a welcome alternative to silent reading.

The editor's allusion to Cicero is revealing. Here was an ancient figure famed for oration despite reaching modern audiences solely through print. The allusion offered a reminder that printed, not spoken, literature was the latecomer to the republic of letters. Nearly all works of literature prior to the sixteenth century had circulated outside of print before their reproduction in book form by later generations.[18] Whereas twentieth- and twenty-first-century debates over the merits of recorded books tend to concentrate on authors who write specifically for print media, the initial accounts in periodicals like *Scientific American* focused on authors diminished by the transition to print. I've noticed that readers who express discomfort toward hearing printed books read aloud seldom express the same unease toward reading oral scripts in print. To put it another way: silently reading Cicero is no less of a compromise than reading aloud Eliot, Dickens, and Thackeray. This hasn't prevented the orator from being read in print, of course. The second book printed on Gutenberg's press was Cicero's *De Officiis*.

The new kind of books proposed by the *New York Times* and *Scientific American* conformed to the predictions made by the talking machine's inventor. It has often been pointed out that Edison failed to grasp the phonograph's entertainment potential owing to his interest in developing it as a dictation device for use by businesses.[19] But Edison did identify other uses for it: playing music, writing letters, teaching elocution, recording courtroom testimony, preserving family archives, and making clocks that announced the time. He also proposed using the phonograph to read aloud:

> Books may be read by the charitably-inclined professional reader, or by such readers especially employed for that purpose, and the record of [each] book used in the asylums of the blind, hospitals, the sick-chamber, or even with great profit and amusement by the lady or gentleman whose eyes and hands may be otherwise employed; or, again, because of the greater enjoyment to be had from a book when read by an elocutionist than when read by the average reader.[20]

One advantage to using the phonograph as a reading machine was its accessibility to both sighted and blind readerships. Tactile alphabets for people with vision impairments required training, whereas anyone could listen to a book.[21] This was an appealing prospect to people who were newly blind as well as to readers who merely feared endangering their eyesight from overuse. Such readers welcomed the phonograph as a means of relieving the disproportionate burden borne by the eyes. The strain placed on them by reading books was commonly held to be responsible for deteriorating eyesight—Milton was often invoked as a cautionary tale.

Disability has always been a driving force behind the technology for recorded books.[22] The fear of ocular degeneration caused by reading underlay the initial discussions of printing for people who were blind in the eighteenth and nineteenth centuries. Valentin Haüy, who developed a system of raised letters in 1784, expressed regret that the method could not be of use to blind authors such as Homer and Milton.[23] Still, even if it may seem obvious to us now, the connection between sound-recording technology and books for those who were blind was not an inevitable one in Edison's time. (Edison's rival Emile Berliner overlooked blind readers altogether.) For much of the nineteenth century, the education of blind people focused on the relationship between sight and touch, not hearing. The distinction between reading with the eyes and reading with the fingers had preoccupied educators ever since the importation of embossed letters to Britain and the United States in the 1820s and early 1830s.[24] A successful campaign by organizations such as the British Foreign Blind Association to promote the use of Louis Braille's script system over other tactile alphabets firmly established braille in both countries by the end of the century.[25]

Yet it is equally important to note that recorded books were never meant for people with disabilities alone. It is a misconception that recorded books began as a format for blind readers before being taken up by a broader readership in the second half of the twentieth century in the form of audiobooks. From the outset the audience for recorded speech reached well beyond those with disabilities. Edison's hypothetical audience included "the average reader" lacking either the time or the inclination to hold a book. His statement is one of the first to characterize reading as a secondary activity intended to accompany other pursuits. More important, it endorsed the professionalization of reading by insisting on the increased "amusement," "enjoyment," and "profit" to be had from listening to a trained reader. There is no idealization here of the silent reader's ability to voice texts for himself or herself. Even if audiences were already reading, Edison implies, they were not reading very well.

Dickens on Tinfoil

Efforts to promote the phonograph as an improved version of the book express the conservatism of the initial attempts to figure out the machine's worth as a reading machine. Despite calls for a new kind of books, the actual accounts of those books adhered closely to traditional formats. Most people used the phonograph to record existing genres (books, lectures, sermons, letters, advertisements) instead of new forms of speech devised specifically for it. Their dependence on the material book suggests that the phonograph and print developed in close relation to one another no matter how insistently journalists placed them in opposition.[26] The phonograph repeated the pattern of other emerging communications technologies by imitating its predecessors, just as Gutenberg's printing press initially produced volumes resembling manuscripts.[27] Such precedents suggest the need for caution when evaluating claims made on behalf of the phonograph to revolutionize the book. In fact, few attempts were made to produce an art form distinct from print until the following century. Far more enticing was the prospect of listening to established authors like Dickens.

Edison intended to capitalize on the demand for recorded books by opening a publishing house in New York. According to him, its catalog would feature "an ordinary 50-cent novel" recorded on six-inch circular plates, among other recitations suitable for home entertainment.[28] Edison claimed to have already received one hundred orders from people who were blind, and he hoped to generate similar demand from other readers. But first it was necessary for Edison to domesticate the phonograph if it was ever to become a household consumer good, as the Edison Speaking Phonograph Company envisioned. He did so by translating the familiar experience of hearing a book read aloud in a public venue to the more intimate space of the home:

> Say I hire a good elocutionist to read David Copperfield or any other work. His words are taken down by machine, and thousands of matrixes of David Copperfield produced. A man can place them in the machine, and lie in bed, while the novel is read to him by the instrument with the finest grade of feeling and accent. He can make it read slow or fast, can stop it when he pleases, and go back and begin again at any chapter he may choose.[29]

Books at bedtime must have been an appealing notion at a time when reading in bed posed very real difficulties, not least of which was hazardous lighting. If the image of a man listening to a book while lying in bed underscores the perceived passivity of the activity, this is counteracted by the recipient's degree of control over the delivery, from its tempo to interruption and replay—features distinguishing mechanical reading from live oration. The intimacy of the scene stands out despite the presence of a mechanical speaker. For most people, reading aloud in the bedroom would have been unthinkable without one.

Edison's marketing campaign sought to domesticate the phonograph by portraying it as a leisure activity in ordinary households. The following vignette features a couple who have purchased an entire Dickens novel on a single sheet of tinfoil: "A man is tired and his wife's eyes are failing, and so they sit around a table and hear the [phonograph] read from this sheet the whole novel with all the expression of a first-class reader. See?"[30] The scene can be read in two ways. In one reading, the scene translates the iconic image of a paterfamilias reading aloud to the family into its technological equivalent—with the upgrade of the mechanical reader's "first-class" delivery. In another, the device relieves the woman from the duty of reading aloud to her husband—a role described by Leah Price as "human audiobooks."[31] (Think of Milton again, this time from the perspective of his daughters.) The couple represents the two types of readers Edison had in mind: one seeking to relax after a day's work and the other on the verge of losing her eyesight. The pun with which the quotation ends invites spectators to visualize themselves in either role.

Dickens's reputation as a performer made him a popular choice with which to illustrate the phonograph's value as a reading machine. Discussions of sound recording frequently cited Dickens's name despite the inconvenient fact that the phonograph was incapable of recording his novels. Edison memorably claimed to be able to record *Nicholas Nickleby* in its entirety on four eight-inch cylinders in 1888.[32] But even then novels were simply too long to record since the standard phonograph cylinder had a maximum playing time of a little over three minutes. The author was nonetheless a shrewd choice since the name of Dickens was shorthand for the novel itself and appealed to a Victorian sensibility that equated "book" and "novel." At a time when the technical limitations of the phonograph prevented the recitation of more than a few lines of verse, it made sense to pitch the conversation toward the ideal rather than the disappointing reality. The two poles on the spectrum of phonograph recording might be said to be "Mary Had a Little Lamb" and *Nicholas Nickleby* owing to their differences in complexity, in length, in form, and in fact, too, since only one of them was actually recorded.

Use of Dickens's name raised issues of performance, adaptation, and even copyright that made him a valuable advertisement for phonographic books. Edison's advocates promoted the phonograph using the genre least associated with recitation (the novel as opposed to poetry or drama). The novel's association with print seemingly set it apart from other genres originally intended for aural reception. Yet Dickens's novels fit both categories since he was among the most theatrical of novelists. Adapting Dickens's novels for recitation risked few objections since the author was renowned for doing just that during his reading tours of America and Britain.[33] The "audio-visual Dickens" familiar to audiences from theatrical performances and staged readings had always exceeded the printed page anyway.[34] To this day Dickens is routinely cited as an author better heard than read.

Recording a British author had the further advantage of sidestepping the thorny issue of copyright. It was uncertain how the issue of phonographic royalties would be resolved or whether publishers might be required to compensate authors for reproducing their work in other media. British writers were not protected by copyright in the United States, of course, until the final decade of the nineteenth century—an oversight notoriously championed by Dickens during his first visit to America.[35] Hence, in the eyes of publishers, a Dickens title represented not just entertainment but *free* entertainment.

There was little consensus as to whether the phonograph would be used to facilitate reading aloud at public venues or in the privacy of one's home. Some foresaw the phonograph replacing the live orator by addressing large groups in public halls or schoolrooms. Mechanical reproduction was especially appealing in environments where it was expensive or impractical to invite speakers. For example, one journalist envisaged the phonograph reciting John B. Gough's temperance stories to a gathering of Nevada miners.[36] Other readers looked forward to solitary forms of reception that would have been impossible without the phonograph. The Dickens vignettes cited above retain the most attractive features of both public oration and private reading by emphasizing the benefits of reading aloud—superior elocution, dramatic delivery, and accessibility—while combining them with features formerly reserved for silent reading—control over one's environment, pace of narration, and solitude. In this sense, the phonograph introduced a distinct form of reading representing the best of both worlds.

A key strategy through which Edison ushered in the new era of recorded sound was by harkening back to older forms of entertainment that had preceded the phonograph. The use of nostalgia to promote the technology diverted attention away from the potential threat it posed to traditions of reading aloud. This is apparent in a *Daily Graphic* cartoon portraying Edison's idealized domestic scene alongside the caption, "The phonograph at home reading out a novel" (Figure 1.3). The scene is reminiscent of the archetypal Victorian image of family entertainment, with the crucial substitution of the phonograph. The

Figure 1.3. "The phonograph at home reading out a novel." From "The Papa of the Phonograph," *Daily Graphic* (New York), April 2, 1878, 1.

family members otherwise conform to conventional roles: father smokes a cigar, mother does needlework, and the two children obediently sit at the table during the recitation. The eyes and hands of the parents are free for labor or leisure, as Edison had promised, while the children respond to the phonograph as if it were a live orator, leaning in and staring at the machine with rapt attention. By aligning itself with a familiar domestic ritual, the bookless scene elides any sense of discomfort toward the displacement of an age-old domestic pastime or of storytelling's commodification. Edison's invention appears instead in the guise of a sensible, laborsaving device. The phonograph is indeed "at home."

The successful advertising campaign inspired one newspaper to predict "a nation of listeners" within thirty years.[37] The economics of publishing cylinders and discs would supposedly expedite America's transition from a reading to a listening nation. Numerous editorials insisted that publishers could produce books more cost effectively using the phonograph than the printing press.

The *Chicago Tribune* wrote of the phonograph, "One application of this quality will revolutionize the whole world of literature."[38] Edison told the paper that he was able to reproduce an entire novel for less than the cost of its print equivalent:

> Now, suppose that a publisher employs one of the most famous elocutionists of the age to talk one of Dickens' best novels upon a phonograph plate. By the stereotype process these plates are reproduced as fast as wanted, and much cheaper than books can be sold. The purchaser buys one of these plates for a mere song, takes it home of an evening, puts it in the machine, gets one of his children to turn the crank, and straightway Mr. [James] Murdock, Mr. [George] Vandenhoff, or Mrs. [Laura] Dainty commences reading the novel to the delighted family.[39]

The prediction is an optimistic one, coming from a source more interested in marketing the phonograph as an alternative to books than in reforming the publishing world. Notably left out of these calculations are the additional expenses of professional actors or elocutionists. The substantial labor costs involved in recording full-length texts—not to mention the three-decker novels of Dickens—are still a prohibitive feature of today's audiobook publishing industry. Commercial recordings of literary texts were all but impossible to make at a time when speakers needed to record each cylinder separately since, despite Edison's talk of stereotyping, there was no straightforward method of duplication prior to Berliner's gramophone in the 1890s.[40] The estimate also neglects to account for the declining costs of book production and the numerous conveniences of print.[41]

Edison's publishing house never managed to record a fifty-cent novel. Still, the press looked ahead to an environment unimpeded by technological limitations. Nearly everyone who responded to Edison's overambitious claims foresaw a time when it would be viable to record entire books—even Dickens. In the words of one starry-eyed journalist, "The library of the future will be one which any man can carry under his arm."[42] Not a bad prediction for 1878. Recorded books were still very much seen as books at that point. No one expected the book's demise, only its conversion into a different format. As Marshall McLuhan long ago pointed out, new media take their content from the media they replace.[43]

The enthusiasm for recorded books is unsurprising in a culture already steeped in oral performance off the page and on the stage. What stands out nevertheless is how one-sided the conversations are in favor of recorded books; rarely does one find a defense of printed books, as one finds so readily among the next century's defenses of the tactile pleasures of holding a material object in one's hands. Nostalgia for the book required a more pressing threat than the tinfoil phonograph.

The Metal Automatic Book of the Future

The phonograph may have remained silent during the ten-year interval between its debut and the first literary recordings of note, but its advocates did not. The silence was broken by an unlikely source—an eccentric essay written in 1883 by the University of Minnesota's Professor Evert Nymanover calling for the replacement of printed books by "whispering machines." What might sound perfectly reasonable to modern readers acquainted with portable listening devices such as iPods and smartphones sounded preposterous to Nymanover's contemporaries. The essay's odd mixture of English, German, and Swedish; its pseudoscientific calculations; and its florid oratory made it an object of ridicule after submission to *Scientific American*. Nymanover compounded the problem by proposing to lodge the machines in people's hats. The unorthodox solution would allow them to continue reading while doing other activities: "Everyone while sitting in the cars, walking in the streets, reclining on beds and sofas, could be perpetually listening to Adam Smith's moral sentiments, Draper's intellectual development, etc., and yet be at the same time talking, resting, working at a carpenter's bench, dressing, promenading, practicing finger-exercises on the piano, or other instruments, and so forth."[44] One activity stands out here: What kind of reader can listen to a book and talk at the same time?

Nymanover's vision of carpenters listening to Adam Smith's *The Theory of Moral Sentiments* and John William Draper's *The History of the Intellectual Development of Europe* reveals lofty expectations for a format that has since come to be associated with distraction. His notion of subliminal self-improvement while the conscious mind is preoccupied with other activities anticipates the twentieth century's faith in listening to self-help books while you sleep—if not its paranoia toward the new forms of government indoctrination portrayed in Aldous Huxley's *Brave New World*.[45] The passage nevertheless offers a glimpse of the direction taken by sound technology in the coming century. The proposal extends Edison's phonograph to mobile situations while at the same time capitalizing on the utilitarian imperative to improve minds and bodies simultaneously. The bizarre presentation made it difficult to take Nymanover's idea seriously, however, and the editors rejected whispering machines as the notion of a crackpot. The University of Minnesota's student magazine wanted the author executed for ludicrously proposing that "a man could get the Encyclopaedia Britannica with every new hat he bought."[46]

Nothing more was heard from Nymanover's whispering machines until R. Balmer of the Bibliothèque Nationale de France published an essay in defense of them in the March 1885 issue of the *Nineteenth Century,* a legitimate forum for intellectual debate in which the idea would be taken seriously. Balmer, while acknowledging the original proposal's eccentricity, defended its core idea: the development of a portable mechanism for reading aloud. Phonographs could be used to imprint entire books on miniature metal cylinders embedded inside an automaton, then inserted into a person's hat and connected to the ear by wires. The tiny reading machine represented, in Balmer's words, the "metal automatic book of the future."[47] Nearly a century ahead of the Walkman, the contraption introduced a way of entertaining urban commuters who were unable to read in crowded public spaces. One magazine observed that "a man might take a walk along a busy street, and have the book of the season read to him."[48]

Mechanical reading appealed to many as a way to democratize the book. The notion may seem counterintuitive since, as we now know, phonographic books were far less accessible than their print counterparts and unlikely to reach the people who would most benefit from them. The expensive equipment alone was a barrier to widespread consumption. Yet the conviction that all members of society should have access to culture was an abiding one.[49] The yearning to hear the author's voice made it easy to forget how dependent that voice's delivery was on a mechanical apparatus that would take decades to turn into a mass consumer good. Advocates saw only the medium's potential to reach an audience whose limited literacy made print inaccessible, or for whom the cost of books was an obstacle.[50]

Numerous illustrations set in industrial and agricultural environments reflect the initial optimism felt toward reaching potential readers denied access to print because of class, literacy, or geography. Balmer's hypothetical machine reached far beyond the average reader: "It would accompany men to the office, to the factory, to the bench, to the field, to the ditch, down into the mines, whispering into their ears greater thoughts and imaginations, strengthening, ennobling, and refining the mind."[51] Machines offered a way to educate housewives and domestic servants, too—candidates accustomed to reading aloud to suit the needs of others rather than for their own enrichment.

Edison even modified his sales pitch to include formerly marginalized readers when he brought out the improved phonograph in 1888, boasting to journalists, "The perfected phonograph is going to do more for the poor man than the printing press."[52] Such paternalism is at odds with the actual record of the phonograph, however, which remained unaffordable for most households until well into the twentieth century. Contrary to a marketing campaign offering entertainment for the middle classes and instruction for the working classes, there is no evidence that miners used the phonograph for self-improvement when given the chance.[53]

Nymanover's device was the first of a sequence of hypothetical reading machines devised over the next quarter century by advocates for those who were blind, engineers, futurists, utopianists, and novelists. Utopian writers in particular paid close attention to mechanized forms of reading since it was difficult to imagine an ideal society in which books did not play a prominent role. The form through which books would reach readers was by no means clear, however. The majority of utopian writers believed that technology would provide the solution to problems of literacy as well as the means to achieving an ideal society. Many of these writers foresaw the library playing a prominent role in public life by providing a communal space for learning or improved access to books through mechanical means such as underground railways and pneumatic tubes.[54] Other writers addressed the growing abundance of print that threatened to exhaust the capacities of libraries—and readers—to manage. Still others dreamed up new kinds of books altogether.

Edward Bellamy was one such writer to rethink the book in the context of new sound-recording technologies. Bellamy is best known for *Looking Backward: 2000–1887*, a science-fiction novel about the transformation of the United States into a socialist utopia in the year 2000. Its account of the book is oddly traditional, however, showing it to be untouched by the technological innovation so pervasive elsewhere in millennial Boston.[55] Bellamy's narrator turns for solace to the Victorian fiction of Dickens, for example, and the one modern narrative he reads is remarkable not for its form but its content. There is no visible difference between the books of the nineteenth and twentieth centuries in Bellamy's utopia. Thankfully, this was not Bellamy's last word on the book of the future. He returned to the topic a year later in the short story "With the Eyes Shut," a radical rethinking of the book written

after the author attended a phonograph demonstration. For Bellamy, the phonograph raised the question, Why imagine the sounds of words when you
could hear them read aloud?

Bellamy's prediction of recorded literature took part in a long tradition of
speculating about how new forms of technology would affect reading habits.
The fantasy of a mechanical talking book predated sound-recording technology by at least two centuries. Cyrano de Bergerac's *Histoire comique en
voyage dans la lune,* a seventeenth-century tale about a rocket trip to the moon,
includes an eyewitness report of a "Book made wholly for the Ears and not the
Eyes" that hangs from the auditor's ears like a pair of pendants.[56] Hearing
the narrative read aloud in a human voice was as easy as winding a spring.
The key difference between de Bergerac's musings and those of postindustrial
writers was the latter group's grounding in actual technology. Reviewers were
quick to point out that Bellamy's fictional depiction of a recorded book was
not nearly as far fetched as the socialist utopia envisioned in *Looking Backward.* The *Western Electrician* boasted that engineers were already working to
recreate the marvels of Bellamy's tale.[57]

"With the Eyes Shut" reflects Bellamy's interest in harnessing technology
to relieve the burdens of labor at a time when the United States was becoming
an increasingly industrialized nation.[58] Like its predecessor, the framed narrative begins with a man who wakes up in a futuristic society transformed by
technology. That society's citizens have little need to read for themselves since
they are read to by an "indispensable," Bellamy's term for the portable phonographic device used to play spoken word recordings of everything from letters to literature.[59] (The name suggests that our dependency on technology
was apparent even in its utopian representations.) The premise reflects the
enthusiasm readers felt toward the ease of listening to recorded books. In other
words, a crucial part of their appeal was the very passivity for which audiobooks are criticized today.[60]

We see this in the story's first scene, which involves an unnamed narrator
who listens to "phonographed books" using a "two-pronged ear-trumpet"
plugged into the railway carriage, allowing him to hear a novel read aloud for
the price of five cents an hour. Here's how Bellamy's narrator describes the
experience of reading with the eyes shut:

A good story is highly entertaining even when we have to get at it by the
roundabout means of spelling out the signs that stand for the words, and
imagining them uttered, and then imagining what they would mean if

uttered. What then shall be said of the delight of sitting at one's ease, with closed eyes, listening to the same story poured into one's ears in the strong, sweet, musical tones of a perfect mistress of the art of story-telling, and of the expression and excitation by means of the voice of every emotion?[61]

The listener's seduction is striking. Bellamy's account purposefully exaggerates the gap between the two modes of reception: the laborious, inefficient deciphering of the printed word in contrast to the effortless reception of words whispered into the ear. The scene operates as a bibliographic litmus test in its staging of the male reader's seduction by the female storyteller, seen either as siren or Scheherazade depending on the spectator's stance toward reading.[62]

In fact, modern critics have singled out "seduction" as the principal hazard of listening to recorded books.[63] The passage's erotic language set the terms of debate in the next century by intimating the potential danger in having a book read to you. The most enduring critique of the recorded book may not be that it is an ineffective way of delivering the text. On the contrary, it is too powerful. The narrator's excitation offers a glimpse of the discomfort toward a feminized mass culture emerging at the beginning of the twentieth century.[64] Print offered an antidote to the reader's excitation by ensuring a critical distance perceived to be impossible—even undesirable, from Bellamy's perspective—when unmediated by the page.

The ergonomics of reading warrant attention since modern audiences seldom think of reading novels as work—at least not to the same degree as an audience for whom books entailed manual as much as mental labor.[65] Utopian writers remind us of the effort required before interpretation even begins: cutting the leaves of a book, turning its pages, holding it open before weary eyes. Bellamy's concern for the reader's physical pleasure conflicts with a later modernist sensibility associating literary value with mental difficulty and discomfort.[66] According to Bellamy's account, the bodily fatigue entailed by reading saps energy best reserved for the brain. In fact, the speculative behavior associated with the very nature of reading is what Bellamy's narrator yearns to move beyond.

Nearly all accounts of phonograph recitals emphasize the ease of listening to books in contrast to the effort involved in reading them. As we have already seen, the strain printed books placed on the eyesight in particular made readers think of books in distinctly physiological terms. One of Bellamy's reviewers looked forward to "the days when [the eyes] are tortured by small type, dim light and weariness are gone forever."[67] Other potential benefits to the body included greater facial expressiveness and even improved posture—sacrificing the book's spine in order to preserve one's own.

The most utopian element of the story may be its faith in technology to improve the reading experience through the help of experts. We see this as a bookshop's customers test out several versions of the same title recited by different speakers, who vary in terms of style and quality. The implication is that literary recitation is a matter best left to the experts. There is no nostalgia for silent reading, no deference to the original text's authority, and no mention of a decline in quality—on the contrary, the voices enhance the work. Bellamy's narrator experiences the difference firsthand when listening to Tennyson's "Claribel" read by baritone, bass, contralto, and soprano speakers. In tomorrow's world, no man of taste would be content with a single rendering of the greatest writers.

Tennyson was an appropriate choice as an author renowned for "word music," a delight in the sound of language (sometimes at the expense of substance, at least according to his critics).[68] Bellamy had previously quoted Tennyson's "Locksley Hall" in *Looking Backward* as a precedent for its prophetic speaker. Here he chooses a poem noted less for its utopian optimism than for its sound effects. Tennyson referred to the poem as "A Melody," and there would be little to the short pastoral lyric were it not for the emphasis on sound to bring out the voices of nature alongside Claribel's grave.[69] Of course, Tennyson was an appropriate choice for another reason: he was among the first poets to record their verse on the phonograph, a year after the publication of Bellamy's tale.[70] Historians are fond of crediting the predictions that Bellamy got right: credit cards, shopping malls, electronic broadcasting, and so forth. Let's add to that list phonograph recordings of Britain's poet laureate.

The End of Books

Utopian fantasies of a mechanical reading machine reflect the era's optimism toward uninterrupted scientific progress. In this context, the printed book's evolution into a new format was welcomed as one of many technological advances meant to improve people's quality of life. The fin-de-siècle French futurists Octave Uzanne and Albert Robida followed Bellamy's lead in imagining how new media would remake the book. Their short tale "The End of

Books" appeared in English translation in *Scribner's Magazine* in 1894 as well as in the French volume *Contes pour les bibliophiles* in 1895. Ironically, the story's author was a self-professed bibliophile. Uzanne was unusual among book collectors in embracing the technological advances that had upended the book trade during the nineteenth century. Instead of rejecting industrialization wholesale, he encouraged the use of industrial techniques to refashion the book into an objet d'art.[71] The story's illustrator, Robida, was less ambivalent about the future and has garnered interest recently for predictions (including radio, television, and video phones) that have turned out to be more accurate than those of his better-known contemporary, Jules Verne.[72]

The tale begins with a conventional science-fiction question: What will society look like a hundred years from now? A group of intellectuals who meet in London to address the question foresee the replacement of the book as a bound object made of paper and ink by the machinery of a post-Gutenberg age. In the narrator's words, "Phonography will probably be the destruction of printing."[73] Yet the story's epitaph for print is misleading. The slogans "the end of books" and "the future of books" have equivalent meanings here since what Uzanne and Robida are describing is the remediation of books—that is, their conversion from one medium into another—in response to competition from rival media.[74]

In the tale's imagined future, books continue to circulate through audiovisual media or what might be called reading machines. The one envisioned here is a miniature phonograph strapped to your shoulder and connected to the ears by a set of flexible tubes—an uncanny harbinger of the modern-day Walkman (Figure 1.4). The spoken word reaches a mass audience through similar phonographic machinery including free listening stations in public squares, vending machines selling recordings of Dickens and Longfellow for the price of a nickel, and a Pullman Circulating Library for the entertainment of railway passengers (Figure 1.5). Modern-day troubadours promote their books by carrying portable phonographs from one apartment building to the next, where residents listen to them through elongated tubes stretching up to their windowsills (Figure 1.6). The original French version of the story includes Robida's sketch of a *bibliothèque universelle phonographique* ("universal phonographic library") capable of playing novels, poetry, history, and philosophy in one's home for an annual subscription of one hundred francs (Figure 1.7). Turning the dial to *"gai"* (comic) or *"triste"* (tragic) even catered to individual tastes for a happy ending.

Figure 1.4. "Phonographic literature for the promenade." From Octave Uzanne and Albert Robida, "The End of Books," *Scribner's Magazine* 16 (August 1894): 228.

Figure 1.5. "Reading on the Limited." From Octave Uzanne and Albert Robida, "The End of Books," *Scribner's Magazine* 16 (August 1894): 230.

Figure 1.6. "The author exploiting his own works." From Octave Uzanne and Albert Robida, "The End of Books," *Scribner's Magazine* 16 (August 1894): 229.

Figure 1.7. "Littérature et musique 'at home.'" From "La fin des livres," in Octave Uzanne and Albert Robida, *Contes pour les bibliophiles* (Paris: Quantin, 1895), plate between 136 and 137.

The story calls attention to how much of our vocabulary for discussing books makes sense only in relation to a particular format for them. Authors in a post-Gutenberg era need no longer be thought of as "writers" at all since they will "talk" their works instead—as the *Times* of London had predicted authors would do as early as 1878.[75] (Ironically, the phonograph's appeal for many writers was as the very dictation tool promoted by Edison for use by businesses.) The term "narrator" likewise has very different meanings depending on whether a book is read aloud or in silence. Auditors would compel authors to renew attention to "the art of utterance" or risk obsolescence. The highest demand would be for the "ravisher of the ear" distinguished by a well-pitched delivery instead of an ornate writing style. Deceased or vocally challenged authors alike could rely on professional voice actors or "favorite Tellers" to narrate their works, as in the cases of, say, Tommaso Salvini's Dante, Henry Irving's Shakespeare, or Sarah Bernhardt's Victor Hugo. Books would never sound the same once the narrative's implied voice began competing with a full cast.

"The End of Books" addresses the question implicitly raised by all accounts of recorded literature: Are reading and listening to books the same thing? Many of the terms used by Uzanne and Robida merely translate a bibliographic vocabulary into a phonographic one: narrator to "phonist," novel to "storygraph." Yet there is no simple translation for the term "reading." Cyrano de Bergerac's seventeenth-century account was already using the term "readers" in quotation marks in order to evade the question of similitude.[76] The absence of a single term to describe the act of listening is a problem evident in all accounts of the recorded book, some of which use the terms "reading" and "listening" interchangeably, others of which use the two terms in opposition in order to register distinct activities. For example, Bellamy describes a society in which "to listen was to read," whereas Uzanne and Robida speak of a future in which "hearers will not regret the time when they were readers."[77]

The textual evidence is proof that even a culture far more assured than our own when it comes to reading aloud struggled to resolve a question that persists to the present day. The inconsistency at least suggests that authors were aware of the troublesome set of questions raised by adapting the book into other media, a process culminating here in illustrated books made with Edison's Kinetograph, one of the earliest cameras used to film motion pictures.[78] The increasingly sophisticated technologies envisioned by Uzanne and Robida acknowledge the inescapable fact that the book was becoming more and more of a multimedia production with every passing year. At the same time, they raise doubts about whether such futuristic books involve the cognitive act of reading at all.

Long live the book. Readers who favored the status quo could take comfort in the skepticism voiced by an anonymous reviewer for the *Bookworm* after the story came out: "No phonogram, however entrancing its tones may be, can ever affect the dominion of the printed page."[79] The publication's very title suggested that the book was unlikely to go away without a struggle. Uzanne stood by his faith in phonography to transform the book, however. Two years after the publication of "The End of Books," Uzanne wondered, "Who might tell us, in effect, what will be the state of Bibliophilia in the year 2000? Will the art of typographic impression still exist at that date, and will the phonograph . . . not definitively replace printed paper and illustration with some advantage?"[80] It is a question that might have been taken straight out of Bellamy's *Looking Backward*. It is also one that we can answer from the perspective of the twenty-first century, when the printed book continues to survive alongside other media despite renewed calls for its demise.[81] Book historians have heard it all before, of course.[82] The post-Gutenberg era has taken longer to get underway than writers such as Uzanne and Robida imagined.

The supersession of the printed book was nevertheless inevitable in the eyes of Balmer, Bellamy, Uzanne, Robida, and many of their contemporaries. Even the nineteenth century's most renowned bibliophile, William Morris, predicted the book's extinction before the end of the next century.[83] These writers used the advent of sound-recording technology as an opportunity to speculate about what form books might take in the future while at the same time calling into question the utility of their current format. The superiority of the spoken page to the silent one was a standard claim made in accounts of the phonograph. As Balmer complained of print, "One half the power of literature is lost. No book is ever read as its author intended it should be read."[84] If readers had settled for print, it was only because no other option had been available until now. New forms of mechanical reproduction invited the book's discontents to formulate alternatives to it, as Balmer would do: "The full realization of what the printed book was intended to do will be the glorious mission of the phonographic reading-machine."[85] This theme—the recorded book as the next stage in the printed book's evolution—appears repeatedly throughout the deliberations over the future of the book taking place in the 1880s and 1890s. According to these accounts, the recorded book was not merely an alternative to the printed book. It was the realization of what the book was always meant to do.

Nostalgia for the book may tell us more about our own time than about the past. The initial responses to the recorded book suggest that modern perspectives are historically anachronistic in their privileging of the printed book over rival media. By contrast, those who took part in the discussions of recorded books taking place during the 1880s and 1890s in America, Britain, and France were quick to point out that the book was itself a technology of recent invention, one that had supplanted manuscript culture before going through its own convulsions. The book's ongoing development was not lost on Balmer. "To stop short at the phonograph," he declared, "would be much the same in its consequence as if the age of Faust and Gutenberg had remained content with its immovable types or the pen of the copyist."[86] Such appeals urged contemporaries to capitalize on a historic event that might turn out to be as pivotal to the history of literature as Gutenberg's press.

Comparisons made by Edison's contemporaries between the printing press and the phonograph helped to reframe the conversation about spoken word recordings as one about the nature of the book itself. A widely circulated account of Balmer's piece in the *Pall Mall Gazette* put the question in the following terms: "Why does not some modern Gutenberg do for the phonograph what has been already done for the printing press?"[87] The mechanical reproduction of the book was at stake here. Just as the press freed the book from its dependence on the scribe, the phonograph represented an analogous liberation from its dependence on print. If such optimism toward the evolution of the book makes many readers uncomfortable today, at a moment when the printed book's longevity is again in doubt, then that is partly because we have become used to associating print with progress and are unsure how to respond to the challenges posed to it by new media.[88]

The conventional narrative proposes that Edison developed the phonograph as a business device before consumers figured out ways of using it for entertainment purposes. This chapter has shown that the sequence was the other way around when it came to talking books. The dream of a talking book—of a Gutenberg for the phonograph—existed long before the technology to make it a reality. Speculation about talking books, whether in the form of bottled authors or whispering machines, arose simultaneously with the advent of phonograph technology and anticipated the completion of an actual talking book by nearly half a century.

If literary critics have been skeptical about the value of the recorded book, relegating it to a minor role in relation to the printed book, the phonograph's first listeners were more enthusiastic about the impact sound-recording technology would have on the republic of letters. The fantasy of recorded literature celebrated the possibilities presented by a new kind of books while at the same time directing attention to the book as a medium with distinct properties, and constraints, of its own. The enthusiasm for mechanical forms of reading suggests the limitations of a reading experience centered exclusively on print. The phonograph promised to change all of that through its preser-vation of the spoken word. Yet the revolution did not happen—at least not during the nineteenth century. Recordings of full-length books had to wait until the 1930s, and portable listening devices stored in our hats until the 1980s. Until then, defenders of the printed book could remain silent as long as talking books did so too.

PART II

Blindness, Disability, and
Talking Book Records

2

A Talking Book in Every Corner of Dark-Land

In 1932, Robert Irwin wrote to the director of the Library of Congress's Books for the Adult Blind Project, "May I ask you, though, what you would think of printing books for the blind on phonograph records?"[1] Irwin believed that it would soon be possible to record an entire book. The American Foundation for the Blind (AFB), of which Irwin was executive director, had spent the previous decade investigating the viability of spoken word recordings for the thousands of people with vision impairments who were unable to read in any other way. It went on to develop the first "talking book," the most significant advance in literacy among blind people since the invention of braille.[2] Yet talking books also raised profound questions about the nature of reading. The most intractable concerned the relationship between speech and print, or, in Irwin's words, "whether a book is still a book when it is printed on phonograph records."[3] Although Irwin's inquiry was primarily a legal one, we might take it as a philosophical one, too, since the talking book's standing has been in dispute ever since sound-recording technology enabled books to speak for themselves. Was a talking book still a book?

The AFB confused matters further by introducing the talking book as both an exact replica of the printed book and an improved version of it. A demonstration titled "What Is the Talking Book?" explained that it was a set of long-playing records on which one could hear a book read aloud.[4] And a promotional record announced, "I am a book whose contents are like those of any other book," before reciting excerpts from the Bible, Shakespeare, and Dickens.[5] Press coverage defined the format in contradictory ways too. Some publications described the talking book as an exact counterpart of the printed book because the narrative was read verbatim; others considered "talking book" a misnomer since it neither was a book nor talked.

Similar confusion surrounded the issue of reading: Was the talking book a way of reading *to* blind people or a way of reading *for* blind people? Blind people themselves described listening to talking books as "reading," not "hearing," since to do otherwise would acknowledge that they were not reading in the same sense as other people.[6] Georgina Kleege describes this distinction as a "stigma" still faced by blind people today.[7] In fact, it may be useful to think of the talking book as a prosthesis rather than a substitute for print since most blind readers had no choice in the matter. According to this way of thinking, the phonograph enabled blind people to read by acting as a surrogate means of vision. One AFB pamphlet asked its recipients, "Will you not do your part to enable the Talking Book to serve as eyes, as far as reading is concerned, by providing one or more machines to the blind in your community?"[8] Debates over aesthetic preferences were irrelevant to a group that was unable to read in any other way. Only a small percentage of blind people could read braille, and volunteer readers were scarce. For the average blind person, talking books meant the difference between reading and not reading at all.

While it is important to think about the talking book in relation to its print predecessors, we should also try to understand the format in its own terms. The talking book only exists because a group of people had no access to books at the beginning of the twentieth century. Media historians have long recognized the link between disability and invention.[9] The book was simply inadequate when it came to meeting the needs of people with disabilities. The obvious solution was to adapt the book into alternative formats suitable for these readers. As Mara Mills has argued, "Media exclusions thus necessitate technological adaptations."[10] The talking book's development thereby challenged conventional notions of the book as a medium exclusively reserved for print and of reading as an activity performed with the eyes instead of a multitude of senses.

This chapter addresses the vexed relationship between orality and print by taking us back to the talking book's origins. Existing accounts of the talking book document its technological, legislative, or institutional history.[11] By contrast, my account recuperates sound technology's social impact by tracing how the first generation to hear books mechanically read aloud encountered, responded to, and shaped the medium in crucial ways. Lisa Gitelman's work on the history of sound recording underscores how new media and their audiences evolve in relation to one another.[12] With this reciprocity in mind, I have sought to recover the voices of the first people to hear talking books in order to better understand the relationship between blindness, literacy, and technology.

The talking book service is commonly held up as a triumphant example of technology's capacity to overcome disability. The real story is more complex. The events documented in the following pages remind us how much resistance advocacy groups encountered—and continue to encounter—while attempting to persuade people of the need, value, and legitimacy of alternatives to printed books. Hence, my account begins with the groups who opposed the talking book (a cost-conscious government, anxious publishers, and even blind people themselves) before moving on to the people who welcomed it as a seemingly miraculous restoration of their ability to read. There is an entire genre devoted to readers' love for books.[13] It's time we heard instead from those readers who had their love of books wrested away from them midlife or who never had the chance to fall in love with books in the first place.

Life in a Bookless World

The first congressional hearing on books for blind adults began on March 27, 1930. The long campaign to supply reading material to people with vision impairments was part of a broader effort to dispel the stereotype of blind dependency. Advocacy groups strove to replace the image of the blind beggar with that of self-sufficient adults capable of leading satisfying lives.[14] Changing the belief that blind people were somehow different from the rest of the population was a crucial step in this campaign. As the superintendent of the Library of Congress's Reading Room for the Blind complained, "The assumption upon the part of certain well meaning but mistaken persons that a blind person is sub-normal as to mentality and therefore only a subject for vocational training must be done away with."[15] The Pratt-Smoot Act contested such assumptions by directing attention to the rich inner lives available to blind people through books.

The Books for the Adult Blind Project provided books in raised type to people who could not read without financial aid. People with impaired vision had only two ways of reading books at the beginning of the twentieth century. They could read books in embossed types like braille or hear them read aloud by friends, relatives, charitable volunteers, or paid readers. Both methods had disadvantages and could be expensive too. Braille books might cost more than twenty times their ink-print equivalents; for example, a reader could purchase *David Copperfield* in print for one dollar or in braille for thirty-five dollars.[16]

Not many people could afford paid readers, and only a fortunate few had access to the recitations held at metropolitan libraries in places like Cincinnati, San Francisco, and Washington, DC.

Advocacy groups conveyed to legislators literacy's importance by asking them to imagine life without books. The technique was simple: tell audiences to shut their eyes in order to feel what it's like to be blind. (This proved to be an effective rhetorical tactic even though it is naïve to think that people can simulate blindness by closing their eyes.[17]) At the hearing held in 1930, Helen Keller appealed to members of Congress to consider how different their lives would be without sight and, as a consequence, the opportunity to read books:

> Have you ever tried to imagine what it would be like not to see? Close your eyes for a moment. This room, the faces you have been looking at—where are they? Go to the window, keeping your eyes shut. Everything out there is a blank—the street, the sky, the sun itself! Try to find your way back to your seat. Can you picture who is sitting in that chair, day in and day out, always in the dark, and only the dark gazing back at you? What you would not give to be able to read again![18]

The thought experiment urged participants to consider being deprived of books at the moment when they were most needed. By establishing a link between blindness and literacy, Keller and other advocates at the hearing insisted that books played a crucial role in blind people's mental health. Testimonials attributed numerous benefits to books including independence, instruction, socialization, stimulation, and relief from severe and prolonged depression. Congress acknowledged the potential gains by awarding the Books for the Adult Blind Project an annual appropriation of $100,000.

Fund-raising campaigns used similar rhetoric to instill empathy in potential donors. One letter asked recipients to imagine closing their eyes forever: "What could a row of books as high as the ceiling mean to you and to me?"[19] The letter noted that over 114,000 men, women, and children in the United States had no access to books since, figuratively speaking, they would never again open their eyes. Such appeals say more about the public's fear of blindness than about the actual experience of sight loss. Another pamphlet reminded readers how easily an accident could deprive them of the ability to read: "What would it do to your life?" Its rhetoric tried to break down the distance between sighted and blind people—between "us" and "them." The pamphlet asked these same readers to contemplate how they would feel if given a second chance: "Shut your eyes for five minutes and try to picture life in a bookless world.

Then think if you were permanently blind what it would mean to have your beloved books come to life—to have a Talking Book that would tell its own story, read itself aloud to you." A fund-raising appeal on behalf of blind people followed: "Will you help us put this power within reach of all who sit in darkness?"[20]

The talking book aimed to bring the benefits of literacy to the thousands of blind people deprived of access to books. In the 1930s, the majority of people with vision impairments were unable to benefit from government-funded libraries in embossed type. Fewer than 20 percent of blind people were able to read braille; even within this group, only a fraction had mastered reading with their fingers well enough to do so without discomfort.[21] The remaining 80 percent of blind people couldn't read raised type. They had never learned to do so, found it too difficult, or suffered from other disabilities. Over half of the blind people in the United States had lost their sight after the age of fifty, when it is difficult to acquire a new language. These people needed an alternative way to read.

The case for federal support was not made on behalf of the civilian blind population alone. Blinded veterans represented another group that urgently needed access to books. Advocacy groups emphasized the nation's responsibilities to the hundreds of soldiers, sailors, and marines who had lost their sight in the First World War.[22] The figure of the war-blinded serviceman played a prominent role in discussions about the government's obligations even though the actual number of blinded veterans was comparatively small. There were estimated to be between 300 and 400 veterans who lost their sight during the First World War (or between 700 and 800 if less severe eye injuries are included) out of a total of 120,000 blind people in America.[23] Yet the patriotic sentiment aroused by these figures, who had sacrificed their bodies defending the country, was crucial to obtaining federal support. Frances Koestler has noted the irony by which the brutality of war was responsible for the benefits enjoyed by millions of blind civilians in its aftermath.[24]

Testimony throughout the congressional hearings invoked the figure of the war-blinded serviceman. Charles Campbell, for example, who had worked with the Red Cross retraining veterans blinded in France, reminded members of Congress how little reading material was available to them:

> I venture to predict that if any member of this committee could live, as I did, for three and a half years with the boys who came out of the trenches without their sight, and if you could have heard them say, "Oh, am I only

to have this book or that magazine?" I predict that you gentlemen would have been startled. And I only ask you to-night when you go home to answer this one question: How would you feel if your newspaper, your magazine, your book was but one out of that present multitude? It is so little, it is so contracted, that it is really pitiful.[25]

Campbell entreated Congress to support the men who lost their sight "for you and for me."[26] The heart-rending speech appealed to the committee's conscience, sense of duty, love of country, and religious obligations. It was one thing to leave charity to the private sector in the case of blind civilians; it was another to neglect the casualties of war.[27] Congress authorized its first appropriation for the purchase of embossed books in 1931. The appropriation was a victory; however, it did little to help the soldiers who couldn't read braille. The very figure singled out for government aid would not benefit from it unless an alternative way of reading could be found.

Revolutionary Changes in Books for the Blind

The idea of a talking book preceded the technology by more than half a century. As we saw in Chapter 1, Thomas Edison proposed using the tinfoil phonograph to read aloud to blind people after its invention in 1877.[28] No blind reader had heard a record without wishing that books might be made available in this way, claimed Irwin.[29] He himself had dreamed of hearing books read aloud ever since hearing a "squeaky Edison Cylinder" for the first time.[30] Other organizations had similar ideas. As early as 1906, for example, the American Library Association considered using the phonograph to read aloud to people who were blind.[31] Phonograph recordings of books remained expensive and impractical, however, as long as records could only play for a few minutes at a time. Irwin failed to interest commercial manufacturers such as the Western Electric Company, Edison Laboratories, or Radio Corporation of America since the potential market was so small. It would take over fifty years to fulfill Edison's wish.

Recorded books became a realistic possibility following technological advances in the film and radio industries. Irwin revived his childhood dream in April 1924, when he was approached by John W. Dyer, a former president of the Edison Phonograph Company. Dyer's father had devised a way of recording up to 15,000 words on each side of a twelve-inch record.[32] This was a substantial improvement over the existing records. The Dyers spent the next year trying to record an entire novel. "This would make the long dreamed of library of phonograph records for the blind entirely practicable," wrote Irwin.[33] After promising results, Irwin wrote to a friend that there would soon be "revolutionary changes in books for the blind."[34] He had to wait another decade for the revolution, however. The breakthrough had yet to come in 1927, when Irwin wrote to various engineers that the first person to record a novel would stand alongside Valentin Haüy and Louis Braille as the greatest benefactors of blind people in history.[35]

The AFB sought a recording format that was simple to use, cheap to manufacture, and adapted to the needs of a blind readership. Ordinary commercial records were unsuitable since they could only play for a few minutes. (Long-playing records were not ready for the commercial market until 1948.) In addition, shellac records were too expensive, heavy, and fragile to ship through the mail. Talking book records needed to be compact and durable; they also needed to be economical enough to compete with braille and, eventually, ink-print books. Engineers struggled to keep pace with Irwin's optimism, however. In October 1930, a representative from the Edison Laboratories demonstrated a test record to the AFB's board of trustees. The record was difficult to hear and prohibitively expensive anyway.

The AFB established its own studio in 1932 to investigate the viability of a talking book library. By this point it had decided that sound recordings were the most practical way to provide reading material for the approximately 85,000 blind people in the United States who were unable to read braille.[36] Many of these people were already accustomed to radios following a campaign begun in 1924 to donate them to blind people.[37] The AFB set up its studio in Grand Central Palace, New York, in order to avoid the prohibitive costs of commercial studios and to resolve technical issues specific to a readership with disabilities. Jackson Kleber's team of engineers focused on three areas: the development of a record sufficiently compact and durable for library circulation, the production of a talking book player adapted for the use of visually impaired people, and the preparation of facilities capable of manufacturing forty to fifty books a year.[38]

Talking books were recorded on twelve-inch phonograph records since this was the largest size that could be shelved conveniently. The double-faced vinylite records contained 150 grooves per inch and played at a slow speed of 33⅓ revolutions per minute (as opposed to the standard rate of 78 rpm).[39]

They held approximately fifteen minutes of speech per side, enabling the average novel to fit on twenty records (Figures 2.1 and 2.2). (Many works required far more: *A Tree Grows in Brooklyn* [32 records], *Gone with the Wind* [80], *War and Peace* [118], and the Bible [169].) Discs were shipped to patrons using sturdy containers and played on specialized equipment in order to avoid sounding like recordings of Daffy Duck.[40] The player itself resembled an ordinary phonograph with controls to adjust the speed, tone, and volume. The success of the initial trials led Irwin to declare, "I believe that the libraries for the blind of the future will be stocked with phonograph records instead of braille books, and that these records will be loaned through the mails just as braille books are today."[41] Irwin announced the initiative at the American Association of Instructors of the Blind's annual convention held in 1932.

The Library of Congress sent the first talking books to readers in October 1934 (Figures 2.3 and 2.4). They included the Bible (the four Gospels, the Psalms), patriotic documents (the Declaration of Independence, the Constitution, George Washington's Farewell Address and Valley Forge Letter to the Continental Congress, Abraham Lincoln's Gettysburg Address and First and Second Inaugural Addresses), and Shakespeare (*As You Like It, Hamlet, The Merchant of Venice*). Irwin and Herman Meyer, who directed the Library of Congress's Books for the Adult Blind Project and wished to establish the program with "something notable," chose as the first recording Samuel Taylor Coleridge's "The Rime of the Ancient Mariner."[42] It was an appropriate choice considering the poem's imitation of an oral form (the ballad) and recitation to a spellbound auditor. In fact, William Wordsworth famously defined the poet as "a man speaking to men" in the preface to the collection featuring Coleridge's poem.[43]

The list featured a mix of classic and contemporary literature for a broad readership. The first novel recorded was Gladys Hasty Carroll's *As the Earth Turns*, a best-selling novel about Maine farm life that had been nominated for a Pulitzer. This was followed by Rudyard Kipling's "The Brushwood Boy" and Cora Jarrett's *Night over Fitch's Pond*. The next three works of fiction were all by British authors: E. M. Delafield's *The Diary of a Provincial Lady*, John Masefield's *The Bird of Dawning*, and P. G. Wodehouse's *Very Good, Jeeves*.[44] The list's composition was a sensitive matter since the AFB sought to treat blind readers like other readers. Hence the list reflected a range of tastes including popular fiction. As we'll see in Chapter 4, the balance between classic

Figure 2.1. A talking book record featuring Tolstoy's *War and Peace*.

Figure 2.2. Complete sets of talking book records for *War and Peace, Gone with the Wind,* the Bible, *The Yearling,* and *One World*.

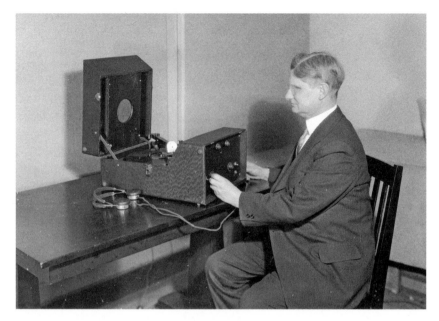

Figure 2.3. Robert Irwin listening to a talking book machine (1934).

Figure 2.4. "Blinded airman listening to talking book" (1944).

and contemporary fiction would be a contentious issue in the decades to come.

Controversy plagued the selection process from the outset since the talking book program received government funding. Meyer deflected potential criticism by ensuring that religious, patriotic, and historic titles always appeared first on the list of titles sponsored by the Library of Congress; the remaining fiction came next.[45] The inaugural titles represented edifying material conducive to self-improvement and good citizenship. Expanding the catalog of popular literature (detective stories, westerns, travelogues, memoirs, and so forth) would have to wait until later, when controversial selections could be attributed to the AFB rather than the Library of Congress.

The Bible was indispensable in more ways than one. It appeased those opposed to the use of federal funding for immoral entertainment (fiction, in other words) while at the same time appealing to a large number of readers. Its presence also helped to secure donations. A fund-raising campaign warned prospective donors that people would be unable to read scripture without the talking book's aid: "Is it not a pity that thousands upon thousands of blind people have never been able to read it by themselves?"[46] Their contributions ensured that the spiritual as well as material needs of blind people were met. Subsequent demonstrations emphasized the talking book's devotional prospects by reciting verse from Isaiah 42:16 about opening the eyes of blind people: "I will make darkness light before them."[47]

The Library of Congress hailed the talking book program as the realization of Edison's plan.[48] In 1934, the AFB asked Congress to include talking books among those receiving federal subsidies. The Pratt-Smoot Act's wording only covered books in raised type, of course, since talking books had yet to be invented when the bill was proposed. An amendment fixed this, making recorded books eligible for federal support. The revised wording specified books "published either in raised characters, on sound-reproduction records, or in any other form."[49] In doing so, it formally acknowledged the ambiguity of the term "books" for a readership that used at least three different kinds of them (talking, raised print, and ink print).

Eye, Ear, and Finger Readers

Talking books encountered resistance not only from legislators but also from commercial publishers and even from blind people themselves. In 1935, Helen

Keller described the talking book as the greatest invention for blind people since braille.[50] Yet the AFB's best-known ambassador had refused to take part in the fund-raising campaign when first approached. Keller replied by cable, "TALKING BOOKS A LUXURY THE BLIND CAN GO WITHOUT FOR THE PRESENT."[51] Her refusal was based on economic, not aesthetic, principles. An avowed socialist, Keller did not wish to solicit money for phonographs amid a severe economic depression that had left millions out of work. Still, Keller's resistance surprised the AFB, which was accustomed to her support of initiatives to expand literacy even when they held few benefits for people who were deaf as well as blind.[52]

Keller agreed to publicize the talking book only after confirming that it did not pose a threat to braille funding (Figure 2.5). Her influence reached all the way to the White House. The Works Progress Administration (WPA) initiative to manufacture talking book machines owed much to Keller's publicity. She memorably wrote to First Lady Eleanor Roosevelt asking for help

Figure 2.5. Helen Keller and Robert Irwin exhibiting a talking book player.

promoting the service: "I am wondering if you would give a tea at the White House to help me send the talking-book to every corner of Dark-land."[53] Her guests at the White House were among the first to hear one.

Keller's hostility was a sign of further opposition to come from braille readers. They had the most at stake if federal funds were diverted to a rival technology. The *Braille Mirror* led the campaign to discredit the competition. As one braille user declared, "With a talking book one cannot *read!*"[54] Others objected to the passivity. "It is a lazy man's way of reading," a woman was told.[55] Braille advocates distinguished between the active experience of reading for oneself and the supposedly passive experience of being read to by another person. One braille reader found "nothing more monotonous than to sit by the hour, warming a chair, listening to the same voice on a phonograph record."[56] Similar accounts criticized "chair-warmers" who were too lazy to read raised type.[57] Braille advocates disapproved of the talking book on aesthetic grounds too. Their objections to "a canned voice" invoked complaints against music's commodification that had been made at the turn of the century by John Philip Sousa.[58]

The Library of Congress assured patrons that recorded books would not supersede braille for two reasons. First, braille was a medium for writing as well as reading; and second, learning it was an "intellectual accomplishment."[59] A supplementary form of reading might even benefit those who preferred to read instructional material with their fingers and recreational material with their ears. Even teachers acknowledged the benefits. For example, the New York Institute for the Education of the Blind recorded several classics after students complained that braille interfered with their ability to appreciate verse. As Irwin observed, "Few even of the students in our schools for the blind acquire sufficient speed in finger reading to enable them to enjoy the rhythm and other beauties of form in such verse as Longfellow's 'Hiawatha' or Scott's 'Lady of the Lake.' "[60] Many teachers already supplemented braille with reading aloud anyway.

The majority of braille readers welcomed talking books. They saw it as a way of expanding access to print for those who couldn't read with their fingers. (One observer attributed opposition to "the mistaken notion that Braille is something holy within itself."[61]) S. Mervin Sinclair, president of the National Association of State Associations and Commissions for the Blind, complained that he had learned the language too late in life to be adept. The "slow, awkward fashion" with which he read gave him little pleasure after spending most of his life as a rapid sight reader: "Your fingers just do not go as fast as your thoughts."[62] Even proficient braille users acknowledged that it was faster to read a talking book than an embossed one. Compare the average reading speed of a talking book at 190 words per minute (wpm) to that of braille at 60 wpm. (The visual average is 250–300 wpm.) Some people read with their fingers as slowly as 20 wpm.[63]

Listening to books was also less physically demanding than braille. The talking book presented an alternative for those who struggled to read with their fingers, suffered from other disabilities, or wanted to read for long periods of time. For manual laborers, reading braille was anything but relaxing. One prospective listener in Washington, DC, wrote, "Although I read Braille very rapidly, I am often too tired after the days [sic] work to run my fingers over a Braille book, and shall enjoy this new leisurely way of enjoying a good book."[64] This prospect appealed especially to people who used braille because they had no other choice. A reader from Mendon, Michigan, complained, "What is worse than the dull drudgery of pawing dull dots through volumes and volumes[?]" He looked forward to talking books because "God did not ordain that we should read with our fingers forever."[65]

Publishers needed to be persuaded of the talking book's benefits too. The AFB's catalog would not be able to include titles published after July 1, 1880, without consent from publishers. While many classics were in the public domain, recent titles were protected by copyright law. The Librarian of Congress warned that relying on pre-1880 titles "would be to deprive the blind, who have sufficient disabilities already, of the contact with the modern world which they crave, which they plead for daily and which the talking book gave promise of providing them."[66] Withheld permission undermined efforts to establish parity between blind and sighted readers. For decades publishers had permitted their titles to be reproduced in braille, but the talking book raised concerns since it could be heard by all readers—maybe even on the radio.

Most publishers granted permission to record copyrighted books in exchange for assurances that the recordings would only be heard by people who were blind. The AFB's agreement with the Authors Guild and the National Association of Book Publishers prohibited commercial use of the records. The AFB agreed to a nominal fee of twenty-five dollars per title to protect the copyright principle; a limit of 300 copies per title; a label marked "solely for the use of the blind" on the face of each record; and, accompanying each set of discs, a letter stipulating the legal terms and forbidding their use by sighted people, at public venues, or on the radio.[67] The strict measures gave rise to the tale of a blind man who ordered his wife and children to leave the house every time he played a record.[68]

Holdouts such as Appleton-Century Company refused to cede any rights until the commercial prospects of recorded books were better understood. "On the whole I think the publishers wish to cooperate," observed Irwin, "but most of them are a little anxious for fear the Talking Book may get out of hand and become a competitor of the ink-type book."[69] Companies wished to avoid setting a legal precedent that would deprive them of future royalties. Irwin noted of the publishers, "They were afraid that too many seeing people would want talking books, and many of the publishers would be put out of business."[70] A. C. Ellis, superintendent of the American Printing House for the Blind, assured publishers that talking books would have little impact on the commercial market since the technology used to make them was already known to the radio and cinema industries. Commerce would proceed independently of any philanthropic initiative. Ellis wrote to the publisher Alfred A. Knopf, "What I am trying to say is that the recording of books for the blind is a small, sheltered undertaking which can have very little influence on the development of a wider use of recorded literature by the seeing."[71] People would find ways to listen to books regardless of whether blind people were listening to them.

Margaret Mitchell was the most prominent author to refuse to allow her novels to be recorded. The Library of Congress made a braille edition of *Gone with the Wind* in 1936. However, recording permission was not sought then because such a large book would be expensive to record (approximately $6,000 as opposed to the average of $1,500) and might be forgotten in a few years anyway. The Librarian of Congress approached Mitchell again in 1940 in response to growing demand for a recording of Mitchell's novel—possibly read by Mitchell herself. Her publisher had already agreed to the request.[72]

The invitation turned into a public relations disaster, however, when Mitchell became suspicious that the Library of Congress had already recorded the novel without her permission. The misunderstanding arose because a catalog sent to her displayed *Gone with the Wind* alongside the titles of other writers who had given their permission. Instead of persuading Mitchell of the project's worthiness, the entry prompted legal action. The library apologized, reassuring Mitchell that her novel, despite being on the prospective list, had not yet been recorded and would not be without her permission. In fact, the library maintained a policy of obtaining the author's permission even after securing the legal right to record any title under revised copyright legislation, which treated phonograph recordings of fiction differently from those of plays, sermons, lectures, and music.

Despite the apology, Mitchell continued to withhold permission on the grounds that her book might be broadcast over the radio.[73] In 1940, Irwin wrote to an attorney, "If you can make available GONE WITH THE WIND, you will have the thanks of an amazingly large number of blind people who have been clamoring for this book ever since it caught the public fancy."[74] She eventually relented. In the end, blind people heard Mitchell's "book of the moment" four years after its original publication.

Oh What a World of Beauty

The AFB received hundreds of letters from the initial recipients of talking book machines. Listening to spoken word recordings represented a revolution in literacy, according to the AFB, enabling people to read books who could not do so in any other way. "Your saying 'It veritably revolutionizes reading for the blind' is as well said as any one can express it," declared one woman. "How in accord I feel with you."[75] Letters written (or dictated) by the recipients of talking book machines reveal how they felt about the new format in terms of its resemblance to ink-print books, its mechanical properties, and its social benefits. This archive preserves a diverse and conflicting set of responses to a question of long-standing interest: What is it like to be a blind reader?

In March 1934, the *Matilda Ziegler Magazine for the Blind* invited correspondence from people who wished to obtain talking book machines. The responses cite the numerous inconveniences and difficulties faced by a group of readers who longed for a technological solution to them. The most optimistic ones expected that talking books would solve problems ranging from difficulty with braille to isolation and inequality. A Chicago subscriber facetiously predicted that "every blind person who is not dead from his shoulders up" would appreciate the machines.[76] Nearly all correspondents expressed dissatisfaction with the existing formats. A Pennsylvanian woman sought to supplement her use of braille since, in her words, "I am one of those who long to hear good reading, but tire of doing it with my fingers."[77] Another woman proposed using the machine when no volunteers were available: "I go out very little and have no one to read to me and I love reading."[78] These people wanted to read more than their disabilities allowed them to.

The following year, *Matilda Ziegler Magazine* sponsored a contest titled "Why I Want a Talking Book Reading Machine."[79] The entries reveal as much about the social obligations tolerated by people with disabilities as they do about the technology. The desire to own a mechanical reading device commonly arose from tensions between these people and the volunteers on whom they depended. Hence, the talking book granted readers like Blanche Logan "glorious independence," allowing her to choose what and when to read.[80] Logan detested asking for help: "No longer will it be necessary for you to ask a friend in an apologetic voice to read you a book you desire to hear."[81] She needn't worry about offending a machine. The talking book relieved the burden of other people's attention, judgment, and disapproval. Della Clark of Stone Ridge, New York, for example, used it to read material that could not be read "by others whose tastes differed from mine."[82]

Charles Magee Adams's prize-winning letter commended the talking book machine for giving readers greater autonomy. A freelance journalist from Milford, Ohio, Adams compared the talking book to the familiar pastime of reading aloud: "In effect, it puts a trained reader at the command of every blind person. Voice fatigue, clashing tastes, and conflicts of available time no longer interfere. The blind person can read whenever, whatever, and as long as he chooses."[83] Calling the machine a "trained reader" reassuringly personified it while at the same time setting it apart as superior.[84] Adams was not alone in welcoming the replacement of flesh-and-blood readers by mechanical surrogates; too often volunteers were the ones who read like machines. Far from lamenting the loss of human contact, blind people looked forward to hearing books read aloud without the obligations.

Letters to the AFB express sheer gratitude on behalf of people who had given up hope of ever reading again. "It is a wonderful thing to be able to read," a woman from California wrote after receiving her machine.[85] People wrote to the AFB within days of receiving their players. A recipient in Knoxville, Tennessee, thanked the organization for her "magical box." While sitting in front of the device, she tells us, "I found my eyes swimming and my throat tightening. It has stirred me more than anything before in Blind Land."[86] Organizations across the country wrote to the AFB on behalf of other readers who were unable to speak for themselves or who struggled to find words to express how they felt about a machine designed to do the talking for them.

Talking books transformed some people's lives. Sight loss had forced many people to stop reading. Alma Wingfield of Madison Heights, Virginia, recalled

how difficult she found the sacrifice: "I have been blind two years, and among
the things which I had to give up on account of the loss of my eye sight I can
truthfully say that I have missed reading more than anything else as I have
not yet mastered the braille system."[87] Talking books allowed people to resume
reading in spite of their vision impairments. One man who used the phonograph to resume reading told the AFB, "You have no idea how much change
this book has made in my life, these talking books."[88] They meant the difference between reading and not reading for many correspondents. A. L. Hammell of Dubuque, Iowa, wrote after receiving his machine, "I can now enjoy
the books which I otherwise would not have done."[89] Hammell represented
an entire class of readers for whom talking books were the only option.
Beneficiaries doubted whether the technology's impact could be appreciated
by people who took books for granted. As Minnie Hicks of Overlea, Maryland, explained, "I cannot give you any idea of what these Talking Books
mean to those of us who cannot read ordinary print."[90]

Other letters expressed childlike enthusiasm. "As I wait for the records to
come," wrote one woman, "I am not unlike the children waiting for Santa
Claus."[91] A man in New York embraced the chance to operate the machine
for himself since he could no longer handle books. He exclaimed, "I could
cry like a child to think that in my life of darkness my hands were still active
to give me some pleasure in life."[92] The talking book's tactility pleased him
even though he now flipped discs instead of pages. Not having read a book in
a decade, a woman from Niobe, New York, did not want to stop after her machine arrived: "I appreciate the books as I have not been able to read a book
for over ten years. I would like to have another book. Send whatever you
have."[93] Which ones hardly mattered. The mere prospect of reading granted
access to imaginative realms from which blind people had long been excluded.
As one reader exclaimed, "Oh what a world of beauty is now open to us."[94]

Blind people had long felt shut out from books. "Books have been sealed
to me for some years," lamented a woman who had lost her sight as an adult.[95]
Talking books seemed to open them up again: "No longer when you touch
the cover of an old classic, must you feel it is a closed book to you."[96] The act
of unveiling was a familiar trope among inspirational writing about blindness and literacy. The cover of *Outlook for the Blind* magazine, for example,
featured a sentimental painting titled *Lifting the Veil of Darkness,* which
showed an angelic woman restoring a blind man's ability to see books
(Figure 2.6).[97] Another common metaphor was the genie in a bottle who could
summon forth a book's contents. One pamphlet assured the talking book's

Figure 2.6. Percy Van Eman Ivory's *Lifting the Veil of Darkness,* featured on every cover of *Outlook for the Blind* from 1923 to 1935.

prospective readers, "You are its master. It is your faithful slave—your genie to command."[98] The metaphor was an empowering one for a group that depended on other people for access to books.

The chance to read again struck many as divine grace. How could the restoration of literacy be anything other than a miracle? A woman wrote after hearing her first set of records, "The Talking Book is a godsend to the blind and I thank Him and all who have made this wonderful thing possible."[99] Others described it as "the miracle of the ages" and "God's blessing to the blind."[100] Isaiah's promise not to forsake the blind had the force of prophesy for beneficiaries of talking books. Bereft readers who had felt cast away by God felt attended to once again. A woman in Denver concluded that "God certainly takes care of his blind."[101] Talking books came in answer to at least one reader's prayer. That woman insisted, "The Lord has made this machine for me alone."[102] It felt as if the Word was spoken directly to these people.

Blindness has always lent itself to metaphors.[103] One of the most common ways of describing blindness was as a conflict between light and darkness. Many people sought to dispel the biblical association of blindness with darkness as a cliché while at the same time continuing to use this imagery to communicate with sighted people. Such figures of speech—think back to "Dark-land"—appear throughout Keller's publicity campaign and her long-standing defense of books as the gateway to an unseen world. Others used the metaphor to convey the difference talking books had made in their own lives. After receiving a turntable from the Navy Unit Gift Committee, Mrs. Norman Reever wrote, "You will never know how happy you have made me. Your kindness will bring much joy and sunshine into my dark life."[104] The phrase conveyed in visual terms what was a profoundly aural experience.

The talking book promised to distribute literacy's benefits to the blind community as a whole. "It will open up the field of literature to thousands of our people," wrote a man in Indiana.[105] Access to books was thought to be a great step forward in the cultural life of blind people as well as toward social equality. A man from Rochester, New York, described the talking book as "the blind person's nearest approach to the regaining of sight."[106] Letters frequently invoked a modest desire for "normalcy." For example, a West Virginian looked forward to participating in the cultural literacy taken for granted by other people: "It will do so much to make us more normal among our sighted friends to be able to discuss and to understand their discussion of books."[107] This correspondent recognized the importance of social inclusion on equal terms. No matter what use blind people made of books, they would at least be able to consult those resources available to everyone else. After listening to Watson Davis's *The Advance of Science*, Frank Armstrong, for one, rejoiced that "we now have access to the same literature as our seeing friends."[108]

Readers disagreed whether talking books should teach people about blindness or distract them from a disability they understood all too well. Helen

Keller's inspirational story was a perennial favorite. Mrs. J. F. Heinkel of Fort Dodge, Iowa, for example, enjoyed *Anne Sullivan Macy: The Story behind Helen Keller,* which she described as a "wonderful story of the perfect blending of those two lives."[109] Another reader from South Dakota urged everyone to listen to Keller's *The Story of My Life.* "Really, I don't believe that I have ever had a book thrill and inspire me quite so much as this wonderful story of dear Miss Keller's life," he wrote. "I hope, that as other blind readers like myself, when they read this book that it will strike a responsive cord [*sic*] in their heart as it has in mine."[110] By contrast, other readers did not want to be inspired or even reminded of their sight loss. A Louisianan woman made a plea for this group: "To those of us who merely wish to be helped keep our minds from the tragedy of blindness, give us something to make us forget for even an hour or two."[111] Escapism was highly valued by many people with disabilities.

Advocacy groups insisted that people who were blind had fewer opportunities to enjoy themselves than other people. Books took on increased importance within this restricted field of leisure. Charles Kuchler was not alone in thinking of talking books as "one of the greatest banishers of the terrible forced idleness under which so many blind people suffer."[112] The AFB's portraits of eligible recipients emphasized the tedium of their lives; one exhibitor recalled an elderly man who spent the entire day twiddling his thumbs and a woman who sat on her bed in silence.[113] A former seaman came to rely on talking books to pass the time. "Having been very active all my life it has been a great hardship to be so completely shut away," he explained. "During the day I keep my mind and hands occupied but dread the long winter evenings."[114] The talking book gave him something to do when there was no one to talk to.

The AFB promoted talking books as a means of "undreamed independence."[115] This was welcome news to the thousands of blind people who relied on the services of family, friends, and charitable volunteers. A Pennsylvanian woman commented, "What a pleasure it will be to do away with the often very unsatisfactory need of sighted readers."[116] Volunteers frustrated even the most patient auditors. Magazines for people with vision impairments regularly lampooned them. Take the well-intentioned Miss Fuss, who, in one sketch, arrives late, chatters ceaselessly, offers unsolicited advice, meddles in private affairs, patronizes people with disabilities, interrupts the reading with commentary, abridges or even censors the material, and then leaves early.[117] Eleanor Brown of Dayton, Ohio, described the talking book as "the greatest emancipator the blind have ever known" for allowing her to read a book according to her own schedule, not someone else's. She writes of the talking book player, "It means that I can read an average sized book in an evening. It means that I can read as long as and as often as I wish."[118] The AFB reported that readers were listening to talking books for up to eight hours at a stretch and staying up all night to finish them.[119]

Talking books accommodated conflicting impulses to escape dependency on other people and to increase contact with them. To this end, the machine's speech mitigated the social isolation endured by many blind people. John Dunney looked forward to hearing the narrator's voice on "the long, lonely nights" in Seattle, and Charles Smith wrote to the Connecticut Board of Education that the player "makes me forget my loneliness."[120] Such readers invoked the venerable tradition of books as the friends of the friendless. Hearing another person's voice provided isolated people contact with the outside world and even a form of virtual companionship. Grace Allen of Orlando, Florida, observed that hearing a talking book "is just like listening to some one read right in the room with one" (Figure 2.7).[121] Charitable organizations used the talking book as a tool for keeping the housebound or "shut-ins" in contact with the community.[122]

Isolated readers depended on the talking book as a friend or even surrogate family. Personifying the narrator as "an unknown friend" suggests how comfortable readers felt toward the machine's displacement of human volunteers.[123] "Never for one moment can I think of it as a machine," wrote one of the many recipients who spoke of talking book players in distinctly human terms.[124] The AFB even introduced the machine as a potential member of the family.[125] Personifying the machine in this way encouraged readers to think of the narrator as an actual person, though some people objected to the use of such intimate terms since the machine was supposed to provide a service to people with disabilities.[126] A number of people claimed that they could no longer live without it. A woman from Philadelphia who referred to "my" talking book machine remarked, "How possessively I refer to it, but honestly, I cannot visualize being without it, it has become such a vital part of my daily living."[127] What Helen Keller initially referred to as a luxury for blind people quickly came to be regarded as a "necessity" by many of them.[128]

The talking book gave some consolation to families too. Mrs. J. D. Bell of Granger, Texas, credited the talking book with entertaining her husband in a household that didn't even have a daily newspaper. The guilt she felt when not attending to him personally was lessened by talking books: "They also

Figure 2.7. John Knight's image appears above the talking book machine while a woman listens to him read.

lift a great load from the minds and hearts of persons associated with the blind, as those of us who are can be happier and go about our own duties with lighter hearts if we know that our loved ones are not sitting in darkness and loneliness."[129] Other relatives reported physical and psychological benefits. One woman's daughter reportedly told her, "Why, Mother, you've become so alive, and so pink and you look a whole year younger since the talking book came."[130] Such changes came as a relief to those concerned about a loved one's mental health.

Nor were the forms of sociability enabled by talking books entirely virtual. Some readers took advantage of the medium to listen to books with other people (Figure 2.8). Married couples or institutionalized people had the best opportunities to do so. But blind people who lived independently listened to books with others too. Copyright restrictions did not stop them from forming reading groups with family and friends. For example, Mattie French wrote to the Connecticut Board of Education about her talking books, "My friends who are living with me like to hear them too, so we have nice evenings together."[131] Civil disobedience turned the solitary act of reading into a social one.

How did talking books compare to silent ones? Few letters explicitly compare the two media. Those that do typically express admiration for the machine's proficiency or even a preference for mechanical recitation. The player

Figure 2.8. Members of the Protestant Guild for the Blind listening to a talking book. Massachusetts, ca. 1940.

exceeded at least one reader's expectations: "I did not imagine that the talking-book would be half so good as it is. I find it to be almost perfect in every possible way and in some ways superior to reading."[132] Devotional texts and other narratives intended to be read aloud seemed ideally suited to the medium. "I find that I enjoy my Bible reading more now than when I used to read it from print," observed one woman. "I seem to feel the meaning of the Word more when I hear it so well read as thru [sic] the Talking Book."[133] Converts typically credited "superior readers."[134] A former librarian and his wife found that Alexander Woollcott's reading enhanced Dickens's novels: "When we read 'A Tale of Two Cities' last winter (which we had not read for forty years), we were charmed and amazed to see how much more clearly *hearing* it read in this manner and how much more distinctly the plot stood out among all its clues and intricacies."[135] The Jordans were typical in engaging books in more than one format.

Talking book players could be used to read as well as to reread. A seventy-year-old man from Sacramento listened closely to the narrator's voice while reading for the second time Dickens's *The Pickwick Papers* and George Eliot's *Romola.* Before losing his sight, he had read them as a child growing up in Chicago. This was not simply nostalgia. Instead, it was a chance to look back on life from the perspective of old age: "The rereading was more than a second witnessing of an old story. It was a reliving of an old necessarily unassimilated experience now widely interpreted by the experience I myself had gathered through the years."[136] The author enjoyed the opportunity to reminisce while at the same time observing crucial differences between sound and print. His letter ends by noting, "I still miss the feel of a book in my hands when reading."[137]

For other people, having their hands freed up was the talking book's most attractive feature. Some used the opportunity to work. Others used it to knit or smoke (Figure 2.9). Talking books allowed Josephine Peters to "keep on working and listening to reading at the same time," and a Pennsylvania housewife found them easy to listen to while raising kids.[138] Others appreciated the chance to unwind. A California woman exclaimed, "To be able to sew or knit, peel potatoes, or make a cake, and at the same time get some reading done is a long-felt desire gloriously fulfilled. Yes, to actually *relax* and read!"[139] Braille readers found it difficult to relax while their hands were engaged. By contrast, people could lie in bed or smoke—or both—while listening. "I can lie down, put on my head phones, light a cigarette or pipe, and

Figure 2.9. Mrs. Elsie Cowan knitting while listening to a talking book.

enjoy the world's finest drama," explained a man in Oregon.[140] He didn't even have to turn the pages.

The talking book library grew rapidly after the initial opposition from legislatures, publishers, and braille readers. In a remarkably short span of time, the debate had shifted from whether the US government had an obligation to provide books for people who were blind to whether the current appropriation would ensure a sufficient number of books were available to them. By the end of June 1935, the talking book library had twenty-seven titles available for use. An increase in the annual appropriation for the Books for the Adult Blind Project ($75,000 of which was now allotted to talking book production) enabled the collection to reach one hundred titles the following year.

Yet the supply was still inadequate when compared with the nearly 15,000 books published every year in the United States. Helen Keller complained of the disparity: "Only 100 titles for 18,000 sightless, unthinkable."[141] A series of increases to the appropriation over the next decade was met with minimal opposition. By 1945, the talking book library had expanded to 1,062 titles. The library's increasing size enabled the majority of readers with vision impairments—including a new generation of war-blinded veterans—to read again. The value of talking books for these readers, at least, was no longer in doubt. For them, a talking book was, in fact, a book.

The talking book had come to be regarded as an indisputable social good by the time the talking book service reached its twentieth anniversary in 1954. President Dwight Eisenhower congratulated it with the declaration, "Freedom to read is essential to our freedom to think and to judge."[142] The United States had gone from a society in which the majority of citizens with impaired vision were unable to read for themselves to one in which the opportunity to read—the liberation from physiological constraints as much as political ones—was taken to be an essential aspect of democracy. Eisenhower's lofty rhetoric suggests just how much was felt to be at stake in the battles over access to print that had already been fought as well as those still to come.

3

How to Read a Talking Book

In 1976, *Dialogue* magazine published a complaint sent to one of the narrators employed by the American Printing House for the Blind. Activists had founded the magazine a decade earlier as a forum in which to discuss issues relevant to the lives of people who were blind. On this occasion, Fred and Miriam Vieni of Westbury, New York, explained the best way to read a talking book:

> We have listened to books for many years. We find that books are most easy to understand when they are read at a normal rate of speech without pauses. Further, just as sighted people bring to the print books they read, their own interpretations, blind people would like to do the same. You, the reader, are the medium which brings the words to us. But if you impose your interpretations onto what you read, you impede our ability to find our own meanings. Therefore, it would be helpful if you would NOT imitate male and female voices, or try to "act" the parts of the characters about whom you read. Straight reading, in a normal tone of voice, at a normal speed, is the most helpful way to help us read in an intelligent and meaningful manner. Blind people who read talking books are not passive recipients of what others pre-digest for us. At least, we would prefer not to be. We want to read actively. This means that the reader should not get in the way of the author's communication with us, his/her readers.[1]

The Vienis objected to any reading style that interfered with their efforts to construe the narrative for themselves. If blind readers were to perform an act equivalent to that performed by other readers, then what was needed was "straight reading," a neutral manner of speaking that added minimal intonation to the narrative in order to approximate the printed page.[2] By asking narrators to stay out of the way, the Vienis' letter suggests that the debate over how to read aloud remained unresolved nearly half a century after the talking book library's inception. Audiences had yet to answer the fundamental question: How should a book sound?

The American Foundation for the Blind (AFB) recognized the importance of presentation if sighted people were to accept the talking book as a legitimate alternative to print. As early as 1933, blind journalist Charles Magee Adams warned the AFB not to overlook it: "As you doubtless recognize, the acceptance of 'Talking Books' by intelligent blind people will depend quite as much on literary considerations as on the mechanical perfection of recording and reproduction. And I am not thinking so much of contents as the way the material is presented."[3] It was not enough to focus on the technical details of sound recording alone. Bibliographic matters were equally important. For Adams, this meant no abridgments, no dramatizations, and, above all, no elocution of the sort objected to five decades later by the Vienis. Before the talking book's first words had been spoken, the AFB already faced a controversy over how to read books.

Disputes over reading styles were more than matters of taste. Behind the disagreements lay persistent questions over the reader's independence. Who exactly was doing the reading: the reader, the speaker, the machine, or the book itself? The talking book had been designed to assist people with disabilities who could not read in any other way and who depended on other people to read aloud to them. Hence, it was unclear whether talking book machines enabled people with vision impairments to read for themselves, by using their ears instead of eyes or fingers, or whether the machine did the reading for them. The very phrase "talking book" invited such confusion. Use of a machine made it appear as if blind people had only to sit back and do nothing. As one radio program asked its audience, "Do you know that books exist which read themselves aloud to blind men and women?"[4] The AFB itself contributed to such misconceptions in its efforts to persuade blind people how easy the equipment was to use. Its promotional record began by announcing, "I am a book that reads itself aloud."[5]

Similar accounts made the talking book appear to be the work of a machine. According to the AFB's annual report, "A blind man or woman sits down, pulls a lever, and the book reads itself to him or her."[6] Suspicions that talking books did all of the work—that reading had been reduced to pulling a lever—are partly responsible for the accusations of passivity that have dogged the format since its inception. "Device Regarded as Boon to Blind, Ill and Lazy," announced one newspaper headline.[7] Characterizations of talking books as the lazy man's way to read lay behind heated disputes among advocacy groups over the appropriate terminology.

As we saw in Chapter 2, many blind people insist on using the word "reading" to describe the act of listening to books, and there have been equally passionate debates over whether to use the term "narrator" or "reader" to describe the agent responsible for reading aloud.[8] Neither term is completely satisfactory, it should be said, since each is ambiguous in its own way. "Narrator" can refer to speakers inside or outside a narrative, for example, and "reader" has similarly contradictory meanings. Whatever the term, the person reading aloud a book plays an inestimable role in its reception.

This chapter ensures that the narrator is not left out of discussions about blindness, literacy, and interpretation. It follows the pursuit of a reading style that was neither too dramatic nor too dull but rather, like Goldilocks's proverbial bowl of porridge, just right. The question "What is a good talking book?" was difficult to answer since the AFB had long sought to make talking books resemble printed ones while at the same time adapting the material to suit the needs of a visually impaired readership. Efforts to remain true to the original book resulted in the AFB's policy of straight narration, a voice that was not overly dramatic or obtrusive, despite the intensely personal affection felt by blind readers toward some narrators, and an equally intense hostility felt toward other narrators. Such conflicts tended to arise when the speaker's age, gender, race, ethnicity, nationality, sexuality, or other discernable traits clashed with the story. For nearly a century, narrators have profoundly influenced a book's reception regardless of whether the speaker was a celebrated public figure or an unknown amateur. No matter how hard narrators may try to cultivate an understated style, they remain the center of attention.

What Is a Good Talking Book?

"What Is a Good Talking Book?" was the question posed in 1938 by *Talking Book Topics,* the AFB's quarterly magazine. Once the talking book library had been established, its studios began to take an interest in quality as well as quantity. William Barbour, a former Broadway actor working for the AFB, singled out three characteristics: clarity, editorial accuracy, and artistic perfection. Above all, a good talking book faithfully reproduced the original book. "We demand that our readers preserve complete fidelity to the text which they are reading," wrote Barbour. "We want those who listen to our books to feel that they are hearing exactly what the author wrote."[9] Exactly: the talking book was treated like the printed book in another medium.

For Barbour and many others, ink-print, talking, and embossed books differed only in conveying information via the eyes, ears, or fingers. The AFB's policy of bibliographic equivalence assured audiences that they were reading the same books as everyone else. This policy also sought to uphold the talking book's legitimacy by aligning it with a familiar format rather than presenting it as something completely new. Listening to books might offer a pleasure all its own, but, if so, that pleasure was a secondary consideration. The goal was to allow blind people to participate in the same activities enjoyed by other people.

Talking books preserved the printed book's features or at least a sense of "bookishness."[10] "Page" was often used instead of "side" to describe records, for example.[11] The talking book was not only a spoken version of the book but also a bookish version of speech. The bibliographic emphasis ensured that talking books would be evaluated in terms of printed ones. Such fidelity rendered the experience of listening to a book as much as possible like that of reading one in print. The AFB embraced fidelity to the point that, in a few cases, narrators were asked to reproduce obvious errors (sometimes even spelling mistakes) in order to ensure that blind readers received the exact same treatment as other readers.[12]

Talking books reproduced every word of the original book. The Library of Congress's "Specifications for Talking Book Records" insisted that the wording be identical: "The Talking Book edition of any work should conform just as closely as possible to the text of the printed edition."[13] Scripts likely to be known by heart—the Bible, historical documents, favorite poems—had to be word perfect. Accuracy was stressed to ensure that talking books were treated as equivalent to ink-print ones. For instance, they recited verbatim the textual apparatus (front matter, acknowledgments, and so forth) skimmed or skipped altogether by the typical reader. The narrator of Bertrand Russell's *A History of Western Philosophy* spent thirteen hours on the fifty-six-page index alone.[14] Chapter headings, epigraphs, and other paratextual features likewise had to be read aloud; manuals instructed narrators to read footnotes at once since records had no page breaks. Educational recordings even cited page numbers in order to convey the source book's layout.

There were limits to the narrator's ability to reproduce the printed page, however. While recorded books adhered to print conventions, publishers acknowledged that some books needed to be adapted for reading aloud. "The narrator must remember that his listener cannot see the page," cautioned the National Braille Association's *Tape Recording Manual*.[15] It advised narrators to clarify textual cues that were easy to miss when read by ear. Words were spelled out for clarity in the cases of technical terms, unusual proper names ("Smyth" instead of "Smith"), and foreign words ("The journey to Aix, capital A-i-x, began at dawn"). Guidelines recommended translating foreign quotations. For example, Alexander Scourby translates the Latin and French in Thackeray's *The History of Henry Esmond*. Similarly, *The Three Musketeers* and *Les Misérables* begin by spelling out the characters' names.

The AFB and other organizations developed elaborate guidelines for converting typographical conventions into sound.[16] The goal was to adhere as closely as possible to the original book's layout while at the same time adapting the material to suit the needs of a disabled readership. The voice's inflection could convey some typographical cues such as italics, ellipses, and parentheses; others needed to be made an explicit feature of the narration. For example, "end of chapter" might be announced even when the narrative ended with a blank space. Such potentially ambiguous moments serve as reminders that the needs of blind readers were not identical with those of sighted readers.

Long novels challenged even the most attentive auditor's memory. One reader complained that Dickens's *David Copperfield* had ninety-two named characters; large casts were difficult to keep track of without being able to flip back through the book's pages.[17] A supplementary record identifying the characters in *War and Peace* prevented this information from disrupting the story. The American Printing House for the Blind's superintendent opposed spelling out names for this reason: "It is difficult enough to read books like the above and I shudder to think what the result would be if we turn these readings into first-class spelling bees."[18] He recommended recording a separate glossary instead.

Talking books stuck closely to print conventions in most cases. However, a pioneering few took advantage of sound technology to show that the talking book could do more than replicate its printed counterpart. Why describe, say, nature when you could hear it for yourself? Leroy Hughbanks, president of the Kansas State Society for the Blind, urged, "Let us stop keeping our microphones in recording studios permanently, and take some of them into the forest and fields, where nature is at her best. Our blind people want to know what certain animals are like. They want to know what noises they make."[19] The microphone's migration outside the studio confirmed that books could make use of other sounds besides the human voice.

The AFB's first attempts to use sound effects proved a hit. One of the most popular albums included actual birdsong. A recording of Cornell ornithologist Albert Brand's *Wild Birds and Their Songs* featured over thirty birds chirping and warbling—reviews described it as a singing book.[20] Naturalist Clarence Hawkes urged blind people, who spent a disproportionate amount of time indoors, to memorize the songs in order to increase their enjoyment outdoors.[21] At least one auditor intended to follow Hawkes's advice, writing, "The study of the voices of these various birds and the recognition of them in the garden of my own home, will add a great joy to my life which, through my blindness has changed in the last year."[22]

Studios tried out sound effects on conventional narratives too. As early as November 1934, Christmas music, chimes, and ghostly noises were added to Dickens's *A Christmas Carol.* The recording began with an actual carol, "God Rest You Merry, Gentlemen." "I got quite excited when I heard one of the recordings today," Irwin told a colleague after playing the Dickens record.[23] Music enlivened other recordings, too, from *John Brown's Body,* which included songs from the Civil War, to Vachel Lindsay's *General Booth Enters into Heaven,* on which the Salvation Army Territorial Staff Band played background music. Best of all, books about musicians could be made with actual music. A recording of Eric Blom's biography of Mozart replaced the original notations with piano music.[24] In 1937, the AFB even began to adapt (using what would today be called audio description) feature films such as Walt Disney's *Snow White and the Seven Dwarfs.*[25] The AFB's president equated listening to these discs with a trip to the cinema.[26]

Plays held obvious appeal. Initially, narrators read them aloud like any other book, with a single speaker performing every role. A woman in Fallbrook, California, enjoyed hearing Shakespeare read by an expert. "I wish I might tell him, whoever he may be, how much pleasure his reading of Hamlet is giving us," she wrote. "It is as though he came right into our Little House and read to us."[27] Not everyone enjoyed hearing plays read like a book, however. The constant switching between characters could be confusing or irritating. Dissatisfaction quickly led to plays being treated as dramatic productions instead of "as books to be read."[28] Fifteen actors replaced the lone narrator, for instance, on Shakespeare's *Love's Labour's Lost.*[29]

Audiences disagreed about the value of sound effects. Advocates saw them as a way to capitalize on the new medium's affordances; after all, the talking book was "a volume writ in sound," not ink.[30] There was no need to remain tethered to print when talking books could play the author's voice, set narratives to music, or dramatize them. One Oregonian described talking books as "like owning a little theatre all your own."[31] Others described sound effects as illustrations for people who couldn't see: "Sighted people have their picture-books, so why should we not have our sound picture-books?"[32] Use of the phrase "sound illustrations" among manuals reinforced this analogy to the printed page.[33] In addition, the AFB's Talking Book Education Project noted that the average student could read three times more quickly with talking books than with braille (the speed of tactile reading was a major cause of the educational disadvantage of blind children).[34]

By contrast, opponents worried that sound effects would turn the talking book into something altogether different from books. Newspaper columnist Alexander Fried suspected as much: "Novels under these conditions will cease to be novels."[35] He urged publishers to leave literature "on the printed page where it belongs." Charles Magee Adams's hostility to the sound effects on *A Christmas Carol* echoed such concerns. Adams may have appreciated showmanship at the theater, "but a Talking Book is not the stage."[36]

Using sound effects for some books raised a difficult question: Why not use them for all titles? After all, the Library of Congress received requests every year from patrons who wanted novels dramatized. In response, the library reaffirmed its mission to reproduce books as accurately and faithfully as possible. It informed one patron, "We regret that we cannot dramatize the books being produced. . . . The Division's responsibility is to reproduce print materials as published so that those who cannot utilize the print may have access to the published works being enjoyed by those around them. Dramatizations would defeat our purpose."[37] Dramatizations were already available through radio, television, and commercial records (at least from the 1950s onward). It wasn't the library's responsibility to make talking books more entertaining than the original ones.

The Inconspicuous Narrator

Fan mail received by talking book narrators vividly captures their hold over the reader's imagination. For many, memories of a book's plot were inextricably bound up with its narrator. The voice is what they remembered. Take the pastor from Baltimore who listened to *Les Misérables* while preparing a sermon on Jean Valjean's travails. Although the pastor had read the novel fifteen years earlier before losing his sight in a hunting accident, it was the first time he had heard it read by Alexander Scourby:

> Then I thought it was a great book, but yesterday I finished on my Talking Book the first two sections which are read by you, and words fail me in attempting to express to you my appreciation for what you have done in the rendition of this story.
>
> You have given the characters personality. I do not know when I have been so stirred. It is one thing to read a book to the blind, another to make them actually feel the pulse and reality of events that move before them.[38]

The fulsome letter raises a key question about the narrator's role that would be debated in the decades to come: Should narrators be unobtrusive or use their theatrical talents to enhance the script? The speaker had to remain a neutral presence—a straight reader—if the talking book was to be seen as comparable to print. Yet audiences yearned for more; they wanted a sense of intimacy felt to be missing from ink-print books. The Library of Congress responded with a compromise: a voice neither overly dramatic nor stultifyingly monotone.

A good narrator was hard to find. The AFB began by interviewing hundreds of professional actors with radio and theater experience. Fewer than ten of these readers possessed the voice, skill, and stamina deemed appropriate for talking books (Figure 3.1).[39] Arthur Helms, the AFB's production director, looked for two characteristics when auditioning potential readers: an agreeable voice and a good delivery. His auditions required candidates to read two five-minute passages, one from a novel and another from a textbook. Helms then replayed the records to find defects including affectations, mannerisms, monotony, breathlessness, or overexertion.[40] Stamina was vital because there was no way of editing mistakes on phonograph records. A narrator had to read for twenty minutes without mispronouncing a single word; nearly every narrator recalled careless mistakes or "fluffs" that had spoiled a record.[41]

Figure 3.1. Alexander Scourby recording James Joyce's *Ulysses.*

Guidelines drawn up by the Library of Congress ensured consistency across talking books. From the outset, the library advocated what I've been calling straight reading, a style of narration neither overly dramatic nor monotonous. Guidelines published in 1937 describe the ideal voice: "The reader is to have a voice both highly articulate and pleasing. He must read sympathetically but with restraint. The reading must not be mechanical nor stilted and must be free from hesitation, coughs or other disturbances."[42] These directions steered speakers toward a middle road between dramatic performance and self-effacement, one that would entertain audiences without straying too far from the impression that a book was being read. Three years later, the revised "Specifications" reaffirmed the narrator's allegiance to the original source: "The reading shall be (a) appropriate to the book, (b) sympathetic but not exaggerated, (c) restrained but not stilted or mechanical, (d) attentive to the sense of the book and skilful in securing proper emphasis."[43] The book's centrality here ensured that narratives held priority over narrators. This was no easy task. The talking book service needed to distance itself from a theatrical style that might undermine its credibility. At the same time, narrators had to be entertaining enough to hold the attention of a broad readership.

Straight reading remained the library's official policy in the years to come. Whereas radio and theater favored a dramatic style, the AFB preferred an undramatic one. In fact, talking book narrators defined themselves *against* commercial entertainers. Manuals disapproved of "over-dramatizing," for example, and the *Talking Book Bulletin* applauded "undramatic" readings as well as "untheatrical" voices.[44] Such anti-theatrical qualities reassured audiences that they were in contact with a facsimile rather than an adaptation of the original book. According to one observer, the AFB insisted that talking books should be read "fast and quite without expression so as to create as far as possible a complete analogy with the setting out of words on a printed page, into which the reader will put his own expression and emphasis."[45] Straight talk did what it could to preserve the page.

One report divided narration into two categories. Interpretive readings treated the script as a dramatic performance. By contrast, an informative one presented material in a neutral manner; its narrators subordinated their personalities when "conveying the written words in audible form."[46] In theory, neutral speech was comparable to print in allowing readers to form their own judgments about how words might sound; it limited the "interpreting factor" between people and the page.[47] Minimizing the narrator's presence allowed audiences to focus their attention on the book instead of the book's narrator.

"Book" still held priority over "talking." Talking books aimed to reproduce printed ones, after all, not to improve them. An informal survey of blind readers led Irwin to declare, "When the record is played, there should be as little indication as possible that the reader is reading from a book."[48] One recent manual defines the narrator as a "transcriber" who copies words from one medium into another. "The narrator is NOT a teacher," it warns. "There must be no editorial comment or imposition of the narrator's views by tone of voice."[49] William Arthur Deacon has described the narrator's obligation to reproduce the original book as faithfully as possible. He recalls making himself "into a panel of glass through which the reader could see the book as if he held it in his own hands."[50] Narrators have aimed for transparency (a notably visual metaphor) since the talking book's earliest days. The goal was to make people forget that a book was being read aloud. At least one narrator proposed that "the ideal recording is the least conspicuous recording; one should not be conscious that he is listening to a record at all."[51] In other words, the best talking books were simply books.

Nevertheless, straight reading required narrators to do more than read aloud the words on a page. They had to figure out an author's intentions too. The early guidelines called for a style of reading that was "appropriate," "attentive," and "sympathetic" to the original book.[52] Subsequent manuals advised narrators to establish a "rapport" with authors in order to convey their styles: Jane Austen required someone with an ear for dialogue, Edgar Allan Poe a feel for suspense, and James Thurber a sense of humor.[53] To this day narrators compare themselves to actors who temporarily adopt another person's identity. "My purpose is to serve the author, in fact to *be* the author," explains Alan Hewitt. "If I am doing my job properly (according to my lights), each of the 184 books I have thus far recorded should have an individual style, not a Hewitt style but the style of that particular author."[54] Successful recordings preserved the illusion that authors were telling their stories directly to the audience.[55]

By contrast, critics accused dramatizations of distorting the original book. Overdramatizing meant that a narrator was acting, not reading. Complaints from as late as the 1970s and 1980s bear this out. One correspondent enjoyed hearing Gordon Gould because "he reads as though he were reading a book and not trying to act out a play."[56] Another preferred it when people "just read normally without the dramatics."[57] All too often dramatic reading made it impossible for people to forget that a book was being read to them. One letter praised a narrator for the "modesty" of his reading: "Your reading did not get in the way of the book, you didn't over-do it or over dramatize."[58] Those who did overdo it were accused of suffering from "the elocution problem."[59] As one correspondent insisted, "Elocution has its place but not in a talking book."[60] Undramatic performances allowed readers to interpret the author's words for themselves just as if they were reading them in print. Any attempt to animate the narrative interfered with this goal. Janet Gawith of Boise, Idaho, complained, "These are not plays, but books. I prefer to imagine the accents and voice quality for myself, not to sit through a distorted version of someone's voice."[61] Again, not plays, but books: the more a narrator's voice stands out, the harder it is to ignore.

Not everyone opposed a dramatic delivery, of course. Catherine Krauss praised Edward Blake's recitation of *Sand Pebbles* precisely because of its theatrical voices. "Despite what anyone may have said to you to the contrary, and believe me they are in the minority, since all the blind people we know on every intellectual level, prefer the dramatic readings," wrote Krauss. "Readings such as you do bring the theater into our homes and it is the only compensation for being without sight."[62] Readers like Krauss sought entertainment in any form, not necessarily books.

The novelist Willa Cather made the most forceful case against dramatization. A minority of authors refused to allow their novels to be recorded for
people who were blind because of copyright concerns. But Cather was unique
in refusing permission on artistic grounds. Her novel *My Ántonia* is the only
title in the Library of Congress's 1937 catalog with an asterisk to mark its can-
cellation.[63] Despite persistent requests, Cather refused to allow her books to
be recorded. As she explained in a letter to Alexander Woollcott, she objected
to any recordings of her novels:

> I am very sorry to seem disobliging but radio and phonograph reproduc-
> tions of my books is a thing I have to fight constantly. It is disastrous in
> every way to a writer who has any conscience or any taste. There is no way
> in which to control these reproductions and the vocalization is often done
> by people with horrid voices and sentimental mannerisms. I cannot ex-
> plain to you in detail how many chances a professional reader has to
> over-stress and over-sentimentalize a writer's work. Of course, if I could
> break my rule at all, I would do it for such a purpose as that you mention
> but I tell you frankly the whole idea of the reproduction of books by sound
> machines is very distasteful to me and the struggle to keep out of the hand
> of sound machine people takes a good deal of my time and energy. Sound
> machines are all very well for the reproduction of music, but I don't want to
> have my books made into records—they are not written for voice
> reproduction.[64]

Although Cather did worry about losing control over the recordings, her primary concerns were aesthetic ones. She feared that overdramatic interpretations would wreck the writing. Words, she insisted, were appropriate only in
the medium for which they were originally intended.

Cather attributed her hostility to a distressing experience that took place
before being contacted by the AFB. In her recollection, Cather and a friend
were having dinner at an Italian restaurant when they heard a radio broadcast of *My Ántonia*. Cather was not impressed. The actor's over-the-top performance reflected a certain kind of elocutionary training, not a feel for the
novel itself. In Cather's words, "They were quiet chapters from a very quiet
book—a mute on the strings."[65] The reading spoiled Cather's meal.

The seemingly minor incident brought to a head Cather's hostility toward
recording in general. As Cather told the Library of Congress in 1944, narrators have too much influence over a text. They control the tempo, stress, and

characterization that, when used irresponsibly, distort a narrative. In other words, Cather was not against reading aloud; she was against reading aloud badly.

My Ántonia called for sensitive narration. Instead, the declamatory voice heard on the radio confirmed Cather's worst fears. She explained to Archibald MacLeish, "I would never have been unwilling to have such records made had I been sure that the recording was done by people who read simply, as our mothers and grandmothers did when they read aloud to us in our childhood."[66] Cather forbade any recordings until shortly before her death, when she allowed several of her novels (including *A Lost Lady* and *Death Comes for the Archbishop*) to be made into talking books. Naturally, she left behind detailed instructions on how to read them.[67]

Good Ol' Americanese

Fit between speaker and script was a delicate matter. Numerous factors went into casting decisions since, as we have seen, narrators profoundly influenced a book's reception in spite of their best efforts to remain neutral. "Readers should be selected for their suitability to particular books," insisted Barbour.[68] Finding a suitable narrator meant matching the speaker to a fictional character's age, class, gender, race, ethnicity, nationality, sexuality, or other audible markers of identity. Irwin's casting decisions, for example, took into account the speaker's biography: "It is not a question of simply having just anybody read a book. We must take into account whose voice, whose temperament, whose background, whose taste, whose outlook on life, whose educational and intellectual equipment will best fit a particular piece of literature."[69] Helen Keller's *Midstream: My Later Life,* Irwin insisted, should be read by a woman who actually knew her. Misfits threatened to come between readers and the page.

The AFB selected voices that would not be too incongruous. "When we choose a reader, we try to fit the voice and manner of speaking to the material," explained a production manager. "Just as we would not ask a British actor to read a Zane Grey Western; at the same time, we would not ask someone with a Texas accent, for example, to read a novel by Charles Dickens."[70] Most recordings reflect this policy: an actual westerner reads *Vengeance Valley,* to name one. Yet getting the right fit was fraught with difficulties. In many cases, readers disagreed over what the appropriate voice should sound like in the first place.

Readers were quick to point out clashes between real and fictional personae. Voicing characters was especially hazardous. The AFB's "Suggested Rules for Talking Book Recorders" advised against the practice since it easily degenerated into caricatures or stereotypes: "Do not indulge in dramatization or in trying to impersonate the persons in conversation. In nine cases out of ten it will be a failure. Women do not all talk in soft voices or in a whisper, and old and strong men do not always roar so that they bring down the roof."[71] Arthur Helms asserted that parts should be "underplayed," if played at all.[72] Otherwise, bad characterization risked turning tragedy into comedy. Use of the same narrators to record different titles compounded the problem since voices became familiar (John Knight recorded 97 of the first 165 titles).[73] Instead of doing the police in different voices, so to speak, manuals recommended a slight change of pitch. This technique has proven to be exceptionally versatile for an audience attuned to even the most minor modulations in speech.

Narrators received increasing scrutiny in the wake of feminism, the civil rights movement, and other campaigns for social equality in the second half of the twentieth century. Controversy over narrator selection may be thought of as the politics of narration: speakers who were too old, too male, or too white drew complaints from readers who expected voices to bear some resemblance to the subject matter and to mark variations in identity. For example, one reader complained of casting mismatches in young adult fiction:

> More care should be taken in selecting readers for books, so that readers are reading books that are appropriate for them to handle. To have that fine reader of western yarns, Bucky Koslow, who sounds like a rough-hewn grampa, reading *Huckleberry Finn,* the first person narration of a child, or Milton Metz, the perfect newscaster, reading the first person narration of a teenager in the re-recording of *The Catcher in the Rye,* is a terrible mismatch between book and reader.[74]

Their voices were hardly inconspicuous. First-person accounts were especially susceptible to mismatch. Audiences did not want to hear old men reading the memoirs of women, teenagers, and other groups who could speak for themselves.

Despite pretensions of neutrality, audiences were acutely aware of the speaker's sex. A disproportionate number of male narrators exacerbated the problem. Women's voices were difficult to record and, for reasons having little to do with technology, unpalatable. A factsheet produced by the AFB at midcentury noted, "Feminine voices have proved neither as satisfactory nor as popular on Talking Book records as those of men."[75] Consequently, women were used as narrators only when required by the material, such as autobiographies of women or stories written from a woman's point of view. Whereas Edward Bellamy fantasized at the end of the nineteenth century about hearing books read aloud by women (as mentioned in Chapter 1), twentieth-century readers preferred men. One reader disliked hearing women as a matter of personal taste.[76] Others accused them of an affected or "sing-song" way of speaking.[77] Still, most patrons agreed that books by and about women should be read by women. Plus, imitations of the opposite sex made some readers uncomfortable. "One thing which really distracts me is when a man tries to talk like a woman, or vice-versa," complained one correspondent.[78] Straight reading could not be straight enough when it came to performing gender.

Impersonation risked a form of minstrelsy when it came to narratives written by or about racial minorities. Complaints about the treatment of marginalized groups became increasingly common in the 1960s and 1970s. Raul Lugo found narrator William Wright offensive, for example: "Mr. Wright's reading style reeks of biggotry [sic], racism, and sexism: His gay characters all lisp, his black people all sound like junkies, and his women all sound like lazy, seductive objects. I find having to sit and listen to this reinforcement of old stereotypes highly offensive."[79] Lisping and other sexually or racially charged methods of characterization indicate how easily a narrator could influence a book's reception. A mere gesture turned a character into a stereotype. The AFB defended Wright on the grounds that the stereotypes arose from the narrative, not the narrator. One of the novels in question, Ben Greer's *Slammer*, for instance, portrayed the grim subject of life in a South Carolina penitentiary. In a letter to the National Gay Task Force, the AFB attributed any prejudicial treatment to the book's author, not its messenger.[80] The Library of Congress refused to censor the material in order to protect blind people's right to read the same books as other people.

Casting narrators according to gender, race, and ethnicity was meant to avoid offensive disparities that might interfere with a reader's concentration. For example, Alvin Marvin DeLaney, a college graduate from Atlanta, Georgia, commended the library's inclusion of African American literature, like *The Book of Negro Humor*, before asking, "So why make it noisome by employing some elderly white spinster who probably wears pince-nez or bifocals and has absolutely no voice for humor at all . . . to singly destroy the book and any effect it might have?"[81] By contrast, a good fit made even the most controversial material palatable. A thirty-seven-year-old African American woman stayed up all night listening to Dick Gregory's *Nigger: An Autobiography* despite usually avoiding anything to do with race.[82] A few voices eluded racial categorization altogether. One correspondent asked actress Eugenia Rawls what color her skin was after hearing her read Gwen Bristow's *Handsome Road.*[83]

Equally heated disputes arose over literature written by foreign authors or set in other countries. One group of readers expected such works to be read by native speakers capable of pronouncing foreign names and phrases. Earl Hyman, for example, received praise for his skillful handling of the dialects in Alex Haley's *Roots.* Cosmopolitan auditors struggled to listen to books read by provincial Americans. Norman Johnson returned books to the library that, as he writes, "were so badly read, and so full of such barbarous mispronunciations, both of English and of other languages with which I am familiar, that I found it quite painful to finish the books."[84] Homegrown narrators did not always possess sufficient expertise or firsthand experience of non-English-speaking countries. The narrator of James Clavell's *Shogun: A Novel of Japan,* for instance, knew very little Japanese. An irritated reader complained that the reader's "butchery of the Japanese language—which occurred at least once every few minutes," resulted in thousands of mispronunciations.[85]

Another group of readers disliked any speech straying from American English. Foreign accents made it difficult for at least one correspondent to follow the storyline.[86] The AFB was well aware of the risks posed by unfamiliar speech. A reader's report on *A Nervous Splendor: Vienna 1888–1889* concluded that the narrator's pronunciation of European languages was "as close to native as is safe for our American audience."[87]

There were disagreements over the best way to recite Shakespeare, Jane Austen, and other English writers. Some felt that American accents spoiled British literature; others refused to listen to anything but American accents. One man insisted that British accents be used for British fiction: "The most common error in narrator selection is assigning some cowboy to a thoroughly English story."[88] He stopped reading Agatha Christie's *The Murder of Roger Ackroyd* because the American narrator was "certainly out of place as an English squire running in and out of Dame Agatha's Tea and Crumpet Shops." Americans imitated foreign accents at their peril. Bert Blackwell received the following complaint for his efforts: "He makes every English-woman, however well educated, sound like a cockney shopgirl."[89]

Complaints also came from readers who expected to hear everything read by Americans. Willard Price of Laguna Hills, California, for one, objected to hearing British novels read in a foreign accent. "The mere fact that they are written by Britons and may be about England is no excuse for making them hard for Americans to understand," complained Price. "Our question is, 'Why can't records meant for Americans be recorded in the American language?'"[90] A woman from Peoria, Illinois, raised a similar objection against British accents: "We are Americans, why subject us to readers who we cannot understand. If it were a Chinese story, would you have it read for us in Chinese?"[91] A number of people struggled with British speech despite its widespread presence on radio, film, and television. The AFB occasionally assigned Americans to British novels to placate this constituency, but only ones who had lost their regional accents.[92] Librarians explained that British accents increased many people's enjoyment of the story by adding a touch of authenticity. Such justifications failed to convince the nativists, however. A man from New Orleans asked, "Why don't you get rid of your stable of English and Irish born readers and hire native U.S. readers[?]"[93]

"Native" readers were not as easy to cast as the man from New Orleans seemed to think. Regional varieties of American speech made it difficult to select one that would satisfy readers in different parts of the country. William Howle, one of the AFB's studio managers, assured correspondents that the organization aimed for regional diversity: "As it is impossible for us to find any one speech pattern that is native to all parts of the country, we try to use a variety of people—some from the East, but others from the West, the Midwest, and the South."[94] Audiences were alert to Yankees reading a southerner's prose and other breaches. Even attempts to match a character's speech could be poorly received. A correspondent from the West Coast complained that Francis Parkman's *The Oregon Trail* was read in an East Coast accent rather than in "good ol' Americanese."[95]

There were even differences of opinion within the talking book service itself. The actors at the AFB's recording studios in New York City often cultivated generic or placeless accents; a visitor from Britain commented on their "de-Americanised voices."[96] By contrast, the American Printing House for the Blind's studios were in Louisville, Kentucky. Edgar Rogers, acting director of Books for the Adult Blind, preferred having books recorded by Broadway actors working for the AFB rather than by staff at the American Printing House, where, in his opinion, "the material is read without brilliance, by cheery-voiced middle-westerners, read as though they were announcing a Wheaties commercial."[97] Yet this very downhome speech appealed to other parts of the country. One reviewer cited Archibald MacLeish's "authentically American" voice (he grew up in Illinois) as proof that books sound best when read by provincials, not metropolitan actors.[98]

Oh, Beautiful Voice

The AFB and Library of Congress's policy of straight reading downplayed the narrator's presence in order to keep attention focused on the book. Yet letter after letter from readers describe intensely personal relationships with narrators. Many correspondents had never written a fan letter before being moved to do so by a particularly brilliant performance. Their letters don't ask to hear less from narrators. They demand to hear more.

Letters describe in detail the difference made by a beloved voice.[99] Favorite narrators were set apart by the following features: a pleasant voice, clear enunciation, accurate pronunciation, good timing, expressiveness, versatility, a command of foreign languages, a sympathetic understanding of the author's intention, and an overall sense of artistry. Good narrators made the reading experience feel as if it were in Technicolor instead of black and white. A man from Sacramento, California, complimented one narrator's reading of *In Trout Country,* an anthology of fishing stories: "You made that book come alive for me."[100] A sensitive reading of Edwin Way Teale's *Journey into Summer* enabled another man to hear the birds, mayflies, and rustling sand dunes.[101] Expert storytelling kept readers on the edge of their seats. The publisher Howard Haycraft wrote, "I can't imagine, for example, how visual reading of *The Day Lincoln Was Shot* could possibly attain the dramatic intensity of Karl Weber's narration on talking books."[102] The right voice could make even a mediocre book enjoyable.

Narrators made audiences think about a book's language in a new way. The narrator of Aleksandr Solzhenitsyn's *The Gulag Archipelago* and William Faulkner's *Absalom, Absalom!* was told, "You bring out even the smallest, most obscure, most elusive and most subtle nuances!"[103] Several readers admitted missing such shades in print. Some even confessed to enjoying books more when read aloud. After hearing Richard Condon's *Winter Kills,* a patient wrote from a veteran hospital in Arizona, "If I was sighted and I had read the book to myself in an easy chair, I know I would not have enjoyed it nearly as much."[104] The relationship worked both ways, of course. If good narrators could redeem bad books, bad narrators could ruin good ones. There are as many anecdotes of readers requesting a narrator's entire run as there are of patrons refusing anything read by a persona non grata.

Patrons frequently chose books by narrator, not by author or title. "In the future may I hope that your editors realize that at least half of the enormous pleasure of our reading is in the quality of voice and diction of the reader?" a fan wrote about Kit Fornier. "From now on, I shall enjoy ANYTHING Miss Fornier is willing to read for me."[105] Other people likewise credited their enjoyment to particular voices. An Arnold Moss fan declared, "I think he could read the phone book or a dictionary and make it a pleasure to hear."[106] Intimacy was inevitable after so much time spent together, insisted one reader: "When we choose a book, we select a reader who reads for many hours, as a companion. I have gone through *War and Peace,* have become the *Idiot,* and have visited the Italian Front to say *A Farewell to Arms* with Alexander Scourby, and have lived through two wars and the Russian Revolution with Norman Rose, my *Doctor Zhivago,* and have found the experience memorable."[107] This reader's Doctor Zhivago owed as much to the narrator as to Boris Pasternak.

Many readers felt as if talking books spoke directly to them. Bucky Kozlow invited people to sit back and enjoy his recording of Joe Franklin's *A Gift for People.* "I liked the powerful, authoritative, dynamic manner in which the book was read," a woman wrote afterward. "You made me feel important; and as I listened to your top-notch recording of this well-written text, I felt as though you were reading this material just for me, personally."[108] Kozlow was hardly an inconspicuous presence. His voice was as memorable as the narrative itself.

Readers compared their relationships with talking book narrators to the public's fascination with film stars. Fans ignored the pretense of neutrality. Instead, they wanted to know the source of the phonograph's disembodied voice. Magazine features with titles like "The Man behind the Voice" appealed to this widespread curiosity.[109] A high school student in Texas wrote to Kozlow, "I'm interested in you as a person as well as a reader."[110] She asked what he did in his spare time and whether he had ever lived in Texas. It was not uncommon for blind readers to request a narrator's photograph. Some even asked to meet their favorite narrators in person. While writing this book, I heard anecdotes about readers bursting into tears upon meeting narrators to whom they had been listening since childhood.

Ethel Everett was one of the narrators given star treatment. She received enough poems from an admiring Indianapolis lawyer to fill an entire album. A poem titled "The Voice" expresses how her suitor felt while listening to Everett:

Oh, beautiful voice in the Talking Book,
    Mellow as sunset in all its hue
    Where a sea of green meets a sky of blue;
Lovely as starlight; clear as a brook
    Flashing and gleaming in royal splendor
    To garnish the rhythms its ripples engender;
Do you know,—can you tell what my thoughts embrace
As we journey along through time and space,
    With you ever leading, page by page,
Delightfully blending each accent and word
    Of poet, philosopher, novelist, sage,
Into such cadence as no one has heard,
    Since sailors were lured from their course in the breeze
    By the singing nymphs of enchanted seas?[111]

"Oh, beautiful voice": it was love at first sound. The comparison between talking books and the siren's song warns how easy it was to be seduced. The poem nevertheless tries to start a dialogue ("can you tell what my thoughts embrace") with a narrator who speaks only in monologues. Despite the AFB's efforts to make narrators inconspicuous, readers persisted in turning storytellers back into real people.

Celebrity recordings offer further evidence that the AFB's policy of straight narration was less straightforward than the studio acknowledged. Despite advocating a neutral reading style that would not come between readers and the page, the AFB recruited distinctive voices—from the book's author to professional actors and public figures—to read aloud. Authors who read their own books, or at least a book's first record, included Stephen Vincent Benét, Edna Ferber, Archibald MacLeish, Thomas Mann, W. Somerset Maugham, Eleanor Roosevelt, Jan Struther, and Alexander Woollcott. Other public figures included Mady Christians, Eva Le Gallienne, Whitford Kane, Otis Skinner, Sybil Thorndike, and Theodore Roosevelt, Jr. The list even included a silent film actor (Bert Lytell).[112] These voices were never meant to be anonymous. Instead, they made the most of the talking book's advantages over the silent page. Distinctive voices enlivened narratives in ways that could only be imagined by readers in other formats. As one of them put it, "To have, for example, Winston Churchill himself thundering out his famous 'Blood, Sweat and Tears' speech gives his words a flavor they could never achieve in cold print."[113]

Blind readers also had the luxury of hearing writers who did not wish to record their books for a commercial market. "Haven't you often wondered how a certain writer, Christopher Morley or Somerset Maugham or Edna Ferber would read something of their own?" asked one AFB representative. "I have. I've wondered what inflections they would give to this or that passage. Whether or not they had any pet words which they liked to linger on. Well, blind people don't need to wonder, for they know."[114] The author's voice seemed to offer a more accurate reading than could be gained from the page alone. After all, typography left much to the reader's discretion.

Skeptics continued to worry, however, that removing such discretion would turn reading into a passive act. What if narrators did all of the work formerly done by the book's reader? After hearing actress Eva Le Gallienne read Oscar Wilde's "The Birthday of the Infanta" and "The Nightingale and the Rose," a man in New Orleans wrote, "I have had both of these read to me so often, but I have always had to imagine the cruelty and the beauty of the Infanta. Tonight all that I had to do was to listen while you did all the imagining for me."[115] For him, Le Gallienne's performance felt closer to the cinema than to the library.

Talking books reproduced ink-print books as faithfully as possible. Yet the author's voice set talking books apart from other books. Hearing the author's voice seemed to bring the reader into closer contact with him or her than was possible through the printed page. As Irwin testified of the author's recitation, "It gives a personal touch with the author, which is very appealing and very interesting to a blind person."[116] The notion perpetuated a fantasy, popular since Edison's time, that sound recording facilitated direct access to the author. Irwin proposed that auditors could even detect the author's personality through tones, inflections, and vocal mannerisms kept off the printed page.[117]

Talking books also gave authors a chance to communicate directly with blind people. Whereas W. Somerset Maugham read the same introduction available in all copies of *Of Human Bondage,* Christopher Morley and Thomas Mann wrote introductions exclusively for talking book records. Before the fable "Where the Blue Begins," Morley's preface compliments the audience for not peeking ahead to see what comes next. He takes the audience into his confidence: "The most perfect patrons are those who listen. . . . Those who listen, often so much wiser than those who only look, will notice that WHERE THE BLUE BEGINS is a wavering and uncertain fable."[118] Hearing the fable read aloud, Morley admitted, exposed flaws that were less pronounced on the page.

Similarly, Mann's preface to *Buddenbrooks* could only be heard by people with impaired vision. He used the opportunity to bridge the divide between spoken and silent literature since reading aloud had played a role in the story's conception and in the epic tradition in which he situated his saga of a German merchant family:

> In the forty years of its life, my youthful work [*Buddenbrooks*] has had many astonishing honors paid it. But none has touched me more than this that has been designed for it here in America; that it is to be recorded, and so, to speak to those whom fate has denied the eyesight to read it. That is very fine and good. For an epic is for the ear more than for the eye. In early times it was said and sung, it was listened to—and, as a matter of fact, this book too was listened to before it was looked at, when the young author read it aloud as he wrote it, to relatives and friends. The epic is closer to music than any other form of literature. It *is* music, the music of life, to which we listen without looking, letting it reach the inward eye through the medium of the ear. May my story, told to those living in darkness, bring them a little inward light, a little joy of the mind.[119]

For the ear more than for the eye: Mann's metaphor of the "inward eye" would have been welcomed by a library intent on promoting equality among readers with different levels of vision. Such cameo appearances allowed audiences to hear the author's voice while simultaneously encouraging them to believe that they were reading the book for themselves.

This chapter began with a controversy in *Dialogue* magazine over how to read a talking book. Audiences faced a choice between an understated style privileging the printed book and a theatrical style that took full advantage of sound-recording technology. Fred and Miriam Vieni came down firmly on the side of what they called straight reading, a neutral delivery that allowed blind readers to be active interpreters of the text. The message to narrators was clear: stay out of the way.

Dialogue had not heard the last from the Vienis, however. After watching the controversy generated by their complaint, the couple wrote a second letter to the magazine. In that one, they shifted attention from the delivery's style to its quality:

> Many people seemed to disagree with some of the points we made in that letter, and this caused us to rethink the issue of Talking Book narration. Upon further reflection we realize that it is not interpretive reading that we oppose, but interpretive reading of poor quality. Over the years we have thoroughly enjoyed books beautifully read by Alexander Scourby, Leon Janney, Norman Rose, Esther Benson, and Barbara Caruso. One of the most moving, dramatic experiences we have encountered was listening to House Jameson reading *You Can't Go Home Again.* But when the choice is between inferior interpretation and straight narration we would choose the unadorned narration.[120]

The Vienis had come to accept a third way, situated between straight and theatrical reading: a dramatic interpretation that coincided perfectly with their own understanding of the book. Accordingly, good narrators bridged the gap between active and passive reading. This elusive solution suggests the difficulties faced by the Library of Congress and the American Foundation for the Blind in choosing a speaking style that remained faithful to the original book while at the same time appealing to a readership expecting to establish a rapport with a narrator who, to them, was much more than just a voice.

4

A Free Press for the Blind

In 1934, the United States Library of Congress established the world's first talking book library in order to provide reading material to people who had lost their sight. The Bible, Shakespeare, and best-selling novels were all recorded on long-playing phonograph records by professional actors. Helen Keller was among those who welcomed talking books as the most significant advance in literacy for blind people since the invention of braille.[1] Countless others joined her in celebrating after the first records went out to readers. As newspapers across the country reported, talking books enabled the nation's 130,000 blind people, many of whom were unable to read braille and depended on other people for access to books, to read for themselves. The press was nearly unanimous in its praise.

But these accounts left out another side of the story. In February 1939, Eleanor Catherine Judd called into question the prevailing narrative of progress. A recent feature in the *New York Times* had given the impression that access to books was no longer a problem. Judd disagreed, pointing out the ongoing frustrations caused by the book selection process. Too often the committee responsible for selecting books chose titles thought to be beneficial for blind people instead of the ones being read by everyone else. Judd protested in a letter to the *Times,* "Why, just because we are sightless, should thousands of us be deprived of current books?"[2] Judd accepted that the library's budget restricted the size of its inventory. What she refused to accept was a congressional committee's authority to decide what blind people should read.

Judd's dissent took part in a long tradition of protest by people with visual disabilities against being treated differently from other readers. Since the first books went out in the mail, blind readers had objected that they did not have access to the same books—namely, popular fiction—as other people. The selection committee's preference for literature published before the twentieth century meant that patrons had no way of reading best sellers like Margaret Mitchell's *Gone with the Wind*. Yet that one book, Judd insisted, would give them more pleasure than all of the Greek tragedies combined.

Questions about the roles of pleasure, edification, and enrichment came up repeatedly during the 1930s, 1940s, and 1950s as the Library of Congress struggled to formulate a book selection policy to meet the needs of a diverse, outspoken readership. The central issue was whether a committee of well-intentioned experts should make decisions about blind people's welfare or whether readers ought to be able to decide for themselves. There was little doubt where Judd stood: "Is it fair? Shouldn't we be given what we want, and not what the committee feels we should have?"[3] Judd spoke for the silent majority in demanding that blind people be given what they want—even if this meant neglecting the best that has been thought and said in favor of titles soon forgotten.

Concerns about the selection of titles are as old as the talking book library itself. Behind such concerns lay suspicions that books were being chosen for reasons other than the reader's preferences. The debates over censorship resembled discussions taking place elsewhere in the blind community about who had the authority to make decisions regarding blind people's welfare. Many still remembered the paternalist style of care imposed on them by government agencies, sometimes disproportionately made up of sighted people, deciding what was good for them.[4] In this case, blind people accused the selection committee of choosing books they did not want and of withholding books they did want.

This chapter addresses the talking book's relation to a broader history of censorship within America's libraries alongside the efforts of blind people to engage in forms of self-advocacy opposing such efforts to restrict their freedom. Specifically, it traces the book selection process from the Librarian of Congress's personal supervision in the 1930s to a committee assembled to choose books that would please librarians, blind readers, and members of Congress and their constituents alike. The talking book library faced the challenge of putting together a representative catalog while at the same time adhering to a budget that allowed few titles to be recorded. The limited inventory meant that every title received heightened scrutiny and might be subject to fierce disputes over its appropriateness. The selection committee was left in the unenviable position of deciding whether books should be chosen on the basis of popular appeal, literary merit, or educational value—the last of which Judd derided as "recordings with a message."[5]

The selection committee also needed to decide what to do about obscene books. In 1949, the library's director of administration was asked, "Is there any kind of censorship exercised by the Library of Congress in the selection of titles to be published for the blind[?]" His answer: "Positively not."[6] Yet archives preserved by the Library of Congress, the National Library Service for the Blind and Physically Handicapped (NLS), and the American Foundation for the Blind (AFB) suggest otherwise. Their holdings reveal that the ethics of library curation, censorship, and disability were more complex matters than custodians of the talking book service led people to believe. Ever since the first books went out to readers, blind people have accused the library of censorship. The selection committee's initial efforts to establish a morally respectable catalog were one reason why people with vision impairments felt denied access to books of their choice. But, as we will see, the Library of Congress went well beyond choosing books with good intentions, preventing blind people from reading books of their choice on some occasions and even prohibiting them—despite the director's denial of censorship—from reading books deemed subversive.

Selection, Not Rejection

The professional librarian's role changed dramatically in the decades leading up to recorded books. Librarians who had once decided which books were safe or beneficial to read now found themselves protecting freedom of inquiry in a democratic society.[7] They gathered, curated, and made accessible the nation's cultural heritage. Yet, in doing so, librarians struggled to balance the responsibilities of selecting titles worthy of inclusion (a process that necessarily involved exclusion too) while at the same time making available the widest range of material possible—even, or especially, when such material was considered to be controversial. The transition from censor to neutral arbiter of the book selection process introduced a new set of challenges to librarians after the 1930s. Foremost among them was the need to work out the relationship among censorship, book selection, and issues of intellectual freedom.

The library profession had established jurisdiction over book selection by the time advances in sound technology made it possible to record books. Still, the selection process generated controversy even before books had spoken a word. The Pratt-Smoot Act of 1931 authorized the Librarian of Congress to coordinate the National Library Service for the Blind and Physically Handicapped.[8] The act's opponents had expressed concerns that nearly all books available to blind people would be chosen by two organizations: the Library of Congress and the American Printing House for the Blind. Skeptics worried that a single individual might restrict the character and scope of reading matter available to all blind people. To prevent this scenario, opponents urged the Library of Congress to establish a committee including representatives who were blind. The chairman of the Braille Readers' League withdrew his opposition to the legislation only after assurances that a rival organization would keep its "hands off" the book selection process.[9]

Book selection remained a contentious issue for decades. The selectors had to balance competing demands to make as many titles available as possible while at the same time deciding which titles to include in, and consequently exclude from, the collection. Their role was poorly understood by the library's patrons, who routinely asked Martin Roberts, director of the Library of Congress's Books for the Adult Blind Project, to explain the selection policy. According to Roberts, the Librarian of Congress received recommendations from four different groups: (a) Library of Congress staff, (b) the Committee of the American Library Association on Work with the Blind and the Book-of-the-Minute Committee, (c) sighted persons with a particular interest in blind welfare, and (d) blind readers themselves. Roberts, who sent over a thousand letters to patrons across the country soliciting their preferences, insisted that "it is at all times the blind reader who is kept in mind" when selecting books.[10]

In 1940, Robert Irwin, the AFB's executive director, formed the General Advisory Committee on Selection of Books for the Blind. The committee included book reviewers for the press, a subcommittee of librarians who worked with blind people, another subcommittee made up of blind readers themselves, and individuals like Helen Keller.[11] By midcentury, the advisory group consisted of more than fifty people.[12] Its seven subcommittees included prominent figures who were blind, Library of Congress staff, regional librarians, representatives of the American Library Association, a Book-of-the-Month Committee, and a Reader's Advisory Group made up of both blind and sighted people.[13] The group's size enabled it to hear a range of opinions, though some members complained that libraries, clubs, and other organizations were given preference over recommendations submitted by blind constituents.[14]

The first talking books reflected a series of compromises and concessions rather than the Library of Congress's ideal reading list. As we saw in Chapter 2, the initial catalog featured a mix of scripture (Gospels and Psalms), patriotic documents (Declaration of Independence, Constitution, and presidential speeches), and Shakespearean drama. The list also included fiction by Gladys Hasty Carroll, E. M. Delafield, Cora Jarrett, Rudyard Kipling, and P. G. Wodehouse. Popular fiction was included despite objections to using government funds for anything other than edifying material. As Irwin wrote to a colleague, "I do want our first group to include books which the rank and file of seeing people would rush to the library to borrow if it were their first chance to read them for themselves."[15] Irwin recognized from the outset that the library's preference for classics would not be well received by readers who wanted to be entertained. The appropriate ratio between classic and contemporary fiction would be a long-standing point of contention.

The inaugural list's emphasis on worthy literature helped to protect the Library of Congress from potential controversy. It reflects three different criteria: the preferences of blind readers; general usefulness; and, finally, appropriateness for distribution with government funds.[16] This last category became increasingly important during debates over censorship. Reference librarian Herman Meyer had it in mind when ensuring that religious, patriotic, and historic titles always appeared first on the list of titles sponsored by the Library of Congress. Those titles needed to be listed ahead of the remaining fiction: "Where you put the rest doesn't matter."[17] Patriotic documents ensured that the federally funded program educated as well as entertained. Georgina Kleege has even suggested that they were meant to instill civic values in a group whose disabilities led them to be thought of as insufficiently American.[18]

The Bible was a safe choice. Despite taking up 169 double-sided records, with a reading time of over eighty-four hours, the Bible is widely recognized in both America and Britain as the most popular talking book ever recorded—the Book of Talking Books.[19] As Chapter 2 noted, it appealed to a large readership while at the same time appeasing those opposed to the use of federal subsidies for recreational reading. Scripture was instructive, widely read, and uniquely suited to reading aloud. As one newspaper reported, the King James Bible combined "the oral virtues of sonorousness and simplicity."[20] And just as religious groups had developed embossed letters in previous centuries to enable blind people to read the scriptures, so too was the recorded Bible hailed as a way of reaching the thousands of blind people who were unable to read it for themselves.[21] Hearing the Bible on a set of records made readers feel as if Isaiah's prophecies about turning darkness into light were meant for them.

The Library of Congress had an obligation to select books appealing to a broad readership. At the same time, it permitted outside groups to sponsor recordings targeted to minority interests. Voluntary organizations ensured that the Bible, for example, was widely distributed despite the library's modest budget. The New York Bible Society and the American Bible Society sold the entire New Testament at the price of twenty-five cents per record to enable blind readers to possess their own Talking Bible (or at least the Gospels and Psalms).[22] The eclectic catalog partly reflected the whims of donors. Irwin admitted that the catalog was governed as much by chance as by ideals: "You see, we have to pass the hat. We go before the Lions Club and ask them to print a book. We may want to print Galsworthy's book, but someone will jump up and say, 'I would like to see God and the Groceryman printed,' and so it is God and the Groceryman. We think it is better than no book at all."[23] Such pragmatism did not always come across to patrons, however, who looked at the catalog and saw only the final choice.

The library's budget was responsible for numerous controversies over book selection. Every title mattered since only a small proportion of printed books could be recorded. "There is no exercise of censorship as such," insisted a 1947 report, before then acknowledging complaints about the exclusion of particular titles.[24] The initial congressional appropriation of $75,000 (raised to $175,000 in 1938 and to $250,000 in 1941) made it difficult to record enough books to satisfy a growing readership. In 1937, Lucille Goldthwaite, a librarian at the New York Public Library, noted that there were only 132 titles available for nearly 900 patrons, each of whom borrowed, on average, three books a month; the number of readers was expected to reach 18,000 by the following year.[25] Book selection remained controversial as long as only a limited number of titles could be recorded to meet their needs.

The selection committee struggled to choose appropriate titles while at the same time maintaining the appearance of an impartial body. Patrons did not always recognize the nuanced distinction between censorship and book selection. One librarian defended the agency from accusations of censorship by describing its role as "a question of selection, not of rejection," when choosing titles to purchase with its limited resources.[26] Still, many readers suspected that finance was not the only factor governing book selection. They accused selectors of paternalism, at best, and censorship, at worst. The first battles over censorship, then, arose from conflicting views over which values should govern book selection.

One controversy arose over the selection committee's investment in books that would be useful ten years in the future instead of in the ephemeral titles wanted right then. The committee aspired to build "a library of permanent worth," which generally meant nonfiction or pre-twentieth-century fiction.[27] An equal split between fiction and nonfiction was another one of its aims. In 1948, more than 50 percent of talking books were in nonfiction categories or qualified as classical literature (mainly nineteenth-century novels by Balzac, Dickens, and others).[28] Many readers objected to this ratio. One complained that the disproportionate amount of nonfiction (as high as 55 percent) ignored most people's preference for recreational reading: "The reading tastes of the blind are not different from the seeing. They like frankly entertaining stories— mystery, adventure, romance—just as well as other people."[29] Blind readers may have shared the same taste in books as other readers but not equal access to them. There was a long waiting list, for example, for Zane Grey's *Riders of the Purple Sage.*

All public librarians faced the problem of choosing between the best books ever written and books of the present moment (alas, the two are rarely the same). The Library of Congress's selectors compared themselves to municipal librarians balancing the needs of constituents against finite resources. Yet most libraries dealt with a public who, unlike blind people, had alternative sources of books. As Goldthwaite observed, "The people we are reaching directly have no other avenue, no other source of reading."[30] Librarians did their best to choose titles likely to stand the test of time, though the candidates picked (Walter Duranty, James Hilton, Anne Morrow Lindbergh, Hugh Walpole) suggest how difficult it could be to predict the staying power of literary reputations.

The selection committee's preference for classical literature led to further controversy as well as a series of objections from blind people hoping to influence the process. "Why can we not have some of the lovely lyrics of modern writers instead of our well known Tennyson?" asked Rosa Barksdale of Shreveport, Louisiana. Barksdale spoke for those who already knew Shakespeare by heart. She wanted to keep up instead with the tastes of sighted friends as well as to escape from her misfortunes. The classics were already available to people unfamiliar with them, she protested: "Is[n't] the need equally great for those of us with stiffening fingers, minds rebellious from starvation, spirits desiring to keep step with thought of the day[?]"[31] The litany of complaints made it difficult to ignore the fact that old books were seldom popular. Irwin admitted, "Time and again I have urged upon the readers their support of the publication of certain of the older classics, like Dickens and Scott, but both the readers and the librarians say, 'Please give us something new, something stimulating, something we have not read before, something our friends are talking about.'"[32] Blind people were interested in reading the same books as everyone else—in most cases, these were not the classics.

Still other readers protested that the titles were too sophisticated. Roberts had a reputation for favoring serious books. As one observer noted, "The Librarian is very highbrow and the A.F.B. have the greatest difficulty in persuading [sic] him to order anything but English classics."[33] Although librarians complained that many titles went over the heads of their readers, such criticism had little effect on Roberts: "His line is that trash is not worth doing."[34] Roberts's attitude, though an extreme one, gestures toward the gulf between the committee and its readership. Resentment drove some readers to boycott the list. As a correspondent reported, "The local blind do not like the selection of reading matter, finding it too high brow; and they have decided to read nothing rather than to have to listen to such as 'Plutarch's Lives' and Pepys' 'Man Against Death,' etc."[35] Such abstentions suggest that some readers would rather forego books altogether than compromise their independence by listening to material deemed good for them.

A final dispute arose over the choice between educational and recreational books—or rather, between what blind people should read and what they actually wanted to read. Many selectors felt that the use of government funds obligated them to purchase books of established merit.[36] Librarian of Congress Herbert Putnam, for one, disapproved of recreational reading, preferring instead books such as Bacon's *Essays*. A survey of approximately 800 blind readers throughout the country seemed to confirm Putnam's preference for serious literature; however, skeptics objected that this group represented a minority of educated readers out of a blind population of approximately 120,000. Calls for a "happy medium" between educational and recreational literature underestimated the depth of feeling on the subject.[37] Still, the selection committee felt that the resulting list would be criticized by one side or the other no matter which titles were chosen.

Many blind people insisted on having access to the same books as everyone else, not those chosen by moral guardians. The loudest demands were for more contemporary fiction. Goldthwaite argued that the talking book library ought to have more recreational titles than equivalent public libraries since blind people relied on books for recreation to a greater extent than sighted people. She urged the Library of Congress to learn from the numerous well-intentioned braille titles left on the shelf unread. "In acquiring books in the new medium," writes Goldthwaite, "it is not a foundation of the world's best literature that is needed, but some good current literature for the use of adults who are already moderately well read."[38] Readers themselves complained more bluntly.

Central to the debate over book selection was the issue of paternalism: whether blind people benefited from having selections made in their best interest or whether they were better off choosing books for themselves. Roberts advocated giving readers what they wanted—as long as they did not want too much fiction. For him, the appropriate ratio was 50 percent popular fiction. The remaining half should be chosen by experts: "There still remains a responsibility upon the librarians for the blind to guide the tastes of their readers to the more enduring and satisfying forms of literature."[39] Yet patrons noticed the difference between steering readers toward books and leaving them off the shelves altogether.

As previous chapters have shown, blind readers were especially sensitive toward book selection since many of them had once depended on other people for access to books. Roberts's policy threatened to continue this dependency by other means. Consequently, many patrons insisted on choosing their own books even if this meant reading trash. Nothing put up journalist Charles Magee Adams's guard more quickly than the suspicion that someone was trying to educate him. He objected that too many talking books were of "the 'improving' sort": "Encouraging a taste for better things is desirable. But trying to force it is something else again."[40]

Blind people insisted on receiving equal treatment—including the right to choose bad books. After all, the majority of blind readers had once been sighted readers, and blindness was a physical, not an intellectual, disability. By the 1950s, the Library of Congress operated on the principle that sighted and blind readers had similar tastes, and that blind people deserved access to the same books as other people.[41] The talking book service made available the same books held in a typical public library. As one report concluded, "No books useful to the sighted are inapplicable to the blind."[42] Yet this equivalence posed challenges, too, since blind readers varied in education, interests, and income to the same extent as other readers (more so, in fact, since this group contained a higher proportion of elderly and disadvantaged people)

while having fewer resources. Whereas public libraries could stock a sufficient number of titles to appeal to a mixed audience, the talking book library's size meant that any choice was likely to offend someone.

Blind readers wanted access to the same contemporary fiction available to
everyone else. Philadelphia's Hallie Baylor, for one, asked the AFB to add more
new fiction than had been included in the catalogs between 1934 and 1937.
She appreciated older books but, at the same time, wished to read the same
ones as her sighted friends. She declared of blind readers, "We are progressive, and we do not like to live solely in the past."[43] Despite a preference for
solitary reading, she could only gain access to *Gone with the Wind* by having
it read aloud to her. Tellingly, her letter appeals to a selection committee made
up of sighted readers: "Just put yourselves in our places, and I am sure you
will readily understand and see that it is only natural that we too do like to
read and keep up with the different new books as well as you do yourselves.
Because we do not see does not make us any different from you along these
lines."[44] Baylor's overt call for empathy implies that blind people were being
held back and even socially excluded out of a misplaced sense of what was
good for them. The result: a reading list that bore little relation to the tastes
of its readers.

Filthy Books

The strained relationship between the United States and the Soviet Union
after the Second World War reached all the way down to the nation's libraries.
The Cold War's defining feature was suspicion of communism. Politicians
used legislative bodies such as the House Un-American Activities Committee to lead anticommunist purges and to investigate subversive activities
by public employees and private citizens.[45] Libraries were vulnerable targets,
and campaigns to remove "subversive" or "immoral" books escalated across
the country. They faced persistent challenges from outside groups who perceived controversial material as a threat to the American way of life.[46] A substantial number of Americans accepted censorship as a necessary protection
against communism.

Librarians responded to such challenges by citing their obligation to select
books representing diverse viewpoints. Since 1939, the American Library Association had championed a professional duty to make available to the public
all sides of controversial issues.[47] In 1948, the association pledged to fight cen-

sorship on the grounds that citizens required access to the full spectrum of opinion in order to make informed decisions. That year, librarians across the country urged the profession to combat censorship in all its forms. The American Library Association's annual conference chose as its theme intellectual freedom.

The Library of Congress had by then become accustomed to defending the talking book catalog from outside interests that sought to shape it according to a particular worldview. Correspondence in 1944 between Archibald MacLeish, then Librarian of Congress, and Reverend John J. Connolly, director of the Catholic Guild for the Blind in Boston, for example, reveals how difficult it could be to assemble a catalog without offending minority interests. Connolly complained that Ernest Hemingway's *A Farewell to Arms* should be excluded from the talking book library because it was offensive to Catholics. "The talking book can be an instrument for good or evil, depending on the type of books selected," declared Connolly.[48]

The objection was taken especially seriously since other Catholic groups, such as the National Organization for Decent Literature, had become influential forces for censorship. MacLeish replied that Hemingway's novel should be understood amid a broader debate over the artist's obligation either to depict life "realistically" or to suppress certain aspects of life.[49] The disagreement reflected the novel's divisive reception throughout the country. Connolly judged the book "offensive to any decent person," whereas MacLeish deemed it one of the century's great novels.[50] The dispute had less to do with the book's merits, on which the two disagreed, than with the appropriateness of including potentially inflammatory titles in the talking book library.

Did the selection committee have a right to exclude offensive books? Hemingway's novel presented an opportunity to make explicit the committee's principles. MacLeish identified two key questions underpinning the debate: (1) whether books included in libraries for blind people should be chosen on a different basis from other libraries; and (2) whether books should be excluded from such collections on the grounds of morality, ethics, or other criteria. MacLeish suspected that blind people would resist any attempts to treat them differently. As he asked Connolly, "Do you feel, that is, that the blind would welcome supervision of their reading of a kind not exercised in the case of sighted readers?"[51] The Books for the Adult Blind Project had originated as part of an effort to give people with visual disabilities equal access to books—not to treat them as a group in need of special protection.

The talking book library did need to be more selective than comparable institutions since it recorded only a fraction of printed books. The committee also had an obligation to choose books that were representative and respectful of various constituents. Connolly argued that, such being the case, "books which are objectively offensive to any racial, religious or national group should not be chosen."[52] For Connolly, Hemingway's book represented a case where its offensiveness outweighed its representativeness.

MacLeish approached the issue from a different angle. He affirmed the right of people who were blind to be treated the same as sighted people when it came to book selection. This meant selecting books on the same basis as other institutions, namely public libraries, even at the risk of offending readers. Of course, the talking book library's size required the committee to choose the "outstanding" ones.[53] Hemingway's novel was a noteworthy, if divisive, title with a sufficient base of admirers to warrant its inclusion, concluded MacLeish.

The correspondence between MacLeish and Connolly shows that the selection committee faced a problem bedeviling all censors: how to exclude offensive material while at the same time protecting literature that deliberately pushed the boundaries of acceptable speech. In 1944, Louise Maurer, who worked for the Library of Congress's Books for the Adult Blind Project, complained about books being judged "bald," by which she meant the frank treatment of a topic—an approach "always considered harmful for the blind."[54] Books rejected for baldness included Gustave Flaubert's *Madame Bovary* and James Joyce's *Dubliners.* That meant the talking book catalog had no Joyce titles since *A Portrait of the Artist as a Young Man* had already been rejected.

In 1947, one Library of Congress staff member (probably Xenophon Smith, director of the library's Division for the Blind) attached a handwritten note to the book selection policy acknowledging that several novels of literary merit had recently been recorded despite "frankness of language," "realistic treatment," or "unpleasantness of situation."[55] They included Betty Smith's *A Tree Grows in Brooklyn;* Lillian Smith's *Strange Fruit;* Thomas Wolfe's *Look Homeward, Angel;* and even an eighteenth-century classic, Laurence Sterne's *Tristram Shandy.* According to the note's author, omitting such titles would have diminished the talking book library's worth. This marked a departure from past policy. In 1942, the library had avoided controversial titles such as John Steinbeck's *The Grapes of Wrath,* a book banned from libraries across the country for its progressive politics and alleged immorality.[56] Steinbeck's novel was not recorded until after the furor subsided.

The need for an explicit talking book selection policy became increasingly apparent after 1945 as disputes shifted from book selection (old or new; non-fiction or fiction; highbrow or lowbrow) toward calls for censorship of obscene, immoral, and subversive books.[57] The American Library Association's annual conference held in June 1947 reviewed the talking book selection policy as part of a panel titled "Obscenity in Books for the Blind." Guidelines reaffirmed the library's mission to supply reading material to people with vision impairments and to treat them exactly the same as sighted readers. Books were to be selected on the basis of literary merit and usefulness, as determined by an advisory committee including both sighted and blind people. The document also outlined the criteria for exclusion: "No literature is reproduced for the blind, under the program, in which the primary interest is erotic or morbid. No books are reproduced because of a popularity which appears to rest merely upon such an interest."[58] While still denying that this qualified as censorship rather than good taste, the library used its government backing to justify excluding erotic and morbid content. The selection committee already refused requests on these grounds for sectarian literature or literature judged to be of poor quality.

Irwin and A. C. Ellis, superintendent of the American Printing House for the Blind, corresponded about the library's new selection policy. Their disagreement reveals the conflicting attitudes toward censorship held by two of the most influential figures responsible for establishing the talking book service in the 1930s. Irwin objected to blind people's dependence on the judgment of a single group since the Library of Congress was their sole source of reading material. Gatekeepers were not immune to political considerations: "Who knows but that books may be excluded because they are anti-Catholic, Anti-Christian Science, Anti-Russian, Anti-British, Anti-Moral or Anti anything else that may offend either a pious or nervous public official or a crotchety Congressman."[59] Talking books had been designed to assist blind readers who depended on other people for access to books. Prejudices threatened their independence.

Irwin noted that readers could always switch off the phonograph. He recalled the case of an elderly woman who listened to every word of *A Farewell to Arms* despite finding the first record offensive. Such incidents prompted him to ask, "Do you really think the Library of Congress should refuse to publish for the blind any book which may be regarded by some old maid, either male or female, as corrupting the blind people's morals[?]"[60] Irwin even considered setting up an independent publishing house to record books rejected by the Library of Congress.

Anecdotes circulated among blind people ensured that they did not forget the bad old days of censorship and even of eugenicist campaigns to keep them from procreating.[61] The American Printing House for the Blind allegedly used to expurgate books to prevent the contamination of blind people's morals. The story was often told of a braille publisher who issued a bowdlerized version of Shakespeare's *Romeo and Juliet* without the love scenes. School superintendents in Minnesota had even considered using an expurgated Bible.[62] Those who resisted censorship efforts were hailed as folk heroes. A renowned librarian at the Wisconsin School for the Blind, for instance, had refused to buy books censored for blind people's use. Such folk tales and anxieties formed the context in which discussions over book selection played out.

Ellis held a more moderate stance, between the two extremes of publishing all offensive material and publishing nothing controversial. While recognizing the blind community's sensitivity toward censorship, Ellis favored recording the many unobjectionable books available instead of fretting about borderline cases. According to Ellis, blind people had other ways to obtain "filth" than through a government-sponsored program. "I resent censorship as much as anyone," declared Ellis, "but I simply can see no justification for recording that stuff on phonograph records to be played at home."[63] It may be true that potentially offensive books of literary value required protection (Irwin maintained that the most offensive talking book ever recorded was the Bible). Yet Ellis opposed publishing controversial books for their own sake: "The Library of Congress, it seems to me, has sponsored too many dirty books which possess neither literary value nor reflect sound scholarship."[64] He felt confident that the library's new selection policy would avoid both extremes.

Concerns that obscene recordings might jeopardize the library's funding were warranted. Elected officials frequently complained about the library's moral standards. At a congressional hearing in 1947, Oklahoma representative George Schwabe protested against talking books with offensive language: "I certainly do not want to be a party to making appropriations for the publication of such books to go out to the blind or to anybody else."[65] At subsequent congressional hearings, Schwabe continued to protest against using federal funds to subsidize obscene, indecent, or blasphemous books. Advocacy groups opposed such restrictions, however, in order to ensure that blind people had the same access to books as other people. In an internal memo, the AFB's Evelyn McKay responded to Schwabe's attacks by asking, "Why should the Director of Books for the Adult Blind, or the members of Congress, undertake to censor the reading matter which blind adults are permitted to have?"[66] The dispute hinged on whether the Library of Congress had an obligation to provide equal access to books for all citizens or to withhold public subsidies for controversial titles opposed by many taxpayers on moral grounds.

The library introduced measures that stopped short of censorship in order to protect readers from unwanted contact with obscenity. Warning labels were one precaution taken by *Talking Book Topics,* a quarterly magazine listing the library's new releases. Such information protected readers like sixty-four-year-old Hazel Hodgdon, who explained, "I am a practicing church member, and while I am not a prude, I don't order the books which are described, 'Explicit descriptions of sex,' because to me sex is a sacred and beautiful thing."[67] Hodgdon, who read up to eighteen books a month, accepted that other readers might not share her preferences. Still, she preferred to avoid sexually explicit scenes: "I like to be able to read without feeling that my mind is being used for a garbage can."[68] Warning labels steered readers like Hodgdon away from objectionable material while at the same time granting other people access to the same stories as sighted readers.

The selection committee occasionally sidestepped the issue of censorship altogether by reproducing potentially offensive books (such as Joyce's *Portrait*) in braille rather than on records. Some justified this maneuver as a way of protecting the reader's privacy since offensive language might be overheard by other people in the room: "When a book containing profane or vulgar expression is read aloud in these circumstances with the loudspeaker on in preference to head phones, it may prove acutely embarrassing to the blind reader."[69] Others felt that hearing profanity read aloud was somehow more offensive than reading it in print. Mrs. Frank Robey of Lincoln, Nebraska, for example, objected to the "dreadful swearing" in Philip Stong's *Buckskin Breeches,* a rough-hewn tale of pioneer life.[70] A librarian defended the book's language while at the same time acknowledging its force: "It is true that these cuss words are more offensive when read aloud than when read silently, and we recognize this fact when selecting books for the 'talking books.'"[71] If language could be more offensive to the ear, it could also be more arousing. Ellis observed a vast difference between braille and spoken word recordings of pornography.[72]

Yet braille was hardly a solution for the people who couldn't read it. Reproducing potentially offensive material solely in this way made it inaccessible to

the majority of people who were blind. The risk of exclusion was especially severe since most blind readers had no other way to obtain books. According to
the selection committee's report on obscenity, publishing controversial literature in braille alone "would constitute a form of censorship which would be
intolerable under the American system of freedom."[73] Such invocations of
democracy suggest how much was felt to be at stake in debates over access to
books.

In June 1948, a controversy over a risqué novel exposed the persistent divide over the issue of censorship even among blind people themselves. The
dispute arose when an unnamed borrower returned Elizabeth Janeway's *Daisy
Kenyon,* a novel about a single woman's romantic engagements in New York
after the Second World War (and later made into a film starring Joan Crawford, Henry Fonda, and Dana Andrews). In a letter to *Talking Book Topics,*
the borrower complained that such indecent material should never have been
recorded in the first place:

> Today I returned the Talking Book DAISY KENYON to the library. It was
> such a filthy story, I did not care to read it or to have people know I read such
> a type of book. This is not the first time I have had to send back books for
> the same reason. I know it is not your fault that such books are made avail-
> able in record form. But I wish you would pass along my feelings about
> them so that money and time would not be spent for such trash. There are
> still many good books of a light nature that would be much better than
> that.[74]

In response, the magazine's editors asked whether readers agreed with this con-
demnation of obscene novels: Should librarians monitor the catalog in order
to protect delicate sensibilities or maintain a hands-off approach at the risk of
offense?

The magazine received twenty-one replies: five in support of the reader's
complaint; sixteen opposed to it or to censorship in any form. Della Clark of
Stone Ridge, New York, was among the "anti-Daisy" faction that condemned
filthy novels. Too much money and time was spent recording books that were
"useless and harmful," according to Clark, especially in a collection that was
restricted in size and supported by taxpayers. "I cannot tell how strongly I
feel upon this subject," she concluded her letter.[75]

By contrast, the "pro-Daisy" faction addressed the broader issue of censorship. Natalie Miller of Evanston, Illinois, protested, "I am not defending that

particular book—but, I am vigorously defending a free press for the blind!"[76] Miller recalled how difficult it had once been for blind people to obtain books widely read by the general public. They required access to the same books as other people if they were to enjoy the right to free inquiry and to safeguard, in Miller's words, "those of us who do our own thinking." After all, *Talking Book Topics* already warned subscribers if a book might be distasteful. Ray Foose of Mahanoy City, Pennsylvania, defended the rights of borrowers who enjoyed novels with a bit of "spice" in them: "Some people care for books of that sort, so why deprive them of that type of story, if they enjoy reading them."[77] Finally, Albert Gayzagian of Watertown, Massachusetts, objected that the library, far from recording too many realistic books, did not record enough of them. He noted the absence of landmarks of modern literature including Theodore Dreiser's *Sister Carrie,* Upton Sinclair's *The Jungle,* John Dos Passos's *U.S.A.* trilogy, and James T. Farrell's *Studs Lonigan* trilogy. Sensitive readers could "continue to live in a world of hearts and flowers, if they choose to do so," protested Gayzagian, without denying people like him the right to judge for themselves.[78]

Going Commie

Librarians faced a growing number of censorship disputes during the Cold War, when many people feared communism was a greater threat to democracy than restricted access to books. In 1947, President Harry Truman established a federal loyalty program intended to purge communist influence from the US government.[79] The Library of Congress voluntarily complied the following year. It began screening employees in the spring of 1948 even though many staff felt loyalty oaths were at odds with their duty to protect freedom of inquiry.[80] Chief Assistant Librarian of Congress Verner Clapp, who was placed in charge of the library's loyalty program, afterward defended people's right to free inquiry as fundamental to the role of research libraries. Speaking at the First Conference on Intellectual Freedom in June 1952, he highlighted the need to protect access to controversial books.[81]

The Library of Congress was especially sensitive to charges of disloyalty since it received funding from the federal government. In February 1953, the conservative magazine *Human Events* accused the Library of Congress's Books for the Adult Blind Project of liberal bias. Its catalog allegedly harbored a disproportionate number of authors suspected of communist sympathies while excluding

Henry Hazlitt, George Sokolsky, Charles Tansill, Freda Utley, and other anticommunists. The Soviet apologist Richard Lauterbach's *These Are the Russians* had been recorded, but not Soviet critic William L. White's *Report on the Russians*. The magazine also characterized two previous Librarians of Congress (MacLeish and Luther Evans) as "liberals." "It is little wonder, in view of the above situation," the editors concluded, "that there are plans being made on Capitol Hill for an investigation of the Library of Congress."[82] Even extreme viewpoints could not be ignored amid the hostile political climate of the 1950s. A handwritten note stapled to the library's copy of *Human Events* warns, "Let's prepare our defense in advance of anyone taking this seriously."[83]

Complaints about books by communists and other subversive material compelled the Library of Congress to take steps to avoid suspicion of disloyalty.[84] In November 1953, Donald Patterson, chief of the library's Division for the Blind, recommended establishing a committee to screen books nominated for recording. According to Patterson's memo, screening all titles from 1932 onward would "guard against inclusion of any which might embarrass us from the points of view of authorship, subversive content or objectionable language."[85] In fact, the book selection policy had always taken into account a title's appropriateness for government subsidy. Material deemed subversive could be excluded under this criterion or, in view of the increased scrutiny from groups such as the American Legion and the Daughters of the American Revolution, by introducing a restriction against communist propaganda.

The following year, the library established a committee to screen books. Its aim was to prevent the recording of books by communist authors, books with subversive content, or books containing language in violation of good taste. Committee members, appointed from the library's staff, were required to write reports explicitly stating the reasons for a book's exclusion. Guidelines given to committee members sought to prevent confusion. (A sample question: What about books written "by someone who goes Commie" after a book's publication?[86]) The guidelines defined communist works to encompass official publications by the Soviet government and the Communist Party as well as works by writers judged to be in sympathy with the party's beliefs. It was the hunt for subversive themes, however, that required committee members to act as literary critics:

> The committee member is cautioned to look for passages which may be described as revolutionary in character, advocating the overthrow of the Gov-

ernment, expressions of sympathy with known Communist ideals or objectives, inflammatory matter or such as may stimulate unrest or dissatisfaction with constituted authority or existing conditions, or language which reflects a proletarian approach to or outlook on national or international affairs.[87]

The guidelines leave little doubt about censorship. A library that began by refusing to record books considered immoral, ephemeral, or of poor quality once again found itself acting as censor by excluding subversive books—thereby ensuring that no blind reader would "go commie." The censorship effort can be taken as a sign either of how extensive anticommunist campaigns had become in the 1950s or that blind readers, whose first government-sponsored books had included patriotic documents such as the Constitution, posed as much of a threat to American sovereignty as other readers.

This chapter's investigation began with the Library of Congress's explicit denial of censorship. Yet, as efforts to choose worthy titles and screen books show, the real story is more complicated since the talking book library faced the same pressures as other libraries to restrict access to books. The committee formed to protect blind people from communism is the only instance of straightforward censorship I've encountered while working among archives held by organizations devoted to blind people's welfare. The irony is that, thanks to the Cold War's far-reaching censorship campaigns, blind readers finally received treatment equal to that of other Americans.

The talking book library evolved alongside other libraries as it went from selecting books in people's best interest to its current role of making available the widest possible selection of books. In 1954, the Library of Congress issued a formal policy on selecting talking books. Henceforth, it intended to build a collection appealing to a diverse readership and, more important, to accommodate this readership's overwhelming preference for popular fiction. By 1970, 90 percent of all of the Library of Congress's best-selling books were issued either in audio or braille.[88] It had struggled as much as other libraries to draw a line between permissible and impermissible publications. As one employee explained, "The book that one finds silly or offensive may bring great pleasure to another."[89] The library's solution: stop making decisions on behalf of blind people and, instead, allow blind people to decide for themselves.

Book selection continued to be fraught with difficulties after the 1950s but never to the same extent as during the McCarthy era. There were several reasons for this. One was the library's improved understanding of blind people's welfare that emerged from book selection controversies. Integrating sighted and blind readers on the selection committee likewise helped to diminish the gap in expectations. The library's talking book service now dealt with the same calls for censorship (moving from subversiveness to "smut") as other libraries rather than with issues of paternalism unique to people who were blind.[90]

In addition, visually impaired people now had other ways to obtain books not recorded by the Library of Congress. The most important of these were recordings made by volunteers using dictation devices such as the Sound-Scriber and, later, tape recorders. Volunteer recording programs emerged after the Second World War to help blinded veterans attend university. From 1950, organizations such as the National Committee on Special Recording (and, later, the National Committee for Recording for the Blind as well as Recording for the Blind, Inc.) worked alongside volunteers to supplement the library's holdings. Finally, record companies began making commercial spoken word recordings for the public in the 1950s—as we'll see in Part III.

Access to books remains a contentious issue as thousands of visually impaired readers (and now people with other physical, learning, and reading disabilities such as dyslexia) still rely on the talking book service.[91] Yet the debate has shifted from the quality to the quantity of books. The Library of Congress continues to avoid censoring material in any way and to allow patrons to decide for themselves what to read. This is a departure from a previous era in which a small group of experts decided what books should be read by blind people—or, as it turned out, what books should not be read by them.

5

From Shell Shock to Shellac

The Royal National Institute of Blind People (RNIB) celebrated the Talking Book Service's fiftieth anniversary in 1985. Its pioneering efforts to record books for a small group of blind and partially sighted individuals had grown into a professional operation reaching nearly half of the estimated 130,000 blind people in Britain.[1] The service by then held nearly 6,000 titles.[2] The Golden Jubilee was marked by a visit from the prime minister, Margaret Thatcher, who had listened to talking books while recovering from eye surgery, as well as a commemorative ceremony in recognition of its 60,000th member.[3]

The Reverend Robert Manthorp, headmaster of Worcester College for the Blind, honored the achievement by recalling how attitudes toward blindness had changed: "Fifty years ago blind persons . . . were, in truth, thought of as being 'not quite nice'; there was something wrong with them, they offended the taste of respectable people and therefore were hidden away behind high walls." The general attitude, he went on to say, was that "blindness is something rather nasty, let's keep away." The Talking Book Service marked a turning point by recognizing the shared interests, capabilities, and humanity of people who couldn't see. Reverend Manthorp credited those who refused to accept that people with disabilities were somehow different from other people—those who, in his words, "refused to believe a man was stupid because he was blind."[4]

The British public's interest in the welfare of blind people was hardly a new phenomenon, however. Sighted people had shown an interest in their literacy since at least the eighteenth century.[5] Inaccessibility to books was a particular concern among philanthropists, educated people, and religious leaders who worried that people would not have access to the Bible. Subsequent generations were equally fascinated by people's acquisition of literacy through the spread of tactile reading methods and the opening of schools for blind pupils.[6] The London Society for Teaching the Blind to Read was established in 1838, and the National Library Service for the Blind was set up in 1882. The Talking Book Service arose out of the public's understanding of the needs of blind people as well as broader cultural shifts related to education, literacy, and what would today be called disability rights activism.

Advocacy groups had long sought accessible reading formats by the time sound technology made it possible to record a full-length book on a set of gramophone records. One publication described "the inability to read" as the greatest handicap imposed by blindness.[7] Embossed books allowed some people to overcome this hardship.[8] But raised type offered no help to people who could not read braille and depended on volunteers to read aloud to them. Their plight received public attention after the return of soldiers who had lost their sight during the First World War, whose number continued to grow as the delayed effects of mustard gas and other chemicals became apparent (Figure 5.1).[9]

Figure 5.1. British troops blinded by tear gas at an advanced dressing station near Béthune, France, April 10, 1918.

War-blinded veterans represented a challenge and an imperative to develop an alternative means of reading for those who were unable to read for themselves.

The war was a catalyst for the reconceptualization of blind veterans and civilians alike.[10] Blinded servicemen returning from the war gave a degree of urgency to problems of literacy that had long been tolerated. Before the war, blindness had been regrettable and unfortunate, but it was not a problem for which the public bore direct responsibility. The war changed all that. The British public owed a debt to the servicemen who had sacrificed their eyesight defending the country. In the absence of state compensation, disabled veterans relied on philanthropic organizations for treatment and rehabilitation.[11] Campaigns to raise funds on behalf of veterans appealed directly to the public's conscience through the prominent display of the wounded soldier's body. For example, St. Dunstan's charity for the rehabilitation of blinded ex-servicemen featured a disabled veteran alongside the caption "BLINDED FOR YOU" (Figure 5.2).[12] Such campaigns reminded the public of its obligation to make the lives of disabled veterans tolerable by supplying them with entertainment including books. Veterans who were unable to read braille, however, required an alternative to print.

Britain's talking books have received less attention from historians than those in the United States despite their parallel trajectories.[13] The following account traces the talking book's development from the initial experiments after the First World War to its debut and reception among blind soldiers and civilians in the mid-1930s. It has been put together using archives held by the RNIB (before its royal charter, the National Institute for the Blind [NIB]) and Blind Veterans UK (formerly St. Dunstan's), the two organizations responsible for establishing Britain's Talking Book Service.[14] My primary goal here is recovery work: to put together an account of the talking book's origins in Britain to stand alongside those written about the United States (as discussed in Chapter 2). Agencies in both countries forged a transatlantic partnership through the exchange of expertise, technology, and titles. Yet, despite shared aims, the two countries worked independently of one another to resolve financial, technological, and aesthetic problems that make each of their stories distinctive.

This chapter starts out by reconstructing the search for an alternative way of reading, then demonstrates the talking book's impact on the lives of people with disabilities. It documents how the first generation of readers, many of whom had given up hope of ever reading again, responded to talking books.

Figure 5.2. Image of a blind soldier used in fund-raising campaigns by St. Dunstan's.

This part of the story recovers the voices of blind readers left out of most histories of books, literacy, and reading practices in the twentieth century.[15] The ensuing pages revisit a debate over the value of recorded books, once again confirming that disputes over the recorded book's legitimacy are as old as the talking book itself. As we will see, prejudicial attitudes were not the only obstacles to progress. The talking book met with equally strong opposition from readers who were themselves blind.

The story told here confronts the central issue raised by the convergence of books, media, and disability in the war's aftermath: Can a book talk? Ambivalence is encapsulated in the very terms "talking" and "book": one promises to reach readers excluded from print, while the other reassures them that they are still in contact with the same narrative as everyone else. The following account demonstrates how talking books evolved in relation to printed ones while at the same time calling into question what reading meant to people during the interwar years in Britain.[16]

The fraught nature of this relationship is evident in people's reluctance to use the term "reading" to describe the act of listening to books. Many accounts use "reading" within quotation marks or neologisms such as "reader-listeners" or "listener-readers." These formulations reflect uncertainty over the exact relationship between reading and hearing a book. They arise from an unresolved set of questions about reading: Is reading inherently visual or can we apprehend books through other sensory organs, including our ears and fingers? How does the speaker's voice affect the process of interpretation? What effect does the machine have on a book's reception? We should not expect the pioneers of the Talking Book Service to be able to answer such difficult questions since they remain unresolved to this day. But questions about aesthetic preferences were beside the point for most blind people in the 1930s. For them, the talking book meant the difference between reading and not reading at all.

The Dream of a Talking Book Library

Books have never been much use to people who cannot see. The history of blind literacy is one of attempts to adapt the printed book into alternative formats as soon as technology made it possible to do so. Dreams of a mechanical reading device have preoccupied auditors ever since Thomas Edison's invention of the phonograph in 1877. This machine and its successors represented a potential prosthesis for blind people by allowing them to read books through another person's eyes.[17]

Captain Ian Fraser first conceived of a talking book while listening to a gramophone at St. Dunstan's: "It ought to be possible, I thought, to record human speech. Theoretically it should be possible to record whole books."[18] Fraser joined St. Dunstan's after being shot through the eyes by a German sniper at the Battle of the Somme in July 1916; he went on to become the organization's chairman at the age of twenty-four. Once there, he began experimenting with a Dictaphone, a device used to record speech onto wax cylinders.[19] Fraser then recorded scraps of poetry and speeches using other devices at a makeshift studio at St. Dunstan's. He wrote in his autobiography, "These were really the first talking-book records, and were the first beginnings of the Talking Book."[20]

Physical disabilities have a history of generating new media.[21] Innovations in sound-recording technology like the long-playing (LP) record presented an opportunity to remake the book for the ears instead of the eyes. Still, veterans had to wait more than a decade after the war for a technological alternative to reading aloud. Spoken word recordings had long been held back by the limited playing time of records. As late as 1932, no gramophone company marketed a record that played longer than five minutes. The LP was not ready for the commercial market until 1948.[22] Blind people benefited from the technology much sooner, however. As early as 1919, Fraser persuaded the Columbia Gramophone Company and Pathephone Company to experiment with recording speech on gramophone discs using speeds slower than the industry standard of 78 rpm (revolutions per minute). "The reproduction was vile," Fraser recalled.[23] Yet the NIB and St. Dunstan's, working with the Gramophone Company (later known as His Master's Voice or HMV) and other firms, eventually succeeded in playing discs at reduced speeds.

Initially, there was little confidence in the gramophone as a long-term solution to the problem of mechanical reading. Experiments conducted by the NIB's Technical Research Committee during the 1920s reflect the group's openness to alternative formats.[24] Over the next decade the committee considered numerous devices: Blattnerphones, Dictaphones, Fotoliptofonos, Libraphones, Marconiphones, Ozaphones, Phonofilms, Readaphones, Telegraphones, and Ecophone Dailygraphs. The committee tried out a range of recording surfaces, too, from wax cylinders and records to film, ribbon, and steel wire.

The alternatives indicated that it might not even be necessary to record speech at all. Headlines like "Ear Books for the Blind" gave the impression that the next breakthrough in literacy would be the musical book, not a talking one.[25] The inventor of the typophone, which played a sound alphabet derived from Morse code, claimed to be able to record an entire novel on an eight-inch phonograph record that fit into one's pocket—a substantial economy at a time when a Dickens novel required over 400 discs.[26] Another promising device was the optophone, which transformed a book's letterpress into musical notes (Figure 5.3).[27] Mary Jameson used this device to become the first blind person to read from an ordinary printed book (Anthony Trollope's *The Warden*).[28] The average person struggled to translate the tones back into words, however. People likewise struggled with tactile reading machines, including

Figure 5.3. A blind man reading a book using an optophone.

the visagraph and photoelectrograph, which made embossed copies of any printed page.[29] They all were rejected as either too impractical or too expensive for the average blind person.

The Technical Research Committee's preference for "speaking films" reflected abiding concerns about investing in a medium that might soon be obsolete.[30] The NIB even refrained from fund raising until it was certain that the gramophone would not be displaced by rival media. As Fraser recalled, "I saw in the talking film a possible way to realise my dream of a Talking Book Library."[31] Ironically, the best fit for the talking book was a medium originally designed for silent entertainment.[32] Film enabled high-quality recordings in a format that was easy to handle, transport, and repair. Narrator mistakes were also easier to fix on film than on records. The NIB's engineering team suspected that talking books would migrate to film once a sufficiently cheap reproducer became available.[33] Many at the American Foundation for the Blind shared this view. As late as 1937, Jackson Kleber, the foundation's chief engineer, advised delegates from the United Kingdom that "the film will be the talking book of the future."[34]

The experiments suggest that we should be wary of a genealogy for the talking book that extends in an unbroken line from Edison's phonograph disc through to modern sound technologies including the cassette tape, compact disc, and digital audio file. The gramophone was chosen on the basis of economic viability, not technical superiority. Its records alone met the Technical Research Committee's twin goals of manufacturing "the pleasantest and most economical type of book to produce" for a group of disabled people with scant resources.[35] In spite of their fragility and bulk, records held practical advantages over other media in terms of cost, audibility, and ease of use. By contrast, none of the film machines tested by the committee were affordable. Blind people living in homes without electricity would not have been able to use one at all.[36]

We should likewise note important differences between American and British talking books. The two countries did not even use the same terminology at first.[37] The NIB's Technical Research Committee recognized the benefits of exchanging records with the Americans in order to establish a larger library than it could achieve by itself.[38] Yet the NIB chose a format differing from that used by the Americans in one key respect: speed. The records used in America played at 33⅓ rpm for approximately fifteen minutes on each side, whereas Britain's records played at 24 rpm for up to twenty-five minutes—a difference that would lead to compatibility issues.

The NIB felt that the Americans had not chosen the most efficient format. Despite recognizing the need for standardization, Fraser insisted on reducing costs too. "Nor must we adhere to the American standard merely because they have set it," Fraser told the Technical Research Committee.[39] British gramophones required special construction for any speed other than 78 rpm. It was therefore in the organization's best interest to produce machines that could play records at an optimal speed (between 16 and 24 rpm, according to engineers) in order to obtain the economic advantages of extended playing time. Twenty-five minutes per side represented a savings of 16 percent over the American record.[40]

In the spring of 1934, the NIB and St. Dunstan's announced their intention to launch the Talking Book Service. As Fraser told readers of the *St. Dunstan's Review,* "I do not want to excite undue hopes, but I think that in the near future it may be possible to establish a Library of Talking Books."[41] The NIB's Technical Research Committee (with whom Fraser had worked for the past decade) had brought the talking book within the bounds of possibility, thanks to electrical recording and other technological advances in the gramophone, radio, and film industries.[42] Talking books could at last be made at a reasonable cost. Fraser had also learned that the American Foundation for the Blind had begun its own venture.

No one knew how appealing talking books would be to a blind readership, many of whom had been accustomed to conventional books before losing their sight. For this reason, familiar bibliographic terms such as "library" and "books" continued to associate the new technology with the reassuring realm of print. The NIB established the Sound Recording Committee, chaired by Fraser, in May 1934 to develop, manufacture, and distribute the machines and records. The NIB and St. Dunstan's, representing blinded ex-servicemen, shared the costs.[43] The committee represented the three largest bodies responsible for blind welfare in the United Kingdom after adding a member from the National Library for the Blind.

The Talking Book Library began at a rudimentary studio in Regent's Park. Fraser described it as "a hut in my own garden, which I used to use as a workshop."[44] There, Anthony McDonald recorded the first talking book made in Britain.[45] McDonald's test readings helped determine the most effective style of reading and the appropriate recording equipment—what Fraser called "the human experiment" as opposed to "the technical experiment."[46] A Watts direct disc recording machine was used to make a limited number of discs, thereby avoiding the prohibitive recording costs of commercial companies.[47] The record labels HMV and Decca transferred the waxes onto a copper master, then returned the pressing for proof listening by a blinded veteran.[48]

The Talking Book Library began a two-year trial period on August 1, 1935. Membership was restricted to those registered as blind and "any others who can give satisfactory evidence of their inability to read ordinary books."[49] Unsurprisingly, the Talking Book Library hardly resembled other libraries. Its books required custom-made machinery in order to be read, and they also cost more to manufacture than printed books (Figure 5.4). According to one estimate, a library of 10,000 volumes would cost £1 million.[50] Funding was scarce since there was no public subsidy. Whereas the United States Library of Congress's talking book library received funding from the government, the NIB and St. Dunstan's relied entirely on private donations from Lord Nuffield, the Carnegie United Kingdom Trust, and the Pilgrim Trust.[51] They were among the many philanthropic organizations helping to rehabilitate wounded veterans in the absence of state support.

Talking books went out to readers on November 7, 1935, nearly one year after the distribution of similar records in the United States. ("Although we started research before the Americans, the Americans rushed into production

Figure 5.4. A talking book player and discs.

before us," Fraser explained.[52]) Each title consisted of a set of twelve-inch shellac discs; the average book took up ten double-sided records, which were shipped at no cost to borrowers, who had only to pay the return postage.[53] Membership was free to anyone who purchased (or received through charity) one of three different models of talking book machines: an electric gramophone, a mechanical model requiring no electricity, or a model designed for use with headphones (Figure 5.5).[54] All three machines could play discs at 24, 33⅓, and 78 rpm. Machines were sold at cost price, ranging from £6 10s. for the electrical model to £3 15s. 4d. for the headphone model.[55] Both the NIB and St. Dunstan's were reluctant to subsidize the machines with public funds until it was certain that gramophones would not be made obsolete; still, St. Dunstan's paid one pound of the cost for veterans.[56] By the end of September 1937, talking book machines had been delivered to 351 blind civilians, 338 St. Dunstaners, and 275 recipients abroad.[57]

The first talking books were Agatha Christie's *The Murder of Roger Ackroyd,* Joseph Conrad's *Typhoon,* and *The Gospel According to St. John.*[58] As a spokesperson recalled, "The Talking Book Library started to circulate books on November 7th, 1935 with the smallest library, I should think, in the world—to wit, three titles."[59] Axel Munthe's *The Story of San Michele* and William Gore's *There's Death in the Churchyard* were among the earliest re-

Figure 5.5. Ian Fraser listening to a talking book.

cordings too, as was the first volume of William Makepeace Thackeray's *The History of Henry Esmond.*

The list adhered closely to the public taste for printed books. Titles were chosen for their broad appeal and resembled those in other popular fiction series begun that same year; Agatha Christie, for example, also featured in the Penguin paperbacks series.[60] Little thought was given to the list's relevance to a blind readership with the exception of *The Story of San Michele,* described as "a modern masterpiece that has a particular interest for all blind people" owing to its author's sight loss.[61] Outside sponsorship influenced the selections as well. The first part of the Bible recorded was *The Gospel According to St. John,* not for its portrait of a blind man absolved of sin, but because the British and Foreign Bible Society offered to pay for it.[62]

The Talking Book Selection Committee was entrusted with the difficult decisions about which titles to include in the catalog. Its policy called for at least 75 percent of the titles to be of permanent value.[63] According to one observer, "The discriminating, but sometimes too austere taste of the classicist, has been tempered with consideration for those weaker brethren who prefer 'a good murder' to Elizabethan verse."[64] The library's modest budget made the selection process highly contentious (as we'll see in Chapter 6). At the end of the library's first year, it held fifty-five complete works (twenty-four recorded in Britain, the other thirty-one in America).[65] Recipients were nearly unanimous in their enthusiasm for the records, though many complained about the limited inventory.

The Coming of the Talking Book

The talking book was not simply a technological challenge. The NIB faced the equally daunting task of promoting it to nonreaders, touch readers, and book publishers, many of whom had reservations about the potential competition to existing books. In fact, they opposed talking books both for being too similar to printed ones and for not being similar enough to them.

In 1936, the NIB introduced the talking book to blind constituencies throughout the country. Demonstrations promoted the machine's benefits while simultaneously reassuring prospective users that it would not disrupt their daily routines. The presentations began with a sales pitch: "The prospect of being able to sit back in a comfortable chair and hear the best, or the worst, literature of the world read to you by a man with a golden voice is extraordinarily attractive."[66] Demonstrations took place before large organizations including the Northern Counties Association for the Blind, the Midland Counties Association for the Blind, and the Union of Counties Associations for the Blind. A loudspeaker was attached to the gramophone in order for the reader's voice to be heard at these public demonstrations. Other people heard the machine at the NIB's headquarters or at reading groups. Forty people attended the readings organized by the North Wales Society for the Blind, for example, and a group at Manchester's National Library for the Blind heard all twenty-two discs of a Thackeray novel.[67]

Some worried that the exhibitions gave a misleading impression since the talking book was meant to replicate the intimacy of solitary reading. The audience at the Home Teachers Conference in York was told, "The Talking book is meant for quiet intimacy. The Reader-Listener will sit back in his own armchair, smoking his pipe, while the Talking Book quietly discourses to him. It is not suitable for talking to a large gathering."[68] The NIB's Sound Recording Committee emphasized the machine's domestic role, as a mechanical reader for the home, since opportunities already existed for public recitation. Fraser encouraged servicemen reading *St. Dunstan's Review* not to be misled: "The Talking Book is a very difficult thing to demonstrate. You cannot get a thoroughly good idea of the value of it by listening for a few minutes to a demonstration in a room with others present. The real value is made obvious only when you have the machine in your home and can listen to a few chapters of a book and get thoroughly into the story; then you realize how excellent the reading is and how the machine meets a long felt need."[69] Fraser's statement recast books as essential to a rich interior life, not a luxury. Talking books alone satisfied an inclination to read in solitude, without other people's help.

The NIB framed the talking book in terms of the familiar practice of reading aloud. Nearly all blind readers had been read to by family, friends, or volunteers. Yet such recitations could be difficult to arrange or an imposition, and professional readers were expensive. As an advertisement in one of St. Dunstan's annual reports explained, "There are few greater pleasures for the blind than reading aloud; but wife and friends are not always available. The TALKING BOOK will supplement the human reader."[70] The final line attempted to defuse anxieties about the human's replacement by a machine. The talking book left existing arrangements intact while presenting additional opportunities for reading on demand: "Clear, agreeable reading aloud whenever this is wanted."[71] Such benefits appealed even to those with access to regular readers.

The "mechanical 'reader aloud'" sought to preserve the activity's intimacy without its awkwardness. To this end, Fraser reassured audiences that the machine was equal and even superior to human speakers:

I have listened to a good many experimental records which have been made and I can assure my fellow St. Dunstaners that if you sit down quietly with a reading machine and listen to a book that interests you, you will get just as much pleasure out of it as if a really competent reader is personally at your service. Indeed, the readers of our records are very much better than most of the friends or family members of the family who have been good enough to read to me in the past, and, what is more, the machine does not get tired, does not want to stretch and look out of the window and scratch its head or poke up the fire or see about something else and, best of all, you do not have to put yourself in the position of asking someone to read to you when they may want to do something else.[72]

Comparisons between talking book machines and human readers served a purpose. As James Lastra has argued, personification helped people to become acquainted with new media.[73] Any unease was neutralized, in this instance, by assurances that "a really competent reader is personally at your service." Such comparisons made the potentially alien machinery seem as human as possible—as did the connotations of the phrase "talking book" itself.

At the same time, the NIB and St. Dunstan's emphasized the machine's superiority. Humans were unreliable, difficult to manage, and not always competent readers. The gramophone eliminated nearly all traces of human fallibility. At least one patron celebrated the fact that "these beautiful readers of our Talking Books are never tired, never argumentative, and never in a hurry, bless them!"[74] The talking book machine made audiences aware of the inconveniences they had tolerated, wittingly or unwittingly, before its arrival. Listening to a family member lost its appeal once you could be read to by professional actors.

The NIB compared the talking book to braille in terms of its historical significance.[75] Various forms of raised type allowed some blind people to share in the cultural benefits brought by literacy. Talking book advocates endorsed a similar independence while at the same time taking care not to infringe on that provided by braille. Still, a small but vocal minority expressed concerns that the talking book would drain already limited funding and distract readers from the arduous process of learning to read raised type (a group discussed in the next section).

Hostility toward the talking book was particularly acute among America's braille readers, whom Fraser described as having "an almost religious conviction about Braille."[76] By contrast, many of Britain's finger readers welcomed the talking book as a supplement to existing methods of reading and as an alternative recreation when their fingers needed a rest. The NIB assured its patrons that the two media were not in competition—"the Talking Book is in no sense a rival to Braille"—since it remained indispensable to those who wished to read in silence, for textbooks, and as a means of writing.[77] Braille alone allowed readers to proceed at their own pace.[78]

Yet the fact remained that most people couldn't read braille. Talking books extended literacy to the 80 percent of the blind population who had no alternative.[79] Most of these people had lost their sight as adults and never learned to read with their fingers. One St. Dunstaner praised the talking book for reaching such cases: "I am sure it solves our greatest problem."[80] Publications for people who were blind recognized braille's benefits and limitations. As one editorial explained, "There is in the learning and use of Braille an intellectual and moral discipline of high intrinsic value. Listening to a gramophone record or to a film will be easier and to some extent on that account less meritorious. But the disc or film record will be a boon to all blind persons on some occasions and to many blind persons on all occasions."[81] One example given was that of a blind man with rheumatoid arthritis.[82] The talking book did have implications for braille readers, but its impact was felt most strongly by other readers.

Publishers objected to talking books for different reasons. Despite obvious differences between talking books and print, they worried about the similarities. Publishers' objections underscored the talking book's ambiguous status as neither a reproduction nor an adaptation of the printed book. The NIB's Sound Recording Committee had initially decided to record titles that were out of copyright, then reversed its stance after promising negotiations with authors and publishers.[83] However, publishers were reluctant to extend the copyright exemptions that had been given to braille since anyone could listen to sound recordings.[84]

In 1936, the International Congress of Publishers addressed the potential hazards facing the publishing industry by what newspapers referred to as "the coming of the 'talking book.' "[85] The congress devoted an entire plenary session to safeguarding authors' rights. Geoffrey Faber, head of the independent publisher Faber and Faber, warned that publishers should prepare for the inevitable competition from gramophone companies: "The commercial 'talking book' is bound to come."[86] In response, conference participants approved a resolution stating that authors should exercise control over mechanical reproductions of their work.

The Publishers Association and the Society of Authors and Playwrights advised members to permit copyrighted work to be recorded by the NIB under strict conditions: a nominal fee of one pound per title, due acknowledgment at the beginning of each recording, a statement of copyright announcing "for the sole use of the blind," an agreement to sell records only to blind people, assurance that the recording would not be used for commercial purposes, and a limit of 300 copies.[87] The Publishers Association insisted that the conditions were necessary to protect their rights in anticipation of the commercial market for talking books.[88] Sales of poetry readings in the United States already hinted at the potential demand for spoken word recordings.

Most authors allowed their novels to be recorded for people who were blind. Yet a small number of refusals indicate how vulnerable authors felt toward copyright infringement. The most prominent skeptic was Rudyard Kipling. Kipling seemed to be the ideal spokesperson for talking books in light of the reputation he commanded among critics and the public alike; the relevance of his military experience and subject matter to the ex-servicemen of St. Dunstan's; and his depiction of blindness in *The Light That Failed*. Stories from *Stalky and Co.* had even been used for test recordings. Hence, it was no surprise when the list of titles to be recorded for the first year's program included *Kim*—a title whose subsequent withdrawal did, in fact, come as a surprise.[89] Kipling had refused permission over concerns that unauthorized sales or radio broadcasts might diminish his royalties.[90] The Kipling estate refused further requests to record *Kim, Stalky and Co.,* and *The Day's Work* after the author's death in 1936. The NIB even failed to obtain permission from Kipling's widow.[91] It succeeded only after a formal letter to Kipling's estate stipulating the elaborate precautions taken to restrict the record's use.[92] The legal wrangling meant that blind veterans had to wait longer than anyone else to read Kipling for themselves.

A Revolution in the Blind World

Fraser wrote to thank Lord Nuffield, the Talking Book Library's most generous benefactor, after the first books went out to readers: "You in turn after Louis Braille have created a revolution in the blind world by starting the TALKING BOOK LIBRARY FOR THE BLIND, and the benefit of this development in the happiness and future usefulness of a blind community which is more alert, more in touch with things, more capable of self-expression and enjoyment of life, is beyond estimation."[93] It was a revolution in both senses of the word: an upheaval in the way people read and what they read. For the rest of his life, Fraser insisted that the talking book represented a second revolution in literacy among blind people.[94] He said of this constituency, "These people are not only cut off from the pleasures of books, but reading means more to them than to others who have so many alternative occupations."[95] This was a plea for what might be called "blind exceptionalism," the notion that blind readers were thought of by others and thought of themselves as a group with distinctive needs, capabilities, and desires that set them apart from other readers.

The best way to measure how blind readers thought about their relationship to books is through their own words. Correspondence received by the NIB and St. Dunstan's allows us to gauge the talking book's reception, from public demonstrations across the country to private sessions in people's homes. Despite scant evidence—a problem faced by all historians of reading and an especially acute one when dealing with a medium that lacks marginalia—I have retrieved a representative sample of their voices from archives. The NIB published extracts from its correspondence with talking book recipients, for example, and Fraser received nearly one hundred letters after the first machines went out.[96] If the available evidence does not confirm whether reading meant more to blind people than to other people, as Fraser alleged, it nevertheless documents the talking book's impact on their lives. As we will see, readers perceived the talking book both as a restoration of the ability to read and as an altogether new way of reading.

Obviously, the talking book had the greatest impact on people who couldn't read in any other way. Testimonials vividly illustrate the plight of those denied access to literature and to a large extent echo those of their American counterparts. Such people associated books with their former lives and, in many cases, had lost hope of ever enjoying them again. One person testified, "I should like to state what great pleasure I derive from the Talking Book. I have been a lifelong invalid, and I used to read a great deal. I also painted, and composed poetry, this latter being the only thing I was able to go on with when I became blind. What joy and interest the 'Talkie' book has brought into my life!"[97] Books reinvigorated this invalid's diminishing sphere of interests and invited comparisons to another form of entertainment (the "talkies") transformed by sound technology.[98]

Other correspondents expressed gratitude at being able to read again. One dumbstruck listener wrote, "Words are totally inadequate to express my gratitude for the Talking Books. How thankful I am for them and the wonderful service!"[99] Like the Americans, many attributed the seemingly miraculous restoration of their ability to read to divine providence. "The books are a wonderful blessing," wrote a grateful reader.[100] A veteran from Carshalton described them as "an absolute God-send to us fellows."[101] Similar explanations invoked the scriptural tradition of viewing blindness in religious terms. Talking books fulfilled Isaiah's promise to turn darkness into light.

Mechanical reading devices offered what blind people most desired: independence. The talking book gave those who did not already have such freedom at their fingertips a chance to read without interference. As Deborah Cohen has shown, many people with disabilities, deprived of employment, pensions, or good health, had to endure the indignities of dependence.[102] At least one reader wondered whether others could appreciate the change: "Sighted readers, and also blind people who can read Braille fluently, can have little conception of what the Talking Book means to us older blind who have hitherto been entirely dependent on kind friends or paid readers to furnish our mental pabulum."[103]

The talking book both read to people and allowed them to read for themselves. An advertisement assured St. Dunstaners that, while the talking machine would do the reading, its operator controlled everything else: "He will work it himself at his own time in his own home."[104] Fraser was not exaggerating the discomfort felt by blind people about burdening family. One of the first recipients of a talking book machine admitted, "It is glorious to be able to sit back and be read to, without even so much as asking the person if they mind doing it."[105] The glory owed as much to the removal of an obligation as to the reading itself.

Such enthusiasm stands out since blind people were thought to have fewer opportunities for recreation than their peers. As Helen Keller pointed out, boredom was the greatest threat.[106] The talking book entertained while also providing a break from tedious, solitary lives. One woman placed the talking book a notch below her marriage in the satisfaction (if not intimacy) it gave her: "The Talking Book is, with the exception of my husband, the greatest joy of my life."[107] Letters vividly describe the pleasure afforded by them. "Oh! the joy of hearing it," wrote a reader after receiving a talking book in the post. "I felt like flying over the moon with pleasure."[108] The impact could be measured quantitatively as well as qualitatively. In 1948, a woman claimed to have read 145 talking books—nearly a quarter of the library's collection.[109]

Pleasure had particular connotations in the First World War's aftermath. Veterans listened to talking books for enjoyment as well as diversion from distressing memories of trench warfare in northern France. Wartime trauma underlies the following letter written from Guildford in 1936 by an ex-soldier named F. G. Braithwaite:

> This is how I enjoy the Talking Book.
>
> Every night at about ten o'clock I shoot the wife off to bed, then make up the fire, draw my armchair near, and, after having got a bottle of Worthington and a cigarette going, I switch on the Talking Book.
>
> Don't you think this is real luxury?
>
> If the book is particularly interesting, it is possible I may have another disc and another Worthington, retiring to bed about midnight, taking care to replace disc in box and empties in proper place.
>
> I have only read two books and thoroughly enjoyed each. Not being able to sleep much, and being very poor at Braille, you can imagine how useful the Talking Book is to me.[110]

The letter might have been written by any man until the final lines reveal it to be the testimony of a soldier who has struggled to learn braille after losing his sight in the war. From shell shock to shellac: the talking book stands alongside alcohol and cigarettes as the soldier's nightly sedative.[111] The machine enabled blinded soldiers to read for themselves at a time when many disabled veterans were unable to participate in domestic life. Here, the soldier asserts his masculinity through the enjoyment of beer, smoking, and marriage.[112] The veteran, despite his injuries, is able to re-create the comforts of home denied to others.

Talking books offered solitary entertainment and even a private space for reflection. A retired teacher listed it as one of three diversions: "The Talking Book, the wireless and my pipe are my only pleasures. I am an old schoolmaster and was a very great reader until I lost my sight. I no longer dread the dreary evenings of the past."[113] Having a way to pass the time relieved another reader, who wrote, "The Library is an immense compensation, largely dispelling the monotony of blindness."[114] Still others looked forward to the diversion when housebound. "I am highly delighted with my machine," announced a man in Hull. "It will help me to pass many a dull moment away, especially in the winter time when I cannot get out."[115] For many blind readers, the passing of time in real life was as important as escaping from it in an imagined one.

As was the case in America, talking books served social as well as aesthetic purposes. The NIB used them, along with the radio, to reduce social exclusion.[116] Talking books offered social interaction, or at least a simulation of it. "Your books come as a faithful friend to visit us," one reader wrote to the NIB.[117] The timeworn metaphor of reading as a form of companionship takes on added poignancy in the context of a disabled readership with limited opportunities for social contact. The most isolated patrons understood this figure of speech literally. For this reason, the NIB characterized the machine's speech as "like the voice of a friend."[118] It would later describe talking books as "the special and unfailing solace of the old and isolated."[119] Simulated companionship was meant to renew the social ties maintained by people before losing their sight.

The NIB treated the talking book as a way to address mental health issues too. In some cases, reading about other people's lives made people value their own. A reader with multiple disabilities described how listening to talking books had renewed his interest in the outside world: "Life becomes interesting again to a man without sight, smell or taste."[120] His response fulfilled the NIB's principal goal: not only to make life bearable (though this was important) but also to engage people with the surrounding world.

The melodramatic terms used by blind people point toward the problem's severity. David Copperfield's famous account of "reading as if for life" takes on greater urgency when applied to a disabled readership suffering from a range of mental health issues.[121] "It is the Talking Book that makes blindness bearable," divulged one reader.[122] For him, talking books were less a way to pass the time than the very reason for doing so. Others described books in even more extreme terms: "My machine has at times meant the difference between life and death to me."[123] Distressed readers turned to talking books for solace in lives otherwise marred by ill health or bereft of social contact.

Appreciative letters also came from the families. One described the "comfort and joy" the records had given a grandmother celebrating her ninetieth birthday.[124] Family members saw firsthand the talking book's impact, especially on those who relied on other people to read aloud to them. A woman confided, "I simply do not know what my husband would have done without the Talking Books."[125] Families struggled to imagine life without them. A mother wrote, "I should just like to say what a boon the Talking Book is to my son; I do not know what he would do without it now."[126] As was the case with other forms of entertainment like radio, a technology that initially generated unease in households quickly came to be seen as indispensable.[127]

The correspondence convinced Fraser, at least, of the talking book's worth. Letters conveyed how people felt about talking books even if only a small percentage of recipients wrote about them. Many had no way of writing to the NIB even if they had wanted to. Still, the congratulatory letters from blinded soldiers confirmed—for Fraser at least—the value of talking books. "Reading their remarks made me think this was one of the best things we had done," concluded Fraser. "I think some hundreds of our men will enjoy this service for the rest of their lives."[128]

Talking Book or Reading Book?

The debate over the recorded book's legitimacy has a long history. Today's version usually takes place between readers who can choose between reading a narrative in print and hearing it read aloud. Georgina Kleege, for one, has described skepticism toward recorded books as a prejudice among sighted people.[129] But talking books have faced opposition since their debut in the 1930s. In fact, the most vocal resistance initially came not from bibliophiles but from blind readers, who were the first to raise questions about the relationship among reading, technology, and self-dependence.

The most impassioned of these debates took place in the *New Beacon,* founded by the NIB to supply information to teachers and care workers supporting blind and partially sighted people. This magazine has preserved dissenting viewpoints among a readership that, owing to the nature of its disabilities, left behind few traces. The spirited attacks on and defenses of talking books in its pages take us beyond the promotional rhetoric of advocacy groups to what blind readers themselves felt about the biggest development in literacy since braille.

The controversy started in February 1937 with Arthur Copland's editorial "Talking-Book or Reading-Book?"[130] A graduate of the Edinburgh School for the Blind, Copland began contributing to the *New Beacon* after writing a prize-winning letter about the prospect of a new braille publication. He went on to cover issues such as careers for people with vision impairments and the psychology of blindness. These pieces gave little warning of the controversy to come when Copland called into question whether talking books were worth the expense.

"Talking-Book or Reading-Book?" acknowledged the enthusiasm for talking books. Fraser had promoted them as the biggest breakthrough since braille, and the *New Beacon* itself heralded their importance.[131] Instead of joining the celebrations, however, Copland asked whether the publicity truly benefited people who were blind. He accused the promotional campaign of "indiscriminate propaganda" that threatened to undermine public support for braille. Despite two centuries of embossed writing, he complained, the talking book had been hailed as an "Open Sesame" to the realm of letters. Couldn't the expenditure in time and money have been invested more prudently in other aspects of blind people's welfare?

Copland voiced prescient concerns about the risks posed by new technologies to an already endangered braille community.[132] At the same time, anxieties about the possibility of new media replacing existing ones, rather than working in conjunction with them, made it difficult for Copland to recognize the talking book's potential benefits for braille and non-braille users alike.[133] The essay's most controversial feature was its portrayal of the talking book as an illegitimate form of reading. For Copland, reading to oneself was superior to being read to by someone else (especially a machine). Silent reading entailed "self-dependence" that could not be matched by the "artificial facility" of hearing a book read aloud. Raised type like braille compelled readers to sound out words for themselves. By contrast, "being read to, however perfectly the reading may be done, necessarily involves the intrusion of a third personality between the author and his public." No mention was made here of blind people's extensive history of listening to books read aloud or of the possibility of the two media coexisting. Copland's objective was to protect braille against all rivals.

The *New Beacon*'s next issue wryly noted that Copland's article had aroused "a lively expression of feeling" on the subject.[134] A forum titled "Talking Book or Reading Book? Some Opinions on the Question" reprinted extracts from the numerous responses. The title's false opposition was the first item challenged by correspondents. W. Percy Merrick of Shepperton opened the forum by declaring, "There is room for both the Talking Book and for Braille reading and writing." A man from Winkleigh, North Devon, raised a similar point, asking, "Why does Mr. Copland make the Talking Book a rival of the Braille Book?" In fact, the staunchest defenses of talking books came from readers who were fluent in braille. C. W. Killingbeck of Chester, for one, objected to the assumption that readers could not enjoy *both* media. Those who read exclusively by ear, he continued, usually do so because they have no other way to read: "Surely the Talking Book wins because it gives literature to those who have it not. As correspondents pointed out, the have-nots included most blind people.

Copland's efforts to undermine the talking book's credibility were based on premises that infuriated the magazine's readership. Responses ranged from the incredulous ("Mr. Arthur Copland's article is quite a shock to me") to the indignant ("I consider it laughable"). To begin with, Copland characterized as a minority the talking book's target audience of aging people who lost their sight late in life.[135] In fact, this group made up a majority of blind people. Many of them had never learned to read braille; as a correspondent pointed out, the National Library had only 11,000 registered braille readers out of a blind population of roughly 30,000.[136] Second, Copland doubted whether the aged and infirm could operate the equipment. Yet gramophones were simple to use; those who struggled to do so would probably benefit most from listening to books. Third, Copland insisted that a lack of privacy would prevent many people from listening to books, though headphones were available (Figure 5.6). Finally, braille had required years of development and

Figure 5.6. Woman listening to a talking book through earphones.

government subsidy. As one of the first St. Dunstaners to receive a talking book player had written, "If this is what they call its 'infancy'—Glory! what will it be when it reaches maturity?"[137] The only allegation to go uncontested was that the exceptional number of soldiers blinded in war was unlikely to happen again.

Copland was not without supporters. Several respondents agreed that talking books posed a threat to braille. Hazel Winter, for one, worried about prospective readers. Learning a new language was difficult work at a time when people who were newly blind were most vulnerable to depression. Braille advocates feared that talking books might tempt potential finger readers to take the easier option of being read aloud to by a machine over the arduous commitment of learning to read by touch. According to Winter, "The Talking Book will be either an inducement to laziness or a mere luxury." She echoed Copland's concerns about resources being siphoned away from other problems facing blind people, including the need for equipment that could read directly from print. More than gramophones were required if blind people were to have freedom of choice in their reading material.

Fraser himself joined the debate. He remained committed to braille despite having spent the past decade developing alternatives to it. Even so, he read with difficulty: "Surely very few of us are so good at Braille that it is really no trouble whatever."[138] Despite reading braille every day, Fraser found it tiring to read for longer than an hour. He added, "The mind moves so quickly that even the Talking Book is too slow. How much more so Braille."

A key issue here is whether a book's identity remains the same across different media. Book historians acknowledge that the medium influences reception, yet few go so far as to deem one mode of reading superior to another.[139] In the *New Beacon,* E. Bates proposed that the medium was *not* the message: "Surely the ordinary book, the Braille book, and the gramophone disc are all, in effect, records—the difference between them being simply that their messages are made intelligible to us through different senses—sight, touch, and hearing respectively?"[140] This stance was controversial. True, the words are identical in all three formats. But readers disagree whether the message stays the same after switching from one medium to another, from print to sound. Defenders of reading as a silent activity believe the question of sensory perception to be a decisive one.

Narrators were to a large extent responsible for Copland's frustration. He associated the books read aloud to him with the "vocal idiosyncrasies" of their readers. For example, it was impossible for him to determine whether one narrator had said "The *cattle* began it" or "The *kettle* began it" (it turned out to be neither).[141] Since the initial experiments in the 1920s, the NIB had been aware of the problems introduced by the narrator's voice. The NIB's Sound Recording Committee had carried out reading trials alongside its technological experiments in order to determine the optimal way of reading. Since either theatricality or monotony would be a distraction, the best readers were usually the least conspicuous ones: "The ideal recorder is one who can sink his own personality and become a part of the mechanism without mechanical effect."[142] Fraser endorsed such neutral voices when replying to Copland: "I do not find the reader intrudes himself between me and the author. I appreciate a good reader, but not for himself. We have aimed, I hope with some success, at choosing readers whose personality is pleasing but not distracting."[143] However, compromise did little to change the minds of those who felt the presence of any reader, no matter how skilled, to be an intrusion.

Other respondents pointed out the advantages of reading aloud. James Wardle of Greenock dismissed the complaints about thick Scottish accents: "Certainly if the reading is bad the idiosyncrasy of the reader may enter in, but the readers I have had the pleasure of listening to in Talking Books (and one of them bearing a very Scotch name) have been so perfect as to obliterate all sense of self, and make one unconscious of any third party."[144] Others enumerated the benefits of hearing texts. Despite having read four different braille copies of St. John's Gospel, the Reverend T. Barnard found that "the Talking Book rendering of the old Gospel is a source of unqualified pleasure and profit." Hearing books held pleasures as well as perils. Another respondent wrote, "It should be pointed out that there are many who, when reading for themselves, can make no sense of certain passages (difficult poems, for instance), which are immediately made clear when heard in the voice and interpretation of a capable reader." Paradoxically, reading aloud could make the page legible.

Talking books held further advantages. Like many of the American readers cited in previous chapters, T. ap Rhys preferred talking books over braille because they freed his hands for other activities: "Who would choose to sit glued to a book, with smoking out of the question, when he had the alternative of imbibing just the same meaning and being free to smoke, move about the room and, in short, give himself up to full enjoyment?" (Figure 5.7). Less enticingly, men and women could also listen while doing household chores.

Figure 5.7. John Jarvis smoking a cigarette while reading a talking book.

"Group-listening" was another pastime facilitated by the turntable, which enabled patrons to listen to recordings with friends and family (Figure 5.8).[145] Such scenes offered a glimpse of the talking book's future as a form of entertainment for all readers. One man's friends even preferred hearing V. C. Clinton-Baddeley's recitations on the wireless over reading Dickens and Thackeray for themselves.[146]

Yet Copland remained unconvinced, and the two sides unreconciled. Debating the narrator's quality and machinery's effectiveness, he insisted in a subsequent issue of the *New Beacon,* sidestepped the principal complaint that talking books invited inertia; they were suited for entertainment, not instruction. No one had challenged his main point, Copland continued, that turning blind readers into "passive buckets, waiting to be pumped into" (a phrase borrowed from Thomas Carlyle) would injure their aspirations toward self-dependence.[147] This was not strictly true. Respondents had, in fact, challenged the equation of braille with self-dependence. Bates, for one, accused Copland of being "obsessed" with self-dependence at the expense of progress.[148] Another reader insisted that nostalgia would not prevent braille from becoming as obsolete as "Caxton's primitive wooden printing blocks."[149]

Figure 5.8. Enjoying a talking book alfresco.

Copland was even accused of attacking "civilisation itself."[150] In other words, the two sides disagreed as to whether the talking book represented a step backward in terms of independence or a step toward the very self-reliance vaunted by Copland. And so the dispute goes on.

The convergence of books, media, and disability in the war's aftermath raised a vexing set of questions about the nature of reading that have yet to be resolved. The most problematic of these questions concern the legitimacy of alternative forms of literacy, rivalries between print media and new media, and definitions of self-sufficiency. Similar questions persist to this day when discussing the printed book's status in an increasingly multimedia environment.

Yet, these questions take on additional urgency when considered in relation to a group of disabled readers who would not otherwise have access to books. The Talking Book Service ensured that blind soldiers and civilians could read even when other people were not available to read to them. In doing so, it confirmed that books can take many forms—even if the appropriateness of these various forms was intensely debated among both blind and sighted readers.

For those used to handling books, it was easy to be misled into thinking that records were hardly books at all. However, the outbreak of the Second World War offered a vivid reminder that talking books were as material as other books since they, too, could be destroyed by the bombs dropped on London during the Blitz. The Talking Book Service depended on a bricks-and-mortar library remaining intact for the storage of its fragile shellac records. The outbreak of war confronted the NIB with a new kind of problem, then, that was not aesthetic, financial, or technological but tactical: how to keep talking books from becoming casualties of war.[151] Donations from the British War Relief Society and the American Foundation for the Blind enabled the service to continue operating throughout the war, even after its studios were twice destroyed by bombing, and to minister to a new generation of blinded soldiers and civilians after the war ended.[152]

The story of the Talking Book Service after the Second World War is less dramatic, and better documented, than in the turbulent decade that preceded it. The expertise, infrastructure, and resources accumulated during the program's first decade ensured that blind people's needs would be met for decades to come. If the Talking Book Service initially concentrated on finding a viable alternative to the printed book, then the story of the modern Talking Book Service has more to do with its expansion in terms of holdings, membership, and access for people with disabilities other than blindness. Successive formats (from long-playing gramophone records to open-reel tape, cassette tapes, compacts discs, and digital files) have kept the Talking Book Service in line with a commercial recording industry that became increasingly interested in recorded literature from the 1950s—as Part III of this book will show.

The Talking Book Service made substantial progress after its modest origins supplying reading material to wounded soldiers. At the end of the Second World War, the service had 1,700 members and 500 books in its library.[153] By January 2005, it had over 40,000 members and a library of over 20,000 titles.

The service now sends out up to 10,000 books per day. This is a dramatic improvement over the situation facing soldiers coming back from the First World War, even if access to books continues to be a problem.[154] Britain's blind and partially sighted people face many difficulties today. The Talking Book Service is part of an ongoing campaign to ensure that access to books is no longer one of them.

6

Unrecordable

M embers of Britain's Talking Book Library inevitably asked: Who chooses the books? The issue of book selection mattered because the library's meager budget permitted it to record only a small percentage of books in print. Unlike other libraries, most of its patrons had no other way of getting books; talking books were the only ones that they could read. The politics of book selection in Britain, as in America, then, was a contentious issue for readers who wished to decide for themselves what to read. Audiences were as interested in who chose the books as in which books were recorded.

Few books nominated for recording posed any problems. But every now and then came along a title deemed unsuitable for the Talking Book Library. *Fandango Rock* was one of those titles. John Masters's 1959 novel described an American pilot's romantic affairs in Spain, intertwined with graphic accounts of bullfighting. Talking Book Librarian Gay Ashton concluded that

> the whole thing is so compounded of lust, blood and violence that it is bound to be offensive to the people in our Library—who are the large majority—and whose standards are Edwardian, if not often Late Victorian. We know our "ideal" book—one which pleases, entertains and makes the listener happy to the point of forgetting his or her afflictions of old age (blindness being but one of their physical handicaps).[1]

Their ideal book was not *Fandango Rock.* Hence, Ashton advised against recording it: "Would sound nauseating aloud."[2]

Other books were also rejected because of potentially offensive content. One was Richard Gordon's farcical novel *Doctor at Sea,* in which sailors acquired sexually transmitted diseases while visiting brothels. A report noted that syphilis's symptoms included loss of eyesight: "Granted this is a subject for humour, I cannot think it would be found funny by our blind people."[3] Another was John Braine's *Room at the Top,* a well-reviewed novel about a former soldier's ambitions in postwar Britain. Its graphic descriptions of sex raised similar concerns: "The sex descriptions in this book are much too crude for reading out loud."[4] None of these books were recorded.

The National Institute for the Blind (NIB, then the Royal National Institute for the Blind [RNIB] after 1953) took complaints about indecency seriously because it depended on public and private sponsors for its funding. Consequences could be severe if grievances reached the institute's leadership or, worse, donors. "What we have to remember, I feel, is the possibility of complaints from listeners," wrote Ashton. "We have had them in the past and some have been addressed to the Sec[retary]-Gen[eral], to the Chairman, and in one instance I recall to Lord Nuffield himself."[5] No one wanted to jeopardize the relationship with a benefactor whose munificence had made it possible to establish the Talking Book Library in the first place. The employees responsible for selecting books worried in particular about allegations reaching donors of public money being spent on "pornography for the blind."[6]

The Talking Book Library was especially sensitive to indecency because hearing such passages read aloud was widely felt to be more intimate—and therefore more offensive—than reading them silently to oneself. Vernon Barlow, the library's general editor, agreed with Ashton on the need for caution when selecting books. And yet, at the same time, Barlow emphasized the need to treat blind people as adults capable of deciding for themselves whether a book is objectionable. After reading Ashton's reports, Barlow replied, "I agree with a good deal of what you say and definitely feel that there are certain books that, although not unprintable, are unrecordable as regards the sex matter contained in them. At the same time we must be careful not to set up any sort of censorship in our minds."[7] The expression "censorship in our minds" suggests more was at stake than simply determining a title's appropriateness. Barlow's intention to select books that would not offend anyone while at the same time avoiding any form of censorship reflects the predicament faced by the Talking Book Library.

This chapter will determine who decided which books to record for Britain's Talking Book Library and on what basis they made those decisions. It shows how the library's selection policy originated with the appointment of a committee of Oxbridge-educated men of letters with a preference for classic literature. Years of pressure from correspondents were necessary before this group would begin to represent the tastes of actual blind readers. Until then, members of the library had to choose from a list of books deemed beneficial for them instead of one including the same books being read by other people.

It would take a series of controversies over taste, representation, and obscenity to compel the library to allow blind people to decide for themselves which books to read. Such disputes (which were taking place at the same time in America) arose because the NIB's efforts to entertain, educate, and even shelter its readership repeatedly came into conflict with its mission to allow blind people to make decisions for themselves. This tension is evident from the earliest debates over the appropriate percentage of contemporary literature on the library's bookshelves to later disputes over censorship that led to protests against being treated like children.

The following account addresses the vexed issue of censorship through close examination of books considered by the library to be "unrecordable." Some books approved for recording turned out to be too difficult to make owing to their use of graphics, nonstandard speech, or experimental styles (Table 6.1). But other books omitted from the catalog raised suspicions that the library was acting as a guardian of public morals. Correspondents frequently accused the library of censorship since many titles were either missing from the collection or altered in some way to avoid causing offense. As we'll see, the library risked such accusations by striving to make the same books available to blind people as were available to other people, while concurrently seeking to accommodate the needs of a readership whose disabilities set them apart from other readers. The result: a book selection policy that officially opposed censorship even as it screened titles for potentially offensive material including blasphemy, profanity, violence, and sex.

The Hundred Best Books

Before a word had been spoken, the NIB's Talking Book Library had to decide who would choose the books. The engineers responsible for making the records did not want to handle debates over what to record on them. The Talking Book Selection Committee was thereby formed to address the fraught issue of choosing titles. Chaired by Ian Fraser, the original committee included

Table 6.1 Unrecordable books (1959–62)

The reasons why books approved for recording were not produced:

Accent or dialect too difficult	Too expensive to produce
Author refused to read	Too fantastic
Book already obsolete	Too harrowing
Critical of National Health Service	Too many characters
Foreign setting	Too many foreigners
Historically inaccurate	Too many subplots
Impossible to read aloud	Too many unpronounceable words
Insufficient demand	Too many voices
Likely to cause offense	Too much blasphemy
Minority appeal	Too much dialogue
No suitable reader	Too much like a guidebook
No woman reader available	Too personal for listeners with fatal illnesses
Of no particular distinction	Too political
Out of print	Too technical
Poorly written	Treatment of blindness deemed insensitive
Sex episodes	Unable to obtain permission to record
Too crude	Unlikely to please
Too dated	Unrecordable
Too difficult	Unsuitable material
Too disturbing	

NIB members along with Secretary-General Waldo McGillicuddy Eagar, General Editor J. de la Mare Rowley, and Secretary-Librarian J. S. Blackmore. The committee also included a graduate of the Royal Normal College and Academy for the Blind, and E. E. Mavrogordato, a barrister and frequent contributor to the *Times Literary Supplement*. St. Dunstan's was represented by blinded ex-officers who acted as "proof listeners" of the completed recordings.

Three initial rules guided the Talking Book Selection Committee's decisions. Books should: (1) be out of copyright (an unresolved legal issue before the Publishers' Association and the Society of Authors and Playwrights granted permission), (2) cover a range of topics and genres, and (3) match the probable tastes of readers—a point on which committee members and their readership clashed in the years to come. Blind readers were consulted from the outset. W. Percy Merrick, for example, advised choosing books "which do not deal with morbid themes and which leave a pleasant taste in the memory."[8] The proportion of blind members to sighted members, however, was another point of contention.

All libraries face the difficulty of choosing books with a limited budget.[9] But the problem was particularly acute for the Talking Book Library since the budget was so small and production expenses so large (a book cost approximately one hundred pounds to record, and thereafter one pound per copy). In most cases, these would be the only books available to patrons, most of whom could not read braille or, unlike other readers, turn to the commercial market. By June 1936, the library had successfully produced twenty-four talking books. Selectors favored titles that had "stood the test of time" (from William Makepeace Thackeray's *Henry Esmond* and Thomas Hardy's *Under the Greenwood Tree* to Baroness Emma Orczy's *The Scarlet Pimpernel* and John Buchan's *The Thirty-Nine Steps*). Since most blind people wanted to read the same books as other people, the committee mixed in a few titles of current interest (including *Brazilian Adventure; Goodbye, Mr. Chips;* and *In the Steps of the Master*) whose "lasting power" was not yet known.[10] However, a limit of only twelve books made it difficult to represent all tastes.

The Talking Book Selection Committee's initial task was choosing the first year's program (recorded at a rate of one title per month). Members resolved that 75 percent of books should be of permanent value and 25 percent of ephemeral value. Rare exceptions like Winston Churchill's *Great Contemporaries* were published without delay. The group also decided to exclude plays and give preference to short books (owing to budgetary constraints on the number of discs that could be recorded). Choices were made on the basis of suggestions and lists submitted by committee members and by correspondents; lists of popular classics and the current best sellers; and "books of the moment."[11] Selections were then made from a precirculated list of titles divided into the categories of fiction (classic, detective stories and thrillers, miscellaneous) and nonfiction (history, biography, travel, religion, miscellaneous).

Major John Hay Beith described the Talking Book Selection Committee's dilemma as follows: "What are the Hundred Best Books in the English language; how could I choose them?"[12] Known to the public through his pseudonym, "Ian Hay," Beith was a Cambridge-educated schoolmaster who had made a reputation writing humorous accounts of life in an army battalion. His recording of *The First Hundred Thousand* made him the first author to read his own book for the service; he began chairing the committee in November 1936. According to Beith, the committee was in the difficult position of choosing a small number of books to record, judging which ones were of lasting value, and satisfying an audience with varied tastes.

Meetings involved winnowing down approximately fifty nominations to twenty titles for recording. On average, roughly 70 percent of the books were fiction. The remaining 30 percent were determined by competition among biography, history, politics, religion, science, travel, and other categories. Selection was all the more contentious because judges had their own agendas. For example, Mavrogordato deliberately chose timeless authors (Shakespeare and Milton) over contemporary ones like Rudyard Kipling. Others held different ideas about what counted as a "classic." Miss O. I. Prince was told that Robert Louis Stevenson's *The Master of Ballantrae,* Thomas Hardy's *The Return of the Native,* and Arnold Bennett's *The Old Wives' Tale* were "modern books" not to be confused with "classic books of the more remote past."[13]

Controversy over book selection inevitably led to scrutiny of the committee itself. Many objected that it did not represent the library's readership. As a result, the committee added new members in order to address its lack of diversity, especially in terms of class, and to improve its proportion of blind soldiers and civilians. In its overrepresentation of Oxbridge-educated selectors, most of whom were not visually impaired, the initial Talking Book Selection Committee bore little resemblance to its constituency. Class was an explicit issue in F. R. Richardson's nomination to join the committee. As the head of Boots Booklovers' Library, a popular subscription service located in pharmacies throughout the United Kingdom, Richardson was thought to be in touch with public taste.[14] Yet, after it was discovered that Richardson was not an "Oxford man" as originally thought, he was interviewed in order "to avoid running any risk of landing the Committee with anyone whose manners compare unfavourably with those of other members," or who, in one member's words, proved to be "below the Oxford level."[15]

There were internal disputes, too, over how representative the group should be. In 1943, committee members debated who should be given preference: literary critics or blind people. Fraser proposed reconstituting the Talking Book Selection Committee in order to include representatives from the NIB, St. Dunstan's, and the National Library; managers from Boots Library, the Times Library, Hodder & Stoughton publishers, and Gollancz publishers; and the editor of the *Times Literary Supplement.* Managers of libraries and publishing houses, it was proposed, might be better guides to popular opinion than critics with refined tastes.[16]

J. de la Mare Rowley (nephew of the poet Walter de la Mare) protested against the changes. Instead, he envisioned the group operating as a kind of "registering body" to approve the recommendations of professional critics. In opposition to Fraser's preference for commercial expertise, Rowley identified three essential qualifications: a love of literature, familiarity with current publications, and exemplary critical faculties. Fraser's commercially oriented group looked very different from Rowley's "purely 'literary men,'" who, along with a well-known writer, included editors of the *World Digest, Times Literary Supplement, News-Chronicle,* and *John O'London's Weekly.*[17] Too often librarians based their judgment on public demand, objected Rowley, and managers possessed more business sense than sensibility.

Rowley's side won the argument. The chairmanship went to Sir John Hammerton, the seventy-three-year-old editor of the *World Digest* described by Rowley as a "man of great culture and a genius at 'selection.'" The result was the privileging of elite literary taste as determined by a small group of experts— essentially a "one man Committee"—over the preferences of blind readers themselves.[18] The shift away from popular taste was apparent in Rowley's exclusion of best sellers and books in high demand since, in his view, these titles reflected successful marketing campaigns rather than literary merit.[19] The new, streamlined structure enabled selections to be made with minimal discussion or input from readers themselves.

Outside sponsorships further distorted the catalog. Beith's goal may have been to choose the hundred best books, but the actual list was dictated as much by budget constraints as by taste. In order to expand the collection, the committee welcomed patronage for titles that would not otherwise have been chosen. For example, the British and Foreign Bible Society paid for *The Gospel According to St. John* because of its ties to the Venerable Bede, whose 1,200th anniversary of death took place the same year that the Talking Book Library opened.[20] (Mavrogordato facetiously suggested generating publicity by bribing a bishop to campaign for St. Luke instead.[21]) Technically, this was the first book chosen for recording since the NIB and St. Dunstan's had yet to establish the Talking Book Selection Committee. The society went on to underwrite recordings of the other Gospels read by BBC announcer Stuart Hibberd.[22] Individual patrons likewise agreed to sponsor designated titles. Naval officer Stephen King-Hall read the Epistle to the Ephesians at his own expense, for example, and newspaper proprietor William Leng paid £200 to record *Every Man's Bible* and *The Pickwick Papers.*

The library's catalog was steered further away from popular taste by the Pilgrim Trust, a charity founded in 1930 to improve the quality of British life. The trust offered to subsidize "books for educated readers."[23] Funds were reserved for "books of the kind which would be of special value to well educated and scholarly-minded blind persons," such as G. M. Trevelyan's *History of England,* Arthur Eddington's *The Expanding Universe,* and Alfred North Whitehead's *Science in the Modern World.*[24] The trust's mission harked back to the previous century's faith in literature as a means of self-improvement and character building. To this end, it provided £1,500 to be spent on serious books, estimated to cost £150 on average owing to their length (for example, *Every Man's Bible* cost £170 to record on sixteen discs). On learning of the donation, the NIB's secretary-general exclaimed, "Long live the high-brows!"[25]

The NIB welcomed such assistance while at the same time cautiously noting that most blind people preferred light entertainment over serious works. Plus, the Pilgrim Trust's conception of eligible books turned out to be even narrower than suspected. It approved J. S. Haldane's *The Philosophy of a Biologist,* G. Lowes Dickinson's *The Greek View of Life,* and Walter Savage Landor's *Imaginary Conversations* but refused to sponsor novels by Dickens, Thackeray, and Walter Scott. A representative telephoned to say that fiction would not be suitable—or at least not fiction of the " 'David Copperfield' type."[26] Instead, Scott's biography was recorded instead of his fiction. The trust's patronage tilted the catalog further away from the tastes of the average reader and resulted in records that were seldom requested.

Poetry presented a dilemma since selectors valued it more than readers. One of the NIB's first commissioned works was the *Talking Book Anthology of Verse* by Elsie Fogerty, founder of the Central School of Speech Training and Dramatic Art.[27] Readers showed little appetite for poetry, however, no matter how expertly read. According to Rowley's estimation, "The number of blind readers interested in poetry is comparatively small, perhaps smaller proportionately than amongst sighted readers."[28] In 1947, 60 out of approximately 1,800 readers (roughly 3 percent) sent in poetry requests.[29] A second anthology, approved in 1961, consisted of poems nominated by this minority and was available for purchase (three pence per record) since many enjoyed replaying them. It consisted mainly of "old favourites" by Robert Browning, Thomas Hardy, Rudyard Kipling, Alfred Tennyson, William Wordsworth, and other mainstays of the school curriculum. No individual poet's albums were in the catalog. One reader's request to include his own poems was rejected as "a dead waste of time and money!"[30]

The library's emphasis on classics over best sellers came under attack in the 1940s and 1950s. Its stance became increasingly difficult to maintain as evidence mounted that readers preferred different books from the ones given to them. Questionnaires confirmed a preference for recent popular fiction. One analysis, based on over 50,000 requests made in 1956, for example, showed that a book's popularity was highest in the first year.[31] This finding undermined the Talking Book Selection Committee's rule of waiting at least a year after a book's publication to record it. ("A book has to prove itself before it is worth recording," explained Fraser.[32])

A second survey provided further evidence that reading tastes failed to match the committee's expectations. Instead, it confirmed that the most popular titles tended to be modern, to have an English background, and to be genre fiction such as detective stories or thrillers. Minimal demand existed for poetry, essays, or even recreational history. In fact, few nonfiction books justified the fifty-copy production threshold that was financially necessary (making fewer copies was actually more expensive because of high overheads and the cost of pressing records). Plus, unused records caused storage problems. The report concluded that books of "minority appeal" should be chosen with these constraints in mind.[33]

In 1959, Ashton, who had worked as the NIB's talking book librarian for nearly two decades, urged the Talking Book Selection Committee to take into account members' needs. Her memo bluntly states, "The blind reader of cultivated literary taste is a minority; the majority demand entertainment."[34] The institute's emphasis on classic literature did not provide these readers access to the same books being talked about by everyone else. The avoidance of best sellers had been a failure, at least in Ashton's experience: "It is a valid viewpoint, but I have not, in 18 years, found it to work out with the Talking Book borrowers. The bulk of our circulation is concentrated on the best-sellers we have produced."[35] Omitting contemporary fiction did not even make economic sense since an initial outlay of £400 for best sellers such as A. J. Cronin's *The Citadel* or Daphne du Maurier's *Rebecca* resulted in a cost of about one shilling per borrower when read by several thousand members. Ashton concluded of Richard Gordon's immensely popular novel *Doctor in the House:* "It may be literary rubbish; it has kept thousands of blind people amused and entertained and still does."[36] Why should the NIB take it upon itself to ensure that books not only entertained but also instructed?

Pressure from readers eventually drove the Talking Book Selection Committee to reform its policy. By the 1960s, the institute's secretary-general openly admitted problems with the previous policy, which gave too much discretion to the whims of committee members. Consequently, many books simply were not read. Readers persistently complained that the catalog did not represent their tastes. Questions like the following were not uncommon: "I would like to know whether the selection committee has any members who are ordinary blind people like myself? If not, what guarantee have we that the books we prefer will be even considered?" The letter was signed, "A dissatisfied reader."[37]

It was not until 1957 that the situation changed, with the formation of a small selection panel (including the editor, the librarian, the chief sound-recording engineer, a blind bookseller, and a St. Dunstaner) that based its choices on statistical analyses of reader requests. This represented a major change from the previous policy of allowing the committee to judge what was in the reader's best interest; now, the reverse was true: "Selection, in other words, is based on what the reader wants."[38] According to one estimate, the new policy led to a 46 percent increase in the average reading rate, from seventeen titles to twenty-seven titles per annum.[39] That year's list of novels nominated for recording includes the note, "not *too* highbrow."[40] Two decades after the founding of the Talking Book Library, a selection policy that had initially sought to elevate readers' tastes reversed its priorities in order to accommodate their actual tastes, no matter the brow.

Ugly Accents

Not all books missing from the Talking Book Library were excluded by choice. Some titles were simply too difficult to record. What could narrators do with Laurence Sterne's *Tristram Shandy* or James Joyce's *Finnegans Wake?* A request for those books met with the reply, "I think one or two of your suggestions would be quite unrecordable."[41]

In 1943, the Talking Book Selection Committee met to address the differences between letterpress and recorded books. The resulting guidelines affirmed that blind people had similar tastes to those of other people and should therefore be given a comparable selection of books. At the same time, converting print into sound introduced unique challenges that could not always be overcome. Books deemed unsuitable for recording included those with too many charts, dialects, diagrams, maps, or statistics; highly technical or pictorial books dealing with the visual arts; and exceptionally long books, which cost too much to produce. The studio refused abridgments as a matter of principle. (A reader who asked for digested material was told by the studio's director, "We do take a firm stand, believing that an author should be reproduced in full and not condensed in any way. [I should hate to feel that I was reading a sort of doctored version of an author.]"[42]) Books of outspoken character might be unsuitable for reading aloud too (a topic to which we'll return).[43] The committee agreed to avoid recording difficult books unless they were exceptional or their absence would deprive blind people of access to books widely discussed by other readers. The reasons for which recordings were never made can be gleaned from the committee's reports as well as correspondence from disgruntled readers.

A shortage of narrators was one of the most common explanations. The library used professional readers, principally BBC announcers, nearly all of whom were men.[44] Women such as Sheila Borrett and Faith Loring were the exception. This was partly because women's voices were more difficult to record than men's voices. One correspondent described them as "just a high-pitched buzzing in my ears."[45] Yet high-pitched or not, women were essential to narrating books by or about women, especially first-person narratives such as Charlotte Brontë's *Jane Eyre* or Diana Cooper's *Autobiography.* Consequently, finding suitable women often delayed production. A man read Beryl Miles's *Candles in Denmark,* for example, after the NIB spent more than a year searching for a woman who could pronounce the Danish words. In fact, it struggled to find narrators to do any voices beyond the mainstream, including women, children, and ethnic minorities. The studio never recorded J. D. Salinger's *The Catcher in the Rye* because its only American reader couldn't do a teenager's voice.

Readers complained when they disliked a voice. This was especially true of those who depended on talking books as their only source of reading material. For example, a subscriber named J. Le Roux listened to books because he couldn't read braille and needed a powerful magnifying glass to read print. He lived alone, frequently bedridden, at a hotel in Cape Town, South Africa. "I often feel terribly lonely and at times it is only the talking books that have saved my sanity," he wrote to the NIB.[46] Le Roux praised some narrators including Jack de Manio, Robert Gladwell, and Andrew Timothy. But most of his three-page letter critiques in detail the shortcomings of other ones since, according to Le Roux, "a good book can be spoilt by a bad reader." He listed them in "order of ugliness." The first reader had a "horrible voice." The second was "rasping, gurgling, grating, gutteral [*sic*]. . . . What an awful gushing reader!" A third made the love passages between young people sound like "the mooing of a frustrated old cow." The library's catalog began listing narrator names after correspondents made it clear how strongly they felt toward them.

Fit between speaker and script became increasingly important to the Talking Book Library's outspoken readership. A speaker's accent or dialect often drew complaints. American accents were a persistent problem since many of the NIB's records came from the United States. Sharing titles was the most economical way to build up the collection, and the two libraries agreed never to duplicate titles except in exceptional circumstances. This saved money, though both countries disliked hearing books read in foreign accents: "You do not like our Oxford brogue and we do not like your Yankee twang."[47] The NIB readership's tolerance was put to the test by American recordings of British fiction. The American Foundation for the Blind conceded that the narrator's woeful imitation of a British accent on P. G. Wodehouse's *Very Good, Jeeves* would irritate them.[48]

The American recordings of Stevenson's *Treasure Island* and John Galsworthy's *Forsyte Saga* led the two countries to reconsider the policy. Both agreed that duplicates might be advisable in cases where the speaker's nationality mattered. The English objected in particular to American plans to record their most famous author: "We have, to be honest, a little hesitation in giving you the monopoly of Shakespeare. I know he is a world possession, but he had the good (or bad) taste to be born and write in England and his passionate lovers may shrink from hearing his words in the voice with an un-English intonation."[49] As a compromise, a producer suggested recording one half of the Bible in an American accent and the other half in an English one.

Britain's readers nevertheless welcomed Yankee accents for American books. Having analyzed talking book requests made in 1957, Ashton explained, "Many Library members here do not like the American reading accent, and our purchases are mainly of books which are native American productions where the accent is congruous, or of 'Westerns' and Gun-men thrillers where it might be said to be essential!"[50] By the 1960s, cowboy tales and "kiss-kiss-bang-bang" westerns were popular enough with young soldiers that two Americans were hired to provide authentic voices.[51]

Dialect was a vexed issue even on British recordings. Books with regional accents (especially Yorkshire, Geordie, and Scots) inevitably led to protests. The selection committee initially avoided Scott and Stevenson because no narrator could cope with the Scottish accent. Even those who could received criticism that authenticity mattered less than "intelligibility."[52] After complaints about Scott's *Redgauntlet,* one committee member recommended avoiding books with "incomprehensible dialect" in the future.[53] The committee agreed to be cautious when selecting books using dialect while at the same time acknowledging that regional accents were often necessary to a book's meaning. Anglicizing pronunciation would make Scott's novels unacceptable to the very people who were their target audience.

Too often, unqualified narrators botched foreign accents. One speaker's French pronunciation drew the complaint, "Surely in Britain with its vast population it must be possible to get sufficient good readers who speak without ugly accents, etc.?"[54] Nevertheless, the NIB struggled. As late as the 1960s, novels set in foreign countries were often rejected as too difficult. Ngaio Marsh's *Died in the Wool* and Nevil Shute's *A Town like Alice,* for example, had too many characters from New Zealand and Australia, some of whom were indigenous. V. S. Naipaul's *The Middle Passage: Impressions of Five Societies, British, French and Dutch, in the West Indies and South America* was similarly rejected because of the number of foreign characters who reveal class prejudice through their speech. The committee eventually decided that books of this type might be read "straight" instead of performed.[55]

Other books were deemed unrecordable for reasons unrelated to taste. Some writing that worked on the page did not fare well off of it. Take Gloria Vanderbilt and Thelma Lady Furness's *Double Exposure: A Twin Autobiography,* which alternated thirty-two times between speakers. The studio worried that audiences would find it difficult to tell them apart even if the speaker's name was announced at the beginning of each track or if separate readers were used. Other narratives contained too many characters for a single speaker to impersonate. Reports on Joseph Heller's *Catch-22* recommended using an experienced narrator in order to keep straight the novel's more than fifty characters. Still other books featured scenarios that were easier to imagine than to perform. The young woman narrating Peter Marchant's *Give Me Your Answer, Do,* for instance, speaks to real people while at the same time whispering to an imaginary horse.

"Too 'guide-booky'" was a criticism leveled against books considered to be useful for sighted readers but not blind ones.[56] Guidebooks concentrated too much on visual aspects of the landscape (including picturesque viewpoints) that were unlikely to engage people who were blind. Many of them relied on illustrations for effect. Ralph Dutton's *The Land of France,* for instance, was rejected because it focused on planning tours through the countryside instead of evoking a feel for it. What the Talking Book Library wanted instead was "a book largely for those confined at home, pleasantly nostalgic for those who may have been there, but also conveying something of the essence of France, its people and places, to those who have not and never will now." In sum, *The Land of France* was "too difficult to 'picture' from one's armchair."[57]

Unrecordable fiction ranged from genre fiction to masterpieces. The staccato dialogue, luridness, and bloody-mindedness of some thrillers worked best in print: "None of these need be a disadvantage when quietly read to oneself, but when read aloud one can easily have too much of the particular slant."[58] Agatha Christie's *And Then There Were None* (originally titled *Ten Little Niggers*) shows how difficult it could be to adapt even suspenseful best sellers into a nonvisual format. The novel's flashbacks and italicized asides proved a challenge. Since phrases along the lines of "he thought to himself" or "she reflected silently" would have to be inserted into the script, the staff recommended choosing a "straight narrative" instead.[59]

The committee recognized the literary merit of books such as Victor Hugo's *The Hunchback of Notre-Dame,* Marcel Proust's *In Search of Lost Time,* and James Baldwin's *Tell Me How Long the Train's Been Gone* that were considered too difficult to record. In fact, the experimental styles of writers like Henry James and Virginia Woolf usually posed the greatest difficulties. "James's style is of course not easy to read aloud," noted a report on *The Portrait of a Lady.* The studio had already rejected *The Wings of the Dove* as too difficult, and its director, Donald Bell, described James's late fiction as "practically unrecordable."[60]

Virginia Woolf's *To the Lighthouse* posed similar challenges through its stream-of-consciousness or interior monologues. The studio had already tried, and failed, to complete *The Waves.* Editors worried in particular about moving between Mrs. Ramsay's allusive inner world and the outer world of social interactions. The extensive addition of "lead-in" and "lead-out" interpolated phrases, thought to be necessary for listeners, risked spoiling the book and perhaps violating the terms of copyright.

All of the examples listed so far had been approved for recording even though many of them were never actually recorded. There was no attempt to block their publication, however. Despite reservations, Bell still approved James's *The Portrait of a Lady:* "I think as a matter of general policy we ought not to reject in advance books which *may* be difficult without having a go at them first."[61] Equal support was given to Woolf's novel, too, despite the introspective narration. "If it is difficult for some listeners, then it is equally difficult in print," wrote Bell. "This is no reason for not recording it."[62] Bell likewise opposed modifying scripts in order to make them accessible. The BBC frequently broadcast stories with interior monologues, he noted, and, personally, he would be "horrified" to find directions inserted into the original novel. More broadly, Bell maintained that the Talking Book Library's duty was to represent the majority's tastes while at the same time recording occasional titles of minority interest. These books, he continued, "must be presented as written."

Pornography for the Blind

If some books were too difficult to record, others were deemed unrecordable lest they offend audiences.[63] As we saw in the previous section, the Talking Book Selection Committee's guidelines stated that outspoken books were not always suitable. Potentially offensive material included blasphemy, profanity, violence, and sex, which, in many cases, were thought to sound harsher when heard with the ear than when read with the eye. The committee took complaints seriously since its readership consisted predominantly of elderly women with a reputation for protesting against indecency (Figure 6.1).[64] Britain's public libraries had long taken it upon themselves to act as guardians of public morals when it came to censoring fiction.[65] At the same time, the committee opposed censorship in order to cater to a broad spectrum of interests and to protect blind people from any sort of paternalism. A ninety-year-old man who complained about books distasteful to his "Victorian" outlook, for example, was told that the institute had to satisfy Elizabethan, Georgian, and Edwardian tastes too.[66]

The biggest challenge to the NIB's tolerant approach came from blind people themselves. "Dirty" or "filthy" books were targets for complaints. Joyce Cary's *A Fearful Joy* was criticized for its "Filthy Nature," for example, and Iris Murdoch's *An Unofficial Rose* was condemned as a "dirty

Figure 6.1. An elderly woman listening to a talking book.

book."[67] A married couple similarly disparaged Ian Fleming's James Bond series as "modern, filthy, sexy books."[68] Indignant readers protested that immoral books used up resources that could be spent on books suitable for everyone.

Objectionable material was thought to be more offensive on the record than on the page. In 1943, the Talking Book Selection Committee's incoming chairman was warned of "the special problem which arises from the objections entertained by some readers to 'outspokenness' which seemed more outspoken when spoken than when written."[69] In other words, hearing another person say offensive things felt more powerful than imagining those very same words to oneself. Books of this sort usually appeared in braille since, according to the studio's director, "there is a distinct difference between reading a book from the printed page and hearing it aloud."[70] Blasphemy caused particular discomfort when spoken aloud.

Despite the NIB's long-standing campaign to treat recorded and letterpress books as equivalent, warnings about outspokenness acknowledged differences in how people experienced the two media—even when the words were the same. Listeners had less control over the record than the page, and they often felt defenseless, even vulnerable, before a speaker. The record's dramatic force was too much for some people. A man who complained about John Eastwood's *The Chinese Visitor* was told, "We are, of course, very well aware that a spoken book is not quite the same as a printed book, and in some cases we have had to cross off our list for recording titles which, although possibly acceptable in print, would be far too embarrassing to read aloud."[71] John Braine's *Room at the Top* and Geoffrey Cotterell's *Go, Said the Bird* were both excluded in order to spare readers discomfort.

Books that were acceptable in print could be distressing to hear out loud. E. L. Withers's *The House on the Beach* was classified as a thriller "the type of which listeners complain so realistic when read aloud as to be disturbing."[72] Similarly, the surgical details in Anne Treger's *Probationer Nurse* (whose dust jacket boasted, "no book for the squeamish") made it appropriate solely for braille.[73] Arthur Koestler's *The Lotus and the Robot* was unsuitable for reading aloud because the descriptions of hatha yoga might disgust listeners—especially ones eating a meal. Alan Sillitoe's *Saturday Night and Sunday Morning* was another book considered "impossible to read aloud" because it described a married woman and her lover attempting a self-induced abortion.[74]

Many people found profanity offensive to hear out loud. As late as the 1970s, a woman complained of Mario Puzo's *The Godfather* and Robert Lait's *Pit,* "I think the language is disgusting."[75] Even readers who were comfortable reading explicit language in print sometimes felt uncomfortable hearing those same words said out loud. Some took coarse speech as a personal affront. A man complained of Sillitoe's novel, "For such language to be spoken aloud in one's home (and probably in the presence of one's wife) is degrading."[76] Nor were novels spared that used profanity judiciously. One woman complained that a "filthy 'four letter' word" in John Updike's *Of the Farm* should be scratched out and replaced with a decent one.[77]

But by far the most controversial topic was sex. Descriptions of sex led to objections against money being wasted on "pornography for the blind."[78] Such correspondents insisted that the Talking Book Selection Committee had a duty to act as gatekeepers. Elderly listeners in particular turned to it for protection from obscenity, if not for themselves then for young people or other supposedly vulnerable groups. An elderly woman from Glasgow, for instance, protested after hearing *The Manchurian Candidate.* "Once again I have received a filthy book, full of sex & violence," she wrote. "I have been forced to the conclusion that someone on your selection panel has a taste for pornographic literature."[79] This woman demanded more censorship, not less: "I put the whole responsibility of this filth seeping into the taking book library entirely on the selection panel."[80] Her letter ended with a threat to contact the press if one more pornographic book reached her—followed by a request for another novel by the same author who had offended her in the first place. Thrillers trafficked in taboo subjects, of course, but even tasteful or artistic depictions of sexuality met with hostility. Another aggrieved reader condemned Marcel Proust's *The Cities of the Plain* as "essays on Prostitution, Homosexualism, and Lesbianism."[81]

Hearing sex described was thought to be especially unpleasant. Alison Lurie's *Love and Friendship* had sex scenes deemed "likely to cause offense when read aloud," and those in *Catch-22* were ruled suitable for silent reading alone.[82] The sex scenes in Muriel Spark's *The Prime of Miss Jean Brodie* were described as "not being read-aloudable."[83] Even Spark's subtle handling of this material was thought to be too explicit when read aloud. A report expressed concerns about "sex innuendo" since the novel's young women used an adult vocabulary without realizing its full implications: "Alright when read silently to oneself, but I would think it very difficult indeed to convey *aloud* the author's intention, without creating in the mind of the listener the adult 'image.'"[84] The library's aging readership made it difficult to overcome generational differences in attitudes toward sex. A volunteer's offer to record a sex education manual was politely declined because the average age of library members was eighty.

Sex was particularly embarrassing when read aloud in other people's company. John Davies made the mistake of listening with his family to W. Somerset Maugham's *Cakes and Ale:* "It was with some considerable dismay that I was forced to listen for a whole track (Track 14) to the most intimate and detailed account of the author's bedtime adventure with his lady friend."

Davies did not object to sexual content, just his lack of control over it: "What I strongly object to is having no alternative but to listen while it is imposed upon me and upon whoever may be listening."[85] There was no easy way to bypass sections of a record as could easily be done with letterpress books. Moreover, indecent material came without warning. "Imagine how embarrassing it is for a blind person to listen to such a book when there are others of the opposite sex around," wrote a listener. "One does not always know when these nasty bits come."[86] Inconveniently, labels warning readers about unsuitable material did not specify exactly where to find it.

In 1937, the Talking Book Library's catalog began including short descriptions of each title. Soon afterward, notices stating "unsuitable for family reading" were introduced to warn patrons about potentially offensive material. Primo Levi's *The Truce* and other exceptionally traumatic books included even more explicit notices. Warning labels served the dual purpose of giving advance notice to people who listened to books in mixed company as well as to readers who objected to risqué material on moral or religious grounds. The warnings were only partially successful, however, since patrons usually ignored them or objected to the mere presence of books requiring them. But at least the committee could cite the warnings when responding to complaints. A man who described *The Death of William Posters* as "disgusting," "deliberately obscene," and "a book where filth is written for filth's sake," for example, conceded that he had listened despite the warning.[87]

Obviously no one was forcing patrons to listen. When a reader complained about adultery in Alan Moorehead's *A Summer Night,* he was told by the librarian, "I suggest that the best way of coping with the difficulty you mention, is to do what you and I no doubt often do when we are listening in to the wireless—switch off."[88] The committee sought to acknowledge offenses while at the same time treating blind readers as independent adults who were capable of making decisions for themselves. Still, one frustrated employee proposed adding the note, "If you object to a book, take it off the machine and return it unfinished; don't finish it and then say it was naughty but I loved every minute."[89]

If warning labels seem like a sensible solution to the problem of indecency, at least one committee member worried that even this measure inappropriately risked influencing the reader's autonomy. The label "unsuitable for family reading" was too sweeping a judgment, in the estimation of Bell, since it applied to books of literary merit. "While this is an agreed formula of long standing, I think, I am just wondering whether it is a little too categorical," wrote Bell in 1967. "After all, who are we to say?"[90] He recommended changing the label to state, "Parts of this recording may be considered unsuitable for family reading." The minor alteration acknowledged the spectrum of opinion among the library's patrons while at the same time avoiding the catalog's division into appropriate and inappropriate books.

The Talking Book Selection Committee operated on the principle that blind people should choose for themselves what books to read. When choosing titles, it aimed to represent a range of tastes, interests, and age groups. This meant choosing books proportionately to suit the tastes of the majority (predominantly elderly women) while at the same time satisfying the interests of various minorities (ranging from young soldiers at St. Dunstan's to university graduates). The Talking Book Library sought to make the same books available to blind readers as could be found at any other library while also serving a readership whose disabilities posed unique hardships. As a result, the library's good intentions frequently came into conflict with its aim to satisfy all readers.

Despite pressure from correspondents, Britain's Talking Book Library has opposed censorship ever since it was founded in the 1930s. Its policy was broadly understood, if never explicitly outlined, in the early years. Hence, complaints from readers presented the NIB with opportunities to formulate, amend, and refine its wavering and inconsistent stance toward censorship. Sometimes editors agreed to minor alterations of the original script; other times they outspokenly refused to tolerate any changes. The stance against censorship did not become official policy until 1968, when a meeting of the RNIB's executive council officially endorsed its opposition to censorship in response to complaints from readers and questions from book selectors over how to resolve such disputes.[91]

Censoring the Talking Book Library would have generated fierce opposition. Many blind people did not want a committee deciding which books should be read or, in this case, should *not* be read by them. Warning labels already allowed people to decide for themselves about a book's suitability. Any attempt to exclude books on the basis of individual complaints would simply lead to a new set of objections. "I am sure we should receive a great many complaints," declared Bell, "if we were even to attempt to censor the material going into the Talking Book Library."[92] Requests for objectionable books to be removed from circulation were uniformly denied. One reader calling for J. B. Priestley's *It's an Old Country* to be excluded was told by Bell that "the majority of blind people would, justifiably, take offence if they thought we were being censorious in our selection because they felt that we were withholding titles which we thought might be unsuitable for them to hear."[93] Plus, the library would be extremely small if it only held books that didn't offend anyone.

Yet, as we have seen, the NIB did take measures to protect readers from offensive material—even depictions of blindness. This was a fraught issue since some people turned to reading in order to escape from their blindness, whereas others identified with blind people, characters, and issues. The library held numerous books on the topic including Ian Fraser's *Whereas I Was Blind,* Russell Criddle's *Love Is Not Blind,* James Kinross's *The Boy from Greece,* and Helen Keller's *Teacher.* In one case, Wally Thomas's *Life in My Hands* was approved for recording despite mixed feelings: "It will certainly appeal to some readers as a plucky fight against blindness; others of course can't bear to know anything more about blindness than their own."[94] (A questionnaire completed in 1936 complained that the word "blind" was repeated too often on the records.) The Talking Book Selection Committee worried that insensitive treatments of blindness would distress listeners. Lyndon Snow's *Moonlight Witchery* and C. Hodder-Williams's *Chain Reaction* were both rejected for this reason. Snow's novel features a woman who marries a blind man out of pity, and *Chain Reaction* ends with a baby born blind as a result of his mother's exposure to radioactive milk.

The committee struggled to choose books that appealed to the majority while at the same time not excluding books of minority interest. Doing otherwise risked returning to the misbegotten policy of choosing which books blind people should read. As Bell informed one would-be censor, "Most blind people I know would take the greatest exception to the thought that they were being treated like children and provided only with those books which were thought to be good for them!"[95] Hence, the catalog included a range of titles from wholesome family sagas to avant-garde experiments in order to satisfy the tastes of a diverse constituency. The committee took into account the difference between speech and writing when judging books to be unsuitable for reading aloud. But, at the same time, the NIB sought to ensure that the books available to blind people were not different from those available to everyone else.

Censorship went beyond decisions to reject titles. Book selection was an equally important issue since, as we have seen, a catalog full of literary classics could just as effectively deny readers access to the books they wanted (namely, the latest best sellers).[96] The library's budget constraints meant that only a handful of books could be recorded. Hence, the books chosen for recording were as important as the books not chosen since they used up scarce resources. Some members criticized the library for "censoring by omission."[97] Controversial books, if not actively excluded, might simply be left off the list in favor of more appealing titles. Equally problematic was the NIB's decision to print controversial titles solely in braille. Although reading by touch was thought to grant greater control over the material, books published in this way were effectively off limits to the majority of blind people who couldn't read braille.

Despite opposing censorship, the NIB occasionally "cleaned up" scripts in ways that might be construed as censorship. In some instances, narrators made minor alterations to books containing explicit material in order to make them suitable for a broad readership. The studio's director had discretion over any changes. For example, requests were approved to "bowdlerize" passages containing "unnecessary filthy talk and four letter words" in Hunter Davies's *The Other Half* and Stanley Winchester's *The Practice*.[98]

Modifying a book's wording, however, made people uneasy. The practice went unacknowledged until 1964, when the committee agreed to insert the following announcement into all edited recordings: "This recording contains some modifications of the author's original text which have been made in order to suit the difference between the written and the spoken word."[99] Still, Bell and the other librarians opposed amending books except as a last resort. In 1965, for example, he refused to approve changes made to Joyce Porter's *Dover Two:*

> The reason for your bowdlerization of this book quite defeats me, but in any case it amounts to censorship, and this we cannot have. We must legislate for *l'homme moyen sensuel,* even though we have a high proportion of old ladies in our membership. I am quite prepared to deal with any complaints you may get. We really cannot rewrite authors' books for them.[100]

Tellingly, the statement alludes to the notorious trial of James Joyce's *Ulysses* in the United States. Judge John M. Woolsey's well-known defense of the novel as a serious work of literature had similarly named *l'homme moyen sensuel* ("person with average sex instincts") as a touchstone by which to judge indecency.[101] The implicit reference to the trial of a book banned in England until 1936, along with Bell's explicit denunciation of censorship, suggest how much was felt to be at stake in protecting blind people's books from outside interference.

In a confidential exchange with the librarian responsible for modifying *Dover Two*, Bell reaffirmed the library's commitment to allow readers to decide for themselves what books to read. "I still say that we cannot take it upon ourselves to trim books in order to anticipate possible offence to some readers," wrote Bell. "We surely must treat our readers as responsible adults (even though some of them may not be) capable of judging for themselves what they read. After all, no reader *has* to listen to anything construable as causing offence."[102] Behind this insistence on the individual's autonomy hovered obscenity laws that had long sought to protect impressionable groups including women, children, and, by implication, people with disabilities who were thought to be less capable than other people of self-control.

The library had been criticized in the past—most vehemently by its own members—for deciding what books should be read by blind people, and its reputation would suffer once again if members perceived the library to be resuming its former role as a paternalistic body. "I am sure that blind people would have every reason for complaint," Bell concluded, "if they were to feel that we were deciding what was good for them to read: it is this aspect of the Institute's image which worries me."[103] Bell was right to be concerned about censorship in the aftermath of high-profile obscenity trials for books like *Lady Chatterley's Lover*.[104] In July 1967, the *Daily Sketch* contacted the RNIB about "the vexed question of censorship." Its reporter wanted to know whether "four-letter words" were removed from talking books.[105] What was the reporter told? That the RNIB never censors books.

This chapter set out to determine who was responsible for the books recorded by the Talking Book Library. It began with a committee's appointment to choose the hundred best books before turning its attention to "unrecordable" books ranging from experimental literature by James and Woolf to outspoken books containing sex, violence, profanity, blasphemy, and other objectionable material. The RNIB professed to oppose censorship while at the same time taking a cautious approach to indecency by using warning labels, excluding distasteful titles, printing controversial narratives solely in braille, or modifying the wording of books to make them suitable for a general audience—actions summed up by one librarian as "censorship of the mind."

The Talking Book Selection Committee had long endorsed allowing blind people to decide for themselves what to read. Its history tells a different story, though, about a group who came to represent the tastes of blind readers only after years of protest from those very same readers. The rise of a commercial market for spoken word recordings during the 1950s would at least give people an alternative way to obtain the books they wanted.

PART III

Audiobooks on and off the Road

7

Caedmon's Third Dimension

Talking books made it possible for thousands of blind and partially sighted people to read again. Since the 1930s, the Library of Congress has recorded entire novels onto long-playing phonograph discs read aloud by professional actors. Spoken word recordings were especially useful to people—from veterans of the First World War to an aging population beset by eye diseases—who had lost their sight midlife and found it difficult to learn braille. Those who could no longer read with their eyes could still read with their ears. In fact, the initiative was so successful that recorded books became linked to disability in the popular imagination. Why listen to books if you can read them?

Commercial audio publishers have been trying to undo the association between blindness and spoken word recordings ever since. Other readers were slow to catch on. Even those who did foresee alternatives to print skeptically wondered whether such behavior would count as reading. As early as 1935, the poet Cecil Day-Lewis contemplated the book's technological makeover. He announced in *Revolution in Writing*, "I can even envisage a day when we shall put a book onto a mechanism as now we put on a gramophone record, and the whole thing will be enacted for us." Technology would usher in a brave new world of multimedia entertainment or what might be thought of as analog media convergence. Yet, with equal foresight, Day-Lewis anticipated the inevitable backlash: "But whether this performance could be called 'literature,' or our share in it 'reading,' are questions quite beyond my reeling imagination."[1] As we've seen in previous chapters, debates over the legitimacy of talking books are as old as the technology used to record them.

Publishers wanting to market spoken word recordings had to convince audiences that recorded books appealed to all people (not just those with

185

disabilities), were a respectable form of reading, and held distinct advantages over the time-honored tradition of print. For spoken word recordings to succeed, it was not enough for them to be print's equal; they had to surpass print in terms of entertainment. Such was the climate when Caedmon Records began recording literature read aloud by authors and actors.

Caedmon's story is well known.[2] In January 1952, Barbara Holdridge and Marianne Mantell went to hear Dylan Thomas read at New York City's 92nd Street Y. Recent graduates from Hunter College, the twenty-two-year-olds had grown restless with minor roles at publishing and record companies. They pooled together $1,800 to establish Caedmon Records (Figure 7.1). After briefly considering medieval music and Shakespeare, they began the series instead with a contemporary poet. Thomas caught their attention with "In the White Giant's Thigh," a sensual poem whose bouncing goosegirls had prompted hundreds of subscribers to cancel subscriptions to the *Atlantic*. The poem had the opposite effect on Holdridge and Mantell, not to mention the large crowds, mostly young women, who attended his readings. That night, they could not get past the other fans to make their business proposition. Instead, Holdridge reached the bohemian poet by telephone at five o'clock one morning as he was coming back from a party. They met a week later at a local restaurant. There, the entrepreneurs made their pitch: a $500 advance against the first 1,000 records, with a 10 percent royalty thereafter, for the rights to one hour of Thomas reading his poems.

Thomas recorded "In the White Giant's Thigh" and four other poems at Steinway Hall on February 22, 1952. There was one problem, however: the poems filled just a single side of the disc. In other words, Caedmon's first record had an A side but no B side. Stuck, Thomas proposed reading a sentimental Christmas story he had recently published in *Harper's Bazaar*. The album was released on April 2 and, after modest initial sales, went on to sell over 400,000 copies by 1960.[3] "A Child's Christmas in Wales" became one of the twentieth century's most popular spoken word recordings (Figure 7.2). To this day, the mere mention of Thomas's story brings a smile to the faces of those who grew up listening to it. It proved that spoken word recordings could be both commercially viable and culturally significant.

Thomas's recitation brought new readers into contact with a story that had aroused little fanfare on the page. Holdridge later attributed the story's success to the switch: "I don't know what would have happened if we had not recorded it. It would have languished at Harper's Bazaar. I don't know

Figure 7.1. Caedmon's founders, Barbara Holdridge and Marianne Mantell, at the office. (Photograph by Rollie McKenna.)

that anyone would have dug it up."[4] Caedmon's impromptu recording session has since been credited with establishing the audiobook industry.[5] In 2002, the Audio Publishers Association marked Caedmon's fiftieth anniversary by honoring Holdridge and Mantell with Audie Awards for Lifetime Achievement.[6]

Caedmon was among the first labels to specialize exclusively in spoken word recordings of literature.[7] The company recorded many of the twentieth century's most influential writers including W. H. Auden, Albert Camus,

Figure 7.2. The album cover for *Dylan Thomas Reading "A Child's Christmas in Wales" and Five Poems* (1952).

Colette, E. E. Cummings, T. S. Eliot, William Faulkner, Robert Frost, Langston Hughes, James Joyce, Thomas Mann, Marianne Moore, Sylvia Plath, Katherine Anne Porter, Ezra Pound, Anne Sexton, Gertrude Stein, Wallace Stevens, May Swenson, Eudora Welty, Tennessee Williams, William Carlos Williams, and W. B. Yeats. The list was the closest anyone had yet come to realizing Thomas Edison's Library of Voices representing the world's best authors. Caedmon was larger and better known, too, than competitors such as Argo and Folkways.[8] By 1959, it had annual revenues of half a million dollars.[9]

Postwar technological developments made Caedmon's success possible. First, the long-playing (LP) vinyl record went on the market in 1948.[10] Full-length novels had been recorded since 1934 for people who were blind; now, commercial labels could likewise record books. LP records held around twenty-two minutes per side, much more than the previous 78 rpm (revolutions per minute) records, which could hold only a few minutes of speech. They were also lighter, stronger, and sounded better than earlier ones. Second, studios began using magnetic tape recording in 1949. Tapes could be edited to improve clarity and to insert sound effects, whereas phonograph records, manufactured from acetate masters, could not be modified.[11] The label eventually benefited from stereophonic sound too. These advances in sound technology made it possible for Caedmon to produce new recordings of writers reading their work in the 1950s and 1960s to market alongside previous series made for radio or on 78 rpm records in the 1930s and 1940s.

Disputes over Caedmon's legacy reflect the perennial struggle of recorded books to achieve cultural legitimacy. National Public Radio recently introduced Caedmon as "a little company with a very high brow."[12] Its records display the tastes of cosmopolitan New Yorkers with an appreciation for difficult modernist writers in particular (Beckett, Joyce, Proust, Stein). Caedmon published all kinds of writing, unlike many of its successors who specialized in poetry, drama, or prose. In retrospect, the catalog resembles nothing so much as a Norton anthology of literature.

At the same time, the label was distinctly middlebrow in its mission to translate traditional forms of high culture into media formats associated with modern pop culture. According to Jacob Smith, Caedmon succeeded in "mass-producing high culture."[13] Caedmon took its place alongside the Book-of-the-Month Club and other organizations aspiring to make literature available to the general public during the postwar period.[14] These groups had a reputation for making challenging works of art palatable to consumers who wanted high culture's prestige without the effort. Such is the dilemma faced by recorded books: Is the content or mode of delivery the decisive factor?

Caedmon faced the formidable challenge of persuading book lovers to start buying records. Audiobooks were not yet familiar when Caedmon began publishing. Instead, Holdridge used terms like "spoken word records" or, if being formal, "recordings of the spoken word."[15] The company's first task was to establish the spoken word recording as a respectable literary category in its own right. Doing so meant clarifying the exact nature of the relationship between printed books and sound recordings: Was one an exact replica of the other or were there distinct advantages to each format? As we'll see, Caedmon marketed its records both as equivalents to the original book and as enhancements of it owing to the addition of voices, music, and other sound effects. Hence the slogan: "Caedmon: a third dimension for the printed page."[16]

Caedmon's records hewed closely enough to books to share their prestige while at the same time innovating enough to justify switching to a phonograph.

To this end, the album sleeves make explicit how Caedmon tried to persuade audiences of the new format's appeal in terms of edification and entertainment. Through liner notes, the editors—and sometimes even the narrators—sought to reassure customers that Caedmon's albums represented both the artworks being reproduced (say, a Virginia Woolf novel) and original works of art in their own right. Reading aloud made spoken word recordings even better than the books—or so Caedmon claimed. In making such statements, Caedmon raised a set of questions about the relationship among literature, voice, and technology that would shape the perception of spoken word recordings for decades to come.

The Bardic Tradition

One of the first advertisements for "talking books" appeared on May 15, 1919, in *Talking Machine World*. It assured readers that talking books were similar to other books, only better: "The Talking Books are real books, with pictures, stories, songs and poems."[17] They were, in fact, real books, just ones with records built into them; the entire book needed to be placed on the turntable.

Since 1917, the Emerson Phonograph Company had been mounting plastic discs on top of illustrated books. After two years, the company began manufacturing children's books made out of four-inch discs fastened to die-cut cardboard animals and other shapes (Figure 7.3). These books were designed as much for the eye as for the ear. Although read by elocutionists, most of the books emphasized the songs, not the text. The company cited several benefits: entertaining children, teaching them to recite, and luring their parents into shops. The public was not ready for talking books, however—at least not ones shaped like hippos and crying babies. The company went bankrupt in 1921.[18]

Caedmon was hardly the first to record literature. As we saw in Chapter 1, Edison's phonograph was used to record statesmen, actors, and poets such as Alfred Tennyson and Robert Browning. The verses of everyone from Milton to John Greenleaf Whittier can be found on records made before Caedmon's time. The Victor label, for example, issued nearly twenty recordings of James Whitcomb Riley in 1912.[19] That same year, Robert Hilliard recorded "Christmas Day in the Workhouse," one of countless dramatic monologues recorded by stage actors.[20] By midcentury, critics were already complaining about too many "poetry records" read by radio crooners and movie stars.[21]

Figure 7.3. The Talking Book Corporation's "I Am a Dancing Girl" (1919).

Harvard University began recording poets, most famously T. S. Eliot, in 1933.[22] The Library of Congress, National Council of Teachers of English, Columbia University, and Yale University all launched similar series in the 1940s and 1950s. Fans could purchase 78 rpm records from these series.[23] (Caedmon reissued many of these recordings.) The records brought poetry to audiences who couldn't attend the live performances. Lloyd Frankenberg, for example, put together an album for people who had never heard the poems read aloud. His ambition was to make books talk: "If only a voice *could* go with the book. Instead of quotations, singing wires: the poets' own inflections magically caught on the page. Or little disks, perhaps, like nursery records, that would slide out of pleats in the binding. With a little machine to be packaged with each copy?"[24] This was a starry-eyed way of describing the recorded poetry anthologies that became popular in Caedmon's time.

Prose could be heard, too, though only in short bursts until long-playing records became available. A. A. Milne's *Winnie the Pooh* was among the *Readings by 12 Famous Authors* issued by the Dominion Company in 1929.[25] James Joyce recorded excerpts from *Ulysses* and *Finnegans Wake,* and Dickens's *A Christmas Carol* could be heard recited by actors including Frank Pettingell, Ernest Chappell, Lionel Barrymore, Charles Laughton, Bransby Williams, and Emlyn Williams. The novels needed to be excerpted, of course, as Zonophone did when recording Little Nell's death as early as 1913.

For decades audiences had listened to spoken word entertainment on the radio. Literature was frequently, if sporadically, read aloud.[26] Orson Welles's *The Mercury Theatre on the Air* adapted classic fiction; Welles even filled dead air by reading passages from his favorite novels.[27] In 1941, the National Broadcasting Company (NBC) adapted Pearl Buck's *This Proud Heart;* James Hilton's *Goodbye, Mr. Chips;* John Steinbeck's *Of Mice and Men;* Kenneth Roberts's *Northwest Passage;* and other best-selling novels into one-hour radio broadcasts.[28] *Poet's Corner, Poet's Gold, Between the Bookends, R Yuh Listenin'?* and similar programs catered to the appetite for verse.[29] In Britain, reading aloud was a key component of the BBC's mission to educate and entertain. It regularly adapted novels for radio and, from 1946, featured authors reading aloud on the Third Programme.[30]

Caedmon, then, was by no means the first to make literary recordings. Yet, as one of the first companies to make them available to a mass audience, Caedmon was tasked with establishing an affinity between books and records. It did so by persuading audiences that spoken word recordings were simultaneously a revival of ancient traditions of reading aloud and one of the twentieth-century's technological breakthroughs.

Invoking a time when bards sang tales to the Greeks helped Caedmon play the roles of both defender of traditional values and hip newcomer.[31] A classicist introduced Caedmon's *Twelve Labors of Heracles* with the reminder, "Long ago, before people knew anything about books or printing, the Greeks enjoyed telling and listening to stories of great heroes of earlier times."[32] The implication was that records enabled modern audiences to do so once again. The liner notes for Homer's *Iliad* insisted that "the author intended it to be heard."[33] "Both epic poems, *Iliad* and *Odyssey,*" declared another album, "were composed for listeners, not readers."[34] According to this line of thought, books were the disruptive technology, not records. Sound recordings merely enabled audiences to hear literature as it had been heard for centuries. Listening to Caedmon's albums was, counterintuitively, a traditionalist gesture, making it possible for audiences to participate in an oral tradition thought to have vanished long ago. Hearing the stories in the original Greek, as some of Caedmon's records allowed them to do, permitted the most authentic encounter possible with Homer.

The Caedmon label sought legitimacy through poetry's oral traditions. Verses by Catullus, Cicero, and Horace were recited in the original Latin as if to invoke the public readings that took place throughout the Roman Empire, where authors presented stories to boisterous crowds known to clap, cheer, and shout at stirring passages. The Greek and Latin verbs for "to read" also mean "to read aloud." Quintus Ennius, the father of Roman poetry, was said by one album to have "fitted his language to the tongue and the ear" since he expected it to be read aloud, not silently.[35] By the fourth century, silent reading was still rare enough that Augustine famously expressed surprise upon finding his teacher Saint Ambrose reading to himself.[36]

Caedmon also sought recognition through its bards. After all, the label's very name derives from an eighth-century cowherd driven to sing by a divinely inspired dream. (Holdridge and Mantell both studied classical literature at Hunter College.) Caedmon's namesake gained his reputation as the first English poet after turning scripture into musical verse. By the 1950s, however, the image of the solitary writer revising intricate verse on the page had long ago replaced that of the wandering minstrel. Caedmon tried to revive the bard by linking spoken word recordings back to this Gaelic pastime. We are told, for example, before hearing *Tristan and Iseult,* "The story comes down to us from the twelfth century, when wandering bards gained a place at the baron's table with such a tale . . . and now, at last, the legend comes full cycle, and is here told again, as once it was, in the bardic tradition of the spoken word."[37] The passage encapsulated Caedmon's ethos: the revival of ancient traditions by modern technology.

Album sleeves implied that ancient literature was diminished by silent reading. Liner notes for the *Canterbury Tales* point repeatedly to their emergence amid an oral culture in which most people still heard stories told to them at the marketplace, church, or home. For them, reading was a public act, not a private one. Reciting Chaucer's tales in Middle English helped to simulate the narrator speaking directly to the original audience, telling tales "as ye may heere."[38] Speakers sought to bring out the distinct sounds of the "vocal company," from the Friar's lisp to the Prioress's nasal singing and the Pardoner's goat voice.[39] The implication: only the ear can fully appreciate such embellishments.

In many cases, scholars were hired to ensure authenticity. Members of the University of Texas's Classics Department read the Latin poems, for example, and a New York University professor recited *Beowulf*. Yet the use of actors on other albums signaled their commercial orientation. Despite reading several *Canterbury Tales* in Middle English, "as Chaucer himself would have spoken it," that album describes Robert Ross as "no scholar but an actor," whose mispronunciations should not distract from Chaucer's story-telling.[40] There was no need to let historical accuracy stand in the way of entertainment.

Turntables were ideally suited to fairy tales, fables, legends, myths, and other stories that have been passed along for centuries by word of mouth. While the previous century's folklorists had translated oral traditions into writing, the twentieth century saw them translated back into speech. Sound technology brought distant storytellers into people's homes. One collection gathered English folk tales told by the fireside; another reproduced storytelling sessions held throughout the Irish countryside. Tales collected from the Pueblos, Navajos, and other Native American tribes harked back to the phonograph's use by ethnomusicologists to preserve American Indian folklore.[41] In fact, Caedmon's tales came from all over the world: China, India, Russia, the West Indies, and African villages. A recording of *Ali Baba and the Forty Thieves* claimed to trace the Arabic tradition of "'told' stories" from the marketplaces of Cairo to the borders of modern-day Pakistan.[42]

As Walter Benjamin reminds us in "The Storyteller," twice-told tales differed from novels in their independence from the book.[43] Benjamin thought that moral counsel in particular had maximum impact when told. Similarly, Aesop's fables were said by Caedmon to be "especially effective when read aloud."[44] The albums emphasize how Jakob and Wilhelm Grimm collected the tales from peasant women who knew them by heart. *Hansel and Gretel* and other albums invoke a time when family entertainment consisted of tales told by the hearthside: "A long time ago, when there was no television to enchant people into silence, mothers and fathers used to read to their children the wonderful tales of Grimm."[45] Television's intrusion into this nostalgic scenario was no accident; reading aloud held particular appeal in the 1950s as an alternative to TV.[46] As Caedmon's charge of mesmerism hints, bookish types viewed television with suspicion despite the efforts of Hollywood's Charles Laughton.[47]

Caedmon made every effort to capitalize on the close relationship that existed between speech and writing before the printing press. But what about books written for silent reading, for the eyes instead of the ears? Caedmon implicitly challenged the historical narrative of a spoken culture evolving into a silent one.[48] Instead, its catalog flaunted oral or hybrid genres (sermons, fairy tales, radio plays, and so forth) exemplifying the ways in which speech continued to influence the arts long after writing's ascendance. Reading aloud did not wither and die on the vine during the nineteenth and twentieth centuries; it persisted and at times flourished.[49]

The ancients were not the only ones demanding to be read aloud. Modern poetry had its own soundtrack. Thomas, Yeats, and Walt Whitman were all described as "bardic"; their poems were meant to be sung.[50] Whitman's album introduced him as

> the solitary singer, whose poems are not for the eye alone to peruse by lamplight. A poem by Whitman may be a whoop and a holler, or a beating of drums, or the ebb of the tide singing to itself among the stones, or a lament in the night, or a cry of ecstasy. But it is cadenced for the voice, and it is meant to be spoken aloud—or sung, in the ancient bardic sense, as the poet used the verb.[51]

Similar to Homer's epics, reading Whitman silently to oneself risked missing out.

Caedmon likewise singled out Mark Twain's distinctive cadences. Twain wrote colloquially, the albums remind us, emphasizing speech and dialect; his "yarn-spinning style" needed to be read aloud for full effect.[52] Caedmon chose many of its titles because they were suited to performance, not because they were great literature. The "Old Times" passages from *Life on the Mississippi* succeed on records, we're told, because the accomplished performer "wrote with an ear for the spoken word."[53]

Caedmon's marketing campaign even enlisted the authors themselves. Take the following lines reprinted in Randall Jarrell's *Poems against War,* a recording made nearly two decades after he served in the Second World War: "My poems are meant to be *read* and *heard* poems . . . I mean, they are not just something on a printed page."[54] The records offered a way for him to reach people beyond the page.

Theater was an obvious fit for Caedmon's catalog. Dramatic recordings ranged from Caedmon's Shakespeare Recording Society, which produced a complete set of Shakespeare's work, to Jean Cocteau's one-act drama, *The Human Voice,* which cast Ingrid Bergman speaking on the telephone to her lover. Caedmon's series joined a venerable tradition of Shakespeare recordings, ranging from individual soliloquies to a full-length *Othello* made in 1944 on eighteen 78 rpm discs. LP records enabled Caedmon to venture beyond the highlights-and-excerpts tradition necessitated by the previous era's technology.

Three ambitious recording series marked the quatercentenary of Shakespeare's birth in 1964: Caedmon's Shakespeare Recording Society, Argo's Marlow Dramatic Society, and Odhams's Living Shakespeare. Douglas Lanier describes the late 1950s and 1960s as a golden age of Shakespeare recordings, when niche productions became economically viable, radio familiarized people with the conventions of spoken productions, and the home became the locus of entertainment media. Phonograph records "converted Shakespearean performance into an experience for the individual listener" that could be played at home without the distractions of actual theaters.[55] They existed midway between page and stage.

At the same time, Caedmon's Shakespeare recordings inadvertently drew attention to the rest of the catalog's theatricality. The American playwright Howard Sackler was among the first Shakespearean directors to use stereophonic sound and other studio techniques to fashion the playwright for the phonograph. Sackler's recordings were renowned for their use of sound effects and musical cues, and he brought these same resources to bear on the production of Caedmon's literary series. Its albums frequently credit both the reader ("read by," "told by," "performed by") and Sackler's direction ("directed by"). His role nods to the close relationship between the rival media of stage and sound recording.

The sermon was another genre better heard than read. Caedmon's sources ranged from John Donne to Father Daniel Berrigan, a Catholic priest sent to federal prison after protesting the Vietnam War. It also recorded *Ol' Man Adam an' His Chillun,* which retold the Biblical stories Roark Bradford heard from African American preachers while growing up in the South.[56] Evangelical fervor motivated churchgoers to get out their tape recorders and spread the Word. In 1947, for example, two men recorded Peter Marshall's sermons for the congregation's elderly people and "shut-ins."[57] They recorded the services every Sunday at a Presbyterian church in Washington, DC, before Marshall was appointed chaplain of the United States Senate. One parishioner told him afterward, "I can listen to your sermons as often as I like."[58] The records preserved the ambience of a live event (Marshall's Scottish burr, the Lincoln chimes, an occasional siren) for a genre whose impact depends on the speaker's voice and delivery as much as his words. The tapes later formed the basis for *The Prayers of Peter Marshall* and the film *A Man Called Peter*.[59]

Caedmon capitalized on the popularity of reading aloud to children, too, through collections ranging from Mother Goose's nursery rhymes to Hans Christian Andersen's fairy tales and Ludwig Bemelmans's *Madeline* series. Notably, *Rootabaga Stories* begins with a note explaining how Carl Sandburg read them aloud to his own children.[60] Children's books were the exception amid the ongoing shift toward silent reading. Dr. Benjamin Spock's *The Common Sense Book of Baby and Child Care,* published in 1946, even featured a section on the importance of reading aloud. (It was no coincidence that Caedmon later issued an album titled *Dr. Spock Talks with New Mothers*.)

Caedmon's marketing campaign even extended to adults who had nostalgic memories of being read to by their parents. For example, a recording of Oscar Wilde's fairy tales appealed to children and adults alike: "Everyone who has known the pleasure of being read aloud to—and everyone who has missed that pleasure—will, we think, be delighted with Caedmon's series of the best of all children's literature."[61] Other albums appealed directly to parents, even volunteering to be surrogate readers for the weary ones. A Brooklyn librarian assured them, "At long last all of the parents, teachers, librarians and babysitters who cannot face reading Curious George aloud for the 50th time can breathe a sigh of relief. Julie Harris will do it for you."[62] The combination of reading and technology was a seductive one for parents who wanted to encourage children to read even when they were too tired, too busy, or too bored to do it themselves.

Reading with the Ear

Reading aloud became increasingly fashionable after the Second World War. Poetry readings grew in number and popularity among both universities and the informal Beat scene.[63] (Donald Hall once described poetry readings as "the main form of publication for American poets."[64]) Yet plenty of holdouts felt that poetry was for the page. For them, print alone made it possible to appreciate the typographical manipulation, linguistic complexity, and sight rhymes possible after Gutenberg. The Spanish Nobel Laureate Juan Ramón Jiménez replied to Caedmon's invitation, "Poetry is not made to read aloud."[65]

Caedmon's records intervened in vehement debates over whether poetry should be seen or heard. Osbert Sitwell's album, for example, recalled a notorious recitation he and Edith Sitwell had given three decades earlier at London's Aeolian Hall. There, the poets stood behind a curtain adorned with a pink-and-white painted face, through which they spoke using a papier-mâché trumpet called a Sengerphone.[66] It was the latest salvo in a long-standing dispute: "Those who felt that poetry needed only to be seen were countered by those who found increased understanding in hearing poetry read aloud by the author."[67] Caedmon's series ensured that poets were heard beyond the platform. The Sitwells' verse, with its fondness for rhythm and wordplay, was especially amenable to an audible format that preserved the spirit of the public readings.

Most of Caedmon's audience felt there to be a difference between reading and hearing poetry. Reading aloud either enhanced a poem's meaning or distorted it; few felt it made no difference whatsoever. The alleged benefits of reading aloud included intimacy, vividness, dramatic force, improved understanding, access to the author's interpretation, and alternative ways of engaging literature. Caedmon's fans spoke about reading aloud using a vocabulary derived from the theater. Basil Rathbone's performance of "The Raven," for instance, made the familiar poem seem new to them.[68] "Bring to life" was a phrase frequently used to describe recordings—as in, the speaker made the letters between George Bernard Shaw and Ellen Terry "come alive in a most pleasing way."[69]

The recordings made it clear how writers imagined their work should sound. According to Caedmon's catalog, "Now it would be possible to recreate the sound of the author's personal interpretation at any convenient moment."[70] Since most listeners were already familiar with the poetry, the records provided an additional way to engage it. Nuances missed on the page could be heard in the author's voice. "We have only to listen to these poets reading their own works to know how important their interpretations are to a full comprehension of the poems," insisted *The Caedmon Treasury of Modern Poets Reading Their Own Poetry*. "The ministerial intonations of Eliot, the passionate orchestrations of Thomas, the very, very precise formulations of Cummings, the easy conversational inflections of Frost, are integral, and lend those subtle clarifications which are beyond the printed page."[71] "Full comprehension": the phrase implied that encounters with the page alone risked a partial, even inadequate grasp of the poems.

Then as now, people tended to think of the eye as the most reliable guide to literature. Caedmon privileged the ear instead. Listening enhanced the intimacy of Kafka's stories, according to one album, by obliging audiences to pay attention: "The eye may skim, losing much of the painstaking artistry of the author's word-images. But the ear will follow each detail with the precision of Kafka's own grim imagination, losing nothing."[72] Such formulations advocated a method of close listening to rival, if not surpass, that of close reading or what one contemporary critic called "slow reading."[73]

Listening closely made difficult scripts accessible to some readers who struggled to understand them in print. Hearing Gerard Manley Hopkins's prosody made sense since Hopkins himself had wanted his poems to be read aloud. As the album points out, he insisted to Robert Bridges, who found the poet's rhythms eccentric and off-putting, that "right, 'dramatic' reading would make his art quite intelligible."[74] This is what Hopkins meant when asking for his verse to be read with the ears. Unbeknownst to Caedmon, Hopkins had even looked forward to a time when sound-recording technology would teach people how to read his verse. Shortly after Edison's invention, Hopkins wrote of its potential use for lyric poems: "With the aid of the phonograph each phrase could be fixed and learnt by heart like a song."[75] Exemplary recordings might even model a poem's correct reading (as those preserved online are sometimes thought to do today). Authoritative recitations appealed to Hopkins since he already relied on a complicated system of superscripts and notations borrowed from music to indicate where the stress should fall in his verse.[76]

Finnegans Wake was another intimidating work singled out by Caedmon. According to the album's liner notes, speech acts as both "concert" and "crutch" in helping readers to appreciate Joyce's linguistic sonority: "With a work like *Finnegans Wake,* it may well be the only way of arriving at an *experience* of the book. Joyce reduces language to pure music; and, hearing it, one slips into a kind of swoon, a not even listening for words, but only the ebb and flow of sound. The reading-aloud is not one more tool to help penetrate the jungle, but a part of the text."[77] Hearing the narrative diverted attention from the book's linguistic density to its musicality. The promised "swoon" represented a different way of engaging with prose found to be incomprehensible at first glance.

But was anything lost in the swoon? Form was a contentious point for skeptics of recorded literature, who worried it would be lost in translation. For Auden, a poem's form was as intimately bound up with its meaning as the body to the soul. He warned that such craft might go unheard: "When one reads a poem in a book one grasps the form immediately, but when one listens to a recitation, it is sometimes very difficult to 'hear' the structure."[78] To prevent this, Auden's liner notes specify whether the poem is an elegy or a villanelle, rhymed or unrhymed, free verse or ballad meter; one cites a word's recurrence in the poem's third and fourth lines (surely an effect detectable by ear too). Auden apologized for the "schoolmasterly" tone of the instructions while at the same time insisting on the need to include them.

Experiments with a poem's appearance were especially tricky to reproduce in other media. Take the vogue for concrete poetry during the late 1950s.[79] The verse reprinted on May Swenson's album sleeve derives much of its meaning from the typographical layout. For example, the poem "Lightning" features a streak of white space running diagonally across the text. Yet the recording compensates for any lost visual effects by adding vocal ones. The voice reading Swenson's poem about shattered love, in which two black lines in the shape of a cross pass through the text, grows in intensity when comparing the lovers to "earth" and "the flower," then "boat" and "the sea." The speaker cries out in a closing line that, according to the sleeve, "embodies the traditional curse of primitive poetry."[80] In this way, the recording turns even the most graphic verse into speech.

Some poems could even be easier to hear. Despite the association between public readings and traditional verse, twentieth-century revivals of the verse-recitation movement emphasized the usefulness of reading aloud in helping people to understand formal experimentation.[81] One album advised newcomers to listen to James Dickey's verse, not to read it, since "the look of these poems on the page is disconcerting."[82] The use of sundered forms, white space, and free verse in what Dickey called "long lines in the air"—a phrase rich in implication for records—all interfered with the reader's efforts to make sense of the poems.

Still, there were limits to what could be translated across media. Certain poems worked on the page alone. One of Caedmon's album sleeves reprinted Christian Morgenstern's "Fisches Nachtgesang," a concrete poem with alternating lines of macrons and breves loosely arranged in the shape of a fish.[83] No attempt was made to record it. What was the narrator supposed to do with a soundless poem?

Nor was lossless translation (as today's tech industry would put it) possible with all books. Alternative ways had to be found to communicate the imagery in children's stories. The authors of the Berenstain Bears stories, for example, wrote additional material for those in which "the transition from picture books to sound recordings seemed lacking."[84]

Multimedia works for grownups posed more serious problems. Consider James Agee and Walker Evans's *Let Us Now Praise Famous Men,* which relies heavily for effect on photographs of sharecropping families in the South. Their gaunt faces are as responsible for the book's impact as the words. Caedmon's records do little more than gesture toward these images, however; the album is essentially Agee without Evans. The liner notes admit, "The powerful impact of these pictures and their part in the full effect of the book can only be suggested to listeners by the two portraits, of George and Annie Mae Gudger, reproduced on the jacket."[85] The disclaimer comes despite Agee's insistence that he wrote the text to be read aloud and to hold subtleties "unavailable to the eye alone."[86]

Other albums sought to break down the border between printed books and spoken word recordings. The two need not be mutually exclusive, after all. Why not enjoy both? A recording of Kurt Vonnegut's *Welcome to the Monkey House* encouraged audiences to read the stories in print before hearing them read aloud. In addition, testimonials noted the benefits of using records to "reread" favorite works of literature. Holdridge and Mantell, for example, discovered in this way new dimensions to Robert Browning: "We ourselves, who have delighted in these poems for so many years, could not have believed that a reading of them would bring out so much more than we had remembered."[87] "Relistening" was encouraged too. The editors recommended playing Faulkner multiple times since each listening revealed something new.

Inviting audiences to follow along in the book was another way to bridge the gap between page and record. Caedmon's editors encouraged this: "We suggest that a proper initiation procedure is to listen with book firmly in hand, following the text as the author reads. For unless this care is taken, even those well acquainted with the novels may find many of the nuances of text and voice gliding past unnoticed."[88] Whereas today's audiobooks advertise the freedom to drive or exercise while listening, Caedmon's implied audience devoted its full attention to the record. (Most of the people I have spoken with did listen to spoken word recordings in this way either at home or in a library.[89]) Doing otherwise risked admitting that spoken word recordings were not high art, as many consumers needed to believe at a time when the cultivation of taste was linked to social mobility.

The booklets accompanying select albums permitted auditors to follow along. A recording of Vachel Lindsay, known to encourage the crowds at live performances to follow on the page, included printed copies "to help the listener better understand the language of the poems."[90] *Finnegans Wake* likewise came with the text, and Peter Marshall's fans could purchase copies of his sermons from Caedmon for twenty-five cents. In each case, the writing preceded the recording. The sequence was usually the other way around for commercially oriented recordings made during this period. Each of the eleven albums of Time-Life's *The Story of Great Music,* for example, came with a sixty-four-page hardcover booklet that no one was expected to read on its own. Other publishers specialized in the "nearly-a-book," an expensively packaged recording with extensive liner notes and illustrations that could not be purchased separately.[91]

Few people denied the appeal of reading aloud despite the ongoing, unresolved debate over the recorded book's legitimacy. Testimonials reprinted on Caedmon's albums highlighted the spoken word's impact on individual readers. Many described being converted. Richard Moore, who produced the WNET/PBS series *The Writer in America,* recalled how hearing Eudora Welty's fiction helped him to understand the importance of conversation to the South:

> When I first read a Eudora Welty short story, I must confess that my tone-deaf Yankee ear didn't really hear the story. Oh, I was impressed with the lively characterizations, the solid structure, and the "social commentary" of the story—it happened to be "Petrified Man"—but I was nowhere near the story itself in my reading. Then, in preparing for a film about Miss Welty, I listened to a recording (a Caedmon recording no less!) of "Why I Live at the P.O.," a Welty story I head read many times. As I listened, I began to "read" the story anew, because a wholly fresh world of sound, of rare good talk, opened up to me. I now try to read all stories, as all good readers should, with the ear as well as the eye.[92]

Moore identifies a key benefit: helping listeners become acquainted with unfamiliar soundscapes, for all audiences have "tone-deaf" ears to one culture or another. In such cases, the reader's imagined voice seldom lives up to the vibrancy of actual speech. "Reading" with the ear instead of the eye gave

Moore a different and, in his view, superior comprehension of the tale. It helped him to think of Welty as a storyteller who drew on the conversations burbling around her while growing up in Jackson, Mississippi. More important, such accounts offered a model for the potential conversion of other listeners—anyone else with a "tone-deaf Yankee ear"—wondering whether Caedmon's albums were worth hearing for themselves.

The Literary World on EP

Caedmon promoted its catalog as a library of great books—what one reviewer deemed "the literary world on EP [extended play]."[93] For those who wanted to read the classics, Caedmon's records reproduced them verbatim. But Caedmon did more than replicate texts. Whereas charities for people with impaired vision worried about unfaithful reproductions being treated as inferior, Caedmon had less at stake in preserving a book's every detail. Many of its recordings did adhere to the original. Yet, not infrequently, Caedmon blithely disregarded fidelity by abridging, adapting, or enhancing the printed text with a dramatic cast and sound effects.[94]

The specter of abridgment haunts the audiobook industry to this day. The limited playing times on cylinders, records, cassettes, and compact discs have long tempted publishers to hold the listener's attention and reduce costs by cutting books short. The audiobook's reputation has suffered as a result. Abridgments seem to confirm suspicions that listening to books is less demanding than reading them. According to this line of thought, audiobook consumers not only allow someone else to read for them; they don't even read every page.

The American Foundation for the Blind and the Royal National Institute of Blind People both prohibited abridgments to ensure that their constituencies received the same credit as everyone else for reading books. Doing otherwise risked being perceived as substandard in terms of literacy. Yet, even though Caedmon routinely abridged the author's work, it showed little anxiety about being taken seriously. The company's justification? Shortening narratives was a commercial necessity, not an aesthetic preference. Caedmon flaunted brevity as a selling point.

Not all publishers chose to abridge books in the 1950s. In fact, competitors used the LP record's extended playing time to record entire novels. The Audio Book Company promoted 16 rpm discs as a technological breakthrough, for example, allowing audiences to hear unabridged books for the first time.

It specialized in classic literature from Plato's *Crito* to *The Autobiography of Benjamin Franklin*. The company's slogan: "Great Literature in High-Fidelity."[95] The albums were bookish, if not actual books. They mimicked bibliographic conventions by replicating book covers, pages, and maps. The twenty-six-record New Testament even smelled like a Bible thanks to its gilt-stamped leather cover.[96]

Similarly, Libraphone advertised entire works of literature. It heralded a new era in artistic production (" 'Talking books' are a New Literary Medium for All") when publishing *The Great Gatsby* unabridged in 1953 (Figure 7.4).[97] Like Caedmon and other commercial labels, Libraphone aimed to expand the market beyond people with vision impairments. To this end, the album sleeve described "reading by ear" to be intimate, but not too intimate: "The effect is that of a personal friend reading aloud—flawlessly, tirelessly, and with dramatic feeling—and yet never intruding his personality between you and the author."[98] Such advertisements sought to create space for recorded books alongside printed ones or other forms of entertainment altogether.

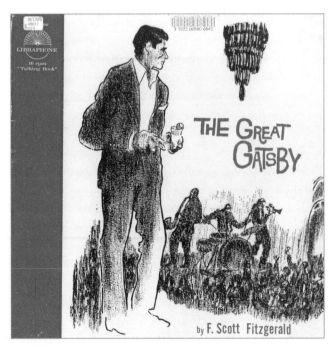

Figure 7.4. Libraphone's *The Great Gatsby* (1953) read by Alexander Scourby.

Caedmon recordings typically fit onto a single or double album sold for $4.95 per disc. The 33⅓ rpm microgroove vinyl records held approximately twenty minutes of material per side. This was an improvement over 78 rpm discs, which played for fewer than five minutes. But, to fit onto an album, most novels still required substantial cuts. What remained: the first four chapters of *Oliver Twist;* an excerpt from *Anna Karenina;* soliloquies from *Ulysses.* Actress-cum-author Ally Sheedy spoke candidly about the process: "To fit the book on to the record, I had to make a few cuts."[99] Stephen Crane's *The Red Badge of Courage* and other albums even directed listeners who wanted the full story to Random House's Modern Library.

More commonly, albums presented abridgment as a kind of curation. *Moll Flanders* was "skilfully shortened," and *Lady Chatterley's Lover* a "choice distillation."[100] Lawrence's album acknowledged the risks in slashing a novel whose craftsmanship had been cited by its author as a defense against charges of sensationalism. Yet Caedmon's "distillation" pledged neither to exploit nor to evade controversial passages. Limiting the point of view to Constance Chatterley, proposed the editors, managed to retain every theme and nuance of Lawrence's poetic style. In other words, the abridged recording sacrificed nothing and maybe even benefited from the cuts.

Other albums claimed to preserve the book's spirit, if not its words. The Shakespeare collection presented "a true essence of *Macbeth,*" not "a chopped-up series of disconnected speeches."[101] The same with Oscar Wilde's *The Picture of Dorian Gray:* "Although necessarily shortened, the book's essence is transmitted perfectly."[102] Again, the recording sacrificed nothing—or so we're told. For the editors, pruning superfluous details enabled audiences to focus on what really mattered. Omitting the "he saids" from the Bible's Book of Job not only sped things along but also highlighted the remaining dialogue's grandeur.[103]

Caedmon showed little remorse about crossing the line between abridgment and adaptation. In fact, quite the opposite: it flaunted departures from the script. Whereas the Library of Congress's talking books were verbatim recordings, and sometimes even reproduced the original book's mistakes, Caedmon set its recordings apart when given the chance. An album of Galway Kinnell's poetry, for example, emphasized the poet's tendency to revise lines during performances. Kinnell's prefatory note described them as improvements:

Most of these changes were made while I was reading the poems to audiences. Standing at the podium, just about to say a line, I would feel come over me a definite reluctance to say it as written. Gradually I learned to trust this reluctance. I would either drop the line altogether (discovering the poem did not suffer from the loss but improved on account of it), or else invent on the spot a revision of it. I would write these changes into my copies of the books and use the altered versions in subsequent readings.[104]

Caedmon's marketing campaign relished such discrepancies even if they risked undermining the rest of the catalog's credibility. As Charles Bernstein has argued, the poet's performance both stands on its own and makes us think differently about the original publication.[105] It instigates a new—and, for many, controversial—way of thinking about poetry as an evolving, exploratory process rather than a finished body of work.

Dramatizations were another way in which Caedmon strayed from the original book. It was common for plays, films, musicals, and other dramatic productions to use full casts; but literary adaptations sometimes did too. An eight-person cast performed P. G. Wodehouse's *Jeeves,* for example, and the Mouse, Mock Turtle, and hookah-smoking Caterpillar heard on *Alice in Wonderland* "sound madder than ever they did between the covers of the book."[106] *Through the Looking-Glass* likewise rounded out the cast with Tweedledum, Tweedledee, and Humpty Dumpty, not to mention a talking Tiger Lily.[107]

Even poetry was susceptible to dramatization. Caedmon recorded 56 of the original 244 poems in Edgar Lee Masters's *Spoon River Anthology.* Instead of a single speaker doing all of the voices, a different one recited each poem. "But where do you find that many actors who can be taught to read poetry with Midwestern accents?" asked the album. "Better to find fifty-six people with good Midwestern accents and teach each one to read a poem." Bona fide Milwaukee citizens played most of the roles. (They were recruited by a professor at the University of Wisconsin.) You can hear an actual banker, barber, farmer, minister, and stockbroker—all good honest folks representing the antithesis of the Broadway stage actor. The album credits the "townspeople of Milwaukee."[108]

Caedmon's records faithfully reproduced their literary heritage while at the same time seeking to exploit the new medium. They did so by embellishing the printed page with sound effects. Whereas talking books made for blind people tried to replicate the printed page, commercial companies had greater latitude to experiment. Traditionalists would stick with print in any case.

In this respect, Caedmon resembled other commercial ventures such as Bubble Books, a series of children's records manufactured in the United States and Britain in 1917. These short, illustrated books came packaged with three five-and-a-half-inch records. The series centered on a lonely boy given a magical pipe, out of which floated bubbles holding Mother Goose characters. Hence the label: "The Harper-Columbia Book That Sings."[109] The editor's moment of inspiration came while composing children's verses and listening to a phonograph at the same time. Advertisements emphasized the novelty of combining books with other media: "Your children have had stories—they've had pictures—and music. But never before have they had all three together."[110] Bubble Books represented a form of entertainment somewhere in between books and toys.[111]

Children's records tapped into a rich oral tradition of nursery rhymes told by mothers everywhere. Yet parents could hardly compete. Carol Channing sang and snapped her fingers while reading the *Madeline* stories, and Boris Karloff's *The Pied Piper* came with "some slithery pied-piper music" taken from a Folkways album.[112] Caedmon's Mother Goose collection even set the nursery rhymes to music composed by Broadway's Hershy Kay, who gave the traditional melodies a makeover using cakewalks, conga rhythms, and jazz. "And has anyone ever before *heard* starlight?" the album asks before playing "Twinkle, Twinkle, Little Star."[113]

Even books for adults used musical accompaniment. A full-cast recording evoked Dickens's London in this way: "What can be better than *A Christmas Carol* with all of the voices, the bells, the music, the laughter and the ghostly shivers recorded imaginatively and faithfully?"[114] Other records added period flourishes. Welsh harpist Osian Ellis played on *Tristan and Iseult,* for example, and *Caedmon's Hymn* featured music played on a small, six-stringed harp modeled after one belonging to an East Anglian king from Caedmon's time. (It made little difference that no one knew what kind of music had actually been played on it.[115]) Of course, the most important sound was the human voice.

Carusos of the Spoken Word

Writers frequently read their work for Caedmon. Hearing the author's voice was an enticing prospect for fans who had few opportunities to do so before publishers began recording literature. As Derek Furr has observed, "Caedmon's purpose was to capitalize on the poetic voice as entertainment."[116] Titles announcing as much—*Arthur C. Clarke Reads His "2001: A Space Odyssey"* or *The Poetry and Voice of Margaret Atwood*—foregrounded the author's presence well into the 1960s and 1970s.[117] The records appealed to those who felt that the author's voice helped them to understand and develop a relationship to literature differently from on the page.

Voice offered the illusion of an author's presence. The *Saturday Review,* for instance, applauded Caedmon's efforts "to lessen the gap between author and reader."[118] Audiences responded to the recorded voice as if the author were speaking directly to them. Whereas readers of print longed for direct contact with the author, spoken word recordings seemed to give them that access. Records felt intimate, even if they were just another form of mediation.

Canny authors made the most of this sentiment. Richard Bach, for example, complained on one album that books prevented him from communing with readers in person: "Recording a book in sound is different. Somehow, reading aloud, I *can* be there for an hour with you, and put to rest an old question: do writers of books really have voices and bodies, and is it possible ever to reach across the space between warm words and cool appearance?"[119] Yes, writers of books really did have voices and bodies. Personal flourishes—from Thomas's slang-ridden quips to Sandburg's angry verbal footnotes—reinforced this sense of contact with an actual person, as did the "word-portrait" obtained by leaving on the microphone while Walter de la Mare chatted with Caedmon's engineer, Peter Bartók.[120] Recordings made outside the studio further helped to capture the atmosphere of a live event. You can hear trucks passing in the background while "Brother Antoninus" (William Everson) delivers his extemporaneous meditations at Wesleyan University.[121]

Thomas Mann's daughter Monika observed that spoken word recordings somehow felt more intimate than other media: "If the photograph or handwriting exude something of a man's character, then the reproduction of his voice does so even more."[122] For her, the public's fascination with authenticity was what drew them to records. The album's liner notes reinforced this notion of personal access. For those of us who missed her father's readings, she conjures a picture: the bespectacled author sitting cross-legged on a velvet-draped chair, one hand holding the manuscript and the other a cigar, foot swaying to the prose's rhythm, head inclined to one side while he strokes his temples. The reading ends, she tells us, with a personal touch: Mann's laugh.

Caedmon emphasized the phonograph's role in making writers accessible to everyone while at the same time providing intimate, one-on-one contact with them. Carl Sandburg's conversational ease and homely speech, displayed during a series of lectures given across the country, made him a popular candidate for recording.[123] Caedmon brought the lectures into the homes of those who missed him: "Now, in this recording he belongs to everyone."[124] Sandburg was a storyteller capable of speaking to adults and children alike. On one album's cover, Hollywood screenwriter Ben Hecht recalled him having "the finest voice I ever heard, reading or talking."[125] Caedmon's live recordings alternated between the two in order to re-create the atmosphere of an overheard conversation, not a staged event. The Lincoln album describes Sandburg's delivery as "the manner of a man reminiscing about a friend."[126] Another album tells of Sandburg staying up late at night with companions, sipping bourbon while strumming a guitar and singing. These portraits framed the listening experience. "The readings on this album have something of the quality of such a session," it promised.[127] Listeners were meant to feel part of the gig.

Caedmon answered the question on many readers' minds: What did authors sound like? There were few chances to hear authors speak in the 1950s. Caedmon's records allowed many readers to hear them for the first time. Hearing an author's accent could be a revelation. Whereas imagined voices might be preternaturally neutral, essentially voices from nowhere, authors' actual voices were marked by distinctive traces of their upbringing or by what Roland Barthes called their "grain."[128]

Donald Hall recalled listening to poetry records when he arrived at Harvard in 1947. This was his first encounter with poets' voices and, consequently, it forced him to adjust the imagined ones in his head. He was especially struck by the British accents of Auden and other cosmopolitan poets, a jarring contrast between what Hall called "the mind's ear" and "the ear's ear."[129] Hearing the real thing enabled him to recalibrate the voice invoked by the page.

Caedmon's records had a similar effect on readers. At one end of the spectrum, Ogden Nash's "Bostonian propriety" supposedly made his satirical light verse all the more amusing.[130] At the spectrum's other end was Faulkner's Mississippi drawl: "the serenity, the deep-south way with words, the unaffected ease with which Faulkner drifts into Yoknapatawpha dialect," and, of course, the author's signature sentences that went on for pages.[131] The author was not always so well received. Toni Morrison found his reading "horrifying."[132]

Sometimes authors read their work in a distinctive way forever setting it apart from the page. J. R. R. Tolkien gave one such performance. While staying at the house of George Sayer in 1952, Tolkien recorded poems from his unpublished manuscript, *The Lord of the Rings,* on a Ferrograph tape recorder in order to hear how they sounded to other people.[133] Caedmon's *The Hobbit* duplicates the riddle scene he read that day in Malvern. More to the point, the album features Elvish poems and songs like "Troll Sat Alone" (loosely set to the English folk tune "The Fox and the Hens"). Hence the album's title: *J. R. R. Tolkien Reads and Sings His "The Hobbit" and "The Fellowship of the Ring."*[134] Similarly, Caedmon's *The Lord of the Rings* contains a passage of Elvish sung to plainchant. Although the book's appendices include instructions on how to read Tolkien's invented language, the album gives fans a chance to hear it spoken by the author himself. Auden singled out the Elvish verse as a reason to listen to Tolkien (even if he was disappointed not to hear Rohan poetry too).[135]

Elvish was one of many languages in Caedmon's catalog. Caedmon has been accused of making high culture accessible to the masses through sound-recording technology. But many of its titles remained inaccessible. Literature recorded in its original language exemplifies one way in which the label refused to compromise artistic integrity in the interest of making material accessible. Audiences could hear Lotte Lehmann recite the *Rosenkavalier* libretto in German, for instance, or Katina Paxinou perform *Oedipus Rex* in Greek. Other untranslated writers include Mann reading in German; Jean Cocteau, Jean Genet, Albert Camus, and Colette in French; Diego Rivera, Pablo Neruda, and Juan Ramón Jiménez in Spanish; George Seferis in Greek; and Yevgeny Yevtushenko in Russian. Caedmon's audience could hear the work of Sophocles, Voltaire, Goethe, Baudelaire, Rilke, Lorca, and Pasternak read aloud too, just not in English.

Albums made in their mother tongues show a marked disregard for commercial considerations—or at least a patron in the form of university libraries. The editors nevertheless tried to persuade customers that great literature needs no translation. One album notes how the American audiences at Yevtushenko's readings "responded to the fervor of his delivery even when they did not understand the words."[136] Others suggest that lyric poetry is capable of moving audiences despite language barriers. "Yet there is impact for the non-German reader in this interpretation of Rilke," explain the editors, "for as lyric it is meant to be heard and a good deal of emotional meaning is apparent simply from the rendition."[137] If few concessions were made to the average American's monolingualism, some albums at least recited the poems in English too.

Caedmon wanted to convince audiences that reading aloud could make the experience of reading great books even better. Albums used words like "revelatory" to intimate hidden dimensions revealed through speech alone. Thus, we are told that "poetry fully alive on the page becomes magically potent" during Archibald MacLeish's performance at Uphill Farm.[138] Newspaper reports describing this reading as "one of the first real phonograph events of 1953" helped Caedmon promote the album as both live performance and timeless art.[139] Favorable reviews emblazoned on Caedmon's other album jackets likewise bolstered the author's dramatic credentials. The *New York Times, High Fidelity,* and *Harper's* all praised T. S. Eliot as a performer: "Eliot is one of the great readers-aloud of this century."[140] (The statement is not as exaggerated as it might seem: Eliot once lectured to a stadium filled with almost 14,000 people.[141])

Yet the case for hearing authors was hardly straightforward. The strongest argument against hearing them was that they could be terrible readers. The Harvard professor who started the first recorded poetry series insisted as much. In his view, people seldom listened to literature because they had few opportunities to hear it done well.[142] Ernest Hemingway's Caedmon album put it best: "You cannot expect a writer to be trained in elocution."[143]

Other albums likewise acknowledged that writers could be poor readers. One concedes, "Not all who write can read; often the spoken word added to the written adds up to nothing much."[144] The liner notes to Judith Merril's album begin with the usual spiel about the tales being better heard than read before acknowledging how rare this is: "That is a statement that cannot always be made about writers doing readings from their own work. So many of the best of them stutter or mumble, or do not seem to understand how to say out loud what they have said so well in print."[145] Not everyone could be Dylan Thomas. Ursula Le Guin recalled her self-consciousness about joining Caedmon's renowned roster. She confessed of *Gwilan's Harp:* "I had to read it in my own God-given croak; and in the corner of my mind, all the while, Dylan Thomas was weeping softly."[146]

Thomas was indisputably the voice of Caedmon Records. No author drew as much attention to the virtues (and vices) of reading aloud. He was the first writer recorded for the series. His records were consistently among the label's best sellers. His lifestyle proved to be as popular as his verse. And the poet's untimely death elevated him to legendary status. In total, Caedmon issued twenty-three records of Thomas's readings.

Thomas's bravura performances exemplified the divide between recordings made for people who were blind and commercial ones sold to the public. Whereas talking books favored straight reading, a style that shied away from the overly dramatic, commercial labels courted authors, actors, and entertainers to enliven the print. Thomas was among the entertainers. As he was fond of saying, the page is for examining how the poem works, the stage for giving the poem the works.[147] The *Saturday Review* felt that his virtuoso recitations made the poetry on the printed page seem dull by comparison.[148] Distinguished music critic Edward Tatnall Canby described "A Child's Christmas in Wales" as "an unforgettable experience in the listening; surely this Christmas story ranks (in its spoken form, at least) among the great expressions of the language."[149] The story attracted little attention before Thomas read it aloud. It was published as a book only after Caedmon's recording came out and has not been out of print since.

Thomas was already a seasoned vocalist before touring America. He regularly appeared on BBC radio series such as *Book of Verse* and the *Third Programme*. Overall, he made more than 150 broadcasts for the BBC. Thomas made a profound impression during his four visits to America between 1950 and his death in November 1953 at the age of thirty-nine. During that time, he read his work at universities and other venues. The typical reading began with an informal speech, followed by verse written by Thomas Hardy and other poets (the "jam" before the "pill" of his own poems, Thomas used to say). Despite describing Thomas's studio sessions in detail, most of Caedmon's albums were posthumously culled from previous recordings made by universities, radio stations, the Library of Congress, the Museum of Modern Art, and the BBC.

Thomas's acquaintances have tried to characterize what made him so distinctive. All of them go right to what Louis MacNeice called the "organ voice."[150] Thomas's booming speech, with its Anglicized accent derived from elocution lessons as a child, and subtle Welsh lilt, perfectly suited for melodious verse, were at least as famous as the poems. Today many of us still find it difficult to read Thomas's poems without hearing the Caedmon voice in our heads. In this sense, he was the perfect advertisement. The *New York Times Book Review* once predicted that Thomas would be the first modern author remembered as both a writer and a reciter of verse.[151]

The chanting made it clear that you were hearing poetry. "I myself chant aloud in a sonorous voice every poem I read," Thomas confided to a friend.[152]

In doing so, he emulated Yeats, who had sought to revive the lost art of chanting verse. Yeats would never open a book again, he once declared, if people knew how to read verse aloud.[153] Despite being described as the best reciter of poetry since Yeats, however, Thomas downplayed his talents, saying of his delivery, "I'm afraid it's second-rate Charles Laughton."[154]

Caedmon's editors described him as a rotund little figure on stage who spoke with an "unforgettable" voice.[155] Paul Kresh called him the "Caruso of the spoken word."[156] Audiences described the recitations using sorcerer's terms such as "enchanting" and "entrancing" to convey how spellbound they felt by his voice. Poet and poems alike were frequently compared to music, their wordplay and lyricism singled out as a pleasure to hear. Too pleasurable, for some. Critics have long debated whether Thomas's verse amounted to more than pretty sounds. Robert Graves, for one, accused Thomas of being too "drunk with melody" to care whether the words made any sense.[157] Naysayers described his performance style as bombastic and old-fashioned.[158] Thomas's full-throated delivery certainly sets him apart from today's preference for understatement at poetry readings.

There were talented readers before Thomas, but his voice was one of the first to reach a mass audience through sound-recording technology.[159] According to one advertisement, "All who have written of Dylan Thomas' recordings agree the voice holds the absolute key to the works. And the works, being those of genius, move profoundly all who hear and read them. At no former time in history has a poet's own voice been treasured and familiar in so many thousands of homes."[160] That last statement would come across as hyperbole except that Thomas's album was, in fact, one of the first spoken word recordings to reach a mass audience of American consumers.[161] Suburban homes throughout the country could play his verse on demand.

Holdridge and Mantell have told interviewers that their aim was to recreate a poem's moment of inspiration.[162] According to this way of thinking (widely shared among oral interpretation departments at American universities), an author's reading recalled, in Proustian fashion, the original sentiments driving the creative act. Yet Thomas, who often mused on the idea, reached the opposite conclusion. During one radio broadcast, he claimed not to be able to remember the original impulses behind his poems; and even if he could, the readings could only "parrot" them. In the following excerpt, Thomas repeats the noble goal only to undermine it:

"And all that a reader-aloud of his own poems can hope to do is to try to put across his own memory of the original impulses behind his poems, deepening, maybe, and if only for a moment, the inner meaning of the words on the printed pages." How I wish I could agree whole-heartedly with that, let alone hope to achieve it![163]

Instead, Thomas warned of the twin perils of mawkish, melodramatic read-ings, on the one hand, and flat, detached readings, on the other hand. It is the dilemma faced by anyone who reads aloud.

Not everyone had Thomas's booming voice even if they wanted to be melo-dramatic. For this reason, Caedmon found replacements to read the work of dead authors, reluctant ones, and those who were poor speakers. It sought to persuade book lovers that literature could be enhanced not only by the au-thor's voice but also by those of professional actors. This was hardly a surprise considering that Caedmon's first recording was of Laurence Olivier delivering a eulogy for King George VI, a tribute described as "beautifully written and yet more beautifully read."[164]

Actors had performed literature since Edison's time. Tennyson recorded his verse, for example, but so did actors and elocutionists including Henry Ainley, Rose Coughlan, Canon Fleming, and Lewis Waller. Caedmon revived this tradition, encouraging actors to read as the authors themselves might have done. "Unless the author himself were to read his poetry, one could never be quite sure of meanings and nuances," explains the anthology *Hearing Poetry.* "The best thought was to find actors of special sensitivity and intelligence, and then to let them thrash out each question with a director who was himself devoted to poetry."[165]

A series that began with a contemporary poet went on to record the clas-sics from Chaucer to Proust, all voiced by actors. When reading *Childe Harold's Pilgrimage,* matinee idol Tyrone Power was said not merely to have recited Byron's verse but to have played Byron himself. The series' emphasis on authorial intention reassured traditionalists while at the same time giving actors scope to entertain less discriminating audiences. Cyril Cusack's *A Por-trait of the Artist as a Young Man* is read in an appropriately sensitive manner, we are told, and Hurd Hatfield's *The Picture of Dorian Gray* faithfully recreates the novel's fin-de-siècle atmosphere.

No one seemed to mind the contradiction in portraying actors as skilled decipherers of an author's intention while at the same time commending their own ingenious insights. For Caedmon, the actor's recording was a work of art in its own right. Its records allowed one to hear multiple renditions of a favorite work, just as one could savor *Hamlet* performed by different troupes, each with its own charm. The *Boston Globe* praised Basil Rathbone for making familiar pieces such as "The Raven" "take on a dramatic tension that makes them seem new."[166] Caedmon stressed the word "interpretation" when describing the work of other actors like Carol Channing and Paul Scofield.

Above all else, actors entertained. They read in ways that would hold the attention of audiences not yet accustomed to reading with their ears. Talking books made for visually impaired people had long stressed the need for a neutral style of reading to avoid interfering with the reader's interpretation. Commercial publishers did not share this concern for letting readers do all of the work. When I asked Holdridge how she felt about dramatizations, she told me, "I wouldn't dream of recording fiction in a 'neutral' voice. What italics, long dashes, ellipses, and exclamation points do on the printed page, the voice must do on the recorded version."[167] Speakers followed the book's cues like a script while at the same time adapting them for the microphone. Such decisions became increasingly important throughout the audiobook industry once spoken word recordings began to compete with other forms of entertainment, namely radio, television, and film, while at the same time seeking to preserve their affiliation with the venerable tradition of the printed word.

Caedmon began making spoken word recordings at a time when few readers had ever considered listening to literature. There were seldom opportunities to do so apart from the odd record of verse. Advances in sound-recording technology made it possible for Caedmon and other labels to make substantial literary recordings that raised perplexing questions about the relationship between books and their successors. Caedmon's mission was to persuade potential customers that spoken word recordings not only reproduced great works of literature verbatim but also enhanced the experience of reading them. It insisted that many tales—from Greek epics to *Leaves of Grass* and *Winnie the Pooh*—were better heard than read. Ancient tales had been composed for oral performance, after all, and the right voice could enrich even modern ones designed for the page. Through Caedmon's records, many people heard for the first time the voices of writers they had been reading for years. Others listened to skilled performers using their vocal talents to discover hidden depths to the writing. In each case, Caedmon sought a balance between venerating the nation's literary heritage and turning books into something new.

Caedmon persuaded enough people to listen to books for the company to succeed, at least in financial terms. The small label established after Thomas's poetry reading grew into a multi-million-dollar company. Holdridge and Mantell sold the label in 1970 to D. C. Heath (owned by Raytheon), who sold the company in 1987 to Harper & Row (now HarperCollins), which continues to release the Caedmon backlist and to produce new recordings. Yet, despite Caedmon's commercial success and the industry's growth during the 1960s and 1970s, skeptics continued to call into question the legitimacy of spoken word albums, just as Cecil Day-Lewis had predicted in 1935.

Nearly half a century later, at a centennial conference held in New York on the topic of the phonograph, publisher Claire Brook ended her presentation by expressing personal discomfort at the prospect of reading being replaced by listening. For her, spoken word recordings were little more than "sound gimmicks" that had become all too common in schools: "I find the fact that Caedmon Records has five science-fiction yarns on its top-ten list for 1977 distressing; it suggests that the time-honored tradition of reading aloud has gone beyond being an intimate family custom or an accommodation for the blind and has instead become a flourishing business servicing those who will not read."[168] Brook's rallying cry acknowledged the proliferation of spoken word recordings while at the same time expressing people's growing discomfort toward the changes in reading habits linked to them. Such anxieties would become even more acute in the following decades as reading moved outside the home and reached new audiences through the next big thing in sound recording: cassette tapes.

8

Tapeworms

Duvall Hecht was stuck in traffic when the idea came to him. Every day he drove one hundred miles from his home in Newport Beach to a brokerage firm in Los Angeles. The two-hour journey got to him. "I became frantic with the commute," he recalled. "It's such a terribly numbing experience."[1] Radio didn't help. He wanted more mental stimulation than could be provided by the Top 40, news, and commercials: "My brain was turning into cottage cheese!"[2] If only there were a better way to pass the time.

Hecht wrote to every organization he could think of for something to listen to while driving. What he found were motivational speeches, marketing seminars, meditation courses, language tutorials, and poetry. Caedmon specialized in literary excerpts, and another company sold Plato's *Phaedrus* along with a handful of other classics. With a typical price of ten dollars for a sixty-minute recording, however, these options were hardly practical for commuters. The only full-length books he could find were made by the Library of Congress exclusively for people with vision impairments. Still, Hecht felt certain that he wasn't alone. Surely other commuters shared his wish for something worthwhile to occupy their minds?

Books on Tape (hereafter BOT), the company founded by Hecht in 1975, went on to become one of the world's largest audio publishers. Hecht's company was the first to focus exclusively on unabridged recordings of books. Its catalog held more full-length books than any other source and provided countless hours of distraction to the nation's drivers. The company's founding principle: Americans wanted to read more books but lacked the time to do so. In response, BOT came up with a way for them to read without disrupting their busy schedules. It did so by turning the mindless activity of driving into an opportunity to hear books read aloud.

The company started out small. Hecht and his wife, Sigrid, initially rented the cassettes out of their home (Figure 8.1). Sales the first year amounted to $17,000. Eight years later, the company posted annual revenues of $1.5 million, and triple that amount by 1987. By then, the company had over 60,000 subscribers. Hecht's hunch had been right that other people on the road sought company too. George Will's nationally syndicated newspaper column compared Hecht to quintessentially American entrepreneurs like Thomas Edison and Henry Ford who converted their dissatisfaction with the world into inventions that benefit the rest of us.[3] Will was one of the company's converts.

BOT grew along with the industry as a whole. By the mid-1980s, mail-order and retail sales of taped books amounted to approximately $170 million, with

Figure 8.1. Duvall and Sigrid Hecht at the offices of Books on Tape.

a yearly growth rate of 10–15 percent.[4] The first industry guide, *On Cassette,* lists nearly 22,000 titles produced by 250 different companies.[5] During a period in which the number of Americans reading books declined by 5 percent, audio publishers found a way to increase the number of people in contact with books.[6]

BOT and other audio publishers gradually changed the reputation of taped books as a way of reading associated exclusively with blind people. The growth of the suburbs, increased commuting distances, and the widespread availability of tape players dramatically expanded the audience for taped books during the 1970s and 1980s. The press reported the trend with headlines like "Books for the Blind and the Busy."[7] In 1984, the *St. Petersburg Times* reported that only 2 percent of recorded books were used by people with vision impairments; people without difficulties seeing accounted for the remaining 98 percent.[8] Listening had once been derided as the lazy man's way to read; nowadays, taped books are for hardworking folks with little time for leisure.

Yet changing people's minds about recorded books was no easy task. BOT's predecessors had faced similar challenges in changing attitudes toward reading. The Library of Congress had to convince people that reading could be done with the ears as well as the eyes and fingers. Similarly, Caedmon needed to persuade audiences that sound technology was compatible with serious literature. BOT faced the biggest challenge yet. It had to convince audiences that books could be read while doing other things at the same time. Could you really read a book behind the wheel of a car?

A Rental Library in Sound

Hecht had no experience in the publishing industry before starting BOT. He wasn't even a devoted reader. "I didn't read a book for 25 years after I got out of Stanford," he told the alumni magazine.[9] He was simply too tired after a full day's work to get past page two. What Hecht did have was an impressive track record of achieving goals. He graduated from Stanford and won an Olympic gold medal for rowing in 1956. But there were plenty of reasons not to take up a new challenge at the age of forty-five. He was working in management for Bateman Eichler, Hill Richards stock brokerage and coaching the UCLA rowing squad. He had a wife and three children. And he had a mortgage.[10] None of this stopped him from selling his 1965 Porsche for $4,500 in order to start his own company.

The first step was to determine whether there really were as many fed-up commuters as Hecht imagined. In 1973, he sent a letter headed "Do you wish you had more time to read?" to 500 people in the Orange County suburbs. The mailing described BOT as a library of best-selling books recorded on cassette tapes that were available for rental through the mail. An encouraging 5 percent of recipients asked for further information. These inquiries confirmed that there was indeed a potential market of discontent drivers with an interest in reading books; even a small percentage of the nation's commuters would be enough to sustain the business. The next steps were to take on partners, raise $10,000 in capital, and begin the protracted pursuit of recording rights.[11] BOT was incorporated on February 11, 1974.[12] The company's subsequent mailing campaign brought its catalog to the attention of 35,000 Los Angeles and Orange County commuters.

Hecht envisioned BOT as "a rental library in sound."[13] Its business model resembled the subscription libraries of the eighteenth and nineteenth centuries, when purchasing books was too expensive for most people.[14] Here's how it worked: Customers signed up by telephoning a toll-free number or replying by mail to the small ads placed in California's newspapers (Figure 8.2). Subscribers paid no dues or initiation fees, and tapes selected from BOT's catalog arrived at their doors in prestamped cardboard boxes for easy return (Figure 8.3). Rental fees ranged from $6.50 to $15.00 in order to compete with the hardback price. Books averaged from eight to twelve hours of listening time and could be kept

Figure 8.2. Classified ad placed in newspapers and magazines throughout the country.

Figure 8.3. Artwork from the cover of Books on Tape's 1983 catalog.

for thirty days without penalty; longer books were split into separate sets of ninety-minute tapes (*War and Peace* required four of them). The company decided to rent tapes because they were too expensive to sell outright. The average recorded book cost close to fifty dollars—roughly four to five times the rental price. Although BOT did sell directly to libraries and customers, most people (over 85 percent) rented. According to Hecht's calculations, renting a book cost under one dollar per hour, slightly less than the price of going to the movies.

BOT saw itself as the audio equivalent to the nation's best-known mail-order book business. "I think it is a nascent 'Book of the Month Club,'" Hecht wrote to a friend in 1974.[15] That company represented a successful business model for distributing books by mail order.[16] Since 1926, the Book-of-the-Month Club had delivered literature to a mass market through the canny use of marketing techniques.[17] Hecht was right in many respects. Both companies made books accessible to audiences neglected by traditional publishers. In different ways, they offered customers a means to keep up with current writing despite the hectic pace of modern life. And, like the Book-of-the-Month Club, BOT appealed to people who wished to present themselves as sophisticated. Listening to books made this group feel as if they were gaining an education as well as a competitive edge in the business world. BOT's marketing campaign implied that listening to books would make its clients smarter, more interesting at parties, and more successful in business. One of the company's proposed mottos: "Successful people everywhere keep up with Books On Tape."[18]

BOT's clientele resembled the typical fiction reader of the 1980s in almost every way.[19] The group's distinguishing characteristic was a desire to read

accompanied by a lack of time, but not resources, to do so. A newsletter described the typical customer profile as follows:

> As a B.O.T. subscriber, chances are you received a B.A. or B.S. ten to
> twenty years ago; went on to graduate school or business, law or medicine;
> now operate as a sole proprietor or upper-level executive in any of a number
> of entrepreneurial activities. You live fifty-two minutes from your office.
> You work fourteen hours a day.
>
> Until B.O.T., there was never any time for books, a fact which made
> you feel more than a little depressed. On any number of occasions you
> have said, "I wish I had more time for reading!"[20]

In 1986, the company's market research identified an affluent clientele living in
areas where incomes, property values, and education levels exceeded the national average.[21] Competitors described their markets in similar terms: affluent,
highly educated professionals in their forties who drive a lot.[22] A librarian in
Washington, DC, described them as "the yuppie type."[23] They were professionals who turned to technology to help cope with demanding schedules.

BOT's first book was George Plimpton's *Paper Lion.* This farcical tale of a
writer trying out for quarterback of the Detroit Lions had originally appeared
in *Sports Illustrated* and afterward been made into a film. The company sought
a narrator from among Los Angeles's pool of aspiring actors. Since audiobook
narration was not yet common, the Hechts placed classified ads in local papers as well as at the nearby South Coast Repertory Theater, where one caught
the eye of Jake Gardiner, who agreed to read for five dollars an hour.[24] In
Hecht's recollection, the first book was made in his living room on a small
open-reel tape recorder.[25] (The amateurish production, marred by mistakes
and erratic volume levels, is a memento of the industry's modest origins.) Afterward, the company reserved a booth at the American Booksellers Association convention to promote its initial offerings: *Paper Lion,* H. L. Mencken's
Happy Days, Nancy Milford's *Zelda,* and Edward Cowan's *Oil and Water.* All
four titles met BOT's criteria: they were widely recognizable, appealing to a
variety of tastes, and fewer than 300 pages long. Most important, the company chose books to which it could obtain the legal rights.[26]

Obtaining permissions was the biggest obstacle to starting the business.
Nearly all books published in the twentieth century required a rights agreement. Yet publishers paid little attention to sound-recording rights because
the market was so small. Hecht recalled of the negotiations, "People in the

publishing business just did not know about rights for recordings."[27] They were often bundled with other subsidiary rights purchased by film studios that had no intention of making tapes; Frederick Forsyth's thrillers were unavailable for this reason.

Even determining who held the rights—author, agent, publisher, estate— could be time consuming. It took Hecht three years to secure the rights to Winston Churchill's memoirs. The company pursued William Faulkner, F. Scott Fitzgerald, Ernest Hemingway, James Joyce, Harper Lee, James Michener, Margaret Mitchell, and Danielle Steele for years too. In 1993, Hecht complained, "We have been trying to obtain rights in Proust's work since the day we started B-O-T!"[28] The company reached agreements with some of these authors; others, never. Willa Cather's will forbid reproducing her books in any form other than print, for example, and Hecht stopped pursuing Ayn Rand after her estate demanded information about the political orientation of BOT's clients.

Hecht estimated that permission was granted for one out of every ten books.[29] The liberal terms of BOT's licensing agreement, however, eventually persuaded enough publishers to release the recording rights. The contract was nonexclusive, could be canceled at any time, and did not conflict with radio, television, or motion picture claims. Authors received an advance royalty of one hundred dollars against earned royalties of 10 percent on all rentals and sales. The Authors Guild approved the terms in 1975. Still, no publisher wanted to be the first one associated with taped books. BOT's breakthrough came after obtaining the rights to Joseph Wambaugh's *The Onion Field,* a best-selling true-crime title that made the company credible in the eyes of publishers (Figure 8.4).

When it came to book selection, BOT cultivated the impression that it valued education as much as entertainment. Hecht described the company's aims in literary rather than commercial terms: "What we are striving to do is to be the source of spoken publication of all important authors of the 19th and 20th centuries."[30] He aspired to record approximately 5,000 titles by the year 2000. The ideal works were not only popular but also culturally significant. The company even had success with classics like Thoreau's *Walden,* an antidote to rush-hour traffic that was among its most requested titles.

Hecht's interest in tasteful curation for a broad readership owed a debt to print series like the Modern Library.[31] Yet the company's lofty aims were at odds with the taped book's middlebrow reputation and the constraints of a

Figure 8.4. Advertisement for *The Choirboys* by Joseph Wambaugh, one of the first major authors to allow his books to be recorded by Books on Tape.

clientele that sat behind the wheel, not a desk. Hecht rejected some books with weak plots or what he described as "hard to read" books.[32] Certain genres were simply not commercially viable. Hecht passed on Edna St. Vincent Millay, a Caedmon favorite, because poetry did not sell. He passed on other titles—a book on Bulgaria's Ferdinand I, for example—for being too specialized. When a subscriber requested literary criticism, Hecht explained that there was no market for it.[33] He described worthy books with poor sales potential as "merit books" that should rarely be added to the catalog.[34]

A few subscribers complained that BOT's catalog tilted toward mainstream best sellers. Their letters requested more women, African American, Native American, and gay writers. Other complaints highlight the perils in trying to provide both serious literature and commercial best sellers. *The Sensuous Woman*—the company's first book to be given an XX rating for explicit sex—drew the ire of those who felt that the catalog marginalized women. Worse, the press treated it as a joke, speculating about awkward moments for drivers and advising men to listen during vigorous exercise. Both women and men (including some of BOT's employees) complained that it was sexist, devoid of literary merit, and a throwback to an earlier era. Hecht assured correspondents that there was no "sexual bias" in the selection process, however, and promised to remedy the underrepresentation of women writers in future catalogs.[35]

Automobile Learning

BOT was born out of America's commuter boom. The number of commuters using private vehicles nearly doubled from forty-three million in 1960 to eighty-three million in 1980.[36] According to the American Automobile Association, Americans spent an average of three and a half hours per week commuting to work; the average was four hours a week in Southern California.[37] Californians possessed nearly nineteen million vehicles and the world's most extensive freeway system. The Los Angeles sprawl exemplified the postwar suburban lifestyle built around the car.[38]

The rest of the country did not lag far behind. By the mid-1980s, newspapers were reporting on "super-commuters" like David Dassaro, who drove nearly 250 miles a day from his home in Shavertown, Pennsylvania, to the bank he worked at in Brooklyn, New York.[39] The majority of commuters drove by themselves. Americans spent more time than ever alone in cars—a trend described by Raymond Williams as "mobile privatisation."[40] It was no coincidence that so many entrepreneurs resolved to start companies while stuck in traffic.

BOT's business model depended on the tape player's widespread availability in homes, in cars, and even on belts. Cassette tapes had been around since the 1960s, though they originally competed with eight-track cartridges. By 1977, tapes had triumphed.[41] Cassettes held several advantages over eight-tracks, especially when used in cars: they were more compact, more reliable, and easier to repair. Car manufacturers rapidly overcame what audio publishers called the "hardware barrier" stalling the growth of their markets.[42] *Travel and Leisure* magazine reported that nearly 3.7 million cassette players for cars were sold in the United States in 1977.[43] More than ten million automotive tape players were sold in 1978, according to the Electronic Industries Association.[44] The *Wall Street Journal* reported that people were turning their cars into "mobile libraries" in which they listened to Shakespeare.[45]

People had always found ways to read books in cars, it should be noted. Some did it the old-fashioned way. The novelist Walker Percy and his wife,

Bunt, took turns reading novels aloud to each other while on the road.[46] Another car-bound couple read to each other all of Dickens in six years.[47] Even solo drivers found ways to hear books. Some of BOT's initial subscribers traveled with their own tape players. Dale Walker, book editor of the *El Paso Times,* listened to *The White Nile* using a Sony cassette recorder set on the passenger seat.[48]

Meanwhile, the market for stereo equipment continued to grow. Only 3 percent of cars were equipped with cassette players in 1975.[49] The Electronics Industries Association estimated that 42.5 million automobiles in America had cassette tape players by the mid-1980s.[50] Sixty percent of households now had automobile tape cassette players.[51] People found tape players easy to use despite the headaches caused by defective tapes. BOT's customer service team spent much of its time advising customers on hardware problems; in 1979, there were up to five complaints a day about faulty cassettes.

America's commuters formed the bulk of BOT's market. One columnist observed that taped books were made for the I-95s of the United States.[52] Publishers estimated that over 90 percent of customers listened to books while driving.[53] *Northeast Woman*'s profile of a "born-again commuter," for example, listed every title heard by a driver who responded to one of BOT's newspaper ads.[54] Commuters viewed spoken word recordings as a way to use time to their advantage. Hecht predicted that there would be no need to recruit bored drivers—they would be desperate to join.

BOT's marketing campaign targeted discontented commuters using radio ads and billboards on congested freeways (Figure 8.5). In addition, the company expanded its campaign from book reviews to *Motorland, Trailer Life, On the Road,* and other travel magazines. By 1986, BOT was spending $30,000 per month on advertising to attract new customers.[55] A memorable radio ad began with a commuter complaining about wasted time before Jill Masters, one of BOT's narrators, intervened with a promise to read *Anna Karenina* to him.[56]

Commuters joined in order to make time behind the wheel useful. One of BOT's first inquiries came from a driver who described the 18,000 miles he had spent on the road as "wasted" time.[57] By contrast, a subscriber characterized his daily two-hour drive as "productive" time.[58] Taped books made it possible to spend these hours improving oneself. "Automobile learning" was the *Wall Street Journal*'s phrase for this emerging industry.[59] Subscribers viewed taped books as superior to radio in terms of cultural enrichment. In just over

Figure 8.5. Books on Tape billboard on a California freeway.

a year, a cardiologist from Long Island listened to twenty books by Dickens, Herman Melville, Joseph Conrad, and other writers left out of his college education.[60] Similarly, a dean at San Francisco's Golden Gate University listened to more than 500 novels while visiting military bases throughout California and Nevada.[61]

Books offered a welcome distraction from the tedium of the open road. Some drivers felt themselves to be on the verge of a nervous breakdown. A man who drove over 35,000 miles annually wrote that BOT's tapes "have kept me sane over these years."[62] Another commuter's daily drive from Pasadena to Century City would have been "unbearable" without them.[63] Taped books helped other drivers avoid road rage.[64] A fifty-seven-year-old salesman from Corona del Mar explained that, when listening to a book, "you really don't pay attention to the commute and it keeps you from getting *frustrated,* shall we say, because of a traffic jam."[65] Listening to books insulated drivers from traffic. Another commuter no longer found the Long Island Expressway "traumatic" now that he could listen to books.[66]

Taped books could even make driving enjoyable. "Rush hour driving has become the high point of my day," wrote one man. The escapism offered by books enabled him to travel—in his mind, at least—away from the Los Angeles freeways. "While surrounded by exasperated drivers in stop-and-go traffic," he continued, "I find myself visiting the Orient with Conrad."[67] Drivers frequently saw books as a form of escape. An Oakland salesman described being "transported" to another world while listening to Dirk Bogarde's autobiography.[68] Foreign settings held particular appeal for drivers. A woman listening to Ken Follett's *The Pillars of the Earth* exclaimed, "I've been able to be far away in early England instead of bored out of my mind with endless roads!"[69]

Commuters were not the only drivers tuned in. People listened while on vacation too. Taped books kept one married couple alert while sightseeing along the West Coast.[70] Listening to *Moby Dick* helped a father grow closer to his twelve-year-old son.[71] And *The Winthrop Woman* so absorbed the Stanley family while driving across the country that they asked for the second set of tapes to be delivered to Niagara Falls, their next stop.[72] Families didn't even need to listen to the same book. All four members of the Glassman family listened to their own books on portable cassette players during long trips.[73] Taped books helped drivers create personal space even on short trips. One request for BOT's catalog contained a handwritten note in its margin: "I drive a car pool with 6 little boys HELP!"[74]

Listening to books behind the wheel raised problems not faced by previous generations. First, some subscribers couldn't hear the narrator's voice above the engine noise.[75] Hecht had to remind narrators to speak loudly since their audience would be driving cars. Women's voices were especially difficult to hear. In 1977, a subscriber complained about Angela Cheyne: "Her voice simply couldn't cope with the noises of driving: the powerful motor, the tire hum and the rush of air (in spite of closed windows)."[76] Low voices were equally difficult to hear. The company stopped using one man because his bass register was unintelligible in cars.

Second, newspapers raised concerns about safety. Could drivers really concentrate on the road while absorbed in a novel? As riveting as books may be, there's little evidence to uphold fears of driver negligence. The *Washington Post* noted that local traffic agencies hadn't received a single report of an accident linked to taped books.[77] The only hazards seemed to be missed exits and late arrivals. Taped books were apparently no more dangerous than the radio, which had triggered similar anxieties after being introduced into cars several decades earlier.[78] In fact, many people claimed that listening to books made them safer drivers. A. K. Murray, editor of *Ohio Motorist* magazine, suggested that stories helped keep drivers awake.[79]

Although most of BOT's customers listened to books while driving, a small but devoted minority listened while doing other things. The sheer range of activities expresses their yearning to make the most of limited amounts of time, in this case by accomplishing two tasks at once. The multitasker challenged the conventional image of reading as a sedentary activity taking place in a comfortable armchair. Customers may have preferred that way of reading, but they found it to be a luxury.

Fortunately for them, the Sony Walkman did for pedestrians what the car stereo did for drivers. Sony introduced the Walkman (originally called the "Sound-About") to the United States in June 1980.[80] This wildly popular handheld device—and, later, competitors such as Toshiba's Walky and Aiwa's CassetteBoy—allowed people to listen to tapes wherever they wished. Whereas Caedmon's records had been designed for home use, much like the stereo or television, portable cassette players took spoken word recordings outside the home. By 1985, half of all Americans owned one.[81] Tape-Worm, an audio publisher in Rockville, Maryland, began selling its cassettes at sporting goods stores in order to reach runners with Walkmans. Many critics have commented on the Walkman's ability to carve out private space within public environments by enabling people to listen to tapes while riding a bus or jogging through the park.[82] Some listeners even tailored their choices to match the surroundings by listening to, say, Charlotte Brontë's *Jane Eyre* in the Yorkshire Dales.[83]

Tapes were ideal for people whose eyes and hands were occupied but whose minds were not. Subscribers to BOT included carpenters, chefs, gardeners, jewelers, knitters, mechanics, painters, photographers, potters, sculptors, and weavers. A woman who manufactured clothing in Maine saw herself taking part in a long tradition: "Following the footsteps of laborers using hand skills such as hat makers and cigar rollers who in the past were read to while they worked, I happily listen to books on tape while sewing my garments."[84]

Homemakers depended on taped books too. A librarian working in Fairfax County, Virginia, observed that unabridged recordings were checked out by both commuters and busy mothers.[85] Some of these mothers turned to audiobooks as a means of contact with a world beyond domesticity or at least a way to reclaim a portion of their schedules for personal interests.[86] Women described listening to books while doing household chores including washing dishes, ironing clothes, and even vacuuming (Figure 8.6). One mother listened to books every evening while walking her two infants.[87]

People who didn't work with their hands still came up with ways to listen to books. The manager of a funeral home in Harlan, Kentucky, admitted, "Nothing can make a long country wake wear on faster, except a chair in a quiet morgue room, and a tiny insert earphone."[88] Devoted readers listened

Figure 8.6. The Audiobook Belt advertised by Blackstone Audio Books.

to books no matter how busy their schedule. A Florida senator listened while deer hunting, and an Oregon woman did so on a farm tractor.[89]

Cases of compulsive listening or audiobibliophilia became increasingly common in the 1980s. Lynett Putterman, an English teacher at Chicago's Roosevelt University, claimed never to be without a tape: "I have a waist belt with holder for my cassette player so that I can go everywhere listening with my hands free. I mean, I listen while I'm in the dentist's chair, waiting for anything, at airports and on planes in dim light where you can't read, at the beach, taking walks or driving, getting a facial or manicure (many a nail's been ruined)."[90] A self-described "addict," Putterman used technology to continue reading when there was no other way to do so.

These Books Talk

Not much is known about individual audio publishers because there were so many of them. *Words on Tape* identified 600 to 800 companies producing spoken word recordings in 1988.[91] Forty or so of those companies made recordings of general interest; the rest were small outfits with narrowly defined specialties and bewilderingly similar names.[92] Many sold motivational tapes or what the industry referred to as "subliminals," self-help books meant to infiltrate the listener's mind.[93] Still, this publishing sector is worth our attention since its studios influenced a book's reception to a greater degree than conventional publishers. Their stances toward dramatization, abridgment, and other controversial editing techniques determined whether a recording resembled the original book or another form of entertainment altogether.

Caedmon, Folkways, Spoken Arts, the Audio Book Company, and the Listening Library had been recording writers for years before BOT's arrival. They could simply transfer their records onto tapes. Other companies emerged at roughly the same time as BOT. Voice Over Books had recorded twenty-three titles by 1974; the following year, Goodwin Talking Books began selling tapes at Britain's petrol stations.[94] Some of these companies flourished; Caedmon had sales of $20 million in 1984.[95] But, as Hecht knew from personal experience, Caedmon didn't serve commuters. It catered to the educational market, favored abridgments or excerpts, and preferred high-profile authors and actors. By contrast, Hecht hired unknown actors to read *The Thorn Birds* and other best sellers that held a driver's attention. The issue of taste set BOT apart from Caedmon, whose marketing director once sniffed, "We would never do 'The Thornbirds.'"[96]

Newcomers specialized in particular niches. The Mind's Eye did dramatizations, complete with music and sound effects (you can hear the pirates grunt on *Treasure Island*), that were played on National Public Radio and its affiliates.[97] Ear Literature offered full-cast recordings. Listen for Pleasure was known as "the Masterpiece Theater of the books-on-cassette business" for its British titles.[98] Ballymote Tape Library mainly offered old-time radio shows that remained popular with drivers.

A number of publishers specialized in the classics because libraries were willing to buy them. When Flo Gibson recorded Edith Wharton's stories, for instance, libraries accounted for over 90 percent of the sales. Gibson's Audio Book Contractors and Classic Books on Cassettes recorded the old favorites, as did Cover to Cover, which specialized in British fiction read by BBC radio presenters. These companies did not vie for rights, since pre-twentieth-century titles were in the public domain, but, as a tradeoff, they had to put up with high competition and low profit margins. By 1990, for instance, there were at least twenty-two recordings of Dickens's *A Christmas Carol*. Still, library sales accounted for substantial revenues and propped up the emerging market. According to a survey conducted in 1985 by the *Library Journal,* more than half of public and academic libraries maintained taped book collections. They purchased anywhere from five to one hundred titles per year; the largest of these held 2,000 titles and spent $77,000 per year on taped books.[99]

Other publishers specialized in particular genres or categories: Alternate World Recordings (science fiction and fantasy), Audio Books (horror and the supernatural), the Audio Press (nature and environmental writing), Audio Renaissance Tapes (spiritualism), Kiddy Kassettes (children's literature), Valley of the Sun Publishing (New Age), and Word Inc. (religion). Those who didn't spread the Word sometimes came up with their own words. Both Embassy Cassette Company and Metacom developed original content. The Audio Book Company even offered the entire Bible alongside its "Listen to Love" romances read straight from unpublished manuscripts.

BOT competed primarily with imitators who also rented books by mail. Its main rival was Recorded Books, a company founded in 1979 as an East Coast alternative to BOT. That company was likewise conceived on the road. A manufacturers' representative named Henry Trentman found himself driving three to four hours between clients. To stave off boredom, he taped Caedmon records and old radio shows and played them on a portable cassette player; however, they were too short for the long commute. He tried out BOT after seeing the company's ad on his American Express bill and then, shortly afterward, launched a similar outfit.[100] Initially, Recorded Books recruited narrators from local dinner theaters. A listing at Washington, DC's Arena Stage caught the eye of Frank Muller, a classically trained actor who went on to become one of the industry's most celebrated narrators. Muller made the company's first recording: Jack London's *The Sea-Wolf.*

BOT and Recorded Books were the leading providers of unabridged recordings in the United States. (Chivers covered the UK market.) They resembled one another in nearly every respect. Their ads appeared side by side in the same publications, and their catalogs contained many of the same books. Both companies' primary sales market was Southern California, then New

York City and Chicago. Size was the key difference. In 1988, BOT's catalog had 2,500 titles; Recorded Books had 300. In fact, BOT was the nation's largest audio publisher in terms of recorded hours. It accounted for approximately 15 percent of the 22,000 titles listed in *On Cassette* for 1986. In order to stand out, BOT and Recorded Books competed for exclusive rights to best sellers. Customers could order *Huckleberry Finn* from either publisher; but they could only rent Tom Clancy's novels from one of them. Surveys by BOT's marketing team confirmed the wisdom of this approach: "Best sellers! This is our real edge over Recorded Books!"[101]

Neither company could prevent its name from being used generically to refer to all taped books. B. Dalton Booksellers maintained a "books on tape" section, for example, despite stocking it with recordings made by competitors. In order to protect its brand, BOT fought against the use of its name as a catchall. In 1973, an availability search by the company's attorneys for the trademark "Best Books on Tape, Inc." had turned up a slew of similar names: Animated Book, Autobooks, BookTape, Books That Talk, Book 'N Tapeworm, Carbooks, My Voicebooks, Phonobook, Singing Book, Telebook.[102] Henceforth, BOT's successful trademark gave it exclusive rights to use "books on tape." Legal judgments protected its name from use by Dove Books on Tape, Books on CD, and Novellas on Tape. The courts likewise ordered Bantam Audio to stop describing its product as "the book on tape."

These rulings did little to stop the press, however, from using the phrase "books on tape" to describe competitors' merchandise. The lack of an industry standard exacerbated the confusion. Hecht advised journalists to use alternatives such as "audio cassettes," "spoken cassettes," or "recorded readings," and some librarians advocated the term "bookcassette."[103] It was not until the early 1990s that publishers settled on "audio books" as a neutral, inclusive term covering books of any length, style, or format (the last was especially crucial as the industry headed toward compact discs).

The first generation of audio publishers sought customers via direct mail because bookstores were reluctant to expand beyond the printed word. Many considered taped books a sideline or refused to stock them at all; as one of Harvard Bookstore's managers explained, "We'd like to sell books only."[104] The taped book's reputation was not helped by its prominence among spinner racks at truck stops and gas stations along the interstate freeways—where drivers can still find them today.

A second wave of audio publishers waited to infiltrate bookstores. In 1981, Newman Publishing began marketing cassettes in stores.[105] The following year Ingram Book Company offered taped books to its retail accounts; the wholesaler's countertop displays allowed customers to hear one-minute samples. By the mid-1980s, the average bookstore carried 85 titles; that number had risen to 120 titles in 1987, by which time nearly three-quarters of independent and regional chains stocked taped books.[106] A handmade sign announcing "These books talk" directed attention to a Californian bookstore's supply.[107] Deseret Books in Logan, Utah, played taped books over the store's speakers. Even holdouts like San Francisco's A Clean, Well-Lighted Place for Books relented once it became apparent that spoken word recordings could account for between 3 and 12 percent of a store's sales.[108] Better yet, tapes didn't compete with book sales; they supplemented them.

Waldenbooks was the first major retailer to embrace cassettes by installing "audio centers" in most of its 980 outlets. Racks holding up to 500 tapes stood at the front of its stores. In 1982, it launched its own line of cassettes, Waldentapes. Retail sales were crucial to publishers. In 1985, one analyst calculated that 63 percent of taped books were bought or rented through stores like B. Dalton and Brentano's.[109] Perennial favorites like Garrison Keillor's *Lake Wobegon Days* helped raise the category's profile. In addition, cross-merchandising—say, Bantam's side-by-side display of paperbacks and tapes of Pat Conroy's *The Prince of Tides*—enticed new customers to audio.

The major publishing houses waited until the mid-1980s to enter the market. Taped books had become big business after years of low-profile, low-profit enterprises catering to schools, libraries, and people with disabilities. The turning point came in 1985, when Warner Publishing, Random House, and Simon and Schuster all opened audio divisions. They focused on abridged books by prestige authors and actors designed to sell in quantities undreamed of by smaller competitors. Random House's initial line featured Toni Morrison's *Song of Solomon,* Gore Vidal's *Lincoln*, and John Updike's *Selected Stories*—all read by the authors themselves—on two-cassette sets sold for $14.95 (Figure 8.7). The big houses held key advantages over the existing audio publishers. Random House's various imprints (Random, Knopf, Pantheon, Villard, and Times Books) already owned many authors' print rights, for example, and Warner had the capital to buy Network for Learning and to partner with BBC Records and Tapes, then estimated to hold over half a million hours of programming. Henceforth,

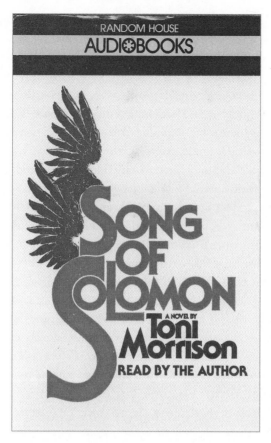

Figure 8.7. Toni Morrison's *Song of Solomon* on two cassettes published by Random House Audiobooks.

the market would be dominated by familiar corporate names rather than quirky upstarts like Hear-a-Book.

The publishing giants had an immediate impact on the market for rights. Publishers had to that point licensed multiple companies to record the same book. Competition among the big publishers for exclusive rights, however, drove up prices. Warner Audio paid $5,000 for Elmore Leonard's *Glitz,* for example, a huge sum in 1985. Advances of that size required sales of more than 70,000 tapes to break even. The following year, Listen for Pleasure paid a six-figure sum for the rights to nineteen Agatha Christie mysteries.[110] Soon, other publishers found themselves paying comparable sums for nonexclusive recording rights to best sellers.

Still, BOT and other publishers specializing in full-length recordings did not see the major houses as competitors. They thought the industry had room for both: abridged books sold through bookstores and full-length ones rented by mail.[111] Big publishers needed to reach a mass market. A spokesperson for Simon and Schuster observed, "If we did what Books on Tape did, we would not be moving enough units, reaching enough customers. It would put us out of business."[112] Whereas big publishers aimed for maximum sales, *Publishers Weekly* described their predecessors as "the small presses of the audio business," companies with limited resources that focused on product development instead of market expansion.[113] Rental programs depended on repeat customers whose loyalty could be won through customer service, not blockbuster sales.

When a dispute arose over rights to Dashiell Hammett's *The Maltese Falcon*, Hecht tried to convince Random House that the two companies were not in competition. (See Table 8.1.) Setting the two products side by side showed the difference. Most publishers used colorful artwork designed to catch the customer's eye; BOT's plain jackets did not vary. Hecht insisted on the benefits of having both versions on the market. Other publishers shared this view: abridged tapes might steer consumers toward the complete recording or even the original book. It was not uncommon for BOT to sublicense recording rights to the unabridged edition from publishers who released their own versions on a single cassette. In fact, the BOT catalog listed its full-length rentals alongside competitors' abridgments—not to mention Caedmon tapes, Spanish language courses, and *Drucker on Management*.

For Hecht, consumers who had yet to hear about the audiobook's existence, not competition, represented the biggest obstacle to his business. The number of taped books sold remained a small fraction of the country's total book sales. Audio publishers fervently believed that people would leap at their merchandise if only they knew about it—or stopped associating it with disability.

BOT's tapes not only looked different from those of the big publishers. They sounded different too. Whereas abridged readings had a reputation for theatrical excess, BOT avoided a dramatic style of narration. Hecht courted authors, many of whom were suspicious of nonprint media, by promising to record their books exactly as written. The company's policy of "straight reading," without dramatic flair or sound effects, tried not to distract attention from the book's words.[114] Narration should be neither melodramatic nor flat, neither flamboyant nor dry. Hecht advised actors to "underread" for the greatest effect.[115]

Table 8.1. Comparing Books on Tape and Random House Audio

Feature	Books on Tape	Random House Audio
Format	Unabridged	Abridged
Narrator	Staff reader	Celebrity
Background	Unenhanced	Enhanced (music, additional voices)
Packaging	Plain wrap	Four-color, highly sophisticated
Distribution	Mail-order only	Bookstores and retail outlets
Acquisition by customer	Rental	Purchase
Length of availability	Always in print	Out of print after a period of time

A reading was considered a failure when narrators intruded between the audience and the page. "These are not dramatizations," a spokeswoman assured librarians. "We regard our recordings as verbal publications in which the author reaches the listener without interference from the reader."[116] In this respect, BOT resembled the Library of Congress's talking book service more than its contemporary rivals. Hecht explicitly warned narrators not to read like Basil Rathbone, whose theatrical cadences had long been a fixture in Caedmon's catalog. There were other sources of entertainment if you wanted acting.

Library Journal once described BOT as the only commercial audio publisher to do "uninterpreted" readings.[117] Narrators restrained themselves in order to permit readers to do the interpreting. For Hecht, straight reading evoked the experience of reading the printed page: "You will put your own excitement in the words, just as you do when you read a novel."[118] Staff cultivated a neutral register in order to focus attention on the prose, not the narrator. Avoiding theatricality, Hecht believed, enabled audiences to lose themselves in the story.

There were no celebrities to distract audiences either. The Laurence Oliviers of the acting world were unaffordable for small publishers and too busy to do unabridged recordings anyway. It would have been unthinkable for celebrities to commit to an entire series of Anthony Trollope's novels—over 300 hours—as BOT's David Case did. Angela Cheyne, Wanda McCaddon, Wolfram Kandinsky, and other narrators recorded hundreds of titles despite being unknown beyond the publishing world. They were what the industry called "anonymous voice talent."[119]

Letters confirm that at least some clients did prefer the bibliocentric approach. One praised BOT's staff for "reading," not "acting" books.[120] Others described forgetting a skilled reader's voice altogether in their absorption. The man who read Mark Twain's *Life on the Mississippi* received praise for his delicate handling of the script: "Not a ham in any way."[121] Although this bookish approach won over loyal subscribers, it was less successful in winning over critics, many of whom made little distinction between different kinds of tapes and took aim instead at the tapes themselves.

Kentucky Fried Literature

Taped books kept a low profile as long as they were used predominantly by people with disabilities and other outliers to the publishing world. They became targets, however, once marquee publishers, authors, and actors entered the business. Traditionalists dismissed taped books as "Kentucky Fried literature"—fast, easy, and innutritious.[122] The metaphor evoked taste in both senses of the word: fast food (a comparison bolstered by the automobile's role in consumption) and, by implication, the type of person who eats fast food. Insinuations that taped books are some kind of shortcut or cheat have kept auditors on the defensive ever since. As noted in the Introduction, listening to books is one of the few forms of reading for which people apologize.

Abridgments were the worst offenders. Whereas Books on Tape and Recorded Books prided themselves on full-length recordings, most audio publishers shortened narratives in order to hold down costs. Consumers could choose between twenty-seven-hour ($144) and three-hour ($15) versions of *Moby-Dick,* for instance. If three hours was too much of a commitment, then a single breathless minute did the job on *10 Classics in 10 Minutes* ($4.95). Best sellers were stripped down to bare plot. For example, James Michener's 868-page *Alaska* ($22.50) appeared simultaneously with its three-hour cassettes ($14.95). A typical abridgment retained less than half of the hardcover book's contents. The Simon and Schuster recording of Tom Clancy's 543-page *The Cardinal of the Kremlin* contained a mere 25,000 words.

For both literary and commercial reasons, BOT refused to trim books. While the employees I spoke with expressed a personal preference for the uncut narrative, long books also appealed to commuters who were looking to fill time, not save it. *Middlemarch* (33 hours), *The Lord of the Rings* (53 hours), and *War and Peace* (70 hours) were ideal companions for long drives. One driver happily spent ten months working through Churchill's *The Second World War* (147 hours).[123] Critics rarely mention such feats of endurance when accusing listeners of having short attention spans.

As previous chapters have shown, recorded books have faced questions about their legitimacy since books began speaking in the 1930s. Now, a debate formerly restricted to people with disabilities shifted to the public arena. Perceptions that the audience consisted of people who were too busy, too tired, or too lazy persisted throughout the 1980s and 1990s. Audio publishers themselves exploited this appeal; for example, E. A. R. Books stood for "Easy Audio Reading." Customers lost credibility, too, by describing themselves as "addicts" and their supplier as "Hooked on Tapes."[124] This vocabulary, though used affectionately, reinforced perceptions of taped books as a passive form of consumption, one more akin to television than to reading.

The specter of television lay behind anxious discussions about reading's future. Traditionalists worried that people might stop reading books altogether if technology made it easy enough for them to do so. Hence, taped books were vilified as the latest in a long line of technological rivals (most notably television, cinema, and eventually computers) to threaten the nation's reading habits. One report expressed concerns that America was turning into "a nation of watchers."[125]

As we have seen, publishers responded to competition from other media in two ways. They either made recordings as bookish as possible or, conversely, modeled them after other forms of entertainment. BOT, Recorded Books, and Listening Library, among others, hewed as closely as possible to print; some publishers even packaged their tapes to resemble hardcover books. Hecht described his subscribers as "book people" who wanted to maintain contact with the world of letters despite busy schedules.[126] Many customers still thought of themselves as book readers and deliberately listened to taped books as an alternative to television. BOT's marketing campaign appealed to such sentiments with slogans like "Let your mind make the movie."[127]

By contrast, Random House, Simon and Schuster, Bantam, Warner, and other big publishers sought to compete with screens, not books. Their tapes were similar in length to the average film and preferably reproduced books that had already been made into television shows or movies. For them, the lines between media were hazy. Ben Kingsley narrated Caedmon's Mahatma Gandhi records, for instance, after playing the Indian leader in Richard Attenborough's film. Sound effects moved books one step closer to other forms of entertainment. To take one example, the Simon and Schuster recording of Clive Barker's *The Inhuman Condition* used stereo to enhance the atmosphere of dread.[128] There was just one problem: the symphonic music distracted from the story's words.[129]

Readers worried then—as they still do today—about technology replacing books. Yet book sales overall benefited from tapes. Listeners were often avid readers who used spoken word recordings as a supplement rather than a substitute for print. People listened to books when they couldn't read them in any other way. Diminishing reading time was a regrettable fact of life. The following testimonial from a BOT subscriber put it best: "I assume that many of your readers feel the same way as I do . . . reading has always been a way of life, the moments I spent with a good book were very special. And then one's life gets so hectic and busy and time for reading becomes more and more rare."[130] For hardworking people, taped books did not replace that special relationship; they preserved it. One grateful customer (echoing the blind readers of a previous generation) wrote, "Thank you, Mr. Hecht, for re-opening the wonderful world of books!"[131]

Time on the road gave commuters a chance to maintain or even increase contact with books. An Indiana woman confessed, "I've ordered 23 books from you . . . which is 22 more than I would have read in the same period."[132] Another woman in Virginia estimated that she read at least thirty-five extra books per year this way.[133] One Kentucky woman carried a tape recorder with her: "I like to read. Period. This way I can do both. I can do housework. I can read books in my spare time. And I can listen to tapes. This way I can read even more."[134] Like other subscribers, she viewed tapes as a continuation of her book reading, not an alternative to it.

Of course, taped books appealed to some people who didn't read at all. One subscriber boasted of hearing over 160 books that he would never have taken the time to read.[135] Busy professionals who spent their days reading work-related documents also turned for recreational reading to taped books, which did not disrupt their schedules or lifestyles. Other people refused to read books in any other way. John Fraser of Scranton, Pennsylvania, had not read a book in ten years (he fell asleep every time he tried) before listening to Milton's biography.[136] Hecht himself claimed to have heard fifty books a year since starting the company—after failing to read a single one during the previous twenty-five.[137]

But were these people actually reading? The industry's growth generated heated disputes over literacy even though this question had been debated for nearly half a century among people with disabilities. Now, scrutiny turned from people who couldn't read in any other way to people who read this way by choice. Advocates described taped books as a way for busy people to continue reading, and even as a gateway to other books, whereas detractors accused them of contributing to the country's literacy woes. Newspapers circulated the warning of Jonathan Kozol, the author of *Illiterate America*. "We will lose something very stirring in the American tradition when we walk upstairs to find our kids listening to Mark Twain on headsets," cautioned Kozol. "Tapes are one more disincentive to literacy."[138] For him, listening to books represented an activity that was distinct from reading and, therefore, bore some blame for the millions of Americans who were unable to read. Serious art required silence; the "quick-fix, toil-free" process of listening bore little resemblance to the slow, laborious work of reading with your eyes.[139]

Most forms of reading accrue a degree of prestige or cultural capital. By contrast, listening to books earned none of the rewards bestowed on reading. Auditors confessed to feelings of shame, as if they did not deserve the respect accorded to readers of books. The editor of one Florida book review admitted how much he enjoyed taped books before the inevitable mea culpa: "At least I'm ashamed of myself."[140] The shame factor reached all the way down to people who had no association with the publishing world. A public relations executive from Alhambra, California, attributed such guilt to a puritan upbringing. "I was taught that one has to work for anything meaningful in life," he remarked. "Taking this shortcut, reading without giving up free time and without doing the work of reading, seems almost devious."[141] He listened anyway.

Press coverage of taped books grew along with the industry. For most of the 1980s, only trade publications such as *Publishers Weekly* and *Library Journal* covered the format. Hundreds of reviews could be found by the decade's end, offering guidance to the more than 38,000 titles now available on cassette. Anticipating raised eyebrows, reviewers preemptively shared their own conversions. Richard Kenyon, the *Milwaukee Journal*'s book editor, described listening with ambivalence:

> Personally, being a person who has always enjoyed reading, I wasn't sure I'd like hearing a book read. I thought it would lose that indefinable intimacy between the word and the eye; that somehow the imagination triggered by a good writer wouldn't be as exercised on tape, and that the echoes of intentionally chosen words and sounds wouldn't be heard in the deep, still chambers of the mind as they are when read.[142]

Kenyon did like listening to books, it turned out, even if it engaged his mind differently than reading did.

Eventually columnists moved beyond confession in order to enumerate the benefits of listening to books. These included heightened appreciation for the writing; a slow, measured pace; an increased sense of intimacy, especially when using headphones; interpretations by professional actors capable of correct pronunciation and a range of accents; and even a childlike pleasure in being read to by another person. Some reviewers found themselves enthralled by authors who held little appeal for them in print (Conrad's and Melville's names were often mentioned). Others found themselves talking back. Gail Forman, an English professor at Maryland's Montgomery College, wrote in the *Washington Post* about her ongoing duel with narrators: "Sometimes I practice imitating their sounds or trying out different ways of emphasizing certain passages, for every reading is an interpretation."[143] Forman was not alone. According to one survey, 70 percent of BOT's subscribers replayed sections of books that they found interesting.[144]

Still, the nation's press coverage by and large focused on the format's legitimacy. It was one thing for people with vision impairments to listen to books; it was another for the average citizen. Nearly every report on the industry's growing popularity raised similar concerns. The *Wall Street Journal*, for example, noted the taped book's commercial success before asking the perennial question: "Is 'listening' as good as reading?"[145] Growing sales figures and public acceptance thereby upheld, instead of putting to rest, the familiar narrative of reading's decline. Portraying taped books as rivals to printed ones neglected to consider whether reading was adapting to and maybe even flourishing in a changing media environment.

Two editorials from the early 1990s signaled that the previous decade's commercial success was unlikely to translate into critical esteem. "Can We Really Read with Our Ears?" was the question posed by the *New York Times*.[146] Rand Richards Cooper's concern with the link between reading and vocalization anticipated that of later critics who drew a line between the two media—even if the words were exactly the same. He doubted whether sound itself was an appropriate medium for books, which depend on texture, syntax, and layout as much as on language for their effects. Cooper's fundamental objection was that listening is pleasurable but passive. Imagining for oneself how the marks on a page might sound—the novel's hypothetical voice as opposed to the tape's real one—is what makes reading so engrossing. For Cooper, this is why books cannot be read while driving. They demand the reader's full attention.

That same year, *Harper's Magazine* published an elegy for reading as we know it. The essay formed part of Sven Birkerts's impassioned defense of the printed book, *The Gutenberg Elegies: The Fate of Reading in an Electronic Age.* Its central question went one step beyond Cooper: "Listening is not reading, but what *is* it?"[147] Birkerts explored whether books were an extension or a simplification of the act of reading. Many of the passive terms—"seduced," "drugged," "lulled"—would seem to confirm Birkerts's hypothesis that listening to books was equivalent to watching television. He especially resented ceding control to external narrators who allowed little space for his own ruminations. The stranger's voice interfered with what Birkerts calls "deep reading," a leisurely absorption in the printed page that borders on the mystical; by contrast, listening reduced books to mere storytelling.[148] Too much was outside the auditor's control to make "deep listening" a realistic prospect. To a large degree Birkerts enjoyed the spell cast over him by taped books. Yet his enjoyment was tempered at all moments by the guilty knowledge that there would be consequences. The essay is an elegy, after all, for forms of concentrated reading that might not survive competition with other, less demanding forms of entertainment. After audiobooks, reading would never be the same.

Hecht founded Books on Tape for the millions of bored commuters stuck on America's highways with nothing to occupy their minds. When the company began, spoken word recordings were used mainly by people with disabilities, devoted Bible readers, and connoisseurs of the arts. BOT helped change the reputation of taped books by marketing them to the nation's growing number of commuters and other professionals who were too busy for books. "Changing the way America reads" was one slogan considered by the company.[149] Drivers who resented hours wasted on the road welcomed taped books as a way to make this time useful.

BOT convinced enough drivers of the benefits of taped books to build a successful business that competed with traditional book publishers. In fact, the BOT brand had become so recognizable that even the shift from cassette tapes to compact discs in the late 1980s made no difference—books on compact disc remained "books on tape" in people's minds. Competitors recognized the brand's value. In 2001, Random House acquired BOT and its backlist of approximately 5,000 books. For Hecht, who had come up with the idea of starting the company over twenty years ago while stuck in traffic, the happy ending might have come straight from the pages of a best seller.

Yet the company's success did little to reassure critics. Suspicions remained that the taped book was an impostor. They saw sound technology less as reading's savior than as the latest threat to the silence and repose necessary for it. BOT tried to win over skeptics by making unabridged recordings that stuck closely to the book and bore little resemblance to the abridgments that turned books into entertainment designed to compete with television, film, and computers. The result was a clientele who thought of themselves as book readers. This made little difference to defenders of the printed word, however, who saw people reading while driving cars, doing dishes, and jogging through parks. For them, taped books raised troubling questions about the nature of reading. The long debate over the format's legitimacy carried on as a result. Taped books may have won over a sizable number of readers. But at least they were sorry.

9

Audio Revolution

In 2006, *Bookseller* magazine hosted a publishing industry seminar on a familiar topic: the relationship between audiobooks and printed ones. For over half a century audio publishers had confronted this issue when deciding how faithfully to reproduce the original book. In most cases, publishers brandished their literary credentials, presenting audiobooks as books. They consistently downplayed the differences. The *Bookseller* panel advocated the opposite approach: play up those differences. It opened with a marketing strategist's plea: "Don't treat audio like it's just a recorded version of a book. This is about product reinvention—a huge opportunity to go for non-book readers."[1] The message suited many publishers in the digital era who have shown little of the previous generation's anxieties about whether their recordings receive the same respect as other books do. In this case, the panel urged audio publishers to declare independence. The seminar's title: "Audio Revolution."[2]

So far my account of the talking book's history has concentrated on its fidelity to the printed book. The last chapter, however, tells the other side to this story. It considers how the convergence of formerly distinct media has encouraged publishers to reconceive audiobooks as something other than a replication of print ones. Instead, companies like Audible—the world's largest audiobook retailer—have begun promoting audiobooks as an independent art form in its own right, one that can do things other books cannot. Whereas publishers traditionally have encouraged a neutral, restrained style of speaking in order to avoid distracting attention from a book's words, many of today's publishers encourage actors to perform. Audible founder and CEO Don Katz is among them. "Several of the companies that made audiobooks, largely to be put in libraries, the actors were told to back off and read bland," Katz once told a reporter. "How crazy is this? They weren't performing. We injected the word performance."[3]

Audible entered the market at a time when audiobooks had become grudgingly accepted, or at least tolerated. (You still hear occasional grumbles from the likes of Harold Bloom.[4]) The Audio Publishers Association (APA) has campaigned on the industry's behalf since 1986. In fact, we have it to thank for the term "audiobook." One of the APA's initial tasks was to decide on a single term from among the many candidates (talking books, books on cassette, spoken word, audio books, audiobooks, AudioBooks).[5] The APA's preferred term, "audio book," covered any sound recording containing at least 51 percent spoken content; preserved on any medium (tape cassettes, compact discs, digital files); and derived from a printed book, another medium, or an original production.[6] Ironically, the term's consolidation officially confirmed that such recordings need not be rooted in books at all. Today the "Audies," the audio industry's equivalent to Hollywood's Oscars, reflect the book's diminished standing among their award categories: solo narration, narration by the author, multivoiced, audiobook adaptation, audio drama, and original work.

The book's declining prestige has contributed to the audiobook's reversal of fortune. In the early days of sound recording, the book was sacred, whereas today print is merely one way to experience storytelling. Describing our era as the "late age of print," as some have done, expresses the book's waning influence within a crowded media ecology.[7] Stories now migrate across different channels, only one of which is books. In addition, the high degree of media convergence characteristic of today's marketplace makes it difficult to separate books, audiobooks, and other media as neatly as we once did. Even the divide between reading a book and watching a film is less antagonistic than it was for previous generations. Literature and the mass media are viewed by many as coconspirators, not mortal enemies, in today's literary culture.[8]

This book's final chapter singles out the qualities setting audiobooks apart from other books. The examples that follow move beyond the audiobook's imitation of print in order to show how its unique capabilities and constraints influence a narrative's reception. The approach taken here will be guided by what N. Katherine Hayles calls "media-specific analysis," in order to avoid treating alternative reading formats as if they were simply books on screen or, in this case, on speakers.[9] Audiobooks aren't reducible to printed ones even when the words are identical. Hence, this chapter investigates how audiobooks use human voices, celebrity readers, sound effects, musical scores, and other devices to distinguish themselves from books and even to compete with radio, television, film, and other digital media. Such experimentation reflects a growing confidence among publishers in the audiobook as an art form in its own right instead of a derivative version of the printed book. In fact, many publishers no longer care whether their recordings are considered "books" at all.

The Audible Player

By the 1990s, audiobooks were no longer a novelty. Spoken word recordings had evolved from an obscure niche product into an established industry. People knew about audiobooks even if they had not actually heard one; as Random House Audio's president explained, "We're no longer selling the public on what audio is."[10] Audio divisions run by the major publishing houses, including Random House, HarperCollins, Simon and Schuster, and Time Warner, accounted for most of the industry's sales, while countless small publishers continued to specialize in particular genres and styles. The large trade houses considered sales of 50,000 the benchmark for success; according to the 10 percent rule, audiobooks could achieve up to a tenth of book sales.[11]

Mail-order catalogs were no longer the only place to find audiobooks. Stores that sold books usually sold them too.[12] "Audio is an accepted bookstore product now," reported a manager at Atlanta's Oxford Books.[13] According to the Book Industry Study Group, audiobook sales grew at five times the rate of those in the consumer book sector.[14] Audiobooks even had stores of their own, including Words in Motion in Chicago, Jimmy B's in Los Angeles, Audio Book World in Raleigh, Earful of Books in Austin, and the Talking Bookshop in London. Redding's Audiobook Superstore in Scottsdale, Arizona, stocked 10,000 titles.[15]

Publishers reached out to customers beyond bookstores by selling their lines in airports, drugstores, toy stores, record shops, and video outlets. Romance Alive titles sold for $5.99 in supermarkets, while Audio Adventures and the Cracker Barrel restaurant chain catered to truckers and long-haul travelers on America's highways. And people continued to get audiobooks from libraries and by mail. The Book-of-the-Month Club and the Literary Guild offered audio alongside their print selections; plus, audiobook clubs run by Columbia House, Doubleday, and the Herrick Company each had more than 150,000 members.[16]

Online retailing offered another way for booksellers to reach customers. Audiobooks.com, the first website dedicated to selling recorded books, appeared in 1994. Small independents such as Big Radio, Plum Choices, and Stuffed Moose Audio established websites before the major publishers. Online catalogs enabled them to promote entire inventories (including backlists and out-of-print titles) that had never fit onto the limited shelf space and spinner racks in retail shops. By 1996, there were nearly two dozen audiobook websites, some of which allowed customers to hear excerpts; nearly all audio publishers had websites by the decade's end. Major book retailers such as Amazon.com, BarnesandNoble.com, and Borders.com sold audiobooks too. It was not long before Amazon began listing multiple formats (hardcover or paperback, cassette or compact disc, abridged or unabridged) for each title.

Today Audible is the world's largest distributor of downloadable audiobooks. But when the company started out, it was by no means clear that Internet downloads were the future of publishing. Audible was founded in New Jersey in 1995 to capitalize on the growing market for spoken word entertainment (AudibleWords was its original name) and commercial opportunities presented by the Internet.[17] By then the online distribution of digital music was already changing the patterns of music consumption and turning the home computer into a virtual jukebox.[18] Audible's website was among the first to allow customers to download spoken word recordings onto their computers.

Audible and a rival company, Audio Highway, pursued different strategies to compete for online market share. Whereas Audible focused on books, signing exclusive contracts with major publishers, Audio Highway featured audio of all sorts, from music to National Public Radio broadcasts. In 1998, Audible's catalog held 1,300 audiobooks; Audio Highway had 90 (only three of which were best sellers). The companies adopted different business models as well. Audible charged as much as fifteen dollars to download books; Audio Highway gave them away for free by bundling up to six minutes of advertisements onto each recording. Audio Highway's superior sound quality came at a cost: it took nearly sixty minutes to download an hour's worth of material from Audio Highway; the same quantity from Audible took only fourteen minutes.[19]

Both companies introduced portable, handheld devices on which to listen to audiobooks downloaded from the Internet. The Audible Player sold for $200 and could hold up to two hours of speech (Figure 9.1). Although short-lived, it served as a bridge to more sophisticated devices such as the Diamond

Figure 9.1. The Audible Player, introduced in 1995.

Rio and eventually the iPods, tablets, and smartphones that, ever since, have enabled users to walk around their neighborhoods enveloped in "sound bubbles."[20] The proliferation of digital devices meant that Audible no longer had to convince customers to pay hundreds of dollars for a single-use audiobook player. Now, anyone with a smartphone has a potential library in their pocket.

Before the Internet, people listened to audiobooks on cassette tapes, as they had done in the 1970s and 1980s when Books on Tape opened for business, and then on compact discs.[21] The Walkman gave way to the Discman. Next, digital technology added to the mix several new formats: downloadable sound files, MP3-CDs (a hybrid format holding up to an entire book on a single disc), and Enhanced CDs or CD+ (another hybrid format adding text, video, and graphics when used on a CD-ROM player).[22]

There were alternatives for people who were uncomfortable mixing books and computers. Since 2005, Playaway or "plug and play" audiobook players have come preloaded with stories; they are essentially disposable MP3 devices containing a single book.[23] Playaways have proven especially popular at public libraries and military bases. The company began supplying American soldiers in Iraq and Afghanistan in April 2007; troops described them as "morale boosters."[24] Whereas soldiers fighting in the Second World War carried Armed Services Editions paperbacks, today's soldiers go to war armed with audiobooks.[25]

The choices benefited consumers—especially those reluctant to adopt new technology—while causing headaches for publishers, who had to manufacture titles in multiple formats or risk losing potential customers. The industry yearned for a single, standard format (a problem shared by the music and video industries) while at the same remaining divided over the viability of Internet downloads. On one side, Audible sought to make bricks-and-mortar stores obsolete; in 1997, it released Regis McKenna's *Real Time,* the first unabridged audiobook published exclusively in digital format.[26] "Born-audio" books came next.[27] Meanwhile, OverDrive, NetLibrary, and Ingram Digital ushered in audiobook downloads to libraries.[28]

On the other side, Simon and Schuster and Bantam Doubleday Dell Audio withheld their titles over concerns about compensation, copyright, and piracy—the same concerns bedeviling print publishing. No one knew yet how consumers would respond to downloads. In 1999, Internet sales accounted for just 2 percent of publishers' business; that number continues to rise but remained at 9 percent in 2005.[29] The following year, CD sales still made up 80 percent of HarperCollins's audio revenue.[30] Most publishers hedged by publishing titles in both traditional and downloadable formats. While publishers continue to move away from tapes and discs, as of 2011 no major publisher had moved entirely to digital stock.

Digital files have obvious advantages: they're easy to buy; they reduce distribution, packaging, and warehouse costs; and they take up less space than other formats. Sound Room's Bible takes up eighty-three CDs ($495) or seven MP3-CDs ($75), whereas the download fits on a single device. But, like e-books, hidden costs limit their profitability. Publishers still have to pay author royalties, actor wages, studio expenses, licensing fees, and digital rights management. The business's scale makes it difficult for audiobooks to compete with rival media such as DVDs sold for roughly the same price. Consumers have long found it baffling that an audiobook recorded on CDs typically costs more than the hardcover book.

Any doubts about the future of audiobook downloads vanished when Amazon purchased Audible in March 2008 for $300 million. Amazon, the world's largest Internet-based retailer, started out as an online bookseller before expanding to music, movies, video games, and practically everything else.[31] The acquisition turned Amazon into the market leader in digital audiobooks, giving it access to Audible's subscriber base, publisher partnerships, and more than 80,000 spoken word recordings.

Audible's success both contributed to and reflects the audio publishing industry's enormous growth over the past decade. At a time when most sectors of the publishing industry were shrinking, annual audiobook sales rose from $480 million in the late 1990s to $1.2 billion by 2012.[32] The widespread use of mobile devices, advances in digital technology, expanding inventories, diminishing production costs, and reduced prices all led to what *Book Business* magazine called "the mainstreaming of audiobooks."[33] Remember, Books on Tape and Recorded Books rented taped books in the 1970s because they were too expensive (fifty to sixty dollars) to buy; the average audiobook now costs twenty dollars.[34] Thousands of free recordings of books in the public domain have even been available from LibriVox since 2005.[35]

Audible's success has generated mixed feelings among publishers. Everyone credits Audible with expanding the market for audiobooks. By 2012, downloads accounted for over half of audiobook sales, and the number of titles produced per year increased from 4,602 in 2009 to nearly 36,000 in 2013.[36] At the same time, publishers are uncomfortable with Audible's virtual monopoly on download sales and its recent move into audiobook production. Audible began producing its own audiobooks after setting up Audible Studios and then, in May 2011, the Audiobook Creation Exchange (ACX), an online clearinghouse bringing together authors, agents, publishers, and rights holders with actors and producers in order to record books. Parties could choose between a pay-for-production deal and a royalty share deal offering favorable rates for giving Audible exclusive distribution rights. More than 10,000 ACX titles were produced in 2013.[37]

Publishers watched their biggest customer turn into their biggest competitor. Backed by Amazon, Audible can use its clout to drive increasingly severe terms in what is already a low-margin industry.[38] Publishers object in particular to the high discounts and unfavorable terms demanded by Audible.[39] (Naxos's director once compared the online retailer to Gazprom, the Russian gas monopoly.[40]) Producers point out that they receive less revenue from downloads than they did from CD sales. In 2013, Strathmore's Nicholas Jones estimated that audio publishers were receiving a 40 percent cut in revenue.[41] Others share concerns that the relentless pressure to economize may result in lower quality by rewarding speed and reducing staff (directors and engineers are becoming increasingly rare as actors move toward home studios).[42] At a recent conference on the audiobook industry, narrators complained that the elephant in the room was money. Many of the narrators I spoke to complained that they were working more hours while making less per hour than they did several years ago. The surest way to make it as an audiobook narrator, it seems, is already to be famous.

The A-List

These days actors spend as much time in the recording studio as the film studio. Everyone from Johnny Depp to Meryl Streep and Oprah Winfrey has narrated an audiobook. Audible's roster resembles a Hollywood film set. In 2013, Audible partnered with actor Tom Hanks and filmmaker Ken Burns to record novels read by actors like *Breaking Bad*'s Bryan Cranston. That series came a year after Audible's A-List Collection, featuring Kate Winslet's take on Emile Zola, Samuel L. Jackson reciting *A Rage in Harlem,* and Nicole Kidman performing Virginia Woolf's *To the Lighthouse.*[43] The A-List itself followed the recruitment of Kenneth Branagh, Tim Curry, Leelee Sobieski, and other moonlighting celebrities for Audible Signature Classics. Hardly a year goes by without a new series of renowned narrators.

Celebrity narrators are one way in which audiobooks have declared their independence from print. Publishers concerned with faithfully reproducing the book tend to favor unknown actors whose voices will not interfere with a story's reception. According to this line of thought, audiences are more likely to concentrate on a book's words if they don't know who is speaking. By contrast, celebrities come between books and readers, making them acutely aware of the voice; the book is no longer the center of attention. As a representative of Silksoundbooks, a website consisting exclusively of recordings by well-known actors, told me, "We focus on the face, not the book."[44] The prominence of celebrities, who are likely to read abridgments instead of the entire narrative, has reinforced suspicions that audiobooks are a degraded form of commerce, not art. In fact, both sides are right: celebrities draw attention to *and* distract attention from the book.

Celebrity narrators have been around as long as talking books. We should not be misled by Audible's marketing campaign into thinking that this is a new idea. Thomas Edison himself proposed recording public figures after he invented the phonograph in 1877. According to him, actors, elocutionists, and vocalists could use it to entertain the solitary reader "without moving from his chair."[45] Henry Irving, Herbert Beerbohm Tree, Ellen Terry, Sarah Bernhardt, and other actors all went on to record speeches from Shakespeare and other plays. The celebrity formula was well established by the time Ginger Rogers recorded *Alice in Wonderland* for Walt Disney in 1944.

Celebrities played an equally conspicuous role in the talking book service for people who were blind. First Lady Eleanor Roosevelt, sportswriter Red Barber, and philosopher Bertrand Russell all recorded books during its first decade. Recognizable voices lent credibility to the recordings and doubled as a public relations campaign. Plus, celebrity voices were popular with visually impaired readers. Despite the Library of Congress's mission to make talking books resemble printed ones, namely by reading them in an understated style, the voices themselves frequently belonged to public figures.[46] The charitable status of the American Foundation for the Blind and, in Britain, the Royal National Institute of Blind People allowed them to secure big names who had little interest in lending their voices to commercial ventures. The tradition of using stage, screen, and radio stars continues to this day. Fund-raising campaigns for talking books are inevitably led by a celebrity.

Complaints about celebrities are equally old. The earliest reviews objected to "radio crooners" and film stars reading sentimental verse set to music.[47] The formula was simple: use a celebrity to signal to audiences that this is art. As early as the 1950s, then, we can already see the battle lines being drawn over the proper way to read aloud. One college teacher complained about the "Big Name" performing instead of reading poems like Gray's *Elegy*.[48] Celebrities displeased literary critics in particular by refusing to subordinate their identities. F. R. Leavis once accused actors of pursuing "elocutionary impressiveness" at literature's expense.[49] However, the disapproval did not stop Caedmon and other audio publishers from hiring famous names.

The use of celebrities intensified after the major publishing houses entered the audiobook business in the 1980s. According to *AudioFile* magazine, recorded books were "the realm of celebrities" for Penguin, Random House, and Simon and Schuster.[50] They had the financial capital to sign up big names to read their titles, or at least abridgments of them. Casting celebrities was a way to enhance the reading experience while at the same time luring customers not otherwise interested in books. Film and television stars might just bring their fans along with them. Random House's initial offerings included Brooke

Adams reading *Dinner at the Homesick Restaurant* ($14.95), Maria Tucci reading *The Stories of John Cheever* ($7.95), and Darren McGavin reading James Michener's *Space* ($14.95) drastically condensed onto two cassettes. All three speakers were known to audiences through screens, not books. Other publishers took notice. In 1987, the Caedmon Cassette line's two best sellers were read by Mel Gibson (Daphne du Maurier's *My Cousin Rachel*) and Kathleen Turner (H. Rider Haggard's *She*).

Celebrity names were an easy way to call attention to the classics. In fact, publishers tell me that it's almost impossible to generate enthusiasm for them without a celebrity. It is now standard practice for publishers to launch series like Blackstone Audio's "The Classics Read by Celebrities" (from Burt Reynolds's *Moby-Dick* to Jamie Lee Curtis's *Little Women*). Pre-twentieth-century literature had the advantage of being out of copyright and, therefore, free to record. However, this meant fierce competition. By the 1990s, fans could hear Mark Twain's *The Adventures of Huckleberry Finn* read by Ed Begley, Dick Cavett, Jackie Cooper, David Crawford, Alfred Gingold, Hal Holbrook, Robert Lewis, Hiram Sherman, Peter Thomas, and Jack Whitaker. When, in 2000, Simon and Schuster launched its series of classics, recordings of *Tom Sawyer* (read by Paul Newman) and *Huck Finn* (read by Jack Lemmon) joined a venerable tradition. Names like theirs helped garner interest in titles that had already been recorded numerous times. Five different recordings of Thomas Hardy's *Tess of the D'Urbervilles* came out in 2008 alone.

The major publishing houses also had the clout to persuade authors to read their books (as Caedmon had been doing by other means since the 1950s). When Random House entered the audio market in 1985, its initial offerings included Toni Morrison's *Song of Solomon*, Gore Vidal's *Lincoln,* Studs Terkel's *The Good War,* and John Updike's *Selected Stories,* all read by the authors themselves. (When questioned about the wisdom in doing so, Updike defensively replied that "there is no perversion to reading a story out loud."[51]) The press attributed the audiobook's growing popularity to the appeal of hearing the voices of Updike, Stephen King, and other writers. One journalist mused, "Why should I just read a sexy story in print when I can have Erica Jong whisper it right in my ear?"[52]

Audio publishers capitalized on the popularity of other, better-funded media through tie-ins to them. In 1955, the Listening Library issued its first recording, Jules Verne's *Around the World in Eighty Days,* during the filming of the novel's Academy Award–winning adaptation. Ever since, publishers have exploited fiction's circulation among other media. In what was dubbed the "Battle of the Emmas," Brilliance, Dove, and HighBridge all released recordings of Jane Austen's novel in advance of the Miramax film adaptation.[53] Major publishing houses with big budgets and best-selling lists were in a strong position to capitalize on media tie-ins. Canny upstarts piggybacked on the screen too, however; a small Los Angeles–based publisher sold more than 25,000 copies of its debut title, *Dances with Wolves,* after releasing it in conjunction with the hit film.[54] Films also made a difference to publisher backlists. When cinemas began showing Tolkien's *The Lord of the Rings* trilogy in 2001, BBC Spoken Word relaunched its twelve-hour dramatization, a series originally broadcast in 1981.

A number of actors stepped off the screen and into the studio. In 1978, Henry Fonda read excerpts from *The Grapes of Wrath* nearly four decades after appearing in the film. "It is especially fitting that Henry Fonda should read these excerpts from *The Grapes of Wrath,*" Caedmon's album explained, "for the noted actor starred as Tom Joad in the 1940 movie version of the novel."[55] Over the next decade film actors regularly took up the microphone. Listen for Pleasure cast Alan Arkin to read *Catch-22* after he played Captain Yossarian in the film adaptation, for example, and Tom Courtenay read *The Loneliness of the Long Distance Runner* following his role as Colin Smith. Today's readers even have the luxury of choosing between recordings linked to different versions of films like *Lolita,* read either by James Mason (the lead in Stanley Kubrick's 1962 adaptation) or Jeremy Irons (who featured in a second one made in 1997).

Actors associated with roles from film and TV series likewise carried over these traits into narration. The actors who played Agatha Christie's Miss Marple, Raymond Chandler's Philip Marlowe, Arthur Conan Doyle's Sherlock Holmes, John Mortimer's Horace Rumpole, and Mickey Spillane's Mike Hammer all narrated audiobook versions of these same roles. Casting distinctive voices across different media prevented the cognitive dissonance of hearing the same character speak in multiple tongues. Such casting worked best with genre fiction in which an iconic figure appeared throughout a series or when an actor became widely associated with a particular role. Leonard Nimoy, an actor synonymous with Spock, narrated an installment of the Star Trek series, for example, and the actor who played John-Boy on *The Waltons* read the novels by Earl Hamner, Jr., on which the television series was based.

Despite the formula's appeal, celebrities were no sure thing. Not all actors are good readers. In one case, reviewers complained that Burt Reynolds had been hired to read Robert Parker's detective series for his heartthrob looks, not his acting talents. Reynolds's gravelly voice hardly suited a young detective, and he mispronounced words, dropping the first "r" from "library."[56] Other actors were firmly linked to specific roles. One review complained that it was impossible to hear Charlton Heston narrate *The Snows of Kilimanjaro* without imagining apes overtaking the mountain.[57] (Heston had starred in *Planet of the Apes*.) Worse, some actors showed up unprepared. Faith in their sight-reading abilities went against the work ethic of professional narrators who undertook hours of research into matters of pronunciation. For example, it becomes apparent when Brad Pitt reads Cormac McCarthy's fiction that he can't speak Spanish (it hurt my ears to hear "jefe" pronounced "jayfay"). Compare that with voice actor Scott Brick, who compiled a glossary of over 2,000 words before reading the made-up language Chakobsa in *Dune*.

Publishers held different views about celebrity voices. A few associated them with an emerging market that had yet to establish itself. In 1987, an editor at Time Warner attributed a gradual shift toward unfamiliar names and longer recordings to the industry's maturation: "The audiobook audience that currently exists is becoming more sophisticated. They would prefer a really good reading by a person they've never heard of over a mediocre reading by someone whose name they know."[58] Other trends might seem to confirm this hypothesis. Digitization has moved the market toward unabridged recordings, for instance, forcing publishers to rerecord titles originally released as abridgments. But, despite predictions to the contrary, the market's growth has led to a profusion of speaking styles, from anonymous, single-voiced readings to full-cast Hollywood dramatizations.

Audio publishers now have the luxury of casting actors from diverse backgrounds too. In the early days, publishers had relied on a narrow vocal range, typically middle-aged white men who worked in broadcasting or on Broadway. Not anymore. "Gone are the days when one white male narrator was the best guy in town," observed a producer for Blackstone Audio in 2012.[59] Nowadays, publishers try to match a book's content to the speaker's voice in terms of age, class, ethnicity, gender, race, nationality, or sexuality in order to avoid what one journalist called "audio drag."[60] Recent productions have cast Puerto Rican actress Rita Moreno to read Sonia Sotomayor's *My Beloved World,* South African actor John Kani for Nelson Mandela's *Conversations with Myself,* and

Torres Strait Islander Rachael Maza for Doris Pilkington's *Follow the Rabbit-Proof Fence*. Emma Donoghue's *Room* is read in the voice of a five-year-old boy—or at least an actress skilled in mimicking a child's voice. And a countertenor narrates Iain Banks's *The Wasp Factory,* a formidable role since the male narrator turns out to be a woman.

The use of multiple voices reflects the continuing drift away from the book. The industry norm is a single narrator whose voice can carry an entire story. This figure mirrors the lone reader who is solely responsible for imagining a book's entire gamut of voices. Theoretically, there's no need for additional narrators since one throat can impersonate a seemingly inexhaustible number of characters. Jim Dale created 134 different voices for a single Harry Potter book, for instance, a record supplanted by Roy Dotrice's 224 voices for *A Game of Thrones.* By contrast, the use of multiple speakers divides a narrative into literal approximations of those voices—as if a single reader's imagination was not enough. Once used exclusively for audio drama, the technique is now routinely used by any book with more than one speaker.

Casting has grown ever more ambitious. As studio budgets have grown, so have the casts. Two speakers (one male, the other female) play the dueling narrators in Gillian Flynn's *Gone Girl.* A multiracial cast of four southern women read Kathryn Stockett's *The Help.* Twelve different speakers visit a comatose woman in Dawn French's *Oh Dear Silvia.* Twenty-three people read *Nelson Mandela's Favorite African Folktales.* Nearly eighty actors read Galaxy Press's *Stories from the Golden Age.* And a cast of over 600 actors makes the Word of Promise's Audio Bible the most ambitious dramatization to date. Many are familiar Hollywood names; the director cast Terence Stamp as the voice of God, for example, after hearing General Zod's booming voice in the Superman films. "Hear the Bible come alive in dramatic audio theater," promises the box set (Figure 9.2).[61] The readings take place over an original score and sound effects illustrating, say, the thud of John the Baptist's beheading.[62]

Other recordings similarly reflect Hollywood's influence. In 2013, Random House Audio issued *World War Z* with the subtitle "(Movie Tie-in Edition)" ahead of the blockbuster film. Historically, audio publishers have lacked the resources to secure any major actors; now a single star is scarcely enough. *World War Z* and other big-budget productions continue to blur the line between audiobooks and rival media by signing up celebrities (in this case, director Martin Scorsese; rapper Common; and cast members from *Star Trek, Battlestar Galactica,* and other sci-fi television series). The audio edition sold over

Figure 9.2. The Word of Promise Audio Bible seventy-nine-CD set.

60,000 copies. These lavish recordings are Hollywood productions in their own right. Books are not their primary competition; they are taking on radio, television, cinema, online videos, and computer games.

Celebrity narrators were an industry fixture long before Audible began casting them. It joined a long tradition of using celebrity names to generate publicity for titles that would otherwise receive little fanfare. Even so, the magnitude of Audible's A-List narrators (Annette Bening, Claire Danes, Colin Firth, Anne Hathaway, Dustin Hoffman, Samuel L. Jackson, Diane Keaton, Nicole Kidman, Meg Ryan, Susan Sarandon, Kate Winslet) suggests a change in scale. As an Amazon subsidiary, Audible has outdone its predecessors in signing talent beyond the small publisher's reach. The A-List reflects Audible's growing influence as well as that of the audiobook market in general. Celebrities who once would have refused to record even abridgments now voice entire novels. Audiobooks have become another form of work for actors alongside radio, television, film, and digital media, which, as we'll see in the next sections, threaten to overtake books as their competition.

Aural Equivalents

Audiobooks have always pulled in two directions at once: imitating printed books and enhancing them through sound effects. The initial publishers of recorded books, from the Library of Congress's Talking Book Library to Books on Tape's cassettes for commuters, stuck closely to print in order to replicate the conventional reading experience. As Tribeca Audio's Paul Ruben recalled of audiobooks, "They were simply viewed as a book read aloud, emphasis on *book.*"[63]

By the 1990s, however, publishers no longer felt beholden to tradition. Like many other formats, audiobooks began by imitating their predecessors, then moved on to forge a distinctive identity. "Audiobooks are no longer just books read out loud," observed Hachette Audio's Anthony Goff. "They have become a separate and legitimate type of entertainment."[64] A growing market, evolving tastes, and technological advances have all contributed to the audiobook's independence. If some audio publishers (especially those aiding people with vision impairments) continue to treat recordings as books, others seek ways to make audiobooks entertaining without regard for their reputation.

Audio publishers have experimented with sound technology for decades. The American Foundation for the Blind added sound effects to some recordings despite striving to keep them as "bookish" as possible. Commercial labels like Caedmon, Books on Tape, and Recorded Books tried out different combinations too. Still, the emphasis remained the printed book, not the performance. Publishers generally shunned theatrical narration as a distraction. Looking back, one librarian noted a sea change: "Of course, audiobook quality has changed dramatically—literally—since the 1980s. While some older recordings were excellent, others were read in a monotone voice—so as not to detract from the author's words, I was told. Disaster! Classics were almost impossible to listen to, and nonfiction was even worse. Deadly, dry, uninviting.

But as the 1990s progressed, all that changed."[65] Whether theatrical performances have improved recordings is debatable. Nevertheless, we can trace the audiobook's evolution away from the page through the translation of visual material into sound—what I'll follow one publisher in calling "aural equivalents"—and the addition of song, music, and other sound effects.

The main impediment to sound recording is the book's appearance. While straightforward narratives lose little in translation, those manipulating the page's layout can be difficult to adapt. There are entire schools of experimental writing that stubbornly resist adaptation into other media.[66] If Friedrich Kittler is right that twentieth-century literature is unfilmable, then much of it should be unrecordable too.[67] Yet this has not stopped audio publishers from remediating the pages of modernist writers such as James Joyce, Virginia Woolf, and Samuel Beckett.

Take *Tristram Shandy,* an icon of formal experimentation. Laurence Sterne's cock-and-bull story famously subverts the conventional novel through its eccentric appearance. What the page looks like is as important as what it says.[68] How, then, should the novel's dashes, squiggly lines, and mottled pages be read aloud? Before throwing up our hands and judging the novel unrecordable, bear in mind that Sterne himself looked forward to reading aloud the section with a marbled page.[69] It is in this spirit that Naxos recorded Sterne's novel, gags and all—but not without warning customers. The following disclaimer appears on Audible's website: "This audiobook tries in a variety of ways to match Sterne's invention with aural equivalents."[70] In other words, the producers do more than copy Sterne's book; they seek out sound effects to achieve the same result in a different medium. Sterne gives us the anti-book; Naxos the anti-audiobook.

Sterne's self-reflexive commentary makes it impossible to forget that we're reading an actual book. Recording studios are left with two options: preserving bibliographic references (we can still pretend we're reading a book, not listening to it) or adapting them into audiobibliographic ones. That way the same devices used to parody the novel can be used to spoof the audiobook. In this case, Naxos's sound effects remind us that an actual book is being read aloud. Instead of erasing the book's existence, the recording highlights its role as prop. We see this when Sterne omits an entire ten-page chapter. Whereas readers deduce this omission through a gap in the book's page numbers, auditors register the absence through the noise of rustling pages. The sounds remind us of the narrator's presence while at the same time offering a rare glimpse into a studio process usually engineered out of the final recording—today's narrators use tablet computers to muffle the turning pages. Just as Sterne makes it impossible to forget that we're reading a book, Naxos makes it impossible to forget that we're listening to one.

Other aural equivalents convey the book's typography. In this case, the narrator's "ahems" and mumbling stand in for the novel's dashes and asterisks. When Uncle Toby hums over a letter, a gesture indicated by over twenty dashes in the novel, the narrator hums out loud. And the audiobook signals the novel's censorship of "Z——s!" by playing a bleep over the word. The acoustics of censorship will be familiar from radio and, in this context, equally humorous since the uncensored word ("Zounds!") is said out loud right before the banned one. Finally, Lesser conveys Corporal Trim's flourish of his stick—graphically represented in the manuscript by a squiggly line—through the swishing noises of an actual stick being waved in the studio. Such effects stand out against the audiobook's conventional background silence.

In Sterne's book, a solid black page mourns Parson Yorick's death. The striking visual effect is an unorthodox way of showing, not telling. Simply describing the page (as some narrators choose to do) faithfully reproduces the original script while at the same time squandering its force. On the Naxos recording, a church bell tolls three times instead, conveying the scene's gravity through the intrusion of a congruently nonverbal element into a verbal narrative. In an even more self-reflexive way, Naxos translates the marbled page by choosing a sound effect uniquely suited to the medium. In this case, we hear radio static increasing in volume instead of a clear transmission: a marbled page, a garbled page.

Sterne is seen by many as a precursor to the twentieth century's experimental writing and its own unruly digressions. Audio publishers must decide what to do with the footnotes used in novels from Nabokov's *Pale Fire* to Kate Atkinson's *Behind the Scenes at the Museum* and Junot Díaz's *The Brief Wondrous Life of Oscar Wao*. David Foster Wallace's writing is renowned for its copious use of footnotes, to the point that even his footnotes themselves have footnotes. For Wallace, these notes are not extraneous but rather self-aware commentary on the way novels work. He once described them as "almost like having a second voice in your head."[71] Whatever the value of such experiments, recording Wallace's books without them would risk losing what the author felt to be essential. Yet such simple bibliographic machinery turns out to be fiendishly difficult to translate into audio. Footnotes are "a nasty problem for an audiobook," Wallace concedes at the beginning of *Consider the Lobster and Other Essays:* "Where do the footnotes go? There is no bottom of the page in an audiobook, obviously."[72]

Wallace's publishers have tried two different solutions: one emphasizing "audio," the other "book." First, the "audio" solution. Audiobooks show little consistency in handling footnotes. Some narrators announce "footnote" at the risk of interrupting the narrative flow. Others record the notes separately. The easiest, and by far most common, option is to leave them out altogether. Wallace resolved the problem by reading in two different voices: one for the main narrative, another for the notes. By using a filter microphone popular on old-time radio shows, he devised an aural equivalent to the visual footnote. This is in stark contrast to the clumsy way he handles ellipses by saying "dot, dot, dot" instead of simply letting his voice trail off.[73]

Next, the "book" solution. Hachette Audio chose a different method for its fifty-six-hour recording of *Infinite Jest,* a 1,076-page maximalist novel crammed with 388 endnotes (one comprising an eight-page filmography of a fictitious director). Hachette's producers decided not to record the endnotes in case they made it too difficult to follow the main narrative. The notes were released as a separate PDF document instead. When Wallace fans objected that any recording calling itself unabridged was obligated to include the notes too, Hachette offered the following explanation:

> Some early listeners have been disappointed that the novel's endnotes are currently available only in text form, to be read. Choosing to include the endnotes as a downloadable PDF file, rather than as a recording by the narrator, was a difficult decision for all involved, and we debated different options at length before beginning production. The audio format allows us great opportunities to showcase Wallace's love of language and grammatical dexterity, to illuminate characters and their relationships, and to bring out some of the unique humor inherent in his work. However, there are also certain limitations to the format, and we needed [to] let go of some of our preconceived notions about the form of *Infinite Jest,* as we must when we adapt any complex work to audio.[74]

For Hachette, adapting Wallace meant leaving out one of the novel's most distinctive features instead of seeking alternative ways—as Wallace himself did—to preserve them. It saw the audiobook's missing bottom page as a constraint, not an opportunity. (Hachette ultimately did issue the notes as a standalone recording that, at nearly eight hours, is longer than most books.)

Audio publishers are by no means alone in confronting the problem of re-mediation. Jennifer Egan's *A Visit from the Goon Squad* includes an entire chapter based on a PowerPoint presentation. While seventy-six slides pose a challenge to audio, keep in mind that they are a challenge for print too, taking up page space and forcing readers to turn the novel sideways. To minimize costs, the novel's slide show appears in black and white, whereas Egan's web-site features a color presentation. In other words, the novel itself is already grap-pling with the problem of how to incorporate other media.

When asked if the slides work on audio, Egan recalled reading them aloud to her writing group: "The language sort of hung in the air in this odd, sort of poetic way. It had an eerie power."[75] (Many listeners disagreed, complaining about the audiobook's black-and-white PDF supplement and tedious reading of graphs.) We might think of Egan's project as a form of transmedia storytelling—telling a story in different ways across multiple media platforms—that capitalizes on the strengths of each one: the novel's prose; the audio-book's sound; and the website's blend of color, sound, and screen—the native environment of PowerPoint, after all.[76] The mobile phone app derived from Egan's novel (Constable & Robinson, £2.99) further undermines these divi-sions by syncing to the text Roxana Ortega's audiobook narration.

Aural equivalents can be equally effective in novels that experiment spar-ingly. The main challenge to reading aloud Zadie Smith's *NW* is mastering London's dialects and accents. Only occasionally does the episodic, stream-of-consciousness novel use pictorial devices. The narrator conveys most of the novel's typographical deviations through a change in pitch. Her voice drops to a whisper when reading "Top-secret: Nathan Bogle," for example, to indi-cate that the entry appears in smaller type than the other items on Leah Hanwell's list.[77] In fact, tedium results from following the prose too closely—by pronouncing every character of an Internet URL, for instance, that readers could take in at a glance. (Other narrators have tried reading long strings of numbers at an exaggeratedly fast pace for comic effect.[78])

Hanwell and Keisha Blake's Web chats are easier on the eyes than the ears since one can see fonts, typos, and emoticons. The section headed "Bye noe" (a mistyping of "bye now") makes sense on the page, a context justifying the speaker's rendering of "!!!!!?????" as "Hmmmm?"[79] In fact, it would be diffi-cult to know that this conversation takes place over computers (also obvious on the page) were it not for the background noise of typing. Sounds are analogous to typefaces here; if such visual effects are bookish, then sound effects are audiobookish. Aural equivalents are especially needed for the novel's poem laid out in the shape of an apple tree. The audiobook has no straightforward way to convey such visual effects. Nevertheless, birdsong played in the background to this passage intimates that we're dealing with exceptional language while at the same time bringing to mind the notion of a tree.

It turns out that some formal devices work even better in audio. In China Miéville's *Embassytown,* the Ariekei aliens speak through two mouths. The novel presents alien names such as Surl/Tesh-echer in fractional notation to indicate the words' simultaneous pronunciation; still, when reading the novel silently, I found myself scanning the names in linear sequence and therefore pronouncing them separately. By contrast, the recording says both names simultaneously. As this illustration suggests, many of the formal experiments that we accept on the page—especially those involving sound—require a degree of imaginative license grudgingly withheld from rival media.

There's nothing stopping authors, either, from adding entirely new material to the recording. Comic writers have begun to do so with increasing brazenness. Many don't even pretend that the two forms of entertainment are the same. Whereas authors have experimented with the book's conventions for centuries, the audiobook's protocols are by comparison relatively unexplored. To take one example, Aziz Ansari threatens to play the introductory smooth jazz—an audiobook cliché—throughout the entire recording of his book. "You didn't think I was gonna let it go this long, did you?" he asks the audience.[80] To take another, Amy Poehler greets us from a recording studio allegedly built at the base of Mount Rushmore, where in between chapters she interviews celebrity guests. Poehler sends up another audio convention—the fantasy of having your book read by a glamorous actor—when Kathleen Turner stops reading chapter one in order to insist that Poehler read it herself.[81]

Nowadays few books are deemed unrecordable. Even the transposed letter in the title of Neal Stephenson's recent novel, he assures us, need not scare away listeners: "*Reamde* is 100 percent audiobook-compliant."[82] Publishers have come up with imaginative solutions to the problem of recording multimedia books once considered suitable only for print. Orion converted the eighty photographs in *Meetings with Remarkable Trees,* for example, into a five-panel inlay containing postage-sized pictures; its producers insist that we do not need to see the trees since graphic descriptions evoke them for us. Orion also replaced the drawings in *Why Men Don't Listen and Women Can't Read Maps* with twenty verbal sketches performed by actors. Children's picture books can be especially difficult to record since they have so few words. In response, Penguin created what it called an "aural picture" of *Spot the Dog* by adding music, extra voices, and the sound of windblown leaves.[83]

There are various ways to handle images, maps, charts, and other visual material. Voice alone can convey graphic content in some cases. Bertrand Russell's *The ABC of Relativity* obliged its narrator to describe the movements of trains using analogies instead of the original diagrams. "The fact that we have not got pictures does not matter," insisted the publisher. "The right enthusiasm can draw pictures in the mind's eye."[84] In other cases, publishers simply skip over the graphics, as Jeff Woodman does when he comes to the drawings, signs, and equations dispersed throughout *The Curious Incident of the Dog in the Night-Time*. Ansari even turns the omissions into a joke. "You may have screwed up," he tells people who bought the audiobook. "I mean you got to hear my lovely voice but . . . no charts."[85] For publishers who do make the effort, multimedia books can be prohibitively expensive to record since narrators must figure out beforehand how to translate pictorial material into aural equivalents. But, as previous examples suggest, few books cannot be adapted into sound. There's even a recording of the *Kama Sutra* (Beautiful Books, £8.99).

Other publishers have taken the opposite approach, turning to hybrid formats somewhere in between books and audiobooks. Audiobook downloads increasingly come with PDF documents containing supplementary material. Listening to economist Thomas Piketty's *Capital in the Twenty-First Century* involves consultation of a separate 106-page supplement preserving the book's graphs and tables. Piketty is not for commuters. The arrangement presupposes a reader willing to navigate between media once considered mutually exclusive. In fact, I usually ignore attachments, taking what I can from the recording alone (if I can read the chart, then I might as well read the book too). Such supplements—which include everything from author interviews to the original book jacket's photograph—offer a reminder that our interaction with books has always been about more than the story itself.

The End of Audiobooks

Listening to books has made me acutely aware of the song lyrics embedded in them. In my experience, people usually read these lyrics as prose or skip them altogether. I'd barely noticed how many books have songs until hearing them. A doleful ballad making Jane Eyre weep did not have the slightest impact on me until Juliet Stevenson sang it. When reading, I usually recognize songs from my lifetime (though pop lyrics are rarely quoted because of copyright restrictions). Songs I don't recognize are mere words on the page, however. Historic melodies would be lost on me without the narrator's guidance. Linda Stephens restores an entire Confederate soundscape to *Gone with the Wind,* for example, by singing "The Bonnie Blue Flag," "When This Cruel War Is Over," "My Old Kentucky Home," "Ole Dan Tucker," and "Go Down Moses."

The original music makes its way onto other audiobooks. Corinna Clendenen's *Double Time* plays tracks by Vampire Weekend and other bands in between chapters.[86] Her audience no longer needs to re-create the songs in their minds from a scrap of verse or play them separately. The "music-enhanced audiobook" (as *AudioFile* described Clendenen's novel) will remain a rarity as long as permissions are expensive and difficult to obtain.[87] Nevertheless, *Double Time* points toward one way in which audiobooks can outdo print.

Audiobook soundtracks typically do not have a source in the original script. Instead, the music has been added to introduce narratives, establish moods, evoke settings, or mark transitions. Sounds can also act as "audio cues," registering key moments through the use of, say, swelling music to indicate a sex scene.[88] Narrators have been known to supply their own music. Rob Inglis did so for *The Hobbit* when he was unable to find all of Tolkien's recordings. Or publishers can commission original music. Full Cast Audio created an entire score for Gail Carson Levine's *Fairest,* a young adult novel set in the musical kingdom of Ayortha. Its composer boasted that "there are more songs in *Fairest* than in any Broadway musical."[89] You can even hear the fourteen hymns Margaret Atwood wrote for God's Gardeners sung to music on a recording of *The Year of the Flood.*

Then there are actual music books. Who wants to read about music you can't hear? Even the Library of Congress's talking book service for blind people considered sound superior to writing when it came to music books; its first Mozart biography replaced the book's notations with piano music.[90] Commercial publishers followed suit with albums like *The History of Classical Music,* which includes 150 musical excerpts. Similarly, musicians enliven Walter Dean Myers's *Blues Journey,* Kate Thompson's *The New Policeman,* and Victor Wooten's *The Music Lesson.* The Medici String Quartet even performs alongside

Alan Bennett on *Hymn,* a memoir of his musical upbringing in Yorkshire—truly a singing book.

Serious readers have long frowned on sound effects as a way of dumbing down books or nudging them toward radio and television. Most publishers use them sparingly to ensure that their recordings are perceived as books, not radio dramatizations.[91] A producer for Warner Audio linked the canned sounds of gravel boxes, slide whistles, and coconut shells to a bygone era: "Today's audiences are too sophisticated for the old-style radio plays."[92] Instead of moving away from sound effects, however, publishers have seized the chance to make books more like radio. Lavish productions target audiences who grew up listening to serials like *The Shadow.* Galaxy Press used over 175,000 sounds, for example, while recording L. Ron Hubbard's pulp fiction.[93] The perpetual soundtrack makes it easy to forget that you're listening to a book.

Audiobooks are even more likely to affiliate themselves with the movies. Some recordings borrow material directly from films. In 1955, Charles Laughton's recording of *The Night of the Hunter* was based on Davis Grubb's novel *and* the United Artists film soundtrack. (Sarah Kozloff describes films converted into spoken word recordings as "audio-izations."[94]) Several decades later, Graham Greene's *The Third Man* (Audio Editions) began with the film's haunting zither music. "It's old radio with new technology," observed the president of Ear Literature.[95]

Vintage radio's homemade sound effects have since given way to the film industry's sound design. Penguin recorded the noises for its Roald Dahl line at Pinewood, one of Britain's oldest film studios—finally readers know what it sounds like to dance on a peach. Galaxy Press uses music to create a "cinematic effect" on its spoken word recordings.[96] And GraphicAudio publishes audiobooks under the tagline "A Movie in Your Mind."[97] Whereas audio publishers once used similar mottoes to differentiate themselves from film—let your imagination do the work, not the screen—GraphicAudio moves in the opposite direction, bringing film elements (celebrity casts, sound effects, original scores) to the reading experience. Its productions either downplay the original books or are based on graphic novels already bearing a tenuous relationship to books.

A number of audio publishers see video, games, and other nonprint media—not books—as their competition. One response: Orson Scott Card turned his novel *Ender's Game* into *Ender's Game Alive,* an "audioplay" performed by nearly thirty actors. Replacing the novel's omniscient narrator with dialogue, background music, and sound effects, the adaptation sits somewhere between the audiobook (even reusing several narrators) and the film adaptation. The producer insists that "this is *not* an audiobook in the usual sense. Nor is it strictly 'radio drama.' . . . It is not the original book or audiobook, and it is not the movie, but in complexity and scale it's more like a feature film."[98] Except that the recording is over seven hours long.

Converging media have made possible new combinations of text and sound, further undermining the boundaries between books, audiobooks, and other media. Digital technology has given rise to "enhanced audiobooks," for example, which are modeled after books but add games, hyperlinks, and audiovisual elements to the text.[99] The first audiobook released as an enhanced CD was Mark Bowden's *Killing Pablo: The Hunt for the World's Greatest Outlaw* (Simon and Schuster Audio, $32).[100] While *Killing Pablo* sounds like a regular audiobook on a CD player, playing it on a computer opens up additional video footage and interviews with law enforcement officials. More recently, Touchpress's *The Waste Land* app (Touch Press, £7.99) for iPads allows audiences to hear the poem read aloud by T. S. Eliot, Alec Guinness, Ted Hughes, Viggo Mortensen, and Fiona Shaw while viewing the original manuscripts.

Such applications resemble multimedia websites as much as books; audio is simply one component. They gesture toward a future in which audiobooks are widely available but increasingly indistinguishable from other media. On that note, Audible is one of many media companies anticipating a rise in "format-agnostic media consumption" among customers who indiscriminately consume stories in audio, textual, and visual media—or even some combination of them.[101] Being asked whether you've read a book is becoming an increasingly difficult question to answer.

Many of today's audiobooks are no longer based on books at all. Companies have begun commissioning works written exclusively for audio. These range from full-cast productions reminiscent of old-time radio plays to multipart science-fiction epics that have long since outgrown their origins among books. Popular series including *Star Trek, Star Wars,* and *Doctor Who* have always been an incoherent mixture of recorded books, original manuscripts, radio dramatizations, and screenplay novelizations with fuzzy boundaries between them. They are characteristic of an era of "postliterary adaptations" derived from sources other than books.[102] If my original definition judged an audiobook to be any recorded book, then dramatic productions that never existed as a book in the first place signal a departure. We're left with "audio" but no "book."[103]

A number of today's publishers aim to sever links to the book altogether by branding their products as "audio entertainment."[104] Original content ranges from radio dramas and podcasts to material intended for book publication that went straight to audio instead—all of which Audible refers to as "non-book-based content."[105] Audible has led the way in commissioning original material, following television distributors such as Netflix in moving from content provided by other companies to original work made under its own imprint. As of 2014, Audible had commissioned and produced approximately thirty original works.

The Chopin Manuscript is one of them. Tellingly, the winner of the Audio Publishers Association's Audiobook of the Year Award in 2008 never existed as a book in the first place. Released only as an audio download, *The Chopin Manuscript* is a serialized thriller written collectively by fifteen different writers and then read by a single narrator.[106] The lead contributor, Jeffery Deaver, went on to write *The Starling Project,* another mystery written exclusively for audio— what the author described as "a nonvisual play."[107] Books would not be mentioned at all here if Deaver's entire career to that point hadn't been spent writing novels. In fact, people who hear *The Starling Project* find it more like watching a film than reading a book.

This book began with the spoken word recordings made after Edison's invention of the phonograph in 1877. It's gone on to trace the tradition from the initial attempts to record books on wax cylinders all the way up to the present moment, at which books no longer seem essential to the audiobook's future—what the *Bookseller* seminar deemed an "Audio Revolution." We're left with two strands of audiobook publishing: one that adheres as closely as possible to printed books; another that strives to outdo them. The use of celebrity readers, multiple narrators, full casts, musical scores, and sound effects once associated with media other than books all signal the audiobook's independence. Caveat auditor: customers should choose titles with care since there is a gulf between the solo narrator and full-cast dramatizations made in Hollywood's image, even if both productions fit comfortably under the label "audiobooks." We are witnessing the format's evolution—if not revolution— in response to rival media, technological developments, and changing tastes. No one knows what the audiobooks of the future will sound like. But we can be sure that they will continue to challenge our understanding of what it means to read a book.

Afterword

SPEED LISTENING

You may be reading this book in print or listening to a recording of it. What you're probably not doing is listening to it being read by an artificial voice—a viable option now that speech synthesis technology has brought these voices to the cusp of humanness. Text-to-speech engines using computer-generated voices are all around us. Today's notebooks, tablets, and smartphones come equipped with synthetic voices that can read out the screen's contents. People who are blind or otherwise print-disabled have long relied on screen readers. Websites like Project Gutenberg offer other people a choice between "human-read" and "computer-generated" audiobooks.[1] And many electronic book readers include a text-to-speech feature allowing any e-book to be turned into an audiobook.

This book began by asking what difference it makes whether we read a book with our eyes or our ears. It ends with a closely related question: Does it make a difference whether the book is read by a human or a robot?

Not long ago this would have seemed like a silly question to ask. For centuries people have tried to simulate the human voice without success. The speaking automata made by eighteenth- and nineteenth-century inventors—from Roger Bacon's Brazen Head to Wolfgang von Kempelen's *Sprachmaschine* and Johannes Faber's Euphonia—modeled themselves on human speech organs and, later, the human ear.[2] Yet no one would mistake these contraptions (even though some had human faces or other body parts) for actual human beings.

Speech synthesis has come a long way since the barely intelligible, robotic voices associated in the popular imagination with Stephen Hawking. The initial efforts to generate artificial speech resulted in voices that sounded unnatural at best. The development of computer-based speech synthesis systems in the 1950s led to the gradual improvement of these voices. Blind people, especially those who had no alternative, were the first to embrace text-to-speech technology as a way of converting print into accessible formats.[3] Subsequent research has brought computer-generated speech ever closer to its goal of mimicking human speech.[4]

A breakthrough came when researchers stopped trying to generate speech ex nihilo and instead began assembling massive databases of real speech that could be carved up and then spliced back together to form new sentences (what's known as concatenative speech synthesis).[5] People who haven't heard the latest synthetic voices are often taken aback by how lifelike they have become. Today these voices sound uncannily human—less Hawking than Hal from *2001: A Space Odyssey*—even if the occasional slip of the tongue (so to speak) still makes it easy to tell the difference between humans and computers.

Speech synthesis has improved to the point that we can anticipate a future in which digital voices will be indistinguishable from human ones. Human speech has so far proven too complex, varied, and nuanced for a computer to replicate. Whereas getting a computer to read words on a page is a relatively straightforward task, getting it to read those words with anything near the expressiveness of a human voice is a challenge of another magnitude. Yet what's called emotional speech synthesis aims to do just that by getting computers to speak a line of text in the same way as a human would.[6] These voices sound increasingly natural, even lifelike.

There are encouraging signs of progress. In 2009, IBM patented a synthetic voice complete with the "ums," "ers," coughs, sighs, and snorts that make narrators all too human.[7] Others allow you to choose a tone (happy, sad, enthusiastic).[8] The latest ones can even be heard taking a breath between sentences. It's telling that voice engines from Anna to Ziggy are referred to by their first names. The idea of falling in love with a voice emanating from one's mobile phone (as depicted in Spike Jonze's 2013 film *Her*) is no longer implausible—even if the technology is a long way from rivaling the voice of Scarlett Johansson.

That film's taboo intimacy suggests one reason why the idea of listening to a synthetic voice makes people uncomfortable. Speech that is *too* lifelike threatens to transgress the boundary between humans and robots. It is one thing to use synthetic voices to access information on our phones; it is another to develop feelings for them. Another source of unease arises from technology's competition with humans. This dystopian tradition goes back at least to John Philip Sousa's objections to talking machines displacing human performers at the expense of "the national throat."[9] What chance do amateur readers stand against the likes of a cyborg Johansson?

Synthetic narration strikes many as a step in the wrong direction, moving us further away from storytelling's roots in ancient Greece or in the bedtime rituals of our childhoods. No one is telling the story any longer in the digital era. It brings to mind the comedian Andy Kaufman's act where he stops reading aloud *The Great Gatsby* on stage only to play a record of himself reading it aloud. Today the punch line would be that Kaufman no longer needs to read the book at all.

Listening to a robot read a novel is hardly an enticing prospect. Most people find it difficult to listen to nonhuman readers for longer than a minute. Too often these voices lack the expressiveness of an actual person. Whereas human narrators have thought about the most appropriate way to read a story, mechanical narrators read every script in the same way. It can be deeply unsettling to hear their unusual pronunciations, odd intonations, and bewildering pauses. One journalist likened this voice to "a dyslexic robot who spent his formative years in Eastern Europe."[10] The unnatural sounds make audiences acutely aware that they're listening to a machine—the sonic equivalent to the uncanny valley effect.[11]

Still, another group of readers, mainly ones who are blind or partially sighted, prefers synthetic voices for these very reasons. (If, by chance, you are listening to this book read by a machine, I'm guessing you're part of this group.) These readers favor computer-generated voices precisely because they do not perform the text; the artificial voice does not distract them from the book's content or lead them to get hung up on a speaker's quirks. It is the least expressive voice possible. More important, computer-generated voices do not interfere with the reader's own construal of the narrative. "With a synthesized voice there's no interpretation," insists one blind woman cited by the *New York Times*.[12] Listening to artificial voices is the closest she's able to get to the experience of reading print.

Other blind readers have shown a comparable level of toleration, if not outright enthusiasm, for synthetic voices. John Hull, who lost his sight in his late forties, explained to me why he considers synthetic voices superior to human ones:

People often ask me if the PC voice irritates me. No, it is not relevant. It is not the sound of the voice that I am listening to but the meaning of the language. Human narrators find it difficult to hide their own emotions when they are reading; the PC has no emotion, only a syntactical inflexion to mark the grammar. The computer is never surprised, baffled, apologetic or embarrassed. The impersonality of the PC is its strength.[13]

Synthetic voices are the antidote to one of the most incriminating charges against the audiobook: that its siren song charms the reader into a state of passive submission. No one would accuse the robot's voice of seduction. In fact, Hull and many other people with vision impairments play synthetic voices at extremely fast rates that sound like gibberish to the untrained ear—speed listening if not speed reading. While I can count on one hand the number of sighted readers I've met who listen to synthetic voices, evidence suggests that these voices are not a personal preference so much as an acquired taste.[14] Nearly all readers prefer natural voices at the outset; it's just that people who are forced to listen to synthetic voices become used to them—maybe even fond of them.

Synthetic voices have the further advantage of being able to read books that are not worth a human reader's time or labor. Only a small percentage (as low as 5 percent) of books published in print each year are then recorded. People who are blind or partially sighted depend on assistive technologies like screen readers to access the other 95 percent. For them, it is a choice between a robot voice and no voice. Most of these books are hardly literature anyway; it makes no difference who reads an economics textbook.

Or maybe it does: the Authors Guild took synthetic readers seriously enough to pen an op-ed in the *New York Times* protesting against the use of text-to-speech on Amazon's Kindle and other electronic readers. According to Roy Blount, Jr., then the guild's president, this option turns every e-book into a latent audiobook. Since the title's audio rights—or synthetic audio rights, as the case may be—have not been purchased, text-to-speech seems to be one more way for authors not to get paid in the new digital economy. Blount found the Kindle's artificial voices to be "quite listenable," even if they fell short of maestros like Jim Dale.[15] In other words, they were good enough that audiences might be tempted to listen to them for free instead of paying to hear flesh-and-blood actors. Amazon relented by allowing publishers to disable the text-to-speech option on specific titles.

The Authors Guild is right to keep an eye on the gradual encroachment of synthetic voices into the publishing industry. The robots are coming for your books! When I spoke to engineers at Google about the technology's future, however, they told me not to think of the issue in terms of robots taking over from humans. Instead, they described a continuum with literature performed by professional actors at one end and, at the other end, the publishing world's leftovers (phonebooks, instruction manuals, last year's travel guides) that no one would ever pay somebody to read. The line will continue to slide marking where people are willing to tolerate robots contra humans.[16] People will probably always prefer to hear literature read aloud by virtuoso performers; Derek Jacobi has nothing to fear from a robotic rhapsode named iOn. Yet more and more people will find synthetic voices satisfactory for those books that are not meant to be life-changing works of art. Skeptics might even succumb to the prospect of hearing dead celebrities (Orson Welles, anyone?) read to them despite knowing the voice isn't real.

The publishing industry faces an era of customized narration in which the speaker's voice will be tailored to suit particular narratives. The shift from human to nonhuman narration will dramatically influence the book's reception as well as ongoing debates over how to read a talking book—what this book's previous chapters have called the politics of narration. Audiences have grown increasingly sophisticated when it comes to judging the fit between narrator and script, especially in terms of sensitive issues like age, class, ethnicity, gender, nationality, race, and sexuality. To the discerning ear, there's no such thing as a neutral voice. Casting controversies might be averted, however, if synthetic speech technology were to give audiences a measure of control over the narrator's identity. Don't like a man reading to you? Swap him for a woman. The voice sounds too white? Switch to a Latino one. Don't like British accents? Choose a Texan instead.

Audiences might even respond to mechanical voices with the same devotion as they do to human ones. A thread running through this book has been the intimate relationships forged between narrators and their audiences despite the studio's best efforts to keep these speakers inconspicuous. This is true of nearly every recording, from talking books narrated in so-called neutral voices to audiobooks read by celebrities. In each case, audiences have been susceptible to intense attachments. The benefits include a sense of intimacy, companionship, and contact—the feeling that someone is speaking directly to you—felt to be missing from encounters with the printed page. What will happen to this relationship when there is no one behind the curtain?

My guess is that people will feel uneasy about synthetic narrators—but only at first. Audiences will eventually grow used to them as they have with the speech engines used by other technologies. They will be entertained and even awed by synthetic voices, then dependent on them. Audiences will expect to be able to customize the speaker's persona to suit their preferences and become increasingly intolerant of unwanted vocal tics among its human counterparts. Knowing that a real person is not actually speaking to them will either have little impact on the relationship's intensity or, perhaps, cause it to blend in with countless other digital interactions. The latter outcome might even return our attention to the words themselves.

The Untold Story of the Talking Book set out to trace the history of recorded books left out of other accounts of our reading lives. In telling the talking book's story, it has sought to move beyond the reductive debate over whether what we do with audiobooks truly counts as reading by calling into question instead what it means to read a book in the first place. Audiobooks have taught me, at least, that reading is even more absorbing, complex, and versatile than is usually thought. We have only to consult the contradictory testimonials of everyone from blind people who defiantly call themselves "readers" to the "nonreaders" listening to Jon Stewart's audiobook.[17] (The latter is a step up, at least, from being called "you lazy piece of shit" by Stewart's fellow comedian Aziz Ansari.[18])

Audiobooks fascinate me precisely because they elicit such intense feelings among readers and appeal to groups that seem to be polar opposites when it comes to taste. As this book has shown, audiobooks are for people who can't read and for people who can't read enough. They are for people who are busy doing other things. They are for people who hang on every word. They are for the technologically savvy. They are for traditionalists. They are for people who want books to be more like the movies. They are for "bookish" people. Audiobooks are for those of us who hate reading. Audiobooks are for those of us who love reading.

NOTES

CREDITS

ACKNOWLEDGMENTS

INDEX

Notes

Introduction

1. The Audio Publishers Association estimates industry retail sales to be $1.47 billion. This figure is cited in its "Annual Survey of Members 2015," Audio Publishers Association, spring 2015, http://www.audiopub.org/resources -industry-data.asp.

2. Audiobooks account for approximately 5 percent of overall revenues among the major trade houses. See John B. Thompson, *Merchants of Culture: The Publishing Business in the Twenty-First Century* (Cambridge: Polity, 2010), 351.

3. James Shokoff refers to audiobooks as "the stepchildren of American letters" in "What Is an Audiobook?," *Journal of Popular Culture* 34, no. 4 (Spring 2001): 171–81. The audiobook's critical history is outlined in Matthew Rubery, ed., *Audiobooks, Literature, and Sound Studies* (New York: Routledge, 2011).

4. Robin Whitten, "Growth of the Audio Publishing Industry," *Publishing Research Quarterly* 18, no. 3 (September 2002): 3–10; 5.

5. See James W. Earl, "King Alfred's Talking Poems," in *Thinking about "Beowulf"* (Palo Alto, Calif.: Stanford University Press, 1994), 87–99.

6. Cyrano de Bergerac, *Voyages to the Moon and the Sun,* trans. Richard Aldington (London: Folio Society, 1991), 79–80; Washington Irving, "The Mutability of Literature," in *The Sketch Book of Geoffrey Crayon, Gent.* (New York: C. S. Van Winkle, 1820), 4:5–27.

7. See Allen Dwight Callahan, *The Talking Book: African Americans and the Bible* (New Haven, Conn.: Yale University Press, 2006).

8. Henry Louis Gates, Jr., "The Trope of the Talking Book," in *The Signifying Monkey: A Theory of African-American Literary Criticism* (New York: Oxford University Press, 1988): 127–69; 165.

9. Margaret Mitchell, *Gone with the Wind*, read by Linda Stephens (Prince Frederick, Md.: Recorded Books, 2001), 41 compact discs; Andrew Mayer and Jim Becker, *10 Classics in 10 Minutes,* read by John Moschitta (New York: Workman, 1986), 1 cassette.

10. On radio's dramatic conventions, see Neil Verma, *Theater of the Mind: Imagination, Aesthetics, and American Radio Drama* (Chicago: University of Chicago

Press, 2012), and Dermot Rattigan, *Theatre of Sound: Radio and the Dramatic Imagination* (Dublin: Carysfort, 2002).

11. Anna Richardson, "Hitchhiker's Guide Top of Audiobooks," *Bookseller,* August 1, 2008, http://www.thebookseller.com/news/hitchhikers-guide-top-audiobooks. The list was published in the *Guardian* on June 28, 2008.

12. On audiobooks as new media, see Iben Have and Birgitte Stougaard Pedersen, "Sonic Mediatization of the Book: Affordances of the Audiobook," *MedieKultur* 54 (2013): 123–40; and Iben Have and Birgitte Stougaard Pedersen, "Conceptualizing the Audiobook Experience," *SoundEffects* 2, no. 2 (2012): 80–95. These ideas are developed at greater length in Iben Have and Birgitte Stougaard Pedersen, *Digital Audiobooks: New Media, Users, and Experiences* (New York: Routledge, 2016), which unfortunately was published after the completion of my manuscript.

13. On Greece's oral tradition, see Albert B. Lord, *The Singer of Tales,* 2nd ed., ed. Stephen Mitchell and Gregory Nagy (Cambridge, Mass.: Harvard University Press, 2000), Eric A. Havelock, *The Muse Learns to Write: Reflections on Orality and Literacy from Antiquity to the Present* (New Haven, Conn.: Yale University Press, 1986), Gregory Nagy, *Poetry as Performance: Homer and Beyond* (Cambridge, Mass.: Cambridge University Press, 1996), and Ruth Scodel, *Listening to Homer: Tradition, Narrative, and Audience* (Ann Arbor: University of Michigan Press, 2002).

14. Marshall McLuhan, *Counterblast* (Toronto, 1954), n.p.

15. Saint Augustine, *Confessions,* trans. Henry Chadwick (Oxford: Oxford University Press, 1992), 92–93.

16. Paul Saenger gives a detailed account of this transition in *Space between Words: The Origins of Silent Reading* (Palo Alto, Calif.: Stanford University Press, 1997).

17. The classic study of the press's impact is Elizabeth L. Eisenstein's *The Printing Press as an Agent of Change: Communications and Cultural Transformations in Early Modern Europe* (Cambridge: Cambridge University Press, 1979).

18. See Marshall McLuhan, *The Gutenberg Galaxy: The Making of Typographic Man* (London: Routledge & Kegan Paul, 1962), and Marshall McLuhan, *Understanding Media: The Extensions of Man* (Cambridge, Mass.: MIT Press, 1994). McLuhan's approach has been called into question by many scholars; for a sample of its shortcomings, see the 2014 special issue of *Journal of Visual Culture* commemorating the semicentennial of *Understanding Media:* "Marshall McLuhan's Understanding Media: Extensions of Man @ 50," ed. Raiford Guins, special issue, *Journal of Visual Culture* 13, no. 1 (April 2014).

19. Gerald Graff, *Professing Literature: An Institutional History* (Chicago: University of Chicago Press, 1987), 36–51.

20. See Christopher Hilliard, *English as a Vocation: The "Scrutiny" Movement* (Oxford: Oxford University Press, 2012), 39–41. John Guillory outlines this method's institutionalization in "Close Reading: Prologue and Epilogue," *ADE Bulletin* 149 (2010): 8–14.

21. Robert Beloof, *The Performing Voice in Literature* (Boston: Little, Brown, 1966), 113. For an account of this shift, see K. B. Valentine, "'New Criticism' and the Emphasis on Literature in Interpretation," in *Performance of Literature in*

Historical Perspectives, ed. David W. Thompson (Lanham, Md.: University Press of America, 1983), 549–65. See also Eugene Bahn, *A History of Oral Interpretation* (Minneapolis: Burgess, 1970).

22. On the role of recitation in education and civic life, see Joan Shelley Rubin, *Songs of Ourselves: The Uses of Poetry in America* (Cambridge, Mass.: Harvard University Press, 2007), and Catherine Robson, *Heart Beats: Everyday Life and the Memorized Poem* (Princeton, N.J.: Princeton University Press, 2012).

23. Walter J. Ong, *Orality and Literacy: The Technologizing of the Word* (London: Methuen, 1982), 11. See also Lucy Bednar, "Audiobooks and the Reassertion of Orality: Walter J. Ong and Others Revisited," *CEA Critic* 73, no. 1 (Fall 2010): 74–85. Walter Benjamin elaborates on the difficulties of storytelling after the First World War in "The Storyteller," in *Illuminations,* ed. Hannah Arendt, trans. Harry Zohn (New York: Schocken Books, 1968), 83–109.

24. Johanna Drucker examines the tradition of typographical experimentation in *The Visible Word: Experimental Typography and Modern Art, 1909–1923* (Chicago: University of Chicago Press, 1994), and Elspeth Jajdelska documents changes in prose style in *Silent Reading and the Birth of the Narrator* (Toronto: University of Toronto Press, 2007).

25. Quoted in Adam Andrew Newman, "How Should a Book Sound? And What about Footnotes?," *New York Times,* January 20, 2006, 33. On the imperative to "find your voice," see Mark McGurl, *The Program Era: Postwar Fiction and the Rise of Creative Writing* (Cambridge, Mass.: Harvard University Press, 2009), 227–70.

26. See Jason Camlot's account of vocalization in "Early Talking Books: Spoken Recordings and Recitation Anthologies, 1880–1920," *Book History* 6 (2003): 147–73.

27. One of the most influential contrasts made between active reading and passive media consumption can be found in *Reading at Risk: A Survey of Literary Reading in America,* Research Division Report 46 (Washington, D.C.: National Endowment for the Arts, 2004), vii.

28. Quoted in Eben Shapiro, "How I Got through Henry James's 580-Page 'Golden Bowl,'" *Wall Street Journal,* May 1, 2015, http://blogs.wsj.com/speakeasy/2015/05/01/how-i-got-through-henry-jamess-580-page-golden-bowl/.

29. Peter Kivy, *The Performance of Reading: An Essay in the Philosophy of Literature* (Oxford: Blackwell, 2009), 135. See also William Irwin's response to Kivy in "Reading Audio Books," *Philosophy and Literature* 33, no. 2 (October 2009): 358–68.

30. Gregg Kavet and Andy Robin, "The Fatigues," *Seinfeld,* season 8, episode 6, aired October 31, 1996, NBC.

31. Thomas A. Edison, "The Phonograph and Its Future," *North American Review* 126, no. 262 (May 1878): 527–36; 533.

32. See Judith Pascoe, *The Sarah Siddons Audio Files: Romanticism and the Lost Voice* (Ann Arbor: University of Michigan Press, 2011), 89–95; and Malcolm Andrews, *Charles Dickens and His Performing Selves: Dickens and the Public Readings* (Oxford: Oxford University Press, 2006).

33. Both versions are available at "David Sedaris Reads from His 'Santaland Diaries,'" *Morning Edition* (December 23, 2013), NPR, http://www.npr.org /2013/12/23/255550048/david-sedaris-reads-from-his-santaland-diaries.

34. Friedrich A. Kittler, *Discourse Networks 1800/1900,* trans. Michael Metteer, with Chris Cullens (Palo Alto, Calif.: Stanford University Press, 1990), 236–37.

35. F. R. Leavis, "Reading Out Poetry," in *Reading Out Poetry; and, Eugenio Montale: A Tribute* (Belfast: Queen's University of Belfast, 1979), 5–29; 6.

36. Mladen Dolar, *A Voice and Nothing More* (Cambridge, Mass.: MIT Press, 2006), 22. Other influential theoretical accounts of the voice include Roland Barthes, "The Grain of the Voice," in *The Responsibility of Forms: Critical Essays on Music, Art, and Representation,* trans. Richard Howard (Berkeley: University of California Press, 1991), 267–77; Stephen Connor, *Dumbstruck: A Cultural History of Ventriloquism* (Oxford: Oxford University Press, 2000); Jacques Derrida, *Of Grammatology,* trans. Gayatri Spivak (Baltimore: Johns Hopkins University Press, 1976); and Kaja Silverman, *The Acoustic Mirror: The Female Voice in Psychoanalysis and Cinema* (Bloomington: Indiana University Press, 1988).

37. See Michele Hilmes, *Radio Voices: American Broadcasting, 1922–1952* (Minneapolis: University of Minnesota Press, 1997), and Susan J. Douglas, *Listening In: Radio and the American Imagination* (Minneapolis: University of Minnesota Press, 2004).

38. Michel Chion examines the acousmatic voice at length in *The Voice in Cinema,* trans. Claudia Gorbman (New York: Columbia University Press, 1999).

39. Toni Morrison, phone conversation with the author, June 28, 2013, available at http://audiobookhistory.wordpress.com/2013/07/29/talking-to-myself-an -interview-with-toni-morrison/.

40. Jerome J. McGann, *The Textual Condition* (Princeton, N.J.: Princeton University Press, 1991), 57.

41. Cathy N. Davidson, "Toward a History of Books and Readers," in *Reading in America: Literature and Social History,* ed. Cathy N. Davidson (Baltimore: Johns Hopkins University Press, 1989), 1–26; 1.

42. David D. Hall, *A History of the Book in America,* 5 vols. (Chapel Hill: University of North Carolina Press, 2000–2009).

43. Michael F. Suarez and H. R. Woudhuysen, "Introduction," in *The Oxford Companion to the Book,* ed. Michael F. Suarez and H. R. Woudhuysen (Oxford: Oxford University Press, 2010), 1:ix–xiii; ix. The entry for "audio book" is on 492–93.

44. This phrase is taken from the title of McLuhan's *The Gutenberg Galaxy.*

45. D. F. McKenzie, *Bibliography and the Sociology of Texts: The Panizzi Lectures, 1985* (London: British Library, 1986), ix.

46. On the relationship between the digital humanities and bibliography, see Jerome McGann, *Radiant Textuality: Literature after the World Wide Web* (Basingstoke: Palgrave, 2001).

47. Andrew Piper, *Dreaming in Books: The Making of the Bibliographic Imagination in the Romantic Age* (Chicago: Chicago University Press, 2009), 5.

48. By contrast, the phonograph features prominently in the work of media historians such as Friedrich A. Kittler, *Gramophone, Film, Typewriter,* trans. Geoffrey Winthrop-Young and Michael Wutz (Palo Alto, Calif.: Stanford University Press, 1999), and Lisa Gitelman, *Scripts, Grooves, and Writing Machines: Representing Technology in the Edison Era* (Palo Alto, Calif.: Stanford University Press, 1999).

49. Robert Darnton, "What Is the History of Books?," in *The Kiss of Lamourette: Reflections in Cultural History* (New York: W. W. Norton, 1990), 107–35.

50. John M. Hull, *Touching the Rock: An Experience of Blindness* (Melbourne: David Lovell, 1990), 152.

51. Andrew Piper considers the link between hands and reading in *Book Was There: Reading in Electronic Times* (Chicago: University of Chicago Press, 2012), 1–23. On touch and vision more broadly, see Constance Classen, *The Deepest Sense: A Cultural History of Touch* (Urbana: University of Illinois Press, 2012), 51–56; and Mark Paterson, *The Senses of Touch: Haptics, Affects and Technologies* (New York: Berg, 2007), 37–57.

52. "Literary Machine," *Illustrated London News,* no. 3789A (December 2, 1911): 951.

53. Carl R. Augusto, *Reflections of a Lifetime Reader: An Address* (Washington, D.C.: National Library Service for the Blind and Physically Handicapped, Library of Congress, 1992), 1.

54. This case is made by Elaine Scarry, *Dreaming by the Book* (New York: Farrar, Straus and Giroux, 1999), 5; and Marie-Laure Ryan, *Narrative as Virtual Reality: Immersion and Interactivity in Literature and Electronic Media* (Baltimore: Johns Hopkins University Press, 2001), 98.

55. Stanislas Dehaene, *Reading in the Brain: The New Science of How We Read* (London: Penguin, 2009), 62. Dehaene reviews subsequent experiments in *"Reading in the Brain* Revised and Extended: Response to Comments," *Mind and Language* 29, no. 3 (June 2014): 320–35.

56. George G. Hruby and Usha Goswami note the risks of "neophrenology" in "Neuroscience and Reading: A Review for Reading Education Researchers," *Reading Research Quarterly* 46, no. 2 (2011): 156–72; 157.

57. Paul B. Armstrong, *How Literature Plays with the Brain: The Neuroscience of Reading and Art* (Baltimore: Johns Hopkins University Press, 2013), 26.

58. Exceptions illustrate the diversity of reading capacities even at the neurological level. Synesthetes like French poet Arthur Rimbaud, for example, perceive a halo of color around certain letters. Dehaene, *Reading in the Brain,* 215–18.

59. Deaf children take three to four years longer than other children to develop minimal reading ability. See Susan Goldin-Meadow and Rachel I. Mayberry, "How Do Profoundly Deaf Children Learn to Read?," *Learning Disabilities Research and Practice* 16, no. 4 (2001): 222–29. Historical accounts include Jonathan Rée, *I See a Voice: A Philosophical History of Language, Deafness and the Senses* (London: HarperCollins, 1999), and Lydia Denworth's memoir, *I Can Hear You Whisper: An Intimate Journey through the Science of Sound and Language* (New York: Dutton Adult, 2014).

60. Barbara Will, *Gertrude Stein, Modernism, and the Problem of "Genius"* (Edinburgh: Edinburgh University Press, 2000), 24.

61. Oliver Sacks, *The Mind's Eye* (London: Picador, 2010), 218.

62. Dr. Seuss, *I Can Read with My Eyes Shut!* (New York: Beginner Books, 1978).

63. Lior Reich, Marcin Szwed, Laurent Cohen, and Amir Amedi, "A Ventral Visual Stream Reading Center Independent of Visual Experience," *Current Biology* 21 (March 8, 2011): 363–68. See also Norihiro Sadato, "How the Blind 'See' Braille: Lessons from Functional Magnetic Resonance Imaging," *Neuroscientist* 11, no. 6 (2005): 577–82.

64. Comparative studies include Anneli Veispak, Bart Boets, and Pol Ghesquière, "Differential Cognitive and Perceptual Correlates of Print Reading versus Braille Reading," *Research in Developmental Disabilities* 34, no. 1 (2013): 372–85; and Beatrice de Gelder and José Morais, eds., *Speech and Reading: A Comparative Approach* (Hove, U.K.: Erlbaum, 1995). On touch as a perceptual system, see Morton A. Heller and Edouard Gentaz, *Psychology of Touch and Blindness* (London: Psychology Press, 2014), 165–72.

65. Susanna Millar, *Reading by Touch* (London: Routledge, 1997), 1.

66. Ella Striem-Amit, Laurent Cohen, Stanislas Dehaene, and Amir Amedi, "Reading with Sounds: Sensory Substitution Selectively Activates the Visual Word Form Area in the Blind," *Neuron* 76 (November 8, 2012): 640–52.

67. Marcela Perrone-Bertolotti et al., "What Is That Little Voice Inside My Head? Inner Speech Phenomenology, Its Role in Cognitive Performance, and Its Relation to Self-Monitoring," *Behavioural Brain Research* 261 (2014): 220–39; 228. See also Marcela Perrone-Bertolotti et al., "How Silent Is Silent Reading? Intracerebral Evidence for Top-Down Activation of Temporal Voice Areas during Reading," *Journal of Neuroscience* 32, no. 49 (December 5, 2012): 17554–62; 17554.

68. The philosophical implications of internal voices are addressed in Don Ihde, *Listening and Voice: Phenomenologies of Sounds,* 2nd ed. (Albany: State University of New York Press, 2007), 137–44; Denise Riley, " 'A Voice without a Mouth': Inner Speech," *Qui Parle* 14, no. 2 (Spring/Summer 2004): 57–104; and Steven Connor, *Beckett, Modernism and the Material Imagination* (Cambridge: Cambridge University Press, 2014), 102–14.

69. On the throat's role, see Garrett Stewart, *Reading Voices: Literature and the Phonotext* (Berkeley: University of California Press, 1990), 1–34.

70. Steven Roger Fischer, *A History of Reading* (London: Reaktion Books, 2005), 330.

71. A sense of this variety can be gained from Shafquat Towheed, Rosalind Crone, and Katie Halsey, eds., *The History of Reading: A Reader* (London: Routledge, 2011), and Leah Price, "Reading: The State of the Discipline," *Book History* 7 (2004): 303–20.

72. Roger Chartier, *The Order of Books: Readers, Authors, and Libraries in Europe between the Fourteenth and Eighteenth Centuries,* trans. Lydia G. Cochrane (Oxford: Polity, 1994), 8. This defense of marginal ways of reading is repeated

nearly verbatim in Guglielmo Cavallo and Roger Chartier, "Introduction," in *A History of Reading in the West,* ed. Guglielmo Cavallo and Roger Chartier, trans. Lydia G. Cochrane (Cambridge: Polity, 1999), 1–36; 4.

73. See Mortimer J. Adler, "The Meaning of 'Reading,'" in *How to Read a Book: A Guide to Self-Education* (London: Jarrolds, [1940]), 25–41; 26. For Adler, "fatigue" is the best indicator of reading: "Reading that is reading entails the most intense mental activity. If you are not tired out, you probably have not been doing the work" (79).

74. N. Katherine Hayles, *How We Think: Digital Media and Contemporary Technogenesis* (Chicago: University of Chicago Press, 2012), 79. See also 55–79. For more on technology's influence, see Naomi S. Baron, *Words Onscreen: The Fate of Reading in a Digital World* (Oxford: Oxford University Press, 2015).

75. Mara Mills, "What Should We Call Reading?," *Flow* 17 (December 2012), http://flowtv.org/2012/12/what-should-we-call-reading/.

76. Philip Hatlen, "Comprehensive Literacy," *Journal of Visual Impairment and Blindness* 90, no. 3 (May–June 1996): 174–75. Rachel Aviv recounts a recent version of the "listening is not literacy" debate in "Listening to Braille," *New York Times,* January 3, 2010, http://www.nytimes.com/2010/01/03/magazine/03Braille-t.html?_r=0.

77. D. W. Tuttle, "An Effective Alternative," *Journal of Visual Impairment and Blindness* 90, no. 3 (May–June 1996): 173–74; 173.

78. Historians have long acknowledged imprecision in the terms "literacy" and "illiteracy." Carl F. Kaestle elaborates on them in "Studying the History of Literacy," in *Literacy in the United States: Readers and Reading since 1880,* ed. Carl F. Kaestle et al. (New Haven, Conn.: Yale University Press, 1991), 3–32.

79. Eileen Hyder explains the stigma associated with alternative reading methods in *Reading Groups, Libraries and Social Inclusion: Experiences of Blind and Partially Sighted People* (Farnham, U.K.: Ashgate, 2013).

80. Georgina Kleege, *Sight Unseen* (New Haven, Conn.: Yale University Press, 1999), 190. Kleege elaborated on her personal experience in a lecture titled "Dear Readers: My History with Aural Texts" given at the "Blindness, Technology, and Multimodal Reading" conference held in London on June 27, 2014. An audio recording is available here: https://blindnessconference.wordpress.com/presentations/.

81. John Hull, e-mail correspondence with the author, May 12, 2014. Peter Kivy similarly describes our external senses (sight, touch, hearing) as "mere instruments" facilitating the mental experience of a novel, in "The Experience of Reading," in *A Companion to the Philosophy of Literature,* ed. Garry L. Hagberg and Walter Jost (Oxford: Blackwell, 2010), 106–19; 107.

82. George Steiner uses the terms "semi-attentive reading" and "pseudo-literacy" in relation to a broad range of audiovisual media in "After the Book?," *Visible Language* 6, no. 3 (Summer 1972): 197–210; 209. For a refutation of passive listening, see Kate Lacey, *Listening Publics: The Politics and Experience of Listening in the Media Age* (Cambridge: Polity, 2013), 3.

83. Stephen Kuusisto, *Planet of the Blind* (London: Faber and Faber, 1998), 49.

84. Florence Nightingale, "Cassandra," in *The Collected Works of Florence Nightingale,* ed. Lynn McDonald (Waterloo, Ontario: Wilfred Laurier University Press, 2008), 11:547–92; 560.

85. Kozol criticizes audiobooks in James Brooke, "Talking Books for Those on the Go," *Des Moines Register,* August 13, 1985, 1. Bloom's comments can be found in Amy Harmon, "Loud, Proud, Unabridged: It Is Too Reading!," *New York Times,* May 26, 2005, G1–G2; Sven Birkerts speaks at length about audiobooks in *The Gutenberg Elegies: The Fate of Reading in an Electronic Age* (New York: Fawcett Columbine, 1994), 141–50.

86. Trish L. Varao Sousa, Jonathan S. A. Carriere, and Daniel Smilek, "The Way We Encounter Reading Material Influences How Frequently We Mind Wander," *Frontiers in Psychology* 4, no. 892 (2013), doi: 10.3389/fpsyg.2013.00892.

87. Poetry readings have received substantial attention since Charles Bernstein, ed., *Close Listening: Poetry and the Performed Word* (Oxford: Oxford University Press, 1998).

88. See, for example, Lesley Wheeler, *Voicing American Poetry: Sound and Performance from the 1920s to the Present* (Ithaca, N.Y.: Cornell University Press, 2008).

89. "A Wonderful Invention—Speech Capable of Indefinite Repetition from Automatic Records," *Scientific American,* November 17, 1877, 304.

90. "V. Talking Books," *National Institute for the Blind Annual Report, 1935–36* (London: National Institute for the Blind, 1936), 17–19; 10.

91. See, for example, Siegfried Volkert and François Van Menxel, eds., *Lesen fürs Hören in Münster: 50 Jahre Westdeutsche Blindenhörbücherei e.V. 1955–2005* (Münster: Westdeutsche Blindenhörbücherei, 2005).

92. Quoted in Elizabeth Mehren and Nancy Rivera, "Audio Books—Fast Food for Mind?," *Los Angeles Times,* August 19, 1985, 1, 3; 1.

93. Jon Stewart, *America (The Audiobook): A Citizen's Guide to Democracy Inaction,* abridged ed., read by the author (Time Warner AudioBooks, 2004), digital audio file.

1. Canned Literature

1. Edward H. Johnson, letter to the editor, *Scientific American* 37 (November 17, 1877): 304. The phonograph's development is described in Oliver Read and Walter L. Welch, *From Tin Foil to Stereo: Evolution of the Phonograph* (Indianapolis: Howard W. Sams, 1976), and Paul Israel, *Edison: A Life of Invention* (New York: John Wiley, 1998). Documents relating to the phonograph's invention are available from the Digital Edition of the Thomas A. Edison Papers Project, http://edison.rutgers.edu. On earlier technologies used to reproduce sound, such as Édouard-Léon Scott de Martinville's phonautograph, see Patrick Feaster, "Framing the Mechanical Voice: Generic Conventions of Early Phonograph Recording," *Folklore Forum* 32, nos. 1–2 (2001): 57–102; and Jonathan Sterne, *The Audible Past: Cultural Origins of Sound Reproduction*

(Durham, N.C.: Duke University Press, 2003), 31–85. Sterne and Mitchell Akiyama address the relationship between phonograph and phonautograph in "'The Recording That Never Wanted to Be Heard' and Other Stories of Sonification," in *The Oxford Handbook of Sound Studies,* ed. Trevor Pinch and Karin Bijsterveld (Oxford: Oxford University Press, 2012), 544–60.

2. "Thus the first words ever spoken into the phonograph were these four simple lines of 'Mother Goose,'" Edison recalled at the turn of the century ("The First Phonograph," *Christian Advocate,* October 26, 1899, 74). The original tinfoil recording of "Mary Had a Little Lamb" no longer exists, though Edison's 1927 reenactment of the original recording is available at http://www.nps.gov/edis /photosmultimedia/upload/EDIS-SCD-02.mp3.

3. Nearly all historical accounts of the phonograph focus on its relation to music. Recent examples include Michael Chanan, *Repeated Takes: A Short History of Recording and Its Effects on Music* (London: Verso, 1995), Timothy Day, *A Century of Recorded Music: Listening to Musical History* (New Haven, Conn.: Yale University Press, 2000), Evan Eisenberg, *The Recording Angel: Explorations in Phonography,* 2nd ed. (New Haven, Conn.: Yale University Press, 2005), and Mark Katz, *Capturing Sound: How Technology Has Changed Music,* rev. ed. (Berkeley: University of California Press, 2010). David L. Morton, Jr., attributes the emphasis on music to the scarcity of spoken word recordings, in *Sound Recording: The Life Story of a Technology* (Westport, Conn.: Greenwood, 2004), xi.

4. Lisa Gitelman provides a detailed account of the 1878 phonograph demonstrations in "Souvenir Foils: On the Status of Print at the Origin of Recorded Sound," in *New Media, 1740–1915,* ed. Lisa Gitelman and Geoffrey B. Pingree (Cambridge, Mass.: MIT Press, 2003), 157–73. See also Patrick Feaster, "'The Following Record': Making Sense of Phonographic Performance, 1877–1908" (PhD diss., Indiana University, 2007), 70–131, http://www.phonozoic.net /following-record.pdf.

5. Russell Miller and Roger Boar's *The Incredible Music Machine* (London: Quartet Books, 1982) is a representative title from this expansive field of scholarship. Recent scholarship has sought to correct the imbalance by showing how the discourse of recorded sound developed in relation to print media. See Jason Camlot, "Early Talking Books: Spoken Recordings and Recitation Anthologies, 1880–1920," *Book History* 6 (2003): 147–73; and Lisa Gitelman, *Always Already New: Media, History, and the Data of Culture* (Cambridge, Mass.: MIT Press, 2006), 25–44.

6. "All about the Phonograph," *Christian at Work,* May 23, 1878, Thomas A. Edison Papers Digital Edition (hereafter cited as TAED), SM029083a.

7. See "Cylinder," in *Encyclopedia of Recorded Sound,* 2nd ed., ed. Frank Hoffmann (New York: Routledge, 2005), 258–63.

8. John M. Picker discusses the Tennyson and Browning recordings in *Victorian Soundscapes* (New York: Oxford University Press, 2003), 110–45. On the establishment of the Library of Congress's talking book service in the 1930s, see Frances A. Koestler, *The Unseen Minority: A Social History of Blindness in the*

United States (New York: David McKay, 1976), 130–52; National Library Service for the Blind and Physically Handicapped, Library of Congress, *That All May Read: Library Service for Blind and Physically Handicapped People* (Washington, D.C.: National Library Service for the Blind and Physically Handicapped, Library of Congress, 1983), 65–219; and Marilyn Lundell Majeska, *Talking Books: Pioneering and Beyond* (Washington, D.C.: National Library Service for the Blind and Physically Handicapped, Library of Congress, 1988).

9. "A Wonderful Invention—Speech Capable of Indefinite Repetition from Automatic Records," *Scientific American,* November 17, 1877, 304.

10. Camlot, "Early Talking Books," 151.

11. See the essays on emerging communications technologies in David Thorburn and Henry Jenkins, eds., *Rethinking Media Change: The Aesthetics of Transition* (Cambridge, Mass.: MIT Press, 2003).

12. Friedrich A. Kittler, *Discourse Networks 1800/1900,* trans. Michael Metteer, with Chris Cullens (Palo Alto, Calif.: Stanford University Press, 1990), 237. My approach shares with media archaeologists an interest in retrieving episodes that have been lost, forgotten, or otherwise neglected by traditional accounts of the mass media. The essays gathered in Erkki Huhtamo and Jussi Parikka, eds., *Media Archaeology: Approaches, Applications, and Implications* (Berkeley: University of California Press, 2011), provide a good introduction to the shared goals of historically oriented media studies.

13. Thomas A. Edison, "The Phonograph and Its Future," *North American Review* 126, no. 262 (May 1878): 527–36; 534.

14. "The Phonograph," *New York Times,* November 7, 1877, 4.

15. Ibid.

16. On the novel's changing reputation, see William B. Warner, *Licensing Entertainment: The Elevation of Novel Reading in Britain, 1684–1750* (Berkeley: University of California Press, 1998), 47–94.

17. "Wonderful Invention," 304. This issue of *Scientific American* reached subscribers as early as November 6 and was widely quoted by the press.

18. John Guillory, "Genesis of the Media Concept," *Critical Inquiry* 36 (Winter 2010): 321–62; 322.

19. See, for example, Roland Gelatt, *The Fabulous Phonograph, 1877–1977,* 2nd rev. ed. (New York: Macmillan, 1977), 44; and Morton, *Sound Recording,* 18.

20. Edison, "The Phonograph and Its Future," 533.

21. Engineers likewise recognized the phonograph's potential to aid blind readers. In March 1878, Alfred Mayer, a physics professor writing a textbook on sound, corresponded with Edison about a portable device for reading books to those who were blind. The blind reader would drag Mayer's handheld unit, made of a stylus attached to a vibrating plate, over indented lines in a metal sheet so that "the page will talk to him." Alfred M. Mayer to Thomas Edison, March 17, 1878, in *The Papers of Thomas A. Edison: The Wizard of Menlo Park 1878* (Baltimore: Johns Hopkins University Press, 1998), 4:190. Underlined in original.

22. Friedrich A. Kittler discusses the relationship between disability and sound recording more broadly in *Gramophone, Film, Typewriter,* trans. Geoffrey

Winthrop-Young and Michael Wutz (Palo Alto, Calif.: Stanford University Press, 1999), 22.

23. Mary Cadwalader Jones, "The Education of the Blind," *Scribner's Magazine* 12 (September 1892): 373–87; 375.

24. Vanessa Warne, " 'So That the Sense of Touch May Supply the Want of Sight': Blind Reading and Nineteenth-Century British Print Culture," in *Media, Technology, and Literature in the Nineteenth Century: Image, Sound, Touch,* ed. Colette Colligan and Margaret Linley (Aldershot, U.K.: Ashgate, 2011), 43–64.

25. See the accounts of the "Battle of the Types" in John Oliphant, " 'Touching the Light': The Invention of Literacy for the Blind," *Paedagogica Historica* 44, nos. 1–2 (February–April 2008): 67–82; and Mary Wilson Carpenter, *Health, Medicine, and Society in Victorian England* (Santa Barbara: Praeger, 2010), 128–48.

26. See Lisa Gitelman, *Scripts, Grooves, and Writing Machines: Representing Technology in the Edison Era* (Palo Alto, Calif.: Stanford University Press, 1999), 13, as well as Gitelman's account of the phonograph as a language machine, ibid., 62–96.

27. Scott D. N. Cook, "Technological Revolutions and the Gutenberg Myth," in *Internet Dreams: Archetypes, Myths, and Metaphors,* ed. Mark Stefik (Cambridge, Mass.: MIT Press, 1996), 67–82.

28. "That Wonderful Edison," *New York World,* March 29, 1878, TAED MBSB10463.

29. "A Marvellous Discovery," *New York Sun,* February 22, 1878, TAED MBSB10378.

30. "Uses of the Phonograph," *Boston Daily Advertiser,* April 15, 1878, 1.

31. Leah Price, *How to Do Things with Books in Victorian Britain* (Princeton, N.J.: Princeton University Press, 2012), 214.

32. Thomas Edison, "The Perfected Phonograph," *North American Review* 146, no. 379 (June 1888): 641–50; 646.

33. On Dickens's reading tours, see Philip Collins, ed., *Charles Dickens: The Public Readings* (Oxford: Clarendon, 1975).

34. The phrase is used in Malcolm Andrews, *Charles Dickens and His Performing Selves: Dickens and the Public Readings* (Oxford: Oxford University Press, 2006), viii.

35. On copyright laws in the nineteenth century, see Meredith L. McGill, "Copyright," in *A History of the Book in America,* vol. 3, *The Industrial Book, 1840–1880,* ed. Scott E. Casper et al. (Chapel Hill: University of North Carolina Press, 2007), 158–78.

36. *Bangor Daily Whig and Courier,* April 10, 1878, 1.

37. "Possibilities of the Phonograph," *Indianapolis News,* March 30, 1878, 4. Reprinted from the *Cincinnati Commercial,* http://www.phonozoic.net/n0038 .htm.

38. "Mr. Edison's Inventions," *Chicago Tribune,* April 3, 1878, 2.

39. Ibid.

40. Walter L. Welch and Leah Brodbeck Stenzel Burt, *From Tinfoil to Stereo: The Acoustic Years of the Recording Industry, 1877–1929* (Gainesville: University Press of Florida, 1994), 78.

41. On the growing book trade in America and Britain, see Carl F. Kaestle and Janice A. Radway, eds., *Print in Motion: The Expansion of Publishing and Reading in the United States, 1880–1940* (Chapel Hill: University of North Carolina Press, in association with the American Antiquarian Society, 2009); and Alexis Weedon, *Victorian Publishing: The Economics of Book Production for a Mass Market, 1836–1916* (Aldershot, U.K.: Ashgate, 2003).

42. "The Phonograph," *Public,* May 2, 1878, Thomas A. Edison Papers Microfilm Edition 25:182.

43. Marshall McLuhan, *Understanding Media: The Extensions of Man* (Cambridge, Mass.: MIT Press, 1994), 8.

44. Quoted in *Ariel* (University of Minnesota) 7, no. 1 (October 9, 1883): 12.

45. The idea of sleep learning, or hypnopaedia, persists in popular culture despite research confirming that learning does not take place during sleep. See Eric Eich, "Learning during Sleep," in *Sleep and Cognition,* ed. Richard R. Bootzin, John F. Kihlstrom, and Daniel L. Schacter (Washington, D.C.: American Psychological Association, 1990), 88–108.

46. *Ariel* (University of Minnesota) 7, no. 1 (October 9, 1883): 12.

47. R. Balmer, "Whispering Machines," *Nineteenth Century* 17 (March 1885), 496–99; 497. At least one French author had already proposed a similar device; see Charles Cros's entry for "petits phonographs," dated August 2, 1878, in *Inédits et Documents,* ed. Pierre E. Richard (Villelongue-d'Aude, France: Atelier du Gué, 1992), 208.

48. "A Whispering Machine," *Cassell's Family Magazine,* 1885, 383.

49. Andre Millard, *America on Record: A History of Recorded Sound* (Cambridge: Cambridge University Press, 1995), 4.

50. See Carl F. Kaestle et al., eds., *Literacy in the United States: Readers and Reading since 1880* (New Haven, Conn.: Yale University Press, 1991), and Patrick Brantlinger, *The Reading Lesson: The Threat of Mass Literacy in Nineteenth-Century British Fiction* (Bloomington: Indiana University Press, 1998).

51. Balmer, "Whispering Machines," 497.

52. "The Phonograph," *Phonographic Magazine* 2, no. 2 (February 1, 1888): 30–31; 31. Reprinted from *New York World.*

53. On uses of the phonograph by the working classes and other marginalized groups, see William Howland Kenney, *Recorded Music in American Life: The Phonograph and Popular Memory, 1890–1945* (New York: Oxford University Press, 1999).

54. Kevin J. Hayes, "The Public Library in Utopia," *Libraries and the Cultural Record* 45, no. 3 (2010): 333–49.

55. Adam Seth Lowenstein discusses the phonograph's absence from Bellamy's original utopian vision in "What *Looking Backward* Doesn't See: Utopian Discourse and the Mass Media," *Utopian Studies* 22, no. 1 (2011): 143–66.

56. Cyrano de Bergerac, *Voyages to the Moon and the Sun,* trans. Richard Aldington (London: Folio Society, 1991), 79–80. Roger Chartier examines the speaking

book's relation to print culture in *Inscription and Erasure: Literature and Written Culture from the Eleventh to the Eighteenth Century,* trans. Arthur Goldhammer (Philadelphia: University of Pennsylvania Press, 2007), 63–82. On the notion of "untimely media," see Siegfried Zielinski, "Modelling Media for Ignatius Loyola: A Case Study on Athanasius Kircher's World of Apparatus between the Imaginary and the Real," in *Book of Imaginary Media: Excavating the Dream of the Ultimate Communication Medium,* ed. Eric Kluitenberg (Rotterdam, Netherlands: NAi Publishers, 2006), 29–54; 30.

57. *Western Electrician,* October 26, 1889, 220.

58. See Howard P. Segal, "Bellamy and Technology: Reconciling Centralization and Decentralization," in *Looking Backward, 1988–1888: Essays on Edward Bellamy,* ed. Daphne Patai (Amherst: University of Massachusetts Press, 1988), 91–105. See also Howard P. Segal, *Technological Utopianism in American Culture* (Chicago: University of Chicago Press, 1985).

59. Edward Bellamy, "With the Eyes Shut," *Harper's New Monthly Magazine* 79 (October 1889): 736–45; 738. Republished in Edward Bellamy, *The Blindman's World and Other Stories* (Boston: Houghton, Mifflin, 1898), 335–65.

60. The essays in Matthew Rubery, ed., *Audiobooks, Literature, and Sound Studies* (New York: Routledge, 2011), provide detailed accounts of the reception given to spoken word recordings.

61. Bellamy, "With the Eyes Shut," 736, 737, 738.

62. On the link between sound technology and women's voices, see John M. Picker, "My Fair Lady Automaton," *Zeitschrift für Anglistik und Amerikanistik* 63, no. 1 (2015): 89–100.

63. Sven Birkerts, *The Gutenberg Elegies: The Fate of Reading in an Electronic Age* (New York: Fawcett Columbine, 1994), 141–50; 143.

64. See Andreas Huyssen, *After the Great Divide: Modernism, Mass Culture, Postmodernism* (Bloomington: Indiana University Press, 1986), 44–62.

65. Three key accounts of the physiology of reading are Nicholas Dames, *The Physiology of the Novel: Reading, Neural Science, and the Form of Victorian Fiction* (Oxford: Oxford University Press, 2007); Adrian Johns, *The Nature of the Book: Print and Knowledge in the Making* (Chicago: University of Chicago Press, 1998), 380–443; and Paul Saenger, *Space between Words: The Origins of Silent Reading* (Palo Alto, Calif.: Stanford University Press, 1997), 1–6.

66. On difficulty as the core aesthetic of modernist writing, see Leonard Diepeveen, *The Difficulties of Modernism* (New York: Routledge, 2003), and Vicki Mahaffey, *Modernist Literature: Challenging Fictions* (Malden, Mass.: Blackwell, 2007).

67. "A Phonographic Era," *Electrical World* 14, no. 15 (October 12, 1889): 243.

68. Morton Luce, *Tennyson* (London: J. M. Dent, 1901), 19. The phrase is originally used in Robert James Mann, *Tennyson's "Maud" Vindicated: An Explanatory Essay* (London: Jarrold & Sons, 1856), 13.

69. Tennyson's poem already had a reputation as a performance piece. In 1973, the English art critic Philip Gilbert Hamerton had used the poem to support his argument that nonnative speakers could never truly master another language's

verse. Hamerton gives the example of a learned Frenchman who reads "Claribel" aloud by pronouncing "Her song the lintwhite swelleth" as "Ere songg ze lintveet svelless." Philip Gilbert Hamerton, *The Intellectual Life* (New York: John B. Alden, 1884), 123–24. The vignette circulated widely among periodicals over the next two decades before being taken up again in the 1900s by the esteemed literary critic Sir Arthur Quiller-Couch, this time with a cod-German accent in place of a French one. Arthur Quiller-Couch, *Studies in Literature* (Cambridge: Cambridge University Press, 1918), 309–11.

70. See Bennett Maxwell, "The Steytler Recordings of Alfred, Lord Tennyson: A History," *Tennyson Research Bulletin* 3 (1980): 150–57.

71. See Willa Z. Silverman, "Books Worthy of Our Era? Octave Uzanne, Technology, and the Luxury Book in *Fin-de-Siècle* France," *Book History* 7 (2004): 239–84.

72. See Robert Hendrick, "Albert Robida's Imperfect Future," *History Today* 48, no. 7 (July 1998): 27–32.

73. Octave Uzanne and Albert Robida, "The End of Books," *Scribner's Magazine* 16 (August 1894): 221–31; 224, 225, 226. The French version appeared as Octave Uzanne and Albert Robida, "La fin des livres," in *Contes pour les bibliophiles* (Paris: Quantin, 1895), 125–45.

74. On the concept of media adaptation, see Jay David Bolter and Richard Grusin, *Remediation: Understanding New Media* (Cambridge, Mass.: MIT Press, 1999).

75. "The Phonograph," *Times* (London), January 17, 1878, 4. Mark Poster elaborates on how authorship is affected by the transition from print to new media in *What's the Matter with the Internet?* (Minneapolis: University of Minneapolis Press, 2001), 43.

76. De Bergerac, *Voyages to the Moon and the Sun,* 13.

77. Bellamy, "With the Eyes Shut," 738; Uzanne and Robida, "The End of Books," 226.

78. See Ray Phillips, *Edison's Kinetoscope and Its Films: A History to 1896* (Westport, Conn.: Greenwood, 1997), 3–27. The role of Edison's Kinetoscope in the development of cinema is documented in Stephen Herbert, ed., *A History of Pre-Cinema,* vol. 3 (London: Routledge, 2000), 132–33.

79. "The End of Books," *Bookworm* 7 (January 1894): 351. Quoted in Elizabeth Eisenstein, *Divine Art, Infernal Machine: The Reception of Printing in the West from First Impressions to the Sense of an Ending* (Philadelphia: University of Pennsylvania Press, 2011), 227.

80. Octave Uzanne, *La nouvelle bibliopolis: Voyage d'un novateur au pays des néo-iconobibliomanes* (Paris: Floury, 1897), 41. Quoted in Silverman, "Books Worthy of Our Era?," 276.

81. Recent examples include Jeff Gomez, *Print Is Dead: Books in Our Digital Age* (London: Macmillan, 2008), and, by implication, Jean-Claude Carrière and Umberto Eco, *This Is Not the End of the Book,* trans. Polly McLean (London: Harvill Secker, 2011).

82. On the long tradition of premature obituaries for the book, see Priscilla Coit Murphy, "Books Are Dead, Long Live Books," in *Rethinking Media Change: The*

Aesthetics of Transition, ed. David Thorburn and Henry Jenkins (Cambridge, Mass.: MIT Press, 2003), 81–93. Paul Duguid considers the book's supersession by new media in "Material Matters: The Past and Futurology of the Book," in *The Future of the Book,* ed. Geoffrey Nunberg (Berkeley: University of California Press, 1996), 63–102.

83. See Morris's remarks quoted in William S. Peterson, *The Kelmscott Press: A History of William Morris's Typographical Adventure* (Oxford: Clarendon, 1991), 313.

84. Balmer, "Whispering Machines," 498.

85. Ibid.

86. Ibid., 499.

87. "Occasional Notes," *Pall Mall Gazette,* February 28, 1885, 3.

88. James Raven warns against associating print culture with the inevitability of progress in *The Business of Books: Booksellers and the English Book Trade, 1450–1850* (New Haven, Conn.: Yale University Press, 2007), 376.

2. A Talking Book in Every Corner of Dark-Land

1. Robert B. Irwin to Herman H. B. Meyer, April 5, 1932, Series 4, Subseries 1, Box 9, Folder 6, Talking Book Archive, American Foundation for the Blind (hereafter cited as AFB). On the Books for the Adult Blind Project, see Eunice Lovejoy, "History and Standards," in National Library Service for the Blind and Physically Handicapped, Library of Congress, *That All May Read: Library Service for Blind and Physically Handicapped People* (Washington, D.C.: National Library Service for the Blind and Physically Handicapped, Library of Congress, 1983), 1–24; 7.

2. Robert B. Irwin, "The Talking Book," in *Blindness: Modern Approaches to the Unseen Environment,* ed. Paul A. Zahl (Princeton, N.J.: Princeton University Press, 1950), 346–53; 347. Irwin is widely credited with coining the term "talking book," which was first used in correspondence in 1932. Dyer used the terms "talking record" and "talking record of a book" in patent number 1,628,658 filed with the United States Patent Office on February 12, 1924; he did not use the phrase "talking book" before 1933, despite presenting himself to clients as "the inventor and patentee of talking books." The earliest use of "talking book" that I have found is in Irwin's letter to Jesse H. Metcalf, May 20, 1932, Series 2, Subseries 1, Box 3, Folder 1, AFB. Irwin may have adopted the term from press coverage in April 1928 of a "talking book" proposed by Dr. Willis R. Whitney, director of the General Electric Company laboratory in Schenectady, New York. Irwin expressed interest in Whitney's "talking book" after reading about it in a New York newspaper (Robert B. Irwin to Willis R. Whitney, April 12, 1928, Series 1, Subseries 1, Box 1, Folder 2, AFB). Whitney's device consisted of a filmstrip attached to a loudspeaker; it was never completed.

3. Robert B. Irwin to Herman H. B. Meyer, April 5, 1932, Series 4, Subseries 1, Box 9, Folder 6, AFB.

4. "What Is the Talking Book?," typescript, n.d., 1–3; 1; Series 3, Subseries 3, Box 7, Folder 5, AFB.

5. "I Am the Talking Book," typescript, February 3, 1937, 1–5; 1; Series 3, Subseries 3, Box 9, Folder 9.1, AFB.

6. On the distinction between reading and hearing, see Howard Haycraft, *Books for the Blind: A Postscript and an Appreciation,* rev. ed. (Washington, D.C.: Library of Congress, Division for the Blind, 1962), 2n2. I have avoided using the phrase "the blind" when possible, though occasionally it will be used as a historical term. The phrase "blind people" is sometimes used instead of "people who were blind" or "people with vision impairments" for reasons of economy. For more on debates over the appropriate terminology used to represent visual impairment, see David Bolt, *The Metanarrative of Blindness: A Re-reading of Twentieth-Century Anglophone Writing* (Ann Arbor: University of Michigan Press, 2014), 16–34.

7. Georgina Kleege, *Sight Unseen* (New Haven, Conn.: Yale University Press, 1999), 190.

8. "Your Part, My Part, that the Blind May Read This Christmas," n.d., Series 3, Subseries 1, Box 5, Folder 10, AFB.

9. See, for example, Friedrich A. Kittler, *Discourse Networks 1800/1900,* trans. Michael Metteer with Chris Cullens (Palo Alto, Calif.: Stanford University Press, 1990), 231.

10. Mara Mills, "The Co-construction of Blindness and Reading," in *Disability Trouble: Ästhetik und Bildpolitik bei Helen Keller,* ed. Ulrike Bergermann (Berlin: b_books, 2013), 195–204; 196.

11. The best history of the talking book program is Frances A. Koestler, *The Unseen Minority: A Social History of Blindness in the United States* (New York: David McKay, 1976), 130–52. Additional accounts include National Library Service for the Blind and Physically Handicapped, Library of Congress, *That All May Read: Library Service for Blind and Physically Handicapped People* (Washington, D.C.: National Library Service for the Blind and Physically Handicapped, Library of Congress, 1983), 79–93; and Marilyn Lundell Majeska, *Talking Books: Pioneering and Beyond* (Washington, D.C.: National Library Service for the Blind and Physically Handicapped, Library of Congress, 1988). There is also an entry for "Talking Books" in the *Encyclopedia of Library and Information Science,* ed. Allen Kent, Harold Lancour, and Jay E. Daily (New York: Marcel Dekker, 1980), 30:71–95.

12. Lisa Gitelman, *Always Already New: Media, History, and the Data of Culture* (Cambridge, Mass.: MIT Press, 2006), 56.

13. See, for example, Nicholas A. Basbanes, *A Gentle Madness: Bibliophiles, Bibliomanes, and the Eternal Passion for Books* (New York: H. Holt, 1999).

14. On the use of spoken word recordings to promote self-sufficiency, see *Pathway to the Mind, Annual Report, 1960* (New York: Recording for the Blind, 1960), 1.

15. Memorandum, Martin Arnold Roberts to Herbert Putnam, December 19, 1929, Box 690, Folder 12.1, Central File, Manuscript Division, Library of Congress (hereafter cited as LOC).

16. Committee on the Library, Books for the Adult Blind: Hearing on H. R. 9042, House, Seventy-First Congress, First Session, March 27, 1930, M. C. Migel, 3.

17. The philosophers Bryan Magee and Martin Milligan examine the perceptual gap between blind and sighted people in *On Blindness: Letters between Bryan Magee and Martin Milligan* (Oxford: Oxford University Press, 1995).

18. Committee on the Library, Books for the Adult Blind: Hearing on H. R. 9042, House, Seventy-First Congress, Second Session, March 27, 1930, Helen Keller, 22.

19. "Notes of the Talking Book for the Blind for Miss Kate Smith," typescript [1935], Series 3, Subseries 1, Box 5, Folder 10, AFB.

20. *The Talking Book Reads Itself to the Blind* (New York: American Foundation for the Blind, [1936]), n.p. The promotional record "I Am the Talking Book" repeated many of these same lines in the first person. Mr. Palmer to Mrs. A. L. Bond, February 3, 1937, Series 3, Subseries 3, Box 9, Folder 1, AFB.

21. Irwin, "Talking Book," 347.

22. On the rehabilitation of disabled soldiers, see Beth Linker, *War's Waste: Rehabilitation in World War I America* (Chicago: University of Chicago Press, 2011), and Ana Carden-Coyne, "Ungrateful Bodies: Rehabilitation, Resistance and Disabled American Veterans of the First World War," *European Review of History* 14, no. 4 (2007): 543–65.

23. This figure is cited in Committee on the Library, Books for the Adult Blind: Hearing on H. R. 168, House, Seventy-Fifth Congress, First Session, January 23, 1937, Robert Irwin, 17. Koestler estimates that approximately 450 veterans were blinded during battle or by diseases contracted while in service. By comparison, the number of war-blinded soldiers among other nations totaled 3,000 in England, 2,800 in France, and 7,000 in Germany. Koestler, *Unseen Minority*, 8, 248.

24. Koestler, *Unseen Minority*, 7.

25. Committee on the Library, Books for the Adult Blind: Hearing on H. R. 9042, House, Seventy-First Congress, Second Session, March 27, 1930, Charles F. F. Campbell, 17.

26. Ibid., 18.

27. On veteran compensation, see Stephen R. Ortiz, *Beyond the Bonus March and GI Bill: How Veteran Politics Shaped the New Deal Era* (New York: New York University Press, 2010).

28. Thomas Edison, "The Phonograph and Its Future," *North American Review* 126, no. 262 (1878): 527–36; 533.

29. Irwin, "Talking Book," 347.

30. Robert B. Irwin to A. C. Ellis, June 13, 1941, Series 1, Subseries 1, Box 1, Folder 5, AFB.

31. *Papers and Proceedings of the Twenty-Eighth General Meeting* (Chicago: American Library Association, 1906), 228–29.

32. Robert B. Irwin to George F. Meyer, April 23, 1924, Series 1, Subseries 1, Box 1, Folder 2, AFB.

33. Robert B. Irwin to Frank L. Dyer, February 2, 1925, Series 1, Subseries 1, Box 1, Folder 2, AFB.

34. Robert B. Irwin to Frank C. Bryan, February 10, 1925, Series 1, Subseries 1, Box 1, Folder 2, AFB.

35. See, for example, Robert B. Irwin to Charles Edison, November 9, 1927, Series 1, Subseries 1, Box 1, Folder 2, AFB.

36. The AFB's experiments with the optophone, photoelectrograph, visagraph, and other devices are described in Frank C. Bryan, "New Devices for the Blind," *Outlook for the Blind* 28, no. 1 (February 1934): 16–18, 36; and Gabriel Farrell, *The Story of Blindness* (Cambridge, Mass.: Harvard University Press, 1956), 130–45. On the evolution of mechanical aids, see Howard Freiberger, "Deployment of Reading Machines for the Blind," *Bulletin of Prosthetics Research* http://www.rehab.research.va.gov/jour/71/8/1/contents.pdf, BPR 10–15 (Spring 1971): 144–56; Franklin S. Cooper, Jane H. Gaitenby, and Patrick W. Nye, "Evolution of Reading Machines for the Blind: Haskin Laboratories' Research as a Case History," *Journal of Rehabilitation Research and Development* 21, no. 1 (1984): 51–87; and Donald Shankweiler and Carol A. Fowler, "Seeking a Reading Machine for the Blind and Discovering the Speech Code," *History of Psychology* 18, no. 1 (2015): 78–99.

37. Koestler, *Unseen Minority*, 83–84.

38. "Talking Book Investigation: An Informal Report of Five Months' Work," typescript, November 8, 1932, Series 4, Subseries 1, Box 9, Folder 6, AFB.

39. See Robert B. Irwin's account of the development of talking book technology in *As I Saw It* (New York: American Foundation for the Blind, 1955), 83–107.

40. "Sample Record for Library of Congress Talking Book Machines," typescript, 1942, 1–7; 4; Box 693, Folder 13.2, LOC.

41. Robert B. Irwin to Frederick P. Keppel, March 26, 1932, Folder "Recorded Books," Archive, National Library Service for the Blind and Physically Handicapped, Washington, D.C. (hereafter cited as NLS). The NLS material is uncataloged.

42. Coleridge's poem was read by John Knight. Robert B. Irwin to Herman H. B. Meyer, March 14, 1934, Folder "Recorded Books," NLS.

43. William Wordsworth, *Wordsworth: The Poems,* ed. John O. Hayden (Harmondsworth, U.K.: Penguin, 1977), 1:877.

44. The initial recordings were read by Gerald Cornell, John Knight, and Fred Uttal. Herman H. B. Meyer, "Books for the Adult Blind," in Library of Congress, *Annual Report, Service for the Blind, 1933–34* (Washington, D.C.: Government Printing Office, 1935), 12–13; 13. The NLS copy of this list contains handwritten marginalia in pencil confirming the sequence of titles recorded. The titles are also listed in National Library Service for the Blind and Physically Handicapped, Library of Congress, *That All May Read,* 81–82. For a full list of recordings made between 1934 and 1935, see "A Complete List of Talking Book Recordings," typescript, n.d., Series 4, Subseries 5, Box 16, Folder 3, AFB.

45. Herman H. B. Meyer to Robert B. Irwin, May 7, 1934, Series 4, Subseries 1, Box 9, Folder 7, AFB.

46. Robert B. Irwin to Mary Colgate, July 10, 1934, Series 3, Subseries 1, Box 5, Folder 9, AFB.

47. Quoted in "The Talking Book Is Born," typescript, ca. 1936, 1–7; 6; Series 3, Subseries 3, Box 7, Folder 6, AFB.

48. For example, see Martin A. Roberts, "Books for the Adult Blind," Library of Congress, *Annual Reports, Service for the Blind and Books for the Adult Blind including the Talking-Book Machine Activity, 1935–36* (Washington, D.C.: Government Printing Office, 1937), 12. For more on the talking book's reception, see the Perkins School for the Blind's scrapbooks of newspaper clippings from 1931–35 and 1935–36, https://archive.org/details/perkinsschoolfo313501perk.

49. "Talking Books and the Pratt-Smoot Law," *Outlook for the Blind* 27, no. 1 (February 1933): 32, 38; and "Pratt-Smoot Law Amended," *Outlook for the Blind* 27, no. 2 (April 1933): 84.

50. "Helen Keller Hails Aid of Talking Books," *New York Times,* June 7, 1935, 2.

51. Radiogram, Helen Keller to M. C. Migel, September 22, 1933, Folder "Braille Production," NLS.

52. Dorothy Herrmann, *Helen Keller: A Life* (Chicago: University of Chicago Press, 1999), 272.

53. Helen Keller to Eleanor Roosevelt, April 20, 1935, in *Helen Keller: Selected Writings,* ed. Kim E. Nielsen (New York: New York University Press, 2005), 178–79; 179.

54. John J. Duffy to the editor of the *Braille Mirror,* "Voices from Brailleland," typescript, June 1933, Series 3, Subseries 3, Box 8, Folder 4, AFB.

55. Esther Chombeau to AFB, ca. 1939, Series 3, Subseries 3, Box 7, Folder 3, AFB.

56. J. Robert Atkinson, "Talking Books Take Flight," typescript, September 29, 1933, 1–6; 6; Folder "Ellis, A. C., Correspondence, 1933," Archive, American Printing House for the Blind (hereafter cited as APH).

57. [J. Robert Atkinson], "Injurious Tactics," typescript, March 1933, 1–3; 2; Series 3, Subseries 3, Box 8, Folder 4, AFB.

58. "Editor's Chair," typescript, *Braille Courier,* April 1934, 1–2; 1; Series 3, Subseries 3, Box 8, Folder 5, AFB. John Philip Sousa objects to "canned music" in "The Menace of Mechanical Music," *Appleton's Magazine* 8 (September 1906): 278–84; 281. See also Patrick Warfield, "John Philip Sousa and 'The Menace of Mechanical Music,'" *Journal of the Society for American Music* 3, no. 4 (2009): 431–63.

59. Library of Congress, *Annual Report, Service for the Blind, 1933–34* (Washington, D.C.: Government Printing Office, 1935), 4.

60. Robert B. Irwin to Frederick P. Keppel, January 18, 1935, Folder "Recorded Books," NLS.

61. A. C. Ellis to Robert B. Irwin, February 12, 1940, Series 4, Subseries 3, Box 14, Folder 4, AFB.

62. Committee on the Library, Books for the Adult Blind: Hearing on H. R. 168, House, Seventy-Fifth Congress, First Session, January 23, 1937, S. Mervin Sinclair, 12.

63. These rates are reported in "Authorizing an Increase in the Annual Appropriation for Books for the Adult Blind," April 12, 1937, Senate, Seventy-Fifth

Congress, First Session, Calendar No. 335, Report No. 324, 2. Berthold Lowenfeld measured the rates in *Braille and Talking Book Reading: A Comparative Study* (New York: American Foundation for the Blind, 1945).

64. Louise Moore to AFB, November 19, 1934, Series 3, Subseries 3, Box 7, Folder 3, AFB.

65. "Extracts from Letters Received from Blind Persons Regarding the Talking Book," typescript, n.d., 1–5; 1; Series 3, Subseries 3, Box 7, Folder 3, AFB.

66. Library of Congress, *Report of the Librarian of Congress for the Fiscal Year ending June 30, 1937* (Washington, D.C.: Government Printing Office, 1937), 295.

67. Memo, "Agreement of the Control of Copyright Talking Books for the Blind," April 20, 1934, Series 1, Subseries 3, Box 2, Folder 6, AFB; and "Talking Books for the Blind Plan of Controlled Distribution," July 8, 1938, Folder "CM 1930s," NLS.

68. Committee on the Library, Books for the Adult Blind: Hearing on H. R. 168, House, Seventy-Fifth Congress, First Session, January 23, 1937, H. R. Latimer, 20.

69. Robert B. Irwin to M. A. Roberts, December 9, 1937, Folder "CM 1930s," NLS.

70. Committee on the Library, Books for the Adult Blind: Hearing on H. R. 168, House, Seventy-Fifth Congress, First Session, January 23, 1937, Robert B. Irwin, 20.

71. A. C. Ellis to Alfred A. Knopf, Inc., February 3, 1938, Box 692, Folder 13.1, LOC.

72. Archibald MacLeish to Mrs. John R. Marsh, April 3, 1940, Box 693, Folder 13.2, LOC.

73. Archibald MacLeish to Margaret Mitchell, April 24, 1940, Box 693, Folder 13.2, LOC.

74. Robert B. Irwin to Benjamin Stern, January 3, 1940, Series 1, Subseries 3, Box 2, Folder 7, AFB.

75. "A Few Unsolicited Letters Received from Blind Persons Who Have Been Lent WPA Talking Book Machines," typescript, n.d., 1–4; 2; Folder "Recorded Books," NLS.

76. "Excerpts from Blind People about the Talking Book Machine," typescript, n.d., 1–3; 3; Series 4, Subseries 1, Box 11, Folder 6, AFB.

77. "Excerpts from Letters from Readers," typescript, 1934, 1–5; 2; Series 4, Subseries 1, Box 11, Folder 6, AFB.

78. Ibid., 3.

79. "Talking Book Contest," *Outlook for the Blind* 29, no. 3 (June 1935): 126.

80. Blanche Logan to AFB, April 18, 1935, Series 3, Subseries 3, Box 7, Folder 4, AFB.

81. Ibid.

82. Della B. Clark to AFB, April 21, 1935, Series 3, Subseries 3, Box 7, Folder 4, AFB.

83. Charles Magee Adams to AFB, April 3, 1925, Series 3, Subseries 3, Box 7, Folder 4, AFB.

84. On the use of personification to domesticate new media, see James Lastra, *Sound Technology and the American Cinema: Perception, Representation, Modernity* (New York: Columbia University Press, 2000), 6–8.

85. "Comments from the Blind," typescript, n.d., Folder "CM 1930s," NLS.

86. Mrs. Norman B. Morrell to AFB, September 30, 1934, Series 3, Subseries 3, Box 7, Folder 3, AFB.

87. "A Few Unsolicited Letters," 3.

88. Quoted in Committee on the Library, Books for the Adult Blind: Hearing on H. R. 168, House, Seventy-Fifth Congress, First Session, January 23, 1937, Robert B. Irwin, 4.

89. "A Few Unsolicited Letters," 3.

90. Minnie E. Hicks to Kent Keller, January 20, 1937, Series 2, Subseries 1, Box 3, Folder 3, AFB.

91. Elsie B. Adams to AFB, January 15, 1937, Series 3, Subseries 3, Box 7, Folder 3, AFB.

92. Quoted in Meyer, "Books for the Adult Blind," 13.

93. "Comments from the Blind."

94. Mattie E. French to Stetson K. Ryan, March 18, 1937, Series 3, Subseries 3, Box 7, Folder 3, AFB.

95. I. M. Hanna to Anne Morrow Lindbergh, December 28, 1936, Series 3, Subseries 3, Box 7, Folder 3, AFB.

96. Blanche Logan to AFB, April 18, 1935, Series 3, Subseries 3, Box 7, Folder 4, AFB.

97. On this journal's history, see Catherine J. Kudlick, "The Outlook of *The Problem* and the Problem with the *Outlook:* Two Advocacy Journals Reinvent Blind People in Turn-of-the-Century America," in *The New Disability History: American Perspectives,* ed. Paul K. Longmore and Lauri Umansky (New York: New York University Press, 2001), 187–213.

98. *Talking Book Reads Itself to the Blind.*

99. Maude G. Nichols, "Service for the Blind," in Library of Congress, *Annual Report, Service for the Blind, 1934–35* (Washington, D.C.: Government Printing Office, 1935), 4.

100. C. E. Seymour to AFB, October 6, 1934, Series 3, Subseries 3, Box 7, Folder 3, AFB; Meyer, "Books for the Adult Blind," in Library of Congress Annual Report, Service for the Blind, 1934–35 (Washington: Government Printing Office, 1935), 12.

101. "A Few Unsolicited Letters," 1.

102. Meyer, "Books for the Adult Blind," 12.

103. See Naomi Schor, "Blindness as Metaphor," *Differences: A Journal of Feminist Cultural Studies* 11, no. 2 (1999): 76–105.

104. Meyer, "Books for the Adult Blind," 12.

105. "Excerpts from Letters Regarding the Talking Book," typescript, 1933, 1–6; 4; Series 3, Subseries 3, Box 7, Folder 3, AFB.

106. J. J. O'Connor to AFB, September 17, 1934, Series 3, Subseries 3, Box 7, Folder 3, AFB.

107. "Excerpts from Blind People about the Talking Book Machine," 3.

108. "A Few Unsolicited Letters," 1.

109. Ibid., 3.

110. Dwight Church to AFB, September 21, 1937, Series 3, Subseries 3, Box 7, Folder 3, AFB.

111. Rosa G. Barksdale to AFB, June 25, 1936, Series 3, Subseries 1, Box 9, Folder 9, AFB.

112. Charles A. Kuchler to *Matilda Ziegler Magazine,* April 19, 1935, Series 3, Subseries 3, Box 7, Folder 4, AFB.

113. "Exhibition Record," typescript, n.d., 1–2; 1; Series 3, Subseries 3, Box 7, Folder 5, AFB.

114. Henry J. Frost to Mrs. James C. Stodder, September 29, 1937, Series 3, Subseries 3, Box 7, Folder 3, AFB.

115. Press release, March 12, 1934, Folder "Ellis, A. C., Correspondence, 1935—AFB (Irwin)," APH.

116. "Excerpts from Letters Regarding the Talking Book," 5.

117. *Talking Book Topics* 4, no. 4 (March 1939): 3–9. The account is based on an actual reader's experience.

118. Eleanor G. Brown to Kent E. Keller, January 16, 1937, Series 2, Subseries 1, Box 3, Folder 3, AFB.

119. American Foundation for the Blind, *The President's Report, 1939* (New York: American Foundation for the Blind, 1939), 4.

120. John T. Dunney to *Matilda Ziegler Magazine,* April 18, 1935, Series 3, Subseries 3, Box 7, Folder 4, AFB; "A Few Unsolicited Letters," 3.

121. Grace Allen to AFB, January 9, 1937, Series 3, Subseries 3, Box 7, Folder 3, AFB.

122. Susan Thornton to *Matilda Ziegler Magazine,* April 15, 1935, Series 3, Subseries 3, Box 7, Folder 4, AFB.

123. Nellie S. Gleason to A. Smith, October 5, 1934, Series 3, Subseries 3, Box 7, Folder 3, AFB.

124. Mrs. Norman B. Morrell to AFB, September 30, 1934, Series 3, Subseries 3, Box 7, Folder 3, AFB. On the treatment of new media as actual people, see Byron Reeves and Clifford Nass, *The Media Equation: How People Treat Computers, Television, and New Media like Real People and Places* (Cambridge: Cambridge University Press, 1996).

125. "Sample Record for Library of Congress Talking Book Machines," 2.

126. Gregory Ziemer, "Talking Book Commemorative Record," typescript, ca. 1959, 1–14; 11; Series 3, Subseries 3, Box 7, Folder 10, AFB.

127. "A Few Unsolicited Letters," 1.

128. Esther Chombeau to AFB, ca. 1939, Series 3, Subseries 3, Box 7, Folder 3, AFB.

129. "A Few Unsolicited Letters," 1.

130. Mrs. Norman B. Morrell to AFB, September 30, 1934, Series 3, Subseries 3, Box 7, Folder 3, AFB.

131. Mattie E. French to Stetson K. Ryan, March 8, 1937, Series 3, Subseries 3, Box 7, Folder 3, AFB.

132. Maude G. Nichols, "Service for the Blind," in Library of Congress, *Annual Reports, Service for the Blind and Books for the Adult Blind including the Talking-Book Machine Activity, 1935–36* (Washington, D.C.: Government Printing Office, 1937), 2.

133. Esther Chombeau to AFB, ca. 1939, Series 3, Subseries 3, Box 7, Folder 3, AFB.

134. "Excerpts from Letters Regarding the Talking Book," 2.

135. Myra B. Jordan to AFB, July 18, 1939, Series 3, Subseries 3, Box 7, Folder 3, AFB.

136. Quoted in Robert B. Irwin to Luther H. Evans, January 29, 1948, Box 691, Folder "Blind 13," LOC.

137. Quoted in ibid.

138. Josephine Peters to Miss A. Smith, February 21, 1937, Series 3, Subseries 3, Box 7, Folder 3, AFB; "Excerpts from Letters Regarding the Talking Book," 6.

139. Esther Chombeau to AFB, ca. 1939, Series 3, Subseries 3, Box 7, Folder 3, AFB. Emphasis in original.

140. C. E. Huntley to AFB, October 12, 1937, Series 3, Subseries 3, Box 7, Folder 3, AFB.

141. Quoted in "Authorizing an Increase in the Annual Appropriation for Books for the Adult Blind," Senate, Report 324, Seventy-Fifth Congress, First Session, 3.

142. Dwight D. Eisenhower to M. Robert Barnett, November 19, 1954, Series 3, Subseries 3, Box 7, Folder 7, AFB.

3. How to Read a Talking Book

1. Miriam Vieni and Fred Vieni to Roy Avers, March 7, 1976, reprinted in "Interpretations," typescript, n.d., Series 3, Subseries 2, Box 7, Folder 1, Talking Book Archive, American Foundation for the Blind (hereafter cited as AFB). More on the magazine's history can be found at http://www.blindskills.com /dialogue.html.

2. See also Georgina Kleege's advice to "read it straight" in *Sight Unseen* (New Haven, Conn.: Yale University Press, 1999), 174. On reading aloud more broadly, see Joan Shelley Rubin, *Songs of Ourselves: The Uses of Poetry in America* (Cambridge, Mass.: Harvard University Press, 2007), and Catherine Robson, *Heart Beats: Everyday Life and the Memorized Poem* (Princeton, N.J.: Princeton University Press, 2012).

3. Charles Magee Adams to AFB, March 27, 1933, Series 3, Subseries 3, Box 7, Folder 4, AFB.

4. "The Talking Book Is Born," typescript, ca. 1936, 1–7; 1; Series 3, Subseries 3, Box 7, Folder 6, AFB.

5. "I Am the Talking Book," typescript, February 3, 1937, Series 3, Subseries 3, Box 9, Folder 1, AFB.

6. "Talking Books," in American Foundation for the Blind, *Annual Report of the President to the Board of Trustees, 1943* (New York: American Foundation for the Blind, 1943), n.p.

7. One of the headlines in "12-Inch Record on Phonograph Reads a Book," *New York Herald-Tribune,* March 24, 1934.

8. On the "narrator" versus "reader" debate, see Catherine Krauss to William P. Howle, October 3, 1977, Series 3, Subseries 2, Box 7, Folder 1, AFB.

9. W[illiam] B[arbour], "What Is a Good Talking Book?," *Talking Book Topics* 4, no. 3 (1938): 8–11; 10.

10. Jessica Pressman discusses the continuities between books and new media in "The Aesthetics of Bookishness in Twenty-First-Century Literature," *Michigan Quarterly Review* 48, no. 4 (Fall 2009): 465–82.

11. Arthur Helms, *Recording Books for the Blind* (New York: American Foundation for the Blind, 1951), 12.

12. On the deliberate perpetuation of errors, see Alan Hewitt, "End of an Idyll for Talking Books: Babbling Books," *Braille Monitor,* May 1981, 131–34. Reprinted from the *New Republic,* November 1, 1980, 14–15.

13. Library of Congress, Project, Books for the Adult Blind, "Specifications for Talking Book Records," February 1, 1940, Box 690, Folder 13, Library of Congress (hereafter cited as LOC). The original specifications were issued on September 28, 1937.

14. Hewitt, "End of an Idyll," 132.

15. National Braille Association, *Tape Recording Manual,* 3rd ed. (Midland Park, N.J.: National Braille Association, 1979), 2.

16. Mrs. W. D. Earnest advises how to record paratextual features including charts, figures, graphs, maps, and mathematical formulae in "Exceptional Uses of Recorded Materials," in *Conference on Volunteer Activities in Recording and Transcribing Books for the Blind: Proceedings, December 1–2, 1952* (Washington, D.C.: Library of Congress, 1954), 25–27. On reproducing pictures, see Yvonne Eriksson, *Tactile Pictures: Pictorial Representations for the Blind, 1784–1940* (Göteborg: Acta Universitatis Gothoburgensis, 1998).

17. Ralph S. Verner to Braille Institute of America, May 21, 1974, Series 3, Subseries 2, Box 7, Folder 1, AFB.

18. A. C. Ellis to Robert B. Irwin, December 22, 1942, Series 4, Subseries 3, Box 14, Folder 5, AFB.

19. Leroy Hughbanks, "The Talking Book—Present and Future," *Outlook for the Blind* 34, no. 4 (October 1940): 131–32; 32.

20. "Book That Talks and Sings," *New York Times,* February 19, 1937, 3. See also "Wild Birds and Their Songs," *Talking Book Topics* 2, no. 4 (March 1937): 8–9; 8; and "A Talking Book of Bird Songs," *New Beacon: A Magazine Devoted to the Interests of the Blind* 21, no. 243 (March 15, 1937): 66. Brand's methods are described in Albert R. Brand, "Recording Sounds of Wild Birds," *Auk* 49, no. 4 (October 1932): 436–39; as well as the opening chapter in Albert R. Brand, *Wild Birds and Their Songs* (New York: Thomas Nelson and Sons, 1934).

21. "Blind Naturalist Praises Bird Book," *Talking Book Topics* 3, no. 1 (June 1937): 14–15.

22. Anna Riedel to AFB, August 15, 1937, Series 3, Subseries 3, Box 7, Folder 3, AFB. Enthusiasm for Brand's birdsongs led to further collaborations with Cornell's ornithologists. See "Report on Talking Books Recorded under the Grant from the W. K. Kellogg Foundation," typescript, December 1943, 1–9, Folder "Recorded Books," Archive, National Library Service for the Blind and Physically Handicapped, Washington, D.C. (hereafter cited as NLS). The NLS material is uncataloged.

23. Robert B. Irwin to Herman H. B. Meyer, November 9, 1934, Series 4, Subseries 1, Box 9, Folder 7, AFB.

24. "New Talking Books Announced," *Talking Book Topics* 6, no. 4 (March 1941): 6–11; 7–8.

25. A[rthur] H[elms], "Something New in Talking Books," *Talking Book Topics* 4, no. 1 (June 1938): 16–17.

26. American Foundation for the Blind, *Annual Report of the President, 1938* (New York: American Foundation for the Blind, 1938), n.p. On cinema in the 1930s, see Andrew Bergman, *We're in the Money: Depression America and Its Films* (New York: New York University Press, 1971), and Ina Rae Hark, ed., *American Cinema of the 1930s: Themes and Variations* (New Brunswick, N.J.: Rutgers University Press, 2007).

27. Rachel Reed to AFB, November 19, 1934, Series 3, Subseries 2, Box 7, Folder 3, AFB.

28. A[rthur] H[elms], "Not Readings, but Plays," *Talking Book Topics* 3, no. 2 (September 1937): 7–11; 7. Reprinted from *New York Herald-Tribune*, June 13, 1937. The AFB permitted "slight editing" for dramatic purposes; however, no unauthorized changes were permitted when recording classic drama.

29. Martin A. Roberts, "The Recordings of Dramas with Casts," in Library of Congress, *Report of the Librarian of Congress for the Fiscal Year ending June 30, 1938* (Washington, D.C.: Government Printing Office, 1939), 10–11. See also "Plays for the Blind," *New York Times*, December 1937, clipping, Series 4, Subseries 1, Box 9, Folder 9, AFB.

30. Untitled pamphlet, n.d., Series 3, Subseries 3, Box 9, Folder 4, AFB.

31. Quoted in "Developments in Recording Dramas with Casts," typescript, ca. 1934, 1–7; 2; Series 3, Subseries 3, Box 8, Folder 5, AFB.

32. C. LaVerne Roberts to Alice M. Smith, May 18, 1937, Series 3, Subseries 3, Box 7, Folder 3, AFB.

33. J. O. Kleber, "Research Information," typescript, November 25, 1936, Series 4, Subseries 5, Box 16, Folder 6, AFB.

34. Berthold Lowenfeld, "The Talking Book," *Talking Book Topics* 5, no. 4 (March 1940): 14–16; 15.

35. Alexander Fried, "Looking About," *San Francisco Chronicle*, ca.1937, clipping, Series 3, Subseries 3, Box 9, Folder 1, AFB.

36. Charles Magee Adams to Robert B. Irwin, March 9, 1935, Series 3, Subseries 3, Box 7, Folder 4, AFB.

37. Mona M. Warner to Maria Sharon Eddington, November 25, 1977, Series 3, Subseries 2, Box 6, Folder 7, AFB.

38. C. E. Seymour to Alexander Scourby, January 29, 1941, Series 4, Subseries 1, Box 10, Folder 1, AFB.

39. A list of narrators used in the first year can be found in "A Complete List of Talking Book Recordings," typescript, November 10, 1935, 1–8, Series 4, Subseries 5, Box 16, Folder 3, AFB.

40. Arthur Helms, "Recording Activities: Techniques of Recording Books for the Blind," in *Conference on Volunteer Activities in Recording and Transcribing Books for the Blind, Proceedings, December 1–2, 1952* (Washington, D.C.: Library of Congress, 1954), 2–6.

41. William Barbour cites examples of humorous mistakes in "Jalna: A Saga of the Studio," *Talking Book Topics* 5, no. 2 (September 1939): 3–9.

42. Library of Congress, Project, Books for the Adult Blind, "Specifications for Talking Book Records," September 28, 1937, Box 690, Folder 13, LOC.
43. Library of Congress, "Specifications for Talking Book Records," 1940.
44. National Braille Association, *Tape Recording Manual*, 14; "The Sound Engineer Says," *Talking Book Bulletin* 4 (March 1936): 3–4; 4; "The 'Voice' of Talking Books," typescript, September 1968, 1–9; 1; Series 3, Subseries 2, Box 6, Folder 7, AFB.
45. Minutes, Sound Recording Subcommittee, October 2, 1934, Folder "Sound Recording Committee 1934–1960" (uncataloged), Royal National Institute of Blind People.
46. Typescript, n.d., Series 3, Subseries 2, Box 7, Folder 2, AFB.
47. Ibid.
48. Robert B. Irwin to Herbert Putnam, October 26, 1938, Series 4, Subseries 1, Box 9, Folder 10, AFB.
49. National Braille Association, *Tape Recording Manual*, 2.
50. Quoted in Billy R. West, *The Art and Science of Audio Book Production* (Washington, D.C.: Government Printing Office, National Library Service for the Blind and Physically Handicapped, 1995), 2.
51. B[arbour], "What Is a Good Talking Book?," 10.
52. Library of Congress, "Specifications for Talking Book Records," 1940.
53. National Braille Association, *Tape Recording Manual*, 24.
54. Alan Hewitt to Alfred Lisi, April 21, 1977, Series 3, Subseries 2, Box 6, Folder 3, AFB. Emphasis in original.
55. For a list of "Talking Book Classics," see B[arbour], "What Is a Good Talking Book?," 10–11. Other popular narrators are cited in "Personalities Who Have Recorded for the Talking Book," typescript, n.d., 1–2, Folder "Braille Production," NLS.
56. Mrs. Edison Dick to Peter E. Hanke, July 7, 1980, Series 3, Subseries 2, Box 6, Folder 2, AFB.
57. Elizabeth Leonard to AFB, February 24, 1973, Series 3, Subseries 2, Box 6, Folder 3, AFB.
58. Timothy Hendel to Robert Evan Jones, February 17, 1976, Series 3, Subseries 2, Box 6, Folder 13, AFB.
59. Chet Avery to Lucy Vecera, May 20, 1974, Series 3, Subseries 2, Box 7, Folder 1, AFB.
60. John E. Robas to LOC, June 14, 1975, Series 3, Subseries 2, Box 7, Folder 1, AFB.
61. Janet Gawith to NLS, November 22, 1978, Series 3, Subseries 2, Box 7, Folder 1.
62. Catherine Krauss to Edward Blake, May 3, 1978, Series 3, Subseries 2, Box 6, Folder 12, AFB.
63. *Talking Book Titles of 1937–1938* (Washington, D.C.: Library of Congress, Project, Books for the Blind, 1938), Box 692, Folder 13-1, LOC.
64. Willa Cather to Alexander Woollcott, February 8, 1935, Houghton Library, Harvard University, HOU b MS Am 1449 247.
65. Willa Cather to Archibald MacLeish, December 11, 1944. Cather's letter is reprinted in "Auspice Willa!," *Talking Book Topics* 14, no. 1 (June 1948): 3–4; 4.

The magazine published an apology in the following issue for inadvertently violating the terms of Cather's will by publishing the letter. See "The Willa Cather Letter: An Apology," *Talking Book Topics* 18, no. 4 (December 1952): 3.

66. "Auspice Willa!," 4.

67. Archibald MacLeish to Alfred Knopf, November 29, 1944, Box 691, Folder 13, LOC.

68. B[arbour], "What Is a Good Talking Book?," 10.

69. Robert B. Irwin to V. W. Clapp, October 21, 1937, Series 4, Subseries 1, Box 9, Folder 9, AFB.

70. William P. Howle to James W. Walker, March 5, 1973, Series 3, Subseries 2, Box 7, Folder 1, AFB.

71. Typescript, n.d., Series 3, Subseries 2, Box 7, Folder 2, AFB.

72. Helms, *Recording Books for the Blind,* 10.

73. "Period May 11, 1934 to 11-10-35," typescript, November 10, 1935, Series 4, Subseries 5, Box 16, Folder 3, AFB.

74. Chet Avery to Lucy Vecera, May 20, 1974, Series 3, Subseries 2, Box 7, Folder 1, AFB.

75. "Some Facts about Reading Talking Books," typescript, n.d., Series 3, Subseries 2, Box 7, Folder 2, AFB. William Barbour explains the reasons behind women's underrepresentation in "The Personality Behind the Voice," *Talking Book Topics* 3, no. 2 (September 1937): 13–15.

76. R. A. Nellis to William P. Howle, August 6, 1976, Series 3, Subseries 2, Box 7, Folder 1, AFB.

77. Philip Leonard to Mary L. Piday, May 12, 1975, Series 3, Subseries 2, Box 6, Folder 13, AFB.

78. Elizabeth Leonard to AFB, February 24, 1973, Series 3, Subseries 2, Box 6, Folder 3, AFB.

79. Raul Lugo to LOC, April 25, 1977, Series 3, Subseries 2, Box 6, Folder 11, AFB.

80. Frank Kurt Cylke to Scott Anderson, December 14, 1977, Series 3, Subseries 2, Box 6, Folder 11, AFB.

81. Alvin Marvin DeLaney to LOC, June 26, 1975, Series 3, Subseries 2, Box 7, Folder 1, AFB.

82. Bette White Minall to Milton Earl Forrest, May 22, 1969, Series 3, Subseries 2, Box 6, Folder 12, AFB.

83. Johnnie Johnson to Eugenia Rawls, n.d., Series 3, Subseries 2, Box 6, Folder 13, AFB.

84. Norman L. Johnson to American Printing House for the Blind (hereafter cited as APH), January 24, 1974, Series 3, Subseries 2, Box 6, Folder 9, AFB.

85. Marya Hunsicker to Frank Kurt Cylke, December 13, 1976, Series 3, Subseries 2, Box 6, Folder 13, AFB.

86. Elizabeth Leonard to AFB, February 24, 1973, Series 3, Subseries 2, Box 6, Folder 3, AFB.

87. Report RC 14874 MT, June 30, 1980, Series 3, Subseries 2, Box 6, Folder 2, AFB.

88. R. A. Nellis to Robert Kost, July 17, 1976, Series 3, Subseries 2, Box 7, Folder 1, AFB.

89. Barbara O. W. Hoeber to Mrs. Werner, February 14, 1973, Series 3, Subseries 2, Box 7, Folder 9, AFB.

90. Willard Price to librarian, Braille Institute of America, October 29, 1974, Series 3, Subseries 2, Box 7, Folder 1, AFB.

91. Louetta R. MacDonald to LOC, June 7, 1973, Series 3, Subseries 2, Box 6, Folder 12, AFB.

92. William P. Howle to R. A. Nellis, July 28, 1976, Series 3, Subseries 2, Box 7, Folder 1, AFB.

93. Frank Church to APH, May 28, 1976, Series 3, Subseries 2, Box 7, Folder 1, AFB.

94. William P. Howle to James W. Walker, March 5, 1973, Series 3, Subseries 2, Box 7, Folder 1, AFB.

95. James W. Walker to LOC, February 16, 1972, Series 3, Subseries 2, Box 7, Folder 1, AFB.

96. "Secretary-General's Visit to United States and Canada. June–July, 1937," typescript, n.d., 11–19; 14; (uncataloged) Blind Veterans UK.

97. Edgar F. Rogers to Luther Evans, July 17, 1944, Box 692, Folder 13-1, LOC.

98. F. Fraser Bond, "Mr. MacLeish Goes on Record," *Talking Book Topics* 6, no. 3 (December 1940): 18–20; 19.

99. A list of actors, celebrities, and public figures who read for the talking book service can be found in the "Beloved Voices" chapter of Frances A. Koestler, *The Unseen Minority: A Social History of Blindness in the United States* (New York: David McKay, 1976), 153–57.

100. William J. Maguire to Bucky Kozlow, June 10, 1976, Series 3, Subseries 2, Box 6, Folder 5, AFB.

101. Timothy Hendel to Robert Evan Jones, February 17, 1976, Series 3, Subseries 2, Box 6, Folder 13, AFB.

102. Howard Haycraft, *Books for the Blind: A Postscript and an Appreciation,* rev. ed. (Washington, D.C.: Library of Congress, Division for the Blind, 1962), 2.

103. George Card to House Jameson, September 2, 1968, Series 3, Subseries 2, Box 6, Folder 13, AFB.

104. R. A. Nellis to Jim Buss, December 15, 1976, Series 3, Subseries 2, Box 6, Folder 12, AFB.

105. Norman L. Johnson to APH, January 24, 1974, Series 3, Subseries 2, Box 6, Folder 9, AFB.

106. Mrs. Thomas Lucas to AFB, n.d., Series 3, Subseries 2, Box 6, Folder 6, AFB.

107. Chet Avery to Lucy Vecera, May 20, 1974, Series 3, Subseries 2, Box 7, Folder 1, AFB.

108. Ruth Vollrath to Bucky Kozlow, April 7, 1982, Series 3, Subseries 2, Box 6, Folder 5, AFB.

109. For example, see the profile of Alwyn Bach in "The Man behind the Voice," *Talking Book Topics* 6, no. 1 (June 1940): 16–19.

110. Christy Willett to Bucky Kozlow, April 7, 1970, Series 3, Subseries 2, Box 6, Folder 5, AFB.

111. [Wilbur Sheron], "The Voice," *Talking Book Topics* 5, no. 4 (March 1940): 18–20; 18–19.

112. Noteworthy readers are listed in "Personalities Who Have Recorded for the Talking Book," typescript, n.d., Folder "Braille Production," NLS; and William Barbour, "We Have the Honor to Present . . . ," *Talking Book Topics* 7, no. 2 (November 1941): 13–14.

113. "Books for the Adult Blind," typescript, n.d., 1–17; 4; Box 690, Folder 12-11, LOC.

114. "Program 2. Talking Book," typescript, n.d., Series 3, Subseries 3, Box 7, Folder 6, AFB.

115. Fraser Bond, "Books That Read Themselves," *New York Times Magazine,* May 14, 1944, 19, 38; 38.

116. Committee on the Library, Books for the Adult Blind: Hearing on H. R. 168, House, Seventy-Fifth Congress, First Session, January 23, 1937, Robert B. Irwin, 74.

117. Fraser Bond, "Famous Authors Read for Nation's Blind," typescript, 1944, 1–5; 2; Series 3, Subseries 3, Box 9, Folder 3, AFB.

118. "Program 2. Talking Book," typescript, n.d., Series 3, Subseries 3, Box 7, Folder 6, AFB.

119. Quoted in Bond, "Famous Authors," n.p. Emphasis in original. A copy of Mann's recording is held in the AFB's Talking Book Archive.

120. "Letters-to-the-Editor," typescript, n.d., Series 3, Subseries 2, Box 7, Folder 1, AFB.

4. A Free Press for the Blind

1. "Helen Keller Hails Aid of Talking Books," *New York Times,* June 7, 1935, 2.

2. Eleanor Catherine Judd, "Choosing 'Talking' Books," letter to editor, *New York Times,* February 4, 1939, 14. Judd is responding to Lawrence Stessin, "Books That Are Heard," *New York Times,* November 27, 1938, 151.

3. Judd, "Choosing 'Talking' Books," 14.

4. See Floyd W. Matson, *Walking Alone and Marching Together: A History of the Organized Blind Movement in the United States, 1940–1990* (Baltimore: National Federation of the Blind, 1990).

5. Judd, "Choosing 'Talking' Books," 14.

6. "Interview with Mr Andreassen Library of Congress on Blind," typescript, September 20, 1949, 1–8; 6; Box 691, Folder 13, Library of Congress (hereafter cited as LOC).

7. Evelyn Geller, *Forbidden Books in American Public Libraries, 1876–1939: A Study in Cultural Change* (Westport, Conn.: Greenwood, 1984).

8. National Library Service for the Blind and Physically Handicapped, Library of Congress, *That All May Read: Library Service for Blind and Physically Handicapped People* (Washington, D.C.: National Library Service for the Blind and Physically Handicapped, Library of Congress, 1983), 7–8.

9. Aksel G. S. Josephson to Herbert Putnam, March 10, 1931, Box 690, Folder "Blind 12-1," LOC. Objections are outlined in "Recommendations Regarding Administration of H. R. 11365 if Passed," typescript, May 15, 1930, Box 690, Folder "Blind 12-1," LOC.

10. Martin A. Roberts, "Books for the Adult Blind," in Library of Congress, *Annual Reports, Service for the Blind and Books for the Adult Blind including the Talking-Book Machine Activity, 1935–36* (Washington, D.C.: Government Printing Office, 1937), 12–29; 21.

11. "Note," *Talking Book Topics* 5, no. 4 (March 1940): 6; and "Selection of Books to Be Recorded," *Talking Book Topics* 6, no. 1 (June 1940): 14–15.

12. Library of Congress, Division for the Blind, *Books for the Blind* (Washington, D.C.: Library of Congress, Division for the Blind, 1951), 2.

13. Francis R. St. John, *Survey of Library Service for the Blind, 1956* (New York: American Foundation for the Blind, 1957), 71.

14. George Smathers to Luther Evans, February 25, 1953, Box 692, Folder "Blind 13," LOC.

15. Robert B. Irwin to Herman H. B. Meyer, March 14, 1934, Folder "Recorded Books," Archive, National Library Service for the Blind and Physically Handicapped, Washington, D.C. (hereafter cited as NLS). The material from NLS is uncataloged.

16. "Selection of Books for the Blind," typescript, December 3, 1947, Box 691, Folder "Blind 13," LOC.

17. Herman H. B. Meyer to Robert B. Irwin, May 7, 1934, Series 4, Subseries 1, Box 9, Folder 7, American Foundation for the Blind (hereafter cited as AFB).

18. Georgina Kleege, *Sight Unseen* (New Haven, Conn.: Yale University Press, 1999), 29. On the disability rights movement and efforts to combat discrimination, see Nancy J. Hirschmann and Beth Linker, eds., *Civil Disabilities: Citizenship, Membership, and Belonging* (Philadelphia: University of Pennsylvania Press, 2015).

19. See, for example, Luther H. Evans, typescript, November 27, 1950, Box 691, Folder "Blind 13," LOC.

20. "The 'Talking Book' Bible," clipping, Box 691, Folder "Blind 13," LOC. On the Bible and oral tradition, see William M. Schniedewind, *How the Bible Became a Book* (Cambridge: Cambridge University Press, 2005), and Allen Dwight Callahan, *The Talking Book: African Americans and the Bible* (New Haven, Conn.: Yale University Press, 2006).

21. On the origins of reading by touch, see John Oliphant, *The Early Education of the Blind in Britain c. 1790–1900: Institutional Experience in England and Scotland* (Lampeter, U.K.: Edwin Mellen, 2007), Gordon Phillips, *The Blind in British Society: Charity, State, and Community, c. 1780–1930* (Aldershot, U.K.: Ashgate, 2004), Pamela Lorimer, *Reading by Touch: Trials, Battles and Discoveries* (Baltimore: National Federation for the Blind, 2002), and Francis A. Koestler, *The Unseen Minority: A Social History of Blindness in the United States* (New York: David McKay, 1976), 91–114.

22. Millard W. Robinson, "New Low Price for Bible Records," *Talking Book Topics* 4, no. 1 (June 1938): 3–4.

23. Harold Bell Wright's *God and the Groceryman* was published in 1927. Committee on the Library, Books for the Adult Blind: Hearing on H. R. 9042, House, Seventy-First Congress, First Session, March 27, 1930, Robert B. Irwin, 14.

24. "Selection of Books for the Blind," typescript, May 23, 1947, 1–3; 3; Box 691, Folder "Blind 13," LOC.

25. Committee on the Library, Books for the Adult Blind: Hearing on H. R. 168, House, Seventy-Fifth Congress, First Session, January 23, 1937, Lucille A. Goldthwaite, 9.

26. Ibid., Herbert Putnam, 8. The distinction is discussed at length in Lester Asheim, "Not Censorship but Selection," *Wilson Library Bulletin* 28 (September 1953): 63–67.

27. Report, "Division for the Blind," typescript, 1949, 1–4; 1; Box 691, Folder 13, LOC.

28. Out of a total of 1,438 talking books, 44 percent were in nonfiction categories, and 150 fiction titles qualified as classic literature. Luther H. Evans to Wilmer C. Smith, October 27, 1948, Box 691, Folder 13, LOC.

29. Charles Magee Adams to Kent Keller, January 20, 1937, Series 2, Subseries 1, Box 3, Folder 3, AFB.

30. Committee on the Library, Books for the Adult Blind: Hearing on H. R. 168, House, Seventy-Fifth Congress, First Session, January 23, 1937, Lucille A. Goldthwaite, 23.

31. Rosa G. Barksdale to AFB, June 25, 1936, Series 3, Subseries 1, Box 9, Folder 9, AFB.

32. Robert B. Irwin to Marjorie Griesser, April 20, 1935, Series 1, Subseries 3, Box 2, Folder 7, AFB.

33. Ian Fraser, "Sir Ian Fraser's Report," June 25, 1936, 1–6; 2; File CRO/139, Folder T55/12/1, Royal National Institute of Blind People.

34. Minutes, Talking Book Selection Subcommittee, May 25, 1937, 1–21; 19; (uncataloged) Blind Veterans UK.

35. Quoted in A. C. Ellis to Robert B. Irwin, February 24, 1937, Series 4, Subseries 3, Box 14, Folder 2, AFB.

36. On efforts to exclude fiction from libraries, see Esther Jane Carrier, *Fiction in Public Libraries, 1900–1950* (Littleton, Colo.: Libraries Unlimited, 1985).

37. Committee on the Library, Books for the Adult Blind: Hearing on H. R. 168, House, Seventy-Fifth Congress, First Session, January 23, 1937, Martin A. Roberts, 27.

38. Lucy A. Goldthwaite, "The Talking Book," *Outlook for the Blind* 31 (February 1937): 13–16; 14.

39. Martin A. Roberts, "Books for the Adult Blind," in Library of Congress, *Report of the Librarian of Congress for the Fiscal Year ending June 30, 1937* (Washington, D.C.: Government Printing Office, 1937), 295–322; 309.

40. Charles Magee Adams to Robert B. Irwin, November 3, 1936, Series 3, Subseries 3, Box 7, Folder 4, AFB.

41. Francis R. St. John, *Survey of Library Service for the Blind, 1956* (New York: American Foundation for the Blind, 1957), 71.

42. "Division for the Blind," 1.

43. Hallie M. Baylor to AFB, May 9, 1937, Series 3, Subseries 3, Box 7, Folder 3, AFB.

44. Ibid.
45. The literature on the Cold War is extensive. Many of the relevant studies are cited by Ellen W. Schrecker, *No Ivory Tower: McCarthyism and the Universities* (New York: Oxford University Press, 1986).
46. See one librarian's response in David K. Berninghausen, "Book-Banning and Witch-Hunts," *American Library Association Bulletin* 42, no. 5 (May 1948): 204–7. On book censorship more broadly, see Paul S. Boyer, *Purity in Print: Book Censorship in America from the Gilded Age to the Computer Age,* 2nd ed. (Madison: University of Wisconsin Press, 2002).
47. On the American Library Association's response to censorship, see Louise S. Robbins, *Censorship and the American Library: The American Library Association's Response to Threats to Intellectual Freedom, 1939–1969* (Westport, Conn.: Greenwood, 1996), and Christine Pawley, *Reading Places: Literacy, Democracy, and the Public Library in Cold War America* (Amherst: University of Massachusetts Press, 2010). On the role of libraries during wartime, see Patti Clayton Becker, *Books and Libraries in American Society during World War II: Weapons in the War of Ideas* (New York: Routledge, 2005).
48. John J. Connolly to Edgar F. Rogers, July 26, 1944, Box 69, Folder 13, LOC. MacLeish replied to the letter during his colleague's absence.
49. Archibald MacLeish to John J. Connolly, August 2, 1944, Box 691, Folder 13, LOC.
50. John J. Connolly to Edgar F. Rogers, July 26, 1944, Box 69, Folder 13, LOC.
51. Archibald MacLeish to John J. Connolly, August 2, 1944, Box 691, Folder 13, LOC. MacLeish describes the librarian's obligation to defend intellectual freedom in "The Librarian and the Democratic Process," *American Library Association Bulletin* 34 (June 1940): 385–88, 421–22.
52. John J. Connolly to Archibald MacLeish, August 8, 1944, Box 691, Folder 13, LOC.
53. Archibald MacLeish to John J. Connolly, August 15, 1944, Box 691, Folder 13, LOC.
54. Memorandum, Louise Maurer to Archibald MacLeish, January 24, 1944, 1–7; 3; Box 691, Folder 13, AFB. Another employee attributed the rejections to potentially limited circulation.
55. Handwritten note attached to "Selection of Books for the Blind," May 23, 1947, 3.
56. Robert van Gelder, "An Interview with Mr. Robert B. Irwin," *New York Times Book Review,* February 8, 1942, 2. See also Rick Wartzman, *Obscene in the Extreme: The Burning and Banning of John Steinbeck's* The Grapes of Wrath (New York: PublicAffairs, 2008).
57. Felice Flanery Lewis outlines the judiciary's obscenity criteria in *Literature, Obscenity, and Law* (Carbondale: Southern Illinois University Press, 1976), 134–84. See also Allison Pease, *Modernism, Mass Culture, and the Aesthetics of Obscenity* (Cambridge: Cambridge University Press, 2000).
58. "Obscenity in Books for the Blind," typescript, June 30, 1947, 1–2; 1; Box 691, Folder 13, LOC.

59. Robert B. Irwin to A. C. Ellis, April 7, 1947, Series 4, Subseries 3, Box 14, Folder 7, AFB.

60. Ibid.

61. See Edwin Black, *War against the Weak: Eugenics and America's Campaign to Create a Master Race* (New York: Four Walls Eight Windows, 2003), 145–58.

62. Koestler, *The Unseen Minority,* 124.

63. A. C. Ellis to Robert B. Irwin, April 9, 1947, Series 4, Subseries 3, Box 14, Folder 7, AFB.

64. Ibid.

65. Quoted in Evelyn C. McKay to C. Warren Bledsoe, August 12, 1947, Series 2, Subseries 1, Box 3, Folder 6, AFB.

66. Evelyn C. McKay to C. Warren Bledsoe, August 12, 1947, Series 2, Subseries 1, Box 3, Folder 6, AFB.

67. Hazel Hodgdon to LOC, June 27, 1975, Series 3, Subseries 2, Box 6, Folder 12, AFB.

68. Ibid.

69. "Selection of Books for the Blind," May 23, 1947, 3.

70. Quoted in Verner W. Clapp to Carl T. Curtis, November 10, 1952, Box 692, Folder 13, LOC.

71. Verner W. Clapp to Carl T. Curtis, December 8, 1952, Box 692, Folder 13, LOC.

72. A. C. Ellis to Robert B. Irwin, April 9, 1947, Series 4, Subseries 3, Box 14, Folder 7, AFB.

73. "Obscenity in Books for the Blind," 2.

74. Letter to the editor, *Talking Book Topics* 14, no. 1 (June 1948): 5.

75. "Daisy, Daisy . . . ," *Talking Book Topics* 14, no. 2 (September 1948): 4–5; 4.

76. Ibid., 4.

77. Ibid., 5.

78. Ibid.

79. See Richard M. Freeland, *The Truman Doctrine and the Origins of McCarthyism, Foreign Policy, Domestic Politics, and Internal Security, 1946–1948* (New York: Knopf, 1972), 123–50; David Caute, *The Great Fear: The Anti-Communist Purge under Truman and Eisenhower* (New York: Simon and Schuster, 1978); and Michael J. Hogan, *A Cross of Iron: Harry S. Truman and the Origins of the National Security State, 1945–1954* (Cambridge: Cambridge University Press, 1998), 254–65.

80. On loyalty oaths and the Library of Congress, see Robbins, *Censorship,* 40–47. The McCarthy era is discussed in Richard Fried, *Nightmare in Red: The McCarthy Era in Perspective* (New York: Oxford University Press, 1990), and Ellen W. Schrecker, *Many Are the Crimes: McCarthyism in America* (Boston: Little, Brown, 1998).

81. On Clapp's presentation, see William S. Dix and Paul Bixler, eds., *Freedom of Communication: Proceedings of the First Conference on Intellectual Freedom, New York City, June 28–29, 1952* (Chicago: American Library Association, 1954), 38–68.

82. "Books for the Blind," *Human Events* 10, no. 7 (February 18, 1953): 2, clipping, Box 692, Folder "Blind 13," LOC.

83. Note, February 24, 1953, Box 692, Folder "Blind 13," LOC.

84. Louise S. Robbins documents the case of a public librarian who lost her job in 1950 for circulating communist material in *The Dismissal of Miss Ruth Brown* (Norman: University of Oklahoma Press, 2000).

85. Memo, Donald G. Patterson to Burton W. Adkinson, November 3, 1953, Box 692, Folder "Blind 13," LOC.

86. Memo, Donald G. Patterson to Burton W. Adkinson, March 6, 1953, Box 692, Folder "Blind 13," LOC.

87. Memo, Donald G. Patterson to Burton W. Adkinson, February 16, 1954, Box 692, Folder "Blind 13," LOC.

88. Koestler, *The Unseen Minority,* 160.

89. William P. Howle to Bertha M. Wilcox, March 12, 1975, Series 3, Subseries 2, Box 7, Folder 1, AFB.

90. On attitudes toward the Library of Congress's talking book program after 1950, see the interviews with librarians, students, educators, and users of library services in Leslie Eldridge, ed., *Speaking Out: Personal and Professional Views on Library Service for Blind and Physically Handicapped Individuals* (Washington, D.C.: National Library Service for the Blind and Physically Handicapped, 1982).

91. The eligibility criteria are listed in Title 36 Code of Federal Regulations, Sec 701.10 "Loans of Library Materials for Blind and Other Physically Handicapped Persons," http://www.loc.gov/nls/sec701.html.

5. From Shell Shock to Shellac

1. This figure is cited in Andrew Timothy, "Introduction," typescript, September 16, 1985, Folder "Talking Books—50th Anniversary," Royal National Institute of Blind People (hereafter cited as RNIB). RNIB's archive was in Stockport and mostly uncataloged at the time of my consultation. It was relocated to London in October 2012.

2. Lucille Hall to David Tytler, July 23, 1985, Folder "Talking Books—50th Anniversary," RNIB.

3. Thatcher borrowed eight talking books while recovering from eye surgery in 1983. "Prime Minister Marks 50th Anniversary of Talking Books," June 21, 1985, Folder "Talking Books—50th Anniversary," RNIB. The events are listed in "Suggested Programme for Thanksgiving Service," September 16, 1985, Folder "Talking Books—50th Anniversary," RNIB.

4. Untitled typescript, September 17, 1985, Folder "Talking Books—50th Anniversary," RNIB. On attitudes toward intellectual disability, see Deborah Cohen, *Family Secrets: Shame and Privacy in Modern Britain* (Oxford: Oxford University Press, 2013), 87–123.

5. Robert Heller, "Educating the Blind in the Age of Enlightenment: Growing Points of a Social Service," *Medical History* 23, no. 4 (1979): 392–403.

6. See Gordon Phillips, *The Blind in British Society: Charity, State, and Community, c. 1780–1930* (Aldershot, U.K.: Ashgate, 2004), and John Oliphant, *The Early Education of the Blind in Britain c. 1790–1900: Institutional Experience in England and Scotland* (Lampeter, U.K.: Edwin Mellen, 2007).

7. Ian Fraser, "The Talking Book," *St. Dunstan's Review for Blinded British Soldiers, Sailors and Airmen* 20, no. 212 (October 1935): 2–3; 2.

8. On tactile reading in Britain, see John Oliphant, " 'Touching the Light': The Invention of Literacy for the Blind," *Paedagogica Historica* 44, nos. 1–2 (February–April 2008): 67–82; Mary Wilson Carpenter, *Health, Medicine, and Society in Victorian England* (Santa Barbara: Praeger, 2010), 128–48; Vanessa Warne, " 'So That the Sense of Touch May Supply the Want of Sight': Blind Reading and Nineteenth-Century British Print Culture," in *Media, Technology, and Literature in the Nineteenth Century: Image, Sound, Touch,* ed. Colette Colligan and Margaret Linley (Aldershot, U.K.: Ashgate, 2011), 43–64; and Heather Tilley, "Touching the Book: Embossed Literature for Blind People in the Nineteenth Century," exhibition website, Birkbeck School of Arts, 2013, http://blogs.bbk.ac.uk/touchingthebook/.

9. Causes of blindness during the war included wounds, concussions, skull fractures, inflammatory diseases of the eye, interstitial keratitis, retinal detachment, optic nerve degeneration, and syphilis. For a comprehensive list, see Arnold Lawson, *War Blindness at St. Dunstan's* (London: Henry Frowde and Hodder & Stoughton, 1922).

10. On attitudes toward disabled veterans, see Seth Koven, "Remembering and Dismemberment: Crippled Children, Wounded Soldiers, and the Great War in Great Britain," *American Historical Review* 99, no. 4 (October 1994): 1167–1202; Joanna Bourke, *Dismembering the Male: Men's Bodies, Britain and the Great War* (London: Reaktion Books, 1996), 31–75; Jeffrey S. Reznick, *Healing the Nation: Soldiers and the Culture of Caregiving in Britain during the Great War* (Manchester: Manchester University Press, 2004); Ana Carden-Coyne, *Reconstructing the Body: Classicism, Modernism and the First World War* (Oxford: Oxford University Press, 2009); and Julie Anderson, *War, Disability and Rehabilitation in Britain: "Soul of a Nation"* (Manchester: Manchester University Press, 2011).

11. On postwar care, see Deborah Cohen, *The War Come Home: Disabled Veterans in Britain and Germany, 1914–1939* (Berkeley: University of California Press, 2001).

12. Tony Allen cites other uses of this phrase for fund-raising campaigns in *St. Dunstan's and the Great War* (York, U.K.: Holgate, 1999). See also David M. Lubin, "Losing Sight: War, Authority, and Blindness in British and American Visual Cultures, 1914–22," *Art History* 34, no. 4 (September 2011): 796–817. On the history of St. Dunstan's, see David Castleton, *Blind Man's Vision: The Story of St. Dunstan's in Words and Pictures* (London: St. Dunstan's, 1990), David Castleton, *In the Mind's Eye: The Blinded Veterans of St. Dunstan's* (Barnsley, U.K.: Pen and Sword Military, 2013), Julie Anderson and Neil Pemberton, "Walking Alone: Aiding the War and Civilian Blind in the Inter-war Period,"

European Review of History 14, no. 4 (December 2007): 459–79, and Julie Anderson, "Stoics: Creating Identities at St. Dunstan's 1914–1920," in *Men After War*, ed. Stephen McVeigh and Nicola Cooper (New York: Routledge, 2013), 79–91.

13. The only history of the RNIB's Talking Book Service is the brief account in Mary G. Thomas, *The Royal National Institute for the Blind, 1868–1956* (Brighton, U.K.: Brighton Herald, 1957), 66–69. RNIB's website (http://www .rnib.org.uk/) features additional information, as does Robert Kirkwood's Insight Radio program "75 Years of Talking Books" (2010), http://www .insightradio.co.uk/.

14. In 2002, RNIB changed its name from the Royal National Institute for the Blind to the Royal National Institute of Blind People.

15. See, for example, Joseph McAleer, *Popular Reading and Publishing in Britain, 1914–1950* (Oxford: Clarendon, 1992), and Robert James, *Popular Culture and Working-Class Taste in Britain, 1930–1939: A Round of Cheap Diversions?* (Manchester: Manchester University Press, 2010).

16. See D. L. LeMahieu's account of gramophones, newspapers, cinema, and other forms of entertainment in *A Culture for Democracy: Mass Communication and the Cultivated Mind in Britain between the Wars* (Oxford: Clarendon, 1998).

17. James Lastra discusses technology's capacity to extend human faculties in *Sound Technology and the American Cinema: Perception, Representation, Modernity* (New York: Columbia University Press, 2000), 6.

18. Ian Fraser, *My Story of St. Dunstan's* (London: George G. Harrap, 1961), 106.

19. [Sharp], "Talking Books for the Blind," March 14, 1938, 1–5; 3; Folder "Demonstrations and Talks on Talking Book Machines," RNIB.

20. Ian Fraser, *Whereas I Was Blind* (London: Hodder & Stoughton, 1942), 100.

21. Friedrich A. Kittler attributes the origins of media to "physiological deficiency" in *Discourse Networks 1800/1900,* trans. Michael Metteer, with Chris Cullens (Palo Alto, Calif.: Stanford University Press, 1990), 231.

22. On the LP's development, see Richard Osborne, *Vinyl: A History of the Analogue Record* (Farnham, U.K.: Ashgate, 2012). See also Peter Martland, *Recording History: The British Record Industry, 1888–1931* (Lanham, Md.: Scarecrow, 2013).

23. Fraser, *My Story of St. Dunstan's,* 106. See also Don Roskilly, "Talking Books in the United Kingdom," *St. Dunstan's Review* 828 (March 1991): 16–17; 17.

24. Edward J. Pyke, the NIB's technical officer, describes the equipment tested in "Sound-Recording for the Blind: A History of Experiment," *New Beacon* 20, no. 230 (February 15, 1936): 37–38; and Edward J. Pyke, "Sound-Recording for the Blind: A History of Experiment," *New Beacon* 20, no. 231 (March 15, 1936): 67–68.

25. Raymond Francis Yates, "Ear Books for the Blind: A Great Invention That Makes It Possible to Produce an Entire Book on a Single Phonographic Record," *Popular Science Monthly* 98, no. 5 (May 1921): 24.

26. "New Device Enables Blind to 'See' by Ear," *New York Times,* June 27, 1920, 1, 3; 1.

27. The optophone's history is described in Michael Capp and Phil Picton, "The Optophone: An Electronic Blind Aid," *Engineering Science and Education Journal* 9, no. 3 (June 2000): 137–43; and Mara Mills, "Optophones and Musical Print," *Sounding Out!*, January 5, 2015, http://soundstudiesblog.com /2015/01/05/optophones-and-musical-print/.

28. Mary Jameson recounts her use of various models in "The Optophone: Its Beginning and Development," *Bulletin of Prosthetics Research* 10, no. 5 (Spring 1966): 25–28.

29. See "Blind Reading Print by Sound," *Nature* 129 (January 9, 1932): 52; "Blind Can Now 'See' Print and Pictures," *Popular Science Monthly* 120, no. 6 (June 1932): 43; and "Science and Invention Begin to Aid the Blind," *Literary Digest* 117, no. 18 (May 5, 1934): 20.

30. "Excerpts of the Technical Research Committee Minutes Dealing with Sound Recording," typescript, n.d., 1, File CRO/119, Folder T55/51A, RNIB.

31. Fraser, *Whereas I Was Blind*, 101.

32. On the transition from silent to sound cinema, see Rick Altman, *Silent Film Sound* (New York: Columbia University Press, 2004), Charles O'Brien, *Cinema's Conversion to Sound: Technology and Film Style in France and the U.S.* (Bloomington: Indiana University Press, 2005), Douglas Gomery, *The Coming of Sound: A History* (New York: Routledge, 2005), and Michel Chion, *Film, a Sound Art,* trans. Claudia Gorbman (New York: Columbia University Press, 2009).

33. The minutes for a meeting held in April 1936 note, "It was quite possible that films would succeed gramophone discs for all uses." Appendix to minutes, Sound Recording Committee, April 28, 1936, File CRO/203, Folder T55/9, RNIB. Trials with alternative formats, such as Gaumont British Company's thousand-foot two-track film and reproducing machine, continued throughout the service's first decade.

34. Robert Irwin, M. C. Migel, and other representatives of the American Foundation for the Blind met with the Sound Recording Committee at St. Dunstan's on August 8, 1934. Quoted in memorandum, "Secretary-General's Visit to United States and Canada. June–July, 1937," typescript, n.d., 11–19; 11; Blind Veterans UK (hereafter cited as BVUK). BVUK's documents are uncataloged.

35. Waldo McGillicuddy Eagar to the secretary, Advisory Committee on the Welfare of the Blind, Ministry of Health, June 15, 1935, File CRO/203, Folder T55/9, RNIB.

36. On the comparative merits of discs and film, see P. Wilson, "Talking Books," *Gramophone* 13, no. 150 (November 1935): 252–53.

37. "Spoken books" was the phrase used to describe recorded literature in the United Kingdom before the adoption of the phrase "talking books" from the Americans. The NIB and St. Dunstan's used the phrase "talking book" in quotation marks as early as April 9, 1934. Memo, Granville Robbins to Ian Fraser, April 9, 1934, BVUK. A subsequent letter from the NIB to the Ministry of Health refers to "what is already known in America as 'The Talking Book for the Blind.'" Waldo McGillicuddy Eagar to the secretary, Advisory Committee

on the Welfare of the Blind, Ministry of Health, June 15, 1935, File CRO/203, Folder T55/9, RNIB.

38. "V. Talking Books," *National Institute for the Blind Annual Report, 1935–36* (London: National Institute for the Blind, 1936), 17–19; 18.

39. Ian Fraser, "Notes on the Talking Book Library by Captain Sir Ian Fraser," typescript, dictated August 1934, 1–7; 6, T55/51A File, RNIB.

40. Pyke, "Sound-Recording," March 15, 1936, 67.

41. Ian Fraser, "Talking Books," *St. Dunstan's Review* 18, no. 196 (April 1934): 2.

42. On the use of electrical recording from the 1920s, see Peter Copeland, *Sound Recordings* (London: British Library, 1991), and David L. Morton, Jr., *Sound Recording: The Life Story of a Technology* (Westport, Conn.: Greenwood, 2004).

43. The formal arrangements between the NIB and St. Dunstan's are set out in a letter from Waldo McGillicuddy Eagar to Ian Fraser, February 25, 1936, BVUK.

44. Ian Fraser, "Chairman's Notes," *St. Dunstan's Review* 647 (December 1973): 2–3; 2.

45. Anthony McDonald is credited as the first narrator in ibid. McDonald made test recordings of Winston Churchill's *My Early Life: A Roving Commission,* Rudyard Kipling's *Stalky and Co.,* and other titles. He became the organization's first commissioned reader at the rate of £1.1.0 per master record. Minutes, Sound Recording Subcommittee, October 16, 1934, BVUK.

46. Ian Fraser, "Memorandum on Sound Recording," July 2, 1934, 1–4; 3; File CRO/802, Folder T55/18, RNIB.

47. Memorandum, P. W. Willins, "Recording Experiments in Connection with the Proposed Library for the Blind," April 7, 1934, BVUK. On the development of Watts's machine, see Agnes H. Watts, *Cecil E. Watts: Pioneer of Direct Disc Recording* (London: William Clowes & Sons, 1972), 11–12.

48. "Sound Recording," typescript, February 12, 1935, BVUK.

49. Minutes, Sound Recording Subcommittee, October 9, 1935, 1–6; 5; BVUK. A formal set of rules ("Talking Book Library for the Blind: Rules") is included in the appendix to a report on the meeting between the Sound Recording Committee and the American Foundation for the Blind, August 13, 1934, BVUK.

50. Appendix to minutes, Sound Recording Committee, April 28, 1936, File CRO/203, Folder T55/9, RNIB.

51. The most substantial support came from Lord Nuffield, who, after a preliminary gift of £5,000 in 1936, went on to provide a total of £37,500 in the service's first decade. The Carnegie United Kingdom Trust granted an additional £500 per annum, for three years, toward research.

52. Ian Fraser to Neville Pearson, March 4, 1936, BVUK.

53. The Post Office Amendment Act of 1936 extended braille postage rates to talking book packages. The postal concession ensured transmission up to a maximum cost of twopence for a weight of eleven pounds. The Import Duties Advisory Committee also added to the Free List gramophone records for the use of blind people. "The Talking Book for the Blind," typescript, n.d., 1–6; 4; File CRO/203, Folder T55/9, RNIB.

54. By December 7, 1935, the Sound Recording Committee had dispatched 119 machines (47 electrical, 34 mechanical, and 38 headphone models). Edward J. Pyke, "Progress Report," December 17, 1935, included as appendix 1, minutes, Sound Recording Committee, December 18, 1935, BVUK.

55. "IV. Talking Books," *National Institute for the Blind Annual Report, 1936–37* (London: National Institute for the Blind, 1937), 21–23; 23.

56. Ian Fraser explains the decision to charge veterans in "Chairman's Notes," *St. Dunstan's Review* 24, no. 261 (March 1940): 1–3; 1.

57. "Report on Talking Book Developments February, 1936–September, 1937," typescript, September 24, 1937, File CRO/203, Folder T55/9, RNIB.

58. Minutes, Sound Recording Subcommittee, July 24, 1935, BVUK. I have been unable to locate any documents confirming whether the first recording was Christie or Conrad, though circumstantial evidence leads me to believe that it was Christie. The numbers of copies (thirty for *Roger Ackroyd*, twenty for all others) are listed in the accounts paid to HMV. "Recordings, Records and Masters Included in Accounts Paid," February 18, 1936, File CRO/736, Folder T55/53A, RNIB.

59. [Sharp], "Talking Books," 3.

60. See Alistair McCleery, "The Paperback Evolution: Tauchnitz, Albatross and Penguin," in Nicole Matthews and Nickianne Moody, eds., *Judging a Book by Its Covers: Fans, Publishers, Designers, and the Marketing of Fiction* (Aldershot, U.K.: Ashgate, 2007), 3–17.

61. [Sharp], "Talking Books," 3. Munthe's memoir was originally meant to be the first talking book. Waldo McGillicuddy Eagar to John Murray, June 12, 1935, Folder "Publisher Negotiations," RNIB.

62. Minutes, Sound Recording Subcommittee, February 17, 1937, Folder "Sound Recording Committee 1934–1960," RNIB. On the Bible's representation of blindness, see John M. Hull, *In the Beginning There Was Darkness: A Blind Person's Conversations with the Bible* (London: SCM, 2001).

63. Minutes, Talking Book Selection Subcommittee, April 25, 1935, BVUK.

64. "The Talking Book Arrives," *New Beacon* 19, no. 224 (August 15, 1935): 201–4; 202.

65. The initial titles recorded in Britain are listed in minutes, Talking Book Selection Subcommittee, April 25, 1935, BVUK. There is a pencil tick next to each of the four titles that had already been recorded. The list is reprinted in "The Talking Book Arrives," 202; and "Report of the Year's Work," *National Institute for the Blind Annual Report, 1935–36* (London: National Institute for the Blind, 1936), 9–19; 18. On the exchange of records with the American Foundation for the Blind, see "Correspondence Dealing with the Sale and Exchange of English and American Talking Book Records, 13th March, 1934 to 20th February, 1936," March 7, 1936, File CRO/139, Folder T55/12/1, RNIB.

66. Ernest Whitfield, "Notes for Dr. Whitfield's Speech to the Union of Associations for the Blind, Clothworkers' Hall, Thursday, 12th March 1936," typescript, 1–4; 1; File CRO/119, Folder T55/51, RNIB.

67. "Progress Report," December 17, 1935, File CRO/203, Folder T55/9, RNIB; "Bulky Books," *Manchester Evening Chronicle,* June 26, 1936, clipping, RNIB.

68. Waldo McGillicuddy Eagar to Joseph Challinor, October 2, 1935, Folder "Demonstrations and Talks on Talking Book Machines," RNIB.

69. Ian Fraser, "Chairman's Notes," *St. Dunstan's Review* 20, no. 219 (May 1936): 1–2; 2.

70. "The Talking Book," *Nineteenth Annual Report of St. Dunstan's for Year Ended March 31st, 1934* (London: Executive Council of St. Dunstan's, 1934), 14.

71. Ibid.

72. Fraser, "The Talking Book," 3.

73. On the tropes of simulation and inscription used for new media, see Lastra, *Sound Technology and the American Cinema,* 5–8.

74. Letter to the editor, *New Beacon* 22, no. 259 (July 15, 1938): 193–94; 193.

75. "IV. Talking Books," *National Institute for the Blind Annual Report, 1936–37,* 21.

76. "Secretary-General's Visit to United States and Canada, June–July, 1937," typescript, n.d., BVUK.

77. "V. Talking Books," *National Institute for the Blind Annual Report, 1935–36,* 19.

78. [Sharp], "Talking Books," 5.

79. "IV. Talking Books," *National Institute for the Blind Annual Report, 1936–37,* 21.

80. "Points from Letters," *St. Dunstan's Review* 21, no. 223 (October 1936): 3.

81. "Spoken Books," *New Beacon* 18, no. 208 (April 15, 1934): 91.

82. "IV. Talking Books," *National Institute for the Blind Annual Report, 1937–38* (London: National Institute for the Blind, 1938), 23–25; 24.

83. Minutes, Talking Book Selection Subcommittee, April 25, 1935, BVUK.

84. Waldo McGillicuddy Eagar to Publishers' Association of Great Britain and Ireland, June 6, 1935, Folder "Copyright and Negotiations with Publishers' Association," RNIB.

85. "'Talking Books,'" *Times* (London), June 10, 1936, 9.

86. Geoffrey Faber, "The Exploitation of Books by Broadcasting and Talking Machine," *Publishers' Weekly* 130, No. 2 (July 11, 1936): 110–114; 114.

87. The full list of conditions can be found in the letter from F. W. Sanders to Waldo McGillicuddy Eagar, September 29, 1936, Folder "Copyright and Negotiations with Publishers' Association," RNIB.

88. F. W. Sanders to Waldo McGillicuddy Eagar, May 30, 1936, Folder "Copyright and Negotiations with Publishers' Association," RNIB.

89. Minutes, Talking Book Selection Subcommittee, November 19, 1935, BVUK.

90. Fraser's discussion of Kipling and the copyright situation with a representative of A. P. Watt is recounted in Fraser, "Notes on the Talking Book Library," 6.

91. Minutes, Talking Book Selection Subcommittee, January 26, 1937, File "Publications Advisory Committee: February 1937 to February 1945," Folder "Book Selection Lists," RNIB.

92. Minutes, Talking Book Selection Subcommittee, May 25, 1937, File "Publications Advisory Committee: February 1937 to February 1945," Folder "Book Selection Lists," RNIB.

93. Ian Fraser to Lord Nuffield, July 22, 1936, BVUK.

94. For example, see Fraser's comments in "Remarks by Lord Fraser of Lonsdale," in *Science and Blindness: Retrospective and Prospective,* ed. Milton D. Graham (New York: American Foundation for the Blind, 1972), 174–77.

95. Ian Fraser to Lord Nuffield, July 22, 1936, BVUK.

96. Fraser, "Chairman's Notes," 1936, 2.

97. "IV. Talking Books," *National Institute for the Blind Annual Report, 1936–37,* 23.

98. See Jeffrey Richards, *The Age of the Dream Palace: Cinema and Society in 1930s Britain* (London: I. B. Tauris, 2010), and John Sedgewick, *Popular Filmgoing in 1930s Britain: A Choice of Pleasures* (Exeter: University of Exeter Press, 2000).

99. "Appreciation of Talking Books," *National Institute for the Blind Annual Report, 1948–49* (London: National Institute for the Blind, 1949), 12–13; 13.

100. "Talking Books," *Royal National Institute of Blind People Report for 1952–1953* (London: Royal National Institute of Blind People, 1953), 16.

101. "Points from Letters," 3.

102. Cohen, *The War Come Home,* 102.

103. Letter to the editor, *New Beacon* 22, no. 259 (July 15, 1938): 193–94; 193.

104. "The Talking Book," *Nineteenth Annual Report of St. Dunstan's,* 14.

105. "The Talking Book Arrives," 203.

106. Helen Keller, "The Heaviest Burden on the Blind," in *Out of the Dark* (New York: Hodder & Stoughton, 1913), 211–18; 212.

107. "Talking Books," *National Institute for the Blind Annual Report, 1939–40* (London: National Institute for the Blind, 1940), 10–12; 10.

108. "Improved Talking Book Service," *Royal National Institute of Blind People Report for 1955–1956* (London: Royal National Institute of Blind People, 1956), 19.

109. "Appreciation of Talking Books," 13.

110. F. G. Braithwaite to Ian Fraser, January 11, 1936. Reprinted in *Twenty-First Annual Report of St. Dunstan's for Year Ended March 31st, 1936* (London: Executive Council of St. Dunstan's, 1936), 14. Fraser discusses Braithwaite's life in *Whereas I Was Blind,* 54–55; and *My Story of St. Dunstan's,* 136–37.

111. The scholarship on trauma and the First World War is extensive. Studies published in the last decade include Peter Leese, *Shell Shock: Traumatic Neurosis and the British Soldiers of the First World War* (Basingstoke, U.K.: Palgrave, 2002), Ben Shephard, *A War of Nerves: Soldiers and Psychiatrists, 1914–1994* (London: Pimlico, 2002), Peter Barham, *Forgotten Lunatics of the Great War* (New Haven, Conn.: Yale University Press, 2004), Edgar Jones and Simon Wessely, *Shell Shock to PTSD: Military Psychiatry from 1900 to the Gulf War* (Hove, U.K.: Psychology Press, 2005), and Fiona Reid, *Broken Men: Shell Shock, Treatment and Recovery in Britain 1914–1930* (London: Continuum, 2010).

112. Bourke, *Dismembering the Male,* 162–70; Cohen, *The War Come Home,* 105.

113. "Appreciation of Talking Books," 13.

114. "Talking Books," *Royal National Institute of Blind People Report for 1952–1953,* 16.

115. "Points from Letters," 3.

116. The British Wireless for the Blind Fund began supplying free radios in 1929. The fund is described in Waldo McGillicuddy Eagar, "Blindness in Great Britain," in *Blindness: Modern Approaches to the Unseen Environment,* ed. Paul A. Zahl (Princeton, N.J.: Princeton University Press, 1950), 26–36; and Mark

Pegg, *Broadcasting and Society, 1918–1939* (London: Croom Helm, 1983), 165. See also Rebecca Scales, "Radio Broadcasting, Disabled Veterans, and the Politics of National Recovery in Interwar France," *French Historical Studies* 31, no. 4 (2008): 643–78.

117. "Talking Books," *Royal National Institute of Blind People Report for 1952–1953,* 16.

118. "Talking Books," *National Institute for the Blind Annual Report, 1939–40,* 10.

119. "Improved Talking Book Service," 19.

120. "The Talking Book Library," *Royal National Institute of Blind People Report for 1954–55* (London: Royal National Institute of Blind People, 1955), 17.

121. Charles Dickens, *David Copperfield* (London: Penguin, 1996), 60.

122. "The Talking Book Library," 17.

123. "The Latest Model of the Talking Book Machine," *Royal National Institute of Blind People Report for 1956–1957* (London: Royal National Institute of Blind People, 1957), 17.

124. "Talking Books," *Royal National Institute of Blind People Report for 1952–1953,* 16.

125. Ibid.

126. "IV. Talking Books," *National Institute for the Blind Annual Report, 1936–37,* 23.

127. On the public's enthusiasm about and anxieties toward new technologies, see Bernhard Rieger, *Technology and the Culture of Modernity in Britain and Germany, 1890–1945* (Cambridge: Cambridge University Press, 2005).

128. Ian Fraser to Neville Pearson, March 4, 1936, BVUK.

129. Georgina Kleege, *Sight Unseen* (New Haven, Conn.: Yale University Press, 1999), 190.

130. Arthur Copland, "Talking-Book or Reading-Book?," *New Beacon* 21, no. 242 (February 15, 1937): 33–35.

131. "The Talking Book Arrives," 201.

132. On the link between emerging technologies and declining braille literacy, see "Braille Is Spreading but Who's Using It?," *BBC News Magazine,* February 13, 2012, http://www.bbc.co.uk/news/magazine-16984742. This article is based on the National Federation of the Blind report, "The Braille Literacy Crisis in America," March 26, 2009, http://www.nfb.org/images/nfb/documents/pdf/braille_literacy_report_web.pdf.

133. See the accounts of emerging technologies in David Thorburn and Henry Jenkins, eds., *Rethinking Media Change: The Aesthetics of Transition* (Cambridge, Mass.: MIT Press, 2003).

134. "Talking Book or Reading Book? Some Opinions on the Question," *New Beacon* 21, no. 243 (March 15, 1937): 68–71; 68.

135. On aging and disability, see Pat Thane, *Old Age in English History: Past Experiences, Present Issues* (Oxford: Oxford University Press, 2000).

136. This figure is cited in "Talking Book or Reading Book? Some Opinions on the Question," 69. Census figures for the blind population in England and Wales from 1851 to 1911 are reprinted in Phillips, *The Blind in British Society,* 321.

137. "Points from Letters," 3.
138. "Talking Book or Reading Book? Sir Ian Fraser's Comments and a Letter from E. Bates," *New Beacon* 21, no. 244 (April 15, 1937): 97–98; 97.
139. See D. F. McKenzie's influential formulation of this concept in *Bibliography and the Sociology of Texts: The Panizzi Lectures, 1985* (London: British Library, 1986), 4. More recent versions can be found in Roger Chartier, *The Order of Books: Readers, Authors, and Libraries in Europe between the Fourteenth and Eighteenth Centuries,* trans. Lydia G. Cochrane (Oxford: Polity, 1994), 89–91; and N. Katherine Hayles, *Writing Machines* (Cambridge, Mass.: MIT Press, 2002), 25.
140. "Talking Book or Reading Book? Sir Ian Fraser's Comments and a Letter from E. Bates," 98.
141. Copland, "Talking-Book or Reading-Book?," 34, 35.
142. "Report of the Year's Work," *Report of the Executive Council of the National Institute for the Blind for the Financial Year Ended 31st March, 1935* (London: National Institute for the Blind, 1935), 19–22; 21.
143. "Talking Book or Reading Book? Sir Ian Fraser's Comments and a Letter from E. Bates," 97.
144. "Talking Book or Reading Book? Some Opinions on the Question," 70.
145. "Talking Book or Reading Book? Sir Ian Fraser's Comments and a Letter from E. Bates," 97. The restriction against use by sighted people included the caveat, "This rule does not debar the overhearing of recordings by members of the family who share the room with the blind person." "Rules," Nuffield Talking Book Library for the Blind, Folder T55/53/1, RNIB.
146. V. C. Clinton-Baddeley delivered the first serial reading of a Dickens novel on radio when *Great Expectations* was read in sixteen installments between January and April 1930. On the history of radio recitations, see Robert Giddings and Keith Selby, *The Classic Serial on Television and Radio* (Basingstoke, U.K.: Palgrave, 2001).
147. Arthur Copland, "Talking-Book or Reading-Book? A Reply," *New Beacon* 21, no. 245 (May 15, 1937): 132–33; 133.
148. "Talking Book or Reading Book? Sir Ian Fraser's Comments and a Letter from E. Bates," 98.
149. "Talking Book or Reading Book? Some Opinions on the Question," 69.
150. Ibid., 71.
151. Recording came to an abrupt halt in 1940, when a bomb demolished the recording studio in Regent's Park. Another air raid in May 1941 damaged the replacement studio. After resuming recording for a second time that August, the library protected its collection by sending three books, instead of the customary two, to the organization's 1,400 members located in various parts of the country. Among the 408 titles evacuated from London was a recently donated recording of Winston Churchill's patriotic broadcast, "The War of the Unknown Warriors." "Talking Books," *National Institute for the Blind Annual Report, 1940–41* (London: National Institute for the Blind, 1941), 12–13; 13.
152. For examples of soldiers listening to talking books after the Second World War, see the profiles of Tommy Gaygan and A. J. M. Milne in Ian Fraser, ed.,

Conquest of Disability: Inspiring Accounts of Courage, Fortitude and Adaptability in Conquering Grave Physical Handicaps (London: Odhams, 1956), 39–50, 134–46.

153. "Talking Books," *National Institute for the Blind Annual Report for 1945–46* (London: National Institute for the Blind, 1946), 18–19; 18.

154. In 2012, the RNIB estimated that only 7 percent of all titles were available in accessible formats including large print, unabridged audio, and braille. *Sight Loss UK 2012: The Latest Evidence* (London: Royal National Institute of Blind People, 2012), 15, http://www.rnib.org.uk/aboutus/Research/reports/2012/Sight _loss_uk_2012.pdf. The report is based on the findings in Helen Greenwood, Sonya White, and Claire Creaser, "Availability of Accessible Publications: 2011 Update," report to RNIB, October 24, 2011, http://www.rnib.org.uk/aboutus /Research/reports/reading/Pages/accessible_publishing_research.aspx. The World Blind Union described the lack of accessible formats as a "book famine." "Committee on the Rights of Persons with Disabilities Day of General Discussion on 'The Right to Accessibility,'" paper presented by the World Blind Union at the Convention on the Rights of Persons with Disabilities, October 7, 2010, 1, http://www2.ohchr.org/SPdocs/CRPD/DGD7102010 /submissions/WBU_II.doc.

6. Unrecordable

1. Memo, G[ay] Ashton to Eric Gillett, July 17, 1959, File CRO/036, Folder T55/32B, Royal National Institute of Blind People (hereafter cited as RNIB).

2. Report, G[ay] Ashton to Donald Bell, April 29, 1963, File CRO/711, Folder T55/32C, RNIB.

3. Memo, G[ay] Ashton to Vernon Barlow, September 24, 1957, Folder T55/32A, RNIB.

4. Ibid.

5. Ibid.

6. Ibid.

7. Memo, Vernon Barlow to G[ay] Ashton, September 25, 1957, Folder T55/32A, RNIB.

8. W. Percy Merrick to Waldo McGillicuddy Eagar, April 25, 1935, File CRO/203, Folder T55/9, RNIB.

9. See Thomas Kelly, *A History of Public Libraries in Great Britain, 1845–1975* (London: Library Association, 1977), and Alistair Black, *A New History of the English Public Library: Social and Intellectual Contexts, 1850–1914* (London: Leicester University Press, 1996).

10. "Library Association Conference Exhibition," June 9, 1936, Folder "Demonstrations and Talks on Talking Book Machines," RNIB, 1–4; 3.

11. Minutes, Talking Book Selection Subcommittee, April 25, 1935, Blind Veterans UK (hereafter cited as BVUK). BVUK's documents are uncataloged.

12. "Ian Hay" [John Hay Beith], "The Talking Book Library for the Blind," in St. Dunstan's, *Twenty-Third Annual Report of St. Dunstan's for Year Ended March 31st, 1938* (London: Shenval, 1938), n.p.

13. J. de la Mare Rowley to O. I. Prince, August 4, 1936, File CRO/203, Folder T55/9, RNIB.

14. F. R. Richardson describes his role as Boots's chief librarian in "The Circulating Library," in *The Book World,* ed. John Hampden (London: Thomas Nelson & Sons, 1935), 195–202. On Boots's circulating library, see Philip Waller, *Writers, Readers, and Reputations: Literary Life in Britain, 1870–1918* (Oxford: Oxford University Press, 2006), 58; and Christopher Hilliard, "The Twopenny Library: The Book Trade, Working-Class Readers, and 'Middlebrow' Novels in Britain, 1930–42," *Twentieth Century British History* 25, no. 2 (2014): 199–220.

15. Waldo McGillicuddy Eagar to Ian Fraser, June 22, 1938, File CRO/203, Folder T55/9, RNIB.

16. Ian Fraser to Waldo McGillicuddy Eagar, February 18, 1943, File CRO/203, Folder T55/9, RNIB.

17. Waldo McGillicuddy Eagar to J. de la Mare Rowley, "Talking Book Selection Committee," July 2, 1943, File CRO/203, Folder T55/9, RNIB.

18. Ibid.

19. J. de la Mare Rowley to Waldo McGillicuddy Eagar, March 18, 1943, File CRO/203, Folder T55/9, RNIB.

20. John R. Temple to Ian Fraser, February 20, 1935, File CRO/203, Folder T55/9, RNIB.

21. E. E. Mavrogordato to Ian Fraser, May 4, 1935, File CRO/203, Folder T55/9, RNIB.

22. Stuart Hibberd describes meeting with Ian Fraser on October 31, 1935, to discuss recording the Bible in *"This—Is London . . ."* (London: Macdonald and Evans, 1950), 119–20.

23. Waldo McGillicuddy Eagar to Ian Fraser, January 30, 1937, File CRO/178, Folder T55/42, RNIB.

24. Waldo McGillicuddy Eagar to Tom Jones, November 4, 1936, File CRO/178, Folder T55/42, RNIB.

25. Waldo McGillicuddy Eagar to Ian Fraser, January 30, 1937, File CRO/178, Folder T55/42, RNIB.

26. Memo, October 15, 1938, File CRO/178, Folder T55/42, RNIB.

27. On speech education in Britain, see Evelyn M. Sivier, "English Poets, Teachers, and Festivals in a 'Golden Age of Poetry Speaking,' 1920–50," in *Performance of Literature in Historical Perspectives,* ed. David W. Thompson (Lanham, Md.: University Press of America, 1983), 283–300.

28. J. de la Mare Rowley to John Hammerton, September 6, 1944, File CRO/203, Folder T55/9, RNIB.

29. G[ay] Ashton to J. de la Mare Rowley, November 14, 1947, File CRO/203, Folder T55/9, RNIB.

30. G[ay] Ashton to Donald Bell, October 25, 1961, File CRO/711, Folder T55/32C, RNIB.

31. "Analysis of the Demand for Talking Books," February 12, 1957, Folder "Book Selection Lists," RNIB.

32. Ian Fraser, "Chairman's Notes," *St. Dunstan's Review,* n.s., 22, no. 235 (November 1937): 1–2; 2.

33. The survey was compiled from 53,594 requests sent by 2,273 members from January to June 1957. At that time, the catalog contained 585 titles (378 fiction; 207 nonfiction). G[ay] Ashton, "Report by the Librarian for the Meeting of the Book Selection Panel on 9th October 1957," BVUK.

34. G[ay] Ashton, memo, February 16, 1959, Folder T55/32B, RNIB.

35. Ibid.

36. Ibid.

37. Mrs. W. Crisp to RNIB, November 12, 1969, Folder T55/32F, RNIB.

38. John Colligan to Ian Fraser, April 26, 1961, File CRO/036, Folder T55/32B, RNIB.

39. Ibid.

40. Memo, G[ay] Ashton to Eric Gillett, January 26, 1961, Folder "Book Selection Lists," RNIB.

41. Donald Bell to D. W. Wadegaonkar, July 16, 1965, File CRO/683, Folder T55/32D, RNIB.

42. A resolution opposing abridgment is noted in the minutes from the Talking Book Selection Subcommittee meeting held on November 25, 1937. The BBC's Books at Bedtime series was not used by the library for this reason. Donald Bell to P. B. Baker, October 15, 1969, Folder T55/32F, RNIB.

43. "Selection of Books for Sound Recording," October 11, 1943, File CRO/203, Folder T55/9, RNIB.

44. Early readers included Bruce Belfrage, Patrick Curwen, Lionel Gamlin, Roland Gillett, Frederick Grisewood, Alan Howland, Edward Le Breton Martin, Alvar Liddel, and Joseph Macleod. They were paid £3.3.0 to record three to four sides per session. See "IV. Talking Books," *National Institute for the Blind Annual Report, 1936–37* (London: National Institute for the Blind, 1937), 21–23; 23; and Ian Fraser, *Whereas I Was Blind* (London: Hodder & Stoughton, 1942), 106.

45. Quoted in Miriam Maisel, "How Talking Books Are Helping Aged Blind," *Northern Despatch* (Priestgate, Darlington, U.K.), April 19, 1965, clipping, Folder T55/38A, RNIB.

46. J. Le Roux to John Colligan, September 12, 1959, File CRO/711, Folder T55/32C, RNIB.

47. Waldo McGillicuddy Eagar to Robert B. Irwin, March 30, 1937, Folder T55/APH, RNIB.

48. Robert B. Irwin to Waldo McGillicuddy Eagar, August 2, 1935, File CRO/139, Folder T55/12/1, RNIB.

49. A survey of twenty-two readers conducted on January 8, 1935, noted that American accents were not considered suitable for the Bible or Shakespeare. Waldo McGillicuddy Eagar to Robert B. Irwin, September 11, 1935, File CRO/139, Folder T55/12/1, RNIB.

50. Report, G[ay] Ashton, February 12, 1958, File CRO/711, Folder T55/32C, RNIB.

51. Memo, G[ay] Ashton to Eric Gillett, May 1, 1961, File CRO/036, Folder T55/32B, RNIB.

52. M. E. Jackson to Donald Bell, January 6, 1969, Folder T55/32F, RNIB.

53. Ian Fraser to G[ay] Ashton, May 15, 1958, File CRO/036, Folder T55/32B, RNIB.

54. J. Le Roux to John Colligan, September 12, 1959, File CRO/711, Folder T55/32C, RNIB.

55. Donald Bell to M. Austen, October 14, 1966, Folder T55/32E, RNIB.

56. G[ay] Ashton to A. Limburg, January 22, 1963, File CRO/711, Folder T55/32C, RNIB.

57. G[ay] Ashton to Eric Gillett, October 10, 1958, File CRO/711, Folder T55/32C, RNIB.

58. Vernon Barlow to A. H. Hill, October 7, 1957, Folder T55/32A, RNIB.

59. G[ay] Ashton to Eric Gillett, April 14, 1958, File CRO/036, Folder T55/32B, RNIB.

60. Donald Bell to G[ay] Ashton, October 8, 1964, File CRO/683, Folder T55/32D, RNIB.

61. Ibid.

62. Donald Bell to Miss Cooch, July 20, 1965, File CRO/683, Folder T55/32D, RNIB.

63. A well-known survey of censorship is Donald Thomas, *A Long Time Burning: The History of Literary Censorship in England* (London: Routledge & Kegan Paul, 1969). See also Paul Hyland and Neil Sammells, eds., *Writing and Censorship in Britain* (New York: Routledge, 1992), Elisabeth Ladenson, *Dirt for Art's Sake: Books on Trial from "Madame Bovary" to "Lolita"* (Ithaca, N.Y.: Cornell University Press, 2007), and David Bradshaw and Rachel Potter, eds., *Prudes on the Prowl: Fiction and Obscenity in England, 1850 to the Present Day* (Oxford: Oxford University Press, 2013).

64. The influence of antivice crusading is charted in Edward J. Bristow, *Vice and Vigilance: Purity Movements in Britain since 1700* (Dublin: Gill and Macmillan, 1977).

65. On censorship and the provision of fiction in public libraries, see Nicholas Hiley, "Can't You Find Me Something Nasty? Circulating Libraries and Literary Censorship in Britain from the 1890s to the 1910s," in *Censorship and the Control of Print in England and France, 1600–1910,* ed. Robin Myers and Michael Harris (Winchester, U.K.: St. Paul's Bibliographies, 1992), 123–47; and Mary Hammond, *Reading, Publishing and the Formation of Literary Taste in England, 1880–1914* (Aldershot, U.K.: Ashgate, 2006), 23–50.

66. D. Porter to Donald Bell, July 20, 1966, Folder T55/32E, RNIB.

67. Edith Clarke to Vernon Barlow, August 17, 1954, Folder T55/32F, RNIB; M. O'Brian to Donald Bell, September 12, 1965, Folder T55/32F, RNIB.

68. J. Knight to Donald Bell, March 15, 1967, Folder T55/32F, RNIB.

69. Waldo McGillicuddy Eagar to J. de la Mare Rowley, July 2, 1943, File CRO/203, Folder T55/9, RNIB.

70. Donald Bell to C. A. Skinner, November 1, 1968, Folder T55/32F, RNIB.

71. Donald Bell to T. J. Boote, November 15, 1971, Folder T55/32G, RNIB.

72. Report, G[ay] Ashton to Donald Bell, April 29, 1963, File CRO/711, Folder T55/32C, RNIB.

73. G[ay] Ashton to Eric Gillett, January 6, 1959, File CRO/036, Folder T55/32B, RNIB.

74. Report, G[ay] Ashton to Donald Bell, April 29, 1963, File CRO/711, Folder T55/32C, RNIB. The British Board of Film Censors' opposition to the adaptation of Sillitoe's *Saturday Night and Sunday Morning* is documented in Anthony Aldgate, *Censorship and the Permissive Society: British Cinema and Theatre, 1955–1965* (Oxford: Clarendon, 1995), 89–119.

75. Jean Harris to Donald Bell, September 21, 1971, Folder T55/32G, RNIB.

76. Henry T. Berry to John Colligan, October 9, 1968, T55/32F, RNIB.

77. Mrs. M. O'Brien to Donald Bell, January 22, 1969, Folder T55/32F, RNIB.

78. Memo, G[ay] Ashton to Vernon Barlow, September 24, 1957, Folder "Book Selection Lists," RNIB.

79. I. McIlvenna to Donald Bell, March 23, 1969, Folder T55/32F, RNIB.

80. I. McIlvenna to Donald Bell, July 2, 1969, Folder T55/32F, RNIB.

81. Dorothea Howard to Donald Bell, February 25, 1969, Folder T55/32F, RNIB.

82. G[ay] Ashton to Donald Bell, April 29, 1965, File CRO/683, Folder T55/32D, RNIB.

83. Report, G[ay] Ashton to Donald Bell, April 29, 1963, File CRO/711, Folder T55/32C, RNIB.

84. G[ay] Ashton to Donald Bell, February 22, 1962, File CRO/711, Folder T55/32C, RNIB.

85. John Davies to Donald Bell, February 18, 1969, Folder T55/32F, RNIB.

86. J. Le Roux to John Colligan, September 12, 1959, File CRO/711, Folder T55/32C, RNIB.

87. Henry T. Berry to John Colligan, August 14, 1968, Folder T55/32F, RNIB.

88. Eric Gillett to H. J. Brough, November 19, 1958, File CRO/036, Folder T55/32B, RNIB.

89. Mrs. Benstead to Donald Bell, June 22, 1970, File CRO/711, Folder T55/32C, RNIB.

90. Donald Bell, memo, "Announcements," December 18, 1967, File CRO/711, Folder T55/32C, RNIB.

91. Minutes, executive council meeting, December 12, 1968, Folder T55/32F, RNIB.

92. Donald Bell to M. A. Cozens, April 30, 1965, File CRO/683, Folder T55/32D, RNIB.

93. Donald Bell to W. J. Braham, June 20, 1969, Folder T55/32F, RNIB.

94. G[ay] Ashton to Leslie Pinder, March 24, 1960, Folder T55/32F, RNIB.

95. Donald Bell to I. McIlvenna, March 28, 1969, Folder T55/32F, RNIB.

96. On censorship, book selection, and public libraries in Britain, see Ann Curry, *The Limits of Tolerance: Censorship and Intellectual Freedom in Public Libraries* (London: Scarecrow, 1997), Ian Malley, *Censorship and Libraries* (London: Library Association, 1990), and Anthony Hugh Thompson, *Censorship in Public Libraries in the United Kingdom during the Twentieth Century* (New York: Bowker, 1975).

97. Donald Bell to I. McIlvenna, March 28, 1969, Folder T55/32F, RNIB.

98. John Colligan to Donald Bell, December 13, 1967, Folder T55/32E, RNIB.

99. Donald Bell to John Colligan, December 15, 1967, Folder T55/32E, RNIB.

100. Donald Bell to G[ay] Ashton, July 20, 1965, File CRO/683, Folder T55/32D, RNIB.

101. Woolsey's judgment was included as an appendix to the first English Bodley Head edition of *Ulysses,* published in 1936. The verdict is discussed at length in Paul Vanderham, *James Joyce and Censorship: The Trials of "Ulysses"* (New York: New York University Press, 1998), and Kevin Birmingham, *The Most Dangerous Book: The Battle for James Joyce's "Ulysses"* (New York: Penguin, 2014). On modernist literature and obscenity, see Allison Pease, *Modernism, Mass Culture and the Aesthetics of Obscenity* (Cambridge: Cambridge University Press, 2000), Florence Dore, *The Novel and the Obscene: Sexual Subjects in American Modernism* (Stanford, Calif.: Stanford University Press, 2005), Celia Marshik, *British Modernism and Censorship* (Cambridge: Cambridge University Press, 2006), and Rachel Potter, *Obscene Modernism: Literary Censorship and Experiment, 1990–1940* (Oxford: Oxford University Press, 2013).

102. Donald Bell, untitled and undated memo, File CRO/683, Folder T55/32D, RNIB.

103. Ibid.

104. On censorship after the 1959 Obscene Publications Act, see John Sutherland, *Offensive Literature: Decensorship in Britain, 1960–1982* (London: Junction Books, 1982).

105. Donald Bell, memo, "Editing of Titles for Recording," July 31, 1967, Folder T55/32E, RNIB.

7. Caedmon's Third Dimension

1. Cecil Day-Lewis, *Revolution in Writing* (London: Hogarth, 1935), 15. Day-Lewis went on to broadcast much of his verse and to advocate radio's usefulness for poets. See C. Day-Lewis, "Broadcasting and Poetry," *BBC Quarterly* 5, no. 1 (Spring 1950): 1–7.

2. See, among other sources, Paul Ferris, *Dylan Thomas* (Harmondsworth, U.K.: Penguin Books, 1978), 300–1; and Andrew Lycett, *Dylan Thomas: A New Life* (London: Weidenfeld & Nicolson, 2003), 326–27.

3. This figure is taken from "Closing the Poetry Gap," *Time,* November 7, 1960, 88.

4. Quoted in Carl Schoettler, "Waxing Poetic," *Baltimore Sun,* August 27, 2002, http://articles.baltimoresun.com/2002-08-27/features/0208270074_1_holdridge-dylan-thomas-young-women.

5. This claim is made in "The National Recording Registry 2008," National Recording Preservation Board of the Library of Congress, http://www.loc.gov/rr/record/nrpb/registry/nrpb-2008reg.html.

6. Shannon Maughan, "A Golden Audio Anniversary," *Publishers Weekly* 249, no. 9 (March 4, 2002): 39–40; 40.

7. A brief history of the company can be found in Helen Roach, "The Two Women of Caedmon," *Association for Recorded Sound Collections Journal* 19, no. 1 (1987): 21–24.

8. See Harley Usill, "A History of Argo: Problems of a Specialist Record Company," *Recorded Sound* 78 (July 1980): 31–43.

9. Ben Cheever, "Audio's Original Voices," *Publishers Weekly* 252, no. 42 (October 24, 2005): 22–23; 22.

10. Andre Millard, *America on Record: A History of Recorded Sound,* 2nd ed. (Cambridge: Cambridge University Press, 2005), 205.

11. Sarah Parry provides a detailed discussion of Caedmon's editing techniques in "The Inaudibility of 'Good' Sound Editing: The Case of Caedmon Records," *Performance Research* 7, no. 1 (2002): 24–33. See also Susan Schmidt Horning, *Chasing Sound: Technology, Culture, and the Art of Studio Recording from Edison to the LP* (Baltimore: Johns Hopkins University Press, 2013).

12. "Caedmon: Recreating the Moment of Inspiration," *Morning Edition,* National Public Radio, December 5, 2002, http://www.npr.org/templates/story/story.php ?storyId=866406.

13. Jacob Smith, *Spoken Word: Postwar American Phonograph Cultures* (Berkeley: University of California Press, 2011), 50.

14. On the formation of middlebrow taste, see Joan Shelley Rubin, *The Making of Middlebrow Culture* (Chapel Hill: University of North Carolina Press, 1992), especially the section on radio, 266–329; and Janice A. Radway, *A Feeling for Books: The Book-of-the-Month Club, Literary Taste, and Middle-Class Desire* (Chapel Hill: University of North Carolina Press, 1997). Subsequent debates are traced in Erica Brown and Mary Grover, eds., *Middlebrow Literary Cultures: The Battle of the Brows, 1920–1960* (Basingstoke, U.K.: Palgrave Macmillan, 2012).

15. Barbara Holdridge, e-mail correspondence with the author, July 24, 2013. This correspondence was published in Matthew Rubery, "Audiobooks before Audiobooks: Matthew Rubery Interviews Barbara Holdridge," *Los Angeles Review of Books,* August 19, 2013, http://lareviewofbooks.org/interview /audiobooks-before-audiobooks.

16. *Jean Cocteau Reads His Poetry and Prose,* Caedmon TC1083, [1962], 1 33⅓ rpm LP record. I have included supplementary information about Caedmon's narrators, directors, and musicians where possible. Most of the liner notes without bylines can be assumed to be by the editors, Holdridge and Mantell. Albums are rarely dated—something Donald Hall complained about more than thirty years ago as an "annoying habit" of Caedmon's.

17. Advertisement, *Talking Machine World,* May 15, 1919, 145.

18. The Emerson series and ones similar to it are documented in Peter Muldavin, "A Brief History of Vintage Children's Records," in *The Complete Guide to Vintage Children's Records: Identification and Value Guide* (Paducah, Ky.: Collector's Books, 2007), 8–16.

19. On Riley's stage career, see Angela Sorby, *Schoolroom Poets: Childhood, Performance, and the Place of American Poetry, 1865–1917* (Durham: University of New Hampshire Press, 2005), 99–125.

20. Robert J. O'Brien, "Literary Recordings," in *Encyclopedia of Recorded Sound in the United States,* ed. Guy A. Marco (New York: Garland, 1993), 392–395.

21. David W. Thompson, "Review: Twentieth Century Poetry in English: Contemporary Recordings of the Poets Reading Their Own Poems," *American Quarterly* 2, no. 1 (Spring 1950): 89–93; 90.

22. See Josephine Packard, "A Discography of the Harvard Vocarium," *Harvard Library Bulletin* 15, nos. 3–4 (Fall–Winter 2004): 1–133.

23. Examples include Lloyd Frankenberg, ed., *Pleasure Dome: An Audible Anthology of Modern Poetry Read by Its Creators,* ML4259 (New York: Columbia Masterworks, [1949]), 1 LP record; and *Twentieth Century Poetry in English: Contemporary Recordings of the Poets Reading Their Own Poems,* (Washington, D.C.: Library of Congress, 1949), 25 LP records. The latter's twelve-inch discs could be purchased for $1.50 per record or $8.25 per five-record album. On the Yale Series of Recorded Poets, see Linda W. Blair, "The Yale Collection of Historical Sound Recordings," *Association for Recorded Sound Collections Journal* 20, no. 2 (1988–89): 167–76.

24. Lloyd Frankenberg, "Preface," liner notes, Frankenberg, *Pleasure Dome.* Emphasis in original. See also Frankenberg's companion book, *Pleasure Dome: On Reading Modern Poetry* (Boston: Houghton Mifflin, 1949).

25. Other noteworthy recordings of literature are listed in Helen Roach's discography, *Spoken Records,* 2nd ed. (New York: Scarecrow, 1966). See also Stephen E. Whicher, "Current Long-Playing Records of Literature in English," *College English* 19, no. 3 (December 1957): 111–21; and David Mason, "British Literary Figures on 78," *British Association of Sound Collections News* 3 (1989): 24–36.

26. A study by Princeton's Office of Radio Research confirmed that most people considered reading books to be more difficult, worthwhile, and educational than listening to them on the radio. Paul F. Lazarsfeld, *Radio and the Printed Page: An Introduction to the Study of Radio and Its Role in the Communication of Ideas* (New York: Duell, Sloan and Pearce, 1940), 178.

27. Paul Heyer, *The Medium and the Magician: Orson Welles, the Radio Years, 1934–1952* (Lanham, Md.: Rowman & Littlefield, 2005), 66. See also James Jesson, "A Library on the Air: Literary Dramatization and Orson Welles's *Mercury Theatre,*" in *Audiobooks, Literature, and Sound Studies,* ed. Matthew Rubery (New York: Routledge, 2011), 44–60.

28. Louis Reid, "Broadcasting Books: Drama, Fiction, and Poetry on the Air," in *Radio and English Teaching: Experiences, Problems, and Procedures,* ed. Max J. Herzberg (New York: D. Appleton-Century, 1941), 176–86; 181. Other recitations are cited in Milton Allen Kaplan, *Radio and Poetry* (New York: Columbia University Press, 1949).

29. Brad McCoy, "Poetry on Radio," in *Encyclopedia of Radio,* ed. Christopher H. Sterling (New York: Fitzroy Dearborn, 2004), 3:1077–81. See also Mike Chasar, *Everyday Reading: Poetry and Popular Culture in Modern America* (New York: Columbia University Press, 2012), 80–122.

30. See Robert Giddings and Keith Selby, *The Classic Serial on Television and Radio* (Basingstoke, U.K.: Palgrave, 2001), and Kate Whitehead, *The Third Programme: A Literary History* (Oxford: Clarendon, 1989).

31. On Greece's oral tradition, see Albert B. Lord, *The Singer of Tales,* 2nd ed., ed. Stephen Mitchell and Gregory Nagy (Cambridge, Mass.: Harvard University Press, 2000), and Adam Parry, ed., *The Making of Homeric Verse: The Collected*

Papers of Milman Parry (Oxford: Clarendon, 1971). See also Rosalind Thomas, *Literacy and Orality in Ancient Greece* (Cambridge: Cambridge University Press, 1992).

32. Pearl Cleveland Wilson, liner notes, Padraic Colum, *The Twelve Labors of Heracles,* read by Anthony Quayle, Caedmon TC1256, [1968], 1 LP record.

33. Pearl Cleveland Wilson, liner notes, *The Iliad of Homer,* read by Anthony Quayle, Caedmon TC1196, [1968], 1 LP record.

34. Pearl Cleveland Wilson, liner notes, Homer, *The Golden Treasury of Greek Poetry and Prose,* read by Pearl Cleveland Wilson, Caedmon TC1034, [1956], 1 LP record. On Homer's reception, see Ruth Scodel, *Listening to Homer: Tradition, Narrative, and Audience* (Ann Arbor: University of Michigan Press, 2002).

35. James Hynd, liner notes, *Classics of Latin Poetry and Prose,* Caedmon TC1296, [1970], 1 LP record.

36. Saint Augustine, *Confessions,* trans. Henry Chadwick (Oxford: Oxford University Press, 1992), 92–93.

37. *The Romance of Tristan and Iseult,* read by Claire Bloom, Caedmon TC1106, [1958], 1 LP record.

38. J. B. Bessinger, Jr., liner notes, Geoffrey Chaucer, *The Canterbury Tales,* read by J. B. Bessinger, Jr., Caedmon TC1151, [1962], 1 LP record.

39. Ibid.

40. Geoffrey Chaucer, *The Canterbury Tales: The Pardoner's Tale and the Nun's Priest's Tale,* read by Robert Ross, Caedmon TC1008, [1956], 1 LP record.

41. See Erika Brady, *A Spiral Way: How the Phonograph Changed Ethnography* (Jackson: University Press of Mississippi, 1999).

42. Amabel Williams-Ellis, liner notes, Amabel Williams-Ellis, *Ali Baba and the Forty Thieves: A Tale from the Arabian Nights,* read by Anthony Quayle, Caedmon TC1251, [1968], 1 LP record.

43. Walter Benjamin, "The Storyteller," in *Illuminations,* ed. Hannah Arendt, trans. Harry Zohn (New York: Schocken Books, 1968), 83–109; 87.

44. Emma D. Sheehy, liner notes, *Aesop's Fables,* read by Boris Karloff, dir. Howard O. Sackler, Caedmon TC1221, [1967], 1 LP record.

45. Liner notes, Jakob Grimm and Wilhelm Grimm, *Grimm's Fairy Tales,* read by Joseph Schildkraut, Caedmon TC1062, [1957], 1 LP record.

46. On television's place in the home, see Lynn Spigel, *Make Room for TV: Television and the Family Ideal in Postwar America* (Chicago: University of Chicago Press, 1992), and James L. Baughman, *The Republic of Mass Culture: Journalism, Filmmaking, and Broadcasting in America since 1941,* 2nd ed. (Baltimore: Johns Hopkins University Press, 1997).

47. Simon Callow describes the public readings in *Charles Laughton: A Difficult Actor* (London: Methuen, 1987), 205–39. Laughton's own account can be found in Charles Laughton, "The Story Teller," in *Tell Me a Story: An Anthology,* ed. Charles Laughton (New York: McGraw-Hill, 1957), 1–2. On Laughton's efforts to bring spoken word performance to network television, see Smith, *Spoken Word,* 59–69. Cecelia Tichi discusses the postwar tension between books and

television in *Electronic Hearth: Creating an American Television Culture* (New York: Oxford University Press, 1991).

48. Influential accounts of this shift can be found in Walter J. Ong, *Orality and Literacy: The Technologizing of the Word* (London: Methuen, 1982), and Marshall McLuhan, *The Gutenberg Galaxy: The Making of Typographic Man* (London: Routledge & Kegan Paul, 1962).

49. Mark S. Morrisson documents modernism's allegiances to the spoken word in *The Public Face of Modernism: Little Magazines, Audiences, and Reception, 1905–1920* (Madison: University of Wisconsin Press, 2001), 54–83.

50. A detailed account of this tradition is given by Sheila Deane, *Bardic Style in the Poetry of Gerard Manley Hopkins, W. B. Yeats and Dylan Thomas* (Ann Arbor: UMI Research Press, 1989).

51. Walt Whitman, *Leaves of Grass,* read by Ed Begley, dir. Howard O. Sackler, Caedmon TC1037, [1959], 1 LP record.

52. John T. Ridley, liner notes, Mark Twain, *Life on the Mississippi,* read by Ed Begley, Caedmon TC1234, [1969], 1 LP record. See also Randall Knoper, *Acting Naturally: Mark Twain in the Culture of Performance* (Berkeley: University of California Press, 1995).

53. Ridley, liner notes, Twain, *Life on the Mississippi.*

54. Quoted in Mary Von Schrader Jarrell, "Randall Jarrell: Anti-War Poems," liner notes, *Randall Jarrell Reads and Discusses His Poems against War,* Caedmon TC1363, [1972], 1 LP record.

55. Douglas Lanier, "Shakespeare on the Record," in *A Companion to Shakespeare and Performance,* ed. Barbara Hodgdon and W. B. Worthen (Malden, Mass.: Blackwell, 2005), 415–36; 420.

56. On the performance of race, voice, and dialect, see Lorenzo Thomas, "The Functional Role of Poetry Readings in the Black Arts Movement," in *Close Listening: Poetry and the Performed Word,* ed. Charles Bernstein (New York: Oxford University Press, 1998), 300–323.

57. Catherine Marshall, liner notes, *Peter Marshall Speaks: Two Sermons,* read by Peter Marshall, Caedmon TC1011, [1955], 1 LP record.

58. Ibid.

59. On Marshall's life, see Catherine Marshall, *A Man Called Peter: The Story of Peter Marshall* (New York: McGraw-Hill, 1951).

60. Liner notes, *Carl Sandburg's Rootabaga Stories,* read by the author, Caedmon TC1089, [1958], 1 LP record.

61. Liner notes, Oscar Wilde, *Fairy Tales,* read by Basil Rathbone, dir. Howard O. Sackler, Caedmon TC1044, [1955], 1 LP record.

62. Marguerite A. Dodson, liner notes, H. A. Rey, *Curious George and Other Stories about Curious George,* read by Julie Harris, Caedmon TC1420, 1972, 1 LP record. The heightened attention to children reflects Caedmon's lucrative involvement in the educational market. Its commitment to reading aloud benefited from the Elementary and Secondary Education Act of 1965, which provided money for schools and libraries to purchase records. According to Caedmon, the albums assisted children who were learning how to read. *Curious*

George Learns the Alphabet and other primers offered an alternative to what it called the "soundless visual training" prevalent in schools. George Riemer, liner notes, *Edward Lear's Nonsense Stories and Poems,* read by Claire Bloom, Caedmon TCp1279, [1970], 1 LP record.

63. On the growth in poetry readings during the 1950s, see Tyler Hoffman, *American Poetry in Performance: From Walt Whitman to Hip Hop* (Ann Arbor: University of Michigan Press, 2011), 123–61.

64. Donald Hall, "Poets Aloud," *Poetry* 139, no. 5 (February 1982): 297–305; 298. Historical overviews of the poetry reading can be found in Peter Middleton, *Distant Reading: Performance, Readership, and Consumption in Contemporary Poetry* (Birmingham: University of Alabama Press, 2005), 61–103; and Lesley Wheeler, *Voicing American Poetry: Sound and Performance from the 1920s to the Present* (Ithaca, N.Y.: Cornell University Press, 2008).

65. Jiménez eventually agreed to record his poetry while a visiting lecturer at the University of Maryland. Liner notes, *Juan Ramón Jiménez Reading His Poetry in Spanish,* Caedmon TC1079, [1961], 1 LP record.

66. Osbert Sitwell, *Laughter in the Next Room: Being the Fourth Volume of "Left Hand, Right Hand!": An Autobiography* (London: Macmillan, 1949), 168–98. See also Laura Severin, *Poetry off the Page: Twentieth-Century British Women Poets in Performance* (Aldershot, U.K.: Ashgate, 2004), 47.

67. Liner notes, *Osbert Sitwell Reading from His Poetry,* Caedmon TC1013, [1953], 1 LP record.

68. Review from the *Boston Globe* quoted in advertisement on slipcase, Edward Everett Hale, *The Man without a Country,* read by Edward G. Robinson, Caedmon TC1178, [1964], 1 LP record.

69. Quoted in advertisement reprinted on slipcase, *Dorothy Parker Stories,* read by Shirley Booth, dir. Howard O. Sackler, Caedmon TC1136, [1962], 1 LP record.

70. *Speaking of the Best for over a Quarter Century: Caedmon, 1952–1977* (New York: Caedmon, 1977), 5.

71. Liner notes, *The Caedmon Treasury of Modern Poets Reading Their Own Poetry,* read by T. S. Eliot, William Butler Yeats, Edith Sitwell et al., Caedmon TC2006, [ca. 1955], 2 LP records.

72. Liner notes, *The Stories of Kafka,* read by Lotte Lenya, dir. Howard O. Sackler, Caedmon TC1114, [1962], 1 LP record.

73. Reuben A. Brower, "Reading in Slow Motion," in *In Defense of Reading: A Reader's Approach to Literary Criticism,* ed. Reuben A. Brower and Richard Poirier (New York: Dutton, 1962), 3–21; 5.

74. Quoted in George N. Shuster, liner notes, *The Poetry of Gerard Manley Hopkins,* read by Cyril Cusack, dir. Howard O. Sackler, Caedmon TC1111, [1958], 1 LP record.

75. Gerard Manley Hopkins to Everard Hopkins, November 5, 1885, in Gerard Manley Hopkins, *Selected Letters,* ed. Catherine Phillips (Oxford: Oxford University Press, 1991), 216–21; 221.

76. On the relationship between speech and verse, see James I. Wimsatt, *Hopkins's Poetics of Speech Sound: Sprung Rhythm, Lettering, Inscape* (Toronto: University of Toronto Press, 2006).

77. Liner notes, James Joyce, *Finnegans Wake,* read by Cyril Cusack and Siobhan McKenna, dir. Howard O. Sackler, Caedmon TC1086, [1959], 1 LP record. Emphasis in the original.

78. W. H. Auden, liner notes, *W. H. Auden Reading in Memory of W. B. Yeats, in Praise of Limestone, Seven Bucolics, and Other Poems,* Caedmon TC1019, [1954], 1 LP record.

79. See the third section of K. David Jackson, Eric Vos, and Johanna Drucker, eds., *Experimental—Visual—Concrete: Avant-Garde Poetry since the 1960s* (Amsterdam: Rodopi, 1996).

80. Grace Schulman, liner notes, *The Poetry and Voice of May Swenson,* Caedmon TC1500, [1976], 1 LP record.

81. See Morrisson, *The Public Face of Modernism,* 56, and Joan Shelley Rubin, "Modernism in Practice: Public Readings of the New Poetry," in *A Modern Mosaic: Art and Modernism in the United States,* ed. Townsend Ludington (Chapel Hill: University of North Carolina Press, 2000), 127–52.

82. Richard Howard, liner notes, *James Dickey Reading His Poetry,* Caedmon TC1333, 1971, 1 LP record.

83. Christian Morgenstern, *The Gallows Songs: A Selection,* trans. Max Knight, read by Ogden Nash, Caedmon TC1316, [1970], 1 LP record.

84. Liner notes, Stan Berenstain and Jan Berenstain, *The Berenstain Bears featuring "The Bears' Picnic" and Other Stories,* read by the authors, music composed by Don Heckman, Caedmon TC1549, 1977, 1 LP record.

85. Harvey Simmonds, liner notes, James Agee and Walker Evans, *Let Us Now Praise Famous Men,* read by Ruby Dee and George Grizzard, Caedmon TC1324, [1970], 1 LP record.

86. Ibid.

87. Liner notes, *Poetry of Robert Browning,* read by James Mason, dir. Howard O. Sackler, Caedmon TC1048, [1956], 1 LP record.

88. Liner notes, *Faulkner Reads from His Works,* Caedmon TC1035, 1954, 1 LP record.

89. I am grateful to the members of the Association for Recorded Sound Collections discussion list who shared with me their personal recollections about listening to Caedmon records.

90. Liner notes, Vachel Lindsay, *Vachel Lindsay Reading the Congo, Chinese Nightingale, and Other Poems,* Caedmon TC1041, [ca. 1956], 1 LP record.

91. Claire Brook, "The Book Publisher and Recordings," in *The Phonograph and Our Musical Life: Proceedings of a Centennial Conference 7–10 December 1977,* ed. H. Wiley Hitchcock (Brooklyn: Institute for Studies in American Music, 1980), 72–77; 73.

92. Richard O. Moore, "Eudora Welty: An Appreciation," liner notes, *Eudora Welty Reads Her Stories "Powerhouse" and "Petrified Man,"* Caedmon TC1626, 1979, 1 LP record.

93. *New York Herald Tribune* quoted in advertisement on slipcase, Katherine Anne Porter, *The Downward Path to Wisdom,* read by the author, Caedmon TC1006, [1952], 1 LP record.

94. Sarah Parry has argued that Caedmon engineered the signal-to-noise ratio so that it "mimicked the black and white of the printed page, effectively

functioning as an analogue to the printed word." "The LP Era: Voice-Practice/Voice Document," *English Studies in Canada* 33, no. 4 (December 2007): 169–80; 175.

95. Advertisement, *Billboard,* June 27, 1960, 23.

96. *Holy Bible: The Complete New Testament* (Benton Harbor, Mich.: Audio Book, 1953), 24 16 rpm records. A profile of this company can be found in Frederic Ramsey, Jr., "Talking Books," *High Fidelity Magazine* (July–August 1953): 29–31, 110. See also Mike Dicecco, "A History of 16-RPM Records, Part Two Audio Books," *Antique Phonograph News,* May–June 2010, http://www.capsnews.org/apn2010-3.htm.

97. Liner notes, F. Scott Fitzgerald, *The Great Gatsby,* read by Alexander Scourby, A 1621 (Long Branch, N.J.: Libraphone, 1953), 3, 16 rpm records.

98. Ibid.

99. Alexandra Elizabeth Sheedy, liner notes, Alexandra Elizabeth Sheedy, *She Was Nice to Mice,* read by the author, Caedmon TC1506, 1976, 1 LP record.

100. Liner notes, James Boswell, *Boswell's London Journal,* read by Anthony Quayle, Caedmon TC1093, [1959], 1 LP record; and liner notes, D. H. Lawrence, *Lady Chatterley's Lover,* read by Pamela Brown, dir. Howard O. Sackler, Caedmon TC1116, [1959], 1 LP record.

101. Liner notes, William Shakespeare, *Great Scenes from "Macbeth,"* read by Anthony Quayle, Gwen Frangcon Davies, Stanley Holloway et al., Caedmon TC1167, [1963], 1 LP record.

102. Liner notes, Oscar Wilde, *The Picture of Dorian Gray,* read by Hurd Hatfield, dir. Howard O. Sackler, Caedmon TC1095, 1959, 1 LP record.

103. *Genesis,* read by Judith Anderson, dir. Howard O. Sackler, Caedmon TC1096, [1959], 1 LP record.

104. Quoted in Grace Schulman, liner notes, *The Poetry and Voice of Galway Kinnell,* Caedmon TC1502, 1976, 1 LP record.

105. Charles Bernstein, "Introduction," in *Close Listening: Poetry and the Performed Word,* ed. Charles Bernstein (Oxford: Oxford University Press, 1998), 3–26; 8.

106. Liner notes, Lewis Carroll, *Alice in Wonderland,* read by Stanley Holloway, Joan Greenwood et al., adapted and dir. by Howard O. Sackler, Caedmon TC1097, [1958], 1 LP record.

107. Liner notes, Lewis Carroll, *Through the Looking-Glass,* read by Stanley Holloway, Joan Greenwood et al., adapted and dir. by Howard O. Sackler, Caedmon TC1098, [1958], 1 LP record.

108. Liner notes, Edgar Lee Masters, *Spoon River Anthology,* read by Julie Harris et al., dir. Howard O. Sackler, Caedmon TC1152, [1965], 1 LP record.

109. Tim Brooks and Merle Sprinzen, *Little Wonder Records and Bubble Books: An Illustrated History and Discography* (Denver, Colo.: Mainspring, 2011), 33.

110. Ibid., 35.

111. See Smith, *Spoken Word,* 13–48.

112. Liner notes, *The Pied Piper and the Hunting of the Snark,* read by Boris Karloff, dir. Howard O. Sackler, Caedmon TC1075, [1960], 1 LP record.

113. Liner notes, *Mother Goose,* read by Celeste Holm, Cyril Ritchard, and Boris Karloff, dir. Howard O. Sackler, music by Hershy Kay, Caedmon TC1091, [1958], 1 LP record. Emphasis in original.

114. Liner notes, Charles Dickens, *A Christmas Carol,* read by Ralph Richardson, Paul Scofield, and cast, dir. Howard O. Sackler, Caedmon TC1135, [1960], 1 LP record.

115. J. B. Bessinger, Jr., liner notes, *Beowulf, Caedmon's Hymn and Other Old English Poems,* read by J. B. Bessinger, Jr., Caedmon TC1161, [1962], 1 LP record.

116. Derek Furr, *Recorded Poetry and Poetic Reception from Edna Millay to the Circle of Robert Lowell* (Basingstoke, U.K.: Palgrave Macmillan, 2010), 21.

117. On reading aloud in the 1960s, see Raphael Allison, *Bodies on the Line: Performance and the Sixties Poetry Reading* (Iowa City: University of Iowa Press, 2014).

118. Quoted in advertisement on slipcase, Porter, *The Downward Path to Wisdom.*

119. Richard Bach, liner notes, Richard Bach, *Illusions: The Adventures of a Reluctant Messiah,* read by the author, Caedmon TC1585, 1978, 1 LP record. Emphasis in the original.

120. Liner notes, *Walter de la Mare Speaking and Reading,* Caedmon TC1046, [1956], 1 LP record.

121. William Everson, *The Savagery of Love: Brother Antoninus Reads His Poetry,* read by the author, Caedmon TC1260, [1968], 1 LP record.

122. Monika Mann, liner notes, Thomas Mann, *Thomas Mann—Dichterlesung,* read by Thomas Mann, Caedmon TC1004, [1952], 1 LP record.

123. On Sandburg's lecture tour, see Penelope Niven, *Carl Sandburg: A Biography* (New York: Charles Scribner, 1991), 386.

124. Liner notes, *Carl Sandburg's Poems for Children,* read by the author, Caedmon TC1124, [1961], 1 LP record.

125. Quoted in William A. Smith, liner notes, *Carl Sandburg Reading Fog and Other Poems,* Caedmon TC1253, [1968], 1 LP record.

126. Advertisement on slipcase, *Carl Sandburg Reading His Poetry,* Caedmon TC1150, [1962], 1 LP record.

127. Smith, liner notes, *Carl Sandburg Reading Fog and Other Poems.*

128. Roland Barthes, *Image, Music, Text* (New York: Hill and Wang, 1977), 185.

129. Hall, "Poets Aloud," 297.

130. Liner notes, *Ogden Nash Reads Ogden Nash,* Caedmon TC1015, [1953], 1 LP record.

131. Liner notes, *William Faulkner Reads the Nobel Prize Acceptance Speech and Selections from "As I Lay Dying," "A Fable," and the "Old Man,"* Caedmon TC1035, 1954, 1 LP record.

132. Toni Morrison, phone conversation with the author, June 28, 2013, available at http://audiobookhistory.wordpress.com/2013/07/29/talking-to-myself-an-interview-with-toni-morrison/.

133. George Sayer, liner notes, *J. R. R. Tolkien Reads and Sings His "The Lord of the Rings," "The Two Towers," "The Return of the King,"* Caedmon TC1478, 1975, 1 LP record.

134. George Sayer, liner notes, *J. R. R. Tolkien Reads and Sings His "The Hobbit" and "The Fellowship of the Ring,"* Caedmon TC1477, 1975, 1 LP record.

135. W. H. Auden, liner notes, J. R. R. Tolkien, *Poems and Songs of Middle Earth,* read by J. R. R. Tolkien, sung by William Elvin, music by Donald Swann, Caedmon TC1231, [1967], 1 LP record.

136. Olga Ley, liner notes, Yevgeny Yevtushenko, *Babii Yar and Other Poems,* read in Russian by Yevgeny Yevtushenko and in English by Alan Bates, dir. Howard O. Sackler, Caedmon TC1153, [1967], 1 LP record.

137. Liner notes, Rainer Maria Rilke, *Die Weise Von Liebe und Tod Das Marienleben,* read by Lotte Lehmann, Caedmon TC1128, [1961], 1 LP record.

138. Liner notes, *Archibald MacLeish Reading from His Works,* Caedmon TC1009, [1953], 1 LP record.

139. Advertisement on slipcase, *Eudora Welty Reading from Her Works,* Caedmon TC1010, [1953], 1 LP record.

140. *Harper's,* quoted on slipcase, *T. S. Eliot Reading Poems and Choruses,* Caedmon TC1045, [1955], 1 LP record. On Eliot's recordings, see Richard Swigg, *Quick, Said the Bird: Williams, Eliot, Moore and the Spoken Word* (Iowa City: University of Iowa Press, 2012), 38–53 and 147–48.

141. David E. Chinitz, *T. S. Eliot and the Cultural Divide* (Chicago: University of Chicago Press, 2003), 183.

142. See Frederick Clifton Packard, "Harvard's Vocarium Has Attained Full Stature," *Library Journal,* January 15, 1950, 69–74.

143. A. E. Hotchner, liner notes, *Ernest Hemingway Reading,* Caedmon TC1185, [1965], 1 LP record.

144. Stephen Lushington, liner notes, *Theodore Roethke Reads His Poetry,* Caedmon TC1351, 1972, 1 LP record.

145. Frederik Pohl, liner notes, Judith Merril, *Survival Ship and The Shrine of Temptation,* read by Judith Merril, Caedmon TC1593, 1978, 1 LP record.

146. Ursula K. Le Guin, liner notes, Ursula K. Le Guin, *Gwilan's Harp and Intracom,* read by the author, Caedmon TC1556, 1977, 1 LP record.

147. This is my paraphrase of a line in John Malcolm Brinnin, *Dylan Thomas in America* (London: Prion Books, 2000), 100.

148. Irwin Edman, *Saturday Review,* quoted on slipcase, *Dylan Thomas Reading from William Shakespeare's "King Lear" and John Webster's "The Duchess of Malfi,"* Caedmon TC1158, [1962], 1 LP record.

149. Quotation from *Harper's* reprinted on slipcase, Dylan Thomas, *An Evening with Dylan Thomas,* read by the author, Caedmon TC1157, [1963], 1 LP record.

150. Quoted in Dylan Thomas, *On the Air with Dylan Thomas: The Broadcasts,* ed. Ralph Maud (New York: New Directions, 1992), 310.

151. William T. Moynihan, "Boily Boy and Bard," *New York Times Book Review,* November 3, 1963, 6, 48.

152. Dylan Thomas to Pamela Hansford Johnson, ca. November 1933, in *The Collected Letters of Dylan Thomas,* ed. Paul Ferris (London: J. M. Dent, 1985), 36–45; 41. Quoted in Paul Kresh, liner notes, *Dylan Thomas Reads the Poetry of William Butler Yeats,* Caedmon TC1353, [1971], 1 LP record.

153. W. B. Yeats, "Speaking to the Psaltery," in *Essays and Introductions* (London: Macmillan, 1961), 13–27; 13. Yeats's chanting features prominently in Ronald Schuchard, *The Last Minstrels: Yeats and the Revival of the Bardic Arts* (Oxford: Oxford University Press, 2008).

154. Quoted in Andrew Lycett, *Dylan Thomas: A New Life* (London: Weidenfeld & Nicolson, 2003), 286.

155. Liner notes, *Dylan Thomas Reading*, vol. 3, Caedmon TC1043, [1953], 1 LP record.

156. Paul Kresh, liner notes, Dylan Thomas, *Return Journey to Swansea*, performed by Dylan Thomas and cast, Caedmon TC1354, [1972], 1 LP record.

157. Robert Graves, *On Poetry: Collected Talks and Essays* (New York: Doubleday, 1969), 148.

158. Furr analyzes Thomas's readings in detail in *Recorded Poetry*, 40–46.

159. On the postwar surge in phonographs, see David L. Morton, Jr., *Sound Recording: The Life Story of a Technology* (Westport, Conn.: Greenwood, 2004), 129–40.

160. Advertisement on slipcase, Thomas, *An Evening with Dylan Thomas*.

161. On the commercial underpinnings of suburban recreation, see Lizabeth Cohen, *A Consumers' Republic: The Politics of Mass Consumption in Postwar America* (New York: Alfred A. Knopf, 2003).

162. For example, see "Caedmon: Recreating the Moment of Inspiration," NPR *Morning Edition*, December 5, 2002, http://www.npr.org/templates/story/story .php?storyId=866406.

163. The passage is from Dylan Thomas, "On Reading One's Own Poems," recorded on September 24, 1949, for the *Third Programme* and reprinted in Dylan Thomas, *The Broadcasts*, ed. Ralph Maud (London: J. M. Dent, 1991), 214–16; 214.

164. Liner notes, *Laurence Olivier on the Death of King George VI*, Caedmon TC1003, 1952, 1 LP record.

165. Liner notes, *Hearing Poetry*, vol. 1, read by Hurd Hatfield, Frank Silvera, Jo Van Fleet et al., dir. Howard O. Sackler, Caedmon TC1021, [1954], 1 LP record.

166. Quoted in advertisement on slipcase, Edward Everett Hale, *The Man without a Country*, read by Edward G. Robinson, Caedmon TC1178, [1964], 1 LP record.

167. Barbara Holdridge, e-mail correspondence with the author, July 24, 2013.

168. Brook, "The Book Publisher and Recordings," 72–77; 75.

8. Tapeworms

1. Quoted in Dennis McLellan, "Taped Books Enter Literary Fast Lane," *Los Angeles Times*, May 12, 1990, N1, N6; N1.

2. "People," *Stanford Alumni Almanac*, January 1981, 8. Hecht shipped his Books on Tape files (hereafter cited as BOT) to me in August 2014. The collection has since been transferred to Stanford University's libraries.

3. George F. Will, "Books on Tape While Away the Miles," *News-Times* (Danbury, Conn.), December 12, 1982, A7.

4. Chauncey Mabe, "Heard Any Good Books Lately?," *Sun-Sentinel*, December 25, 1988, 1D, 5D; 1D.

5. *On Cassette: A Comprehensive Bibliography of Spoken Word Audio Cassettes* (New York: R. R. Bowker, 1985).

6. This figure comes from the Book Industry Study Group, a nonprofit organization in Manhattan. Cited in James Brooke, "Talking Books for Those on the Go," *Des Moines Register,* August 13, 1985, 1.

7. Velma Daniels, "Books for the Blind and the Busy," *News Chief* (Winter Haven, Fla.), April 12, 1981, 10C.

8. Robert Bowden, "Heard Any Good Novels Lately?," *St. Petersburg Times,* August 5, 1984, 1E, 6E; 6E.

9. "People," *Stanford Alumni Almanac,* 8.

10. Duvall Y. Hecht, e-mail correspondence with the author, August 7, 2013.

11. A partnership agreement lists Hecht, James W. McElvany, and Sara A. Ford as the initial contributors. Philip V. Swan and Gilbert E. Haakh were later added as principal partners. Duvall Y. Hecht to James W. McElvany, December 28, 1973, BOT.

12. "Notes to Financial Statements," December 31, 1975, BOT.

13. Quoted in Dale L. Walker, "Books on Tape Record Success," *El Paso Times,* August 23, 1981, 6E.

14. See Edward Jacobs, "Circulating Libraries," in *The Oxford Encyclopedia of British Literature,* ed. David Scott Kastan (Oxford: Oxford University Press, 2006), 2:5–10. Richard Roehl and Hal R. Varian compare this economic model to those used by modern entertainment industries in "Circulating Libraries and Video Rental Stores," *First Monday* 6, no. 5 (May 7, 2001), http://firstmonday .org/ojs/index.php/fm/article/view/854/763.

15. Duvall Y. Hecht to Frank L. Bryant, June 5, 1974, BOT.

16. Despite the model's success, Hecht refused to adopt the "negative option" used by nearly all book clubs. This coercive sales technique automatically ships books to subscribers each month unless they instruct the company to do otherwise.

17. On the company's history and influence, see Janice A. Radway, *A Feeling for Books: The Book-of-the-Month Club, Literary Taste, and Middle-Class Desire* (Chapel Hill: University of North Carolina Press, 1997).

18. Memo, Duvall Y. Hecht, "Possible Mottos," August 11, 1976, BOT.

19. Except in terms of gender: the audience for taped books was thought to be 55 percent male, whereas the majority of fiction readers were women. For a survey of reading habits, see Nicholas Zill and Marianne Winglee, *Who Reads Literature? The Future of the United States as a Nation of Readers* (Cabin John, Md.: Seven Locks, 1990).

20. "We See You!," *Titles in Review,* August 1976, 2, clipping, BOT.

21. Sixty-three percent of BOT's customers lived in areas where the median house value was more than $50,000; nationally, only 28 percent of Americans lived in such areas. These statistics were generated by comparing BOT customers to the 1980 census data. Memo, D. Keane to K. A. Steigerwald, "Books on Tape Analysis," February 12, 1986, BOT.

22. Mickey Friedman, "Books on Tapes: High-Tech Renditions of the Storyteller's Art," *San Francisco Examiner,* June 14, 1982, E3.

23. Jo-Ann Armao, "Books on Tape Setting Commuting on Its Ear," *Washington Post,* October 30, 1989, D1, D5; D5.

24. Jenny Campbell, "All Booked Up? Well, Listen to This . . ." *Orange County Register,* July 28, 1985, L1, L5; L5.

25. Frank Green, "Top Authors Taken along for the Ride," *San Diego Union,* March 12, 1985, clipping, BOT.

26. James W. McElvany to George Borchardt, January 30, 1947, BOT.

27. Quoted in Walker, "Books on Tape," 6E.

28. Duvall Y. Hecht to Kathleen A. Minder, September 28, 1993, BOT.

29. Duvall Y. Hecht to George Kirkpatrick, April 4, 1988, BOT.

30. Quoted in Martha McCarty, "Heard Any Good Books Lately?," *Motorhome Life,* January 1980, 38, 62; 38.

31. See Jay Satterfield, *"The World's Best Books": Taste, Culture, and the Modern Library* (Amherst: University of Massachusetts Press, 2002).

32. Duvall Y. Hecht to Mrs. Gordon Furth, October 11, 1979, BOT.

33. The catalog did include some scholarly titles such as A. L. Rowse's *Milton the Puritan* and *Shakespeare the Man.* Duvall Y. Hecht to T. N. Turner, September 14, 1992, BOT.

34. Duvall Y. Hecht to John Weld, October 25, 1988, BOT.

35. Duvall Y. Hecht to M. Y. Menzel, October 30, 1979, BOT. Curiously, the book's publisher withheld permission from Recording for the Blind. Its director expressed disappointment: "The blind are entitled to their junk, too." Quoted in Peggy Constantine, "Plugging into the Talking-Book Craze," *Sun-Times* (Chicago), June 30, 1985, 24.

36. Alan E. Pisarski, *Commuting in America: A National Report on Commuting Patterns and Trends* (Westport, Conn.: Eno Foundation for Transportation, 1987), 7.

37. Robert Ferrigno, "Pop a Tape in the Deck, Sit Back, Close Your Eyes and . . . Listen to Literature," *Orange County Register,* February 17, 1986, C1, C7; C1.

38. See Kenneth T. Jackson, *Crabgrass Frontier: The Suburbanization of the United States* (Oxford: Oxford University Press, 1985), 246–71.

39. Trout Pomeroy, "Super-Commuters: When They Head to Work, the Trip Is Long-Distance," *Times Leader* (Wilkes-Barre, Pa.), August 14, 1985, D1.

40. Raymond Williams introduces the term in Raymond Williams, *Television: Technology and Cultural Form,* 2nd ed., ed. Ederyn Williams (London: Routledge, 1990), 26 (italics in original); and explains its relevance to traffic in Raymond Williams, *Towards 2000* (London: Chatto and Windus, 1983), 188.

41. On the cassette tape's impact, see David L. Morton, Jr., *Sound Recording: The Life Story of a Technology* (Westport, Conn.: Greenwood, 2004), 153–65; and Andre Millard, *America on Record: A History of Recorded Sound,* 2nd ed. (Cambridge: Cambridge University Press, 2005), 313–27.

42. Doron P. Levin, " 'Books' for the Road," *Wall Street Journal,* March 7, 1986, 21.

43. David Abrahamson, "Audio for Autos: What's New in Cassettes?," *Travel and Leisure,* August 1978, 61–62; 61.

44. Robert N. Webner, "Heard a Good Book Lately? Drivers Do So Increasingly," *Wall Street Journal,* August 21, 1979, 23.

45. Ibid.

46. Constance Casey, "A Book in Your Ear," *San Jose Mercury News,* July 28, 1985, 1, 18–19; 1.

47. William Livingstone to Books on Tape, August 15, 1979, BOT.

48. Walker, "Books on Tape," 6E.

49. Levin, " 'Books' for the Road," 21.

50. Bowden, "Heard Any Good Novels Lately?," 6E.

51. Elizabeth Mehren and Nancy Rivera, "Audio Books—Fast Food for Mind?," *Los Angeles Times,* August 19, 1985, 1, 3; 1.

52. Betsy Wade, "Books on Cassettes Are the Last Word for Extended Trips by Car," *Chicago Tribune,* February 14, 1988, 20.

53. Guy Kelly, "Unabridged Tapes at Cutting Edge of Audio Books," *Rocky Mountain News,* June 3, 1990, 24M.

54. Phyllis Zauner, "Heard Any Good Books Lately?," *Northeast Woman* (*Sunday Times Magazine,* Scranton, Pa.), March 8, 1987, 10–11; 11.

55. Memo, Duvall Y. Hecht, "B-O-T Projects," September 8, 1986, BOT.

56. Duvall Y. Hecht to Ted Neale, September 28, 1987, BOT.

57. Letter to the editor, *Titles in Review,* January 1977, 2, BOT.

58. Allen Grossman to Books on Tape, May 16, 1978, BOT.

59. Webner, "Heard a Good Book Lately?," 23.

60. James Worthington, "Making Freeway Time Amount to Something," *Star-News* (Pasadena, Calif.), March 15, 1978, D-2V.

61. Mike Stephens, "Heard Any Good Books Lately?," *Sunday Sun* (San Bernardino, Calif.), August 11, 1985, C1, C7; C1.

62. Jack Spector to Duvall Y. Hecht, March 26, 1992, BOT.

63. Jay Mathews to Duvall Y. Hecht, April 25, 1992, BOT.

64. Michael Bull discusses the car's role as a sanctuary in "Soundscapes of the Car: A Critical Study of Automobile Habitation," in *The Auditory Culture Reader,* ed. Michael Bull and Les Back (New York: Berg, 2003), 357–74.

65. McLellan, "Taped Books," N1.

66. Edwin F. Russell to Duvall Y. Hecht, April 3, 1985, BOT.

67. David Johnston to Duvall Y. Hecht, June 23, 1989, BOT.

68. Dick Kolbert to David Case, April 29, 1993, BOT.

69. Dawn Marie Lemonds to Books on Tape, December 28, 1990, BOT.

70. Helen W. Hall to Duvall Y. Hecht, August 4, 1990, BOT.

71. Sam Adam to Duvall Y. Hecht, November 14, 1984, BOT.

72. David Stanley to Duvall Y. Hecht, August 15, 1990, BOT.

73. Stuart Glassman to Books on Tape, December 17, 1992, BOT.

74. Anne Bice to Books on Tape, 1978, BOT.

75. Karin Bijsterveld tracks changing attitudes toward car noise in "Acoustic Cocooning: How the Car Became a Place to Unwind," *Senses and Society* 5, no. 2 (July 2010): 189–211.

76. Arnold H. Chadderdon to Books on Tape, December 15, 1977, BOT.

77. Armao, "Books on Tape," D5.

78. Recent studies indicate that any cognitive distractions (including listening to radios, phones, or passengers) impair driving performance. A 2013 report commissioned by the AAA Foundation for Traffic Safety concludes that recorded books are "not very distracting," however, and less risky than talking with passengers or using a hands-free cell phone. David L. Strayer et al., *Measuring Cognitive Distraction in the Automobile* (Washington, D.C.: AAA Foundation for Traffic Safety, 2013), 4, https://www.aaafoundation.org/sites/default/files/MeasuringCognitiveDistractions.pdf.

79. Quoted in Webner, "Heard a Good Book Lately?," 23.

80. The Walkman's origins are discussed at length in Paul du Gay, Linda Janes, Hugh Mackay, and Keith Negus, *Doing Cultural Studies: The Story of the Sony Walkman* (London: SAGE, 1997). Michael Brian Schiffer surveys the Walkman's predecessors in *The Portable Radio in American Life* (Tucson: University of Arizona Press, 1991).

81. Mehren and Rivera, "Audio Books," 1.

82. For example, see Iain Chambers, "A Miniature History of the Walkman," *New Formations* 11 (Summer 1990): 1–4.

83. Michael Bull, *Sounding Out the City: Personal Stereos and the Management of Everyday Life* (New York: Berg, 2000), 59–61.

84. Frances Pusch to Books on Tape, August 11, 1995, BOT. On this tradition, see Alberto Manguel's vivid account of the *lectores* at cigar factories in *A History of Reading* (London: HarperCollins, 1996), 109–14.

85. Armao, "Books on Tape," D5.

86. On changing attitudes toward women's labor, see Ruth Rosen, *The World Split Open: How the Modern Women's Movement Changed America* (New York: Penguin, 2000).

87. Lucy Jarrad-McCray to Duvall Y. Hecht, August 2, 1990, BOT.

88. Ron Ball to Books on Tape, 1979, BOT.

89. George Kirkpatrick to Duvall Y. Hecht, December 21, 1987, BOT.

90. Lynett Putterman to Books on Tape, July 14, 1991, BOT.

91. Irene J. Iwan, ed., *Words on Tape: An International Guide to the Audio Cassette Market, 1987/1988* (Westport, Conn.: Meckler, 1988).

92. Sources are listed in *Guide to Spoken-Word Recordings: Popular Literature* (Washington, D.C.: National Library Service for the Blind and Physically Handicapped, Library of Congress, 1987).

93. John Koch, "Some Books Better Heard than Seen," *Boston Globe,* March 29, 1990, 69–70; 69.

94. Lewis Grossberger, "90-Minute Novels Switch on Cassette Set," *New York Post,* April 23, 1974, 4; G. J. Goodwin to Duvall Y. Hecht, December 9, 1976, BOT.

95. BOT rented $1.6 million worth of recordings that year. Barbara Rudolph, "The Audioliterati," *Forbes,* September 10, 1984, 157–58; 157.

96. Quoted in Sara Terry, "How Some Americans Drive, Do Dishes—and 'Read' at the Same Time," *Christian Science Monitor,* November 13, 1980, 1, 10; 10.

97. National Public Radio has made tapes of its broadcasts since 1967, when Congress mandated a nonprofit alternative to commercial radio stations. On the history of public broadcasting, see Michael P. McCauley, *NPR: The Trials and Triumphs of National Public Radio* (New York: Columbia University Press, 2005).

98. Carol Stocker, "Name Your Pleasure—It's Probably on Cassette," *Boston Globe,* August 25, 1985, A21, A24; A24.

99. Ann Burns, "Library Use of Books on Audiocassettes," *Library Journal* 110 (November 15, 1985): 38–39; 38. A statistical review of the library market overall can be found in Hendrik Edelman and Karen Muller, "A New Look at the Library Market," *Publishers Weekly* 231, no. 21 (May 29, 1987): 30–35.

100. Henry Trentman, phone interview with the author, October 14, 2014.

101. Memo, "Customer Service Reaction," Susan Jin to Duvall Y. Hecht, December 18, 1987, BOT.

102. Duvall Y. Hecht to Gilbert E. Haakh, August 20, 1973, BOT.

103. Virgil L. P. Blake, "Something New Has Been Added: Aural Literacy and Libraries," in *Information Literacies for the Twenty-First Century,* ed. Virgil L. P. Blake and Renee Tjoumas (Boston: G. K. Hall, 1990), 203–18; 203.

104. Quoted in David Blaiwas, "Sideline Update: Books on Cassette," *Publishers Weekly* 225, no. 13 (March 30, 1984): 36–40; 37.

105. Mabe, "Heard Any Good Books Lately?," 1D.

106. Herbert Mitgang, "Recorded Books Help Make the Ear Faster than the Eye," *New York Times,* August 27, 1987, C19; Tom Spain, "Good News for the Holidays," *Publishers Weekly* 232, no. 25 (December 18, 1987): 29–30; 29.

107. Blaiwas, "Sideline Update," 39.

108. Ibid., 37.

109. Liz Hart, "Busy Would-Be Readers Find Time for Taped Books," *Houston Post,* November 10, 1985, 10F.

110. Stanley Young, "Heard Any Good Books?," *Los Angeles,* September 1986, 53, 57–59; 57.

111. Brilliance Audio was the exception: its unabridged titles were sold in bookstores but required a special adapter.

112. Quoted in Andy Meisler, "The Full Story," *Orange County Register,* April 19, 1996, 1, 4; 4.

113. John Zinsser, "Word-for-Word," *Publishers Weekly* 231, no. 7 (February 20, 1987): 52, 54; 52.

114. Mary Jane Scarcello, "Tapes Take New Twist," *Daily Pilot* (Newport Beach, Calif.), April 15, 1981, B9.

115. Duvall Y. Hecht to David Case, August 29, 1988, BOT.

116. Sally Swan to Ann Durbin, March 19, 1979, BOT.

117. Mark Annichiarico, "Books on Tape: Speaking Softly and Carrying a Big Backlist," *Library Journal,* November 15, 1994, 38–40; 38.

118. Quoted in John Taylor, "First We Had to Read Books, Now We Can Listen," *L. A. Federal Savings Quarterly* (Winter 1977): 4–5; 4.

119. Young, "Heard Any Good Books?," 58.

120. Jim Renick to Books on Tape, May 17, 1977, BOT.

121. Roy W. Parmenter to Books on Tape, September 28, 1978, BOT.

122. Mehren and Rivera, "Audio Books," 1.

123. "Books on Tape," *New Yorker,* June 25, 1984, 26–28; 28.

124. Alan Golden to Duvall Y. Hecht, March 25, 1992, BOT.

125. Zill and Winglee, *Who Reads Literature?,* 1. On the relationship between television and reading habits, see 69–72.

126. Quoted in McLellan, "Taped Books," N6.

127. Duvall Y. Hecht to William Messer, April 14, 1993, BOT.

128. Clive Barker, *The Body Politic in 3-D Sound* from "The Inhuman Condition," read by Kevin Conway (New York: Simon and Schuster AudioWorks, 1987), 1 cassette, 90 mins.

129. John Gabree, "Audio Books," *New York Newsday,* April 12, 1987, 20.

130. Ellipsis in the original. Carol Fitzgerald and David Fitzgerald to Books on Tape, June 25, 1979, BOT.

131. Janet Sandman to Duvall Y. Hecht, July 30, 1991, BOT.

132. Joan W. McCreary to Books on Tape, ca. 1981. Quoted in "Notes that Have Brightened Our Day," *New Releases,* May 1981, 2, clipping, BOT.

133. Margie Shetterly, "Tapes Spice Routine Chores," *Daily News-Record* (Harrisonburg, Va.), July 17, 1980, 23.

134. Eleanor Flagler, "Book Tapes Lift Drivers Out of Doldrums," *Louisville Times* (Ky), December 4, 1978, C10.

135. Dennis D. Dunn to Robert MacNeil, January 5, 1987, BOT.

136. Zauner, "Heard Any Good Books Lately?," 10.

137. "People," *Stanford Alumni Almanac,* 8.

138. Quoted in Brooke, "Talking Books," 1. Jonathan Kozol criticizes technology in *Illiterate America* (Garden City, N.Y.: Anchor/Doubleday, 1985), 160.

139. Kozol quoted in Brooke, "Talking Books," 1.

140. Mabe, "Heard Any Good Books Lately?," 1D.

141. Michael Hirsley, "Talking Cars May Soon Be Rattling Off Classics," *Gazette Telegraph* (Colorado Springs, Colo.), November 11, 1979, 12E.

142. Richard Kenyon, "The Book Publishers Want Us to Turn Over a New Tape," *Milwaukee Journal,* September 15, 1985, 2.

143. Gail Forman, "It Was a Good Hear," *Washington Post,* January 22, 1988, B5.

144. Helen Aron, "Bookworms Become Tapeworms: A Profile of Listeners to Books on Audiocassettes," *Journal of Reading* 36, no. 3 (November 1992): 208–12; 211.

145. Levin, " 'Books' for the Road," 21.

146. Rand Richards Cooper, "Can We Really Read with Our Ears? The 'Wuthering' Truth about Novels on Tape," *New York Times,* June 6, 1993, 15.

147. Sven Birkerts, *The Gutenberg Elegies: The Fate of Reading in an Electronic Age* (New York: Fawcett Columbine, 1994), 141–50; 145. Emphasis in original. The essay first appeared as "Close Listening: The Metaphysics of an Audiobook" in *Harper's Magazine,* January 1993, 86–94.

148. Birkerts, *The Gutenberg Elegies,* 146. For a cognitive neuroscientist's perspective on the shift away from print-based reading, see Maryanne Wolf and Mirit

Barzillai, "The Importance of Deep Reading," *Educational Leadership* 66, no. 6 (March 2009): 32–37.

149. Duvall Y. Hecht to Ted Neale, January 16, 1995, BOT.

9. Audio Revolution

1. Damian Horner quoted in Joel Rickett, "Talkin' 'bout a Revolution," *Bookseller* 5253 (October 27, 2006): 18.

2. "Highly Audible," *Bookseller* 5253 (October 27, 2006): 6.

3. Quoted in Jenni Laidman, "Audiobooks: Are They Really the Same as Reading?," *Chicago Tribune,* April 6, 2012, http://articles.chicagotribune.com /2012-04-06/entertainment/ct-prj-0408-audiobooks-20120406_1_audiobooks -first-book-audible-com.

4. See Bloom's criticism in Amy Harmon, "Loud, Proud, and Unabridged: It Is Too Reading!," *New York Times,* May 26, 2005, G1–G2. More recent critiques include Verlyn Klinkenborg, "Some Thoughts on the Lost Art of Reading Aloud," *New York Times,* May 16, 2009, http://www.nytimes.com/2009/05/16 /opinion/16sat4.html; and Nicholas Carr's comments in Alexandra Alter, "The New Explosion in Audiobooks," *Wall Street Journal,* August 1, 2013, http://www .wsj.com/articles/SB10001424127887323854904578637850049098298.

5. Preston Hoffman, "A Change of Voice: The Art of the Spoken Word," *Library Journal,* November 15, 1991, 39–43; 40.

6. Sandra M. Gilbert, "JAM Today and Tomorrow? Sandra M. Gilbert Considers the Position of the US Audiobook Market, Past, Present, and Future," *Bookseller* 5031 (June 21, 2002): 10–12; 11.

7. Ted Striphas, *The Late Age of Print: Everyday Book Culture from Consumerism to Control* (New York: Columbia University Press, 2009), 3.

8. See, for example, Jim Collins, *Bring on the Books for Everybody: How Literary Culture Became Popular Culture* (Durham, N.C.: Duke University Press, 2010).

9. N. Katherine Hayles, *Writing Machines* (Cambridge, Mass.: MIT Press, 2002), 29.

10. Quoted in Joanne Tangorra, "Getting the Word Out," *Publishers Weekly* 236, no. 25 (January 5, 1990): 52–53; 52.

11. "New and Notable," *Publishers Weekly* 242, no. 31 (July 31, 1995): 28. See also John B. Thompson, *Merchants of Culture: The Publishing Business in the Twenty-First Century* (Cambridge: Polity, 2010), 351.

12. Laura J. Miller discusses the growth of multimedia sidelines in *Reluctant Capitalists: Bookselling and the Culture of Consumption* (Chicago: University of Chicago Press, 2006), 132.

13. Quoted in Tangorra, "Getting the Word Out," 52.

14. This figure is for 1993 to 1997. Cited in Trudi M. Rosenblum, "From LPs to Downloads," *Publishers Weekly* 246, no. 49 (December 6, 1999): 32–33; 32.

15. Joanne Tangorra, "The Advent of the Audio Store," *Publishers Weekly* 238, no. 20 (May 3, 1991): 48–49; 49.

16. Trudi M. Rosenblum, "Audiobook Clubs and Catalogues Thrive," *Publishers Weekly* 244, no. 36 (September 1, 1997): 37–39; 37.

17. Matthew Thornton, e-mail correspondence with the author, February 24, 2015.

18. David L. Morton, Jr., *Sound Recording: The Life Story of a Technology* (Westport, Conn.: Greenwood, 2004), 190–94.

19. Trudi M. Rosenblum, "Downloading Audio from the Internet: The Future of Audio?," *Publishers Weekly* 245, no. 9 (March 2, 1998): 27–28; 27.

20. Michael Bull, "iPod Use, Mediation, and Privatization in the Age of Mechanical Reproduction," in *The Oxford Handbook of Mobile Music Studies,* ed. Sumanth Gopinath and Jason Stanyek (Oxford: Oxford University Press, 2014), 1:103–17; 115.

21. On compact discs, see Andre Millard, *America on Record: A History of Recorded Sound,* 2nd ed. (Cambridge: Cambridge University Press, 2005), 353–58.

22. On the development of digital audio files, see Jonathan Sterne, *MP3: The Meaning of a Format* (Durham, N.C.: Duke University Press, 2012).

23. Mary Burkey, "Playaway: Grab-and-Go Audio," *Booklist,* January 1 and 15, 2009, 106.

24. Press release, "Department of Defense Provides Audiobooks for Soldiers on the Front Lines," Playaway, May 27, 2008. See also Craig Morgan Teicher, "Playaway's Military Victory," *Publishers Weekly* 255, no. 35 (September 1, 2008): 20. On the military's use of portable listening devices, see Jonathan Pieslak, *Sound Targets: American Soldiers and Music in the Iraq War* (Bloomington: Indiana University Press, 2009).

25. See John Y. Cole, ed., *Books in Action: The Armed Services Editions* (Washington, D.C.: Library of Congress, 1984), and John B. Hench, *Books as Weapons: Propaganda, Publishing, and the Battle for Global Markets in the Era of World War II* (Ithaca, N.Y.: Cornell University Press, 2010), 52–54.

26. Cited in Rosenblum, "From LPs to Downloads," 33.

27. In 2006, for example, Brian Luff's "audio novel" *Sex on Legs* was published solely as a downloadable audiobook. BBC Audiobooks began commissioning original books exclusively for audio production in 2007. Anna Richardson, "BBC Commissions Audio-Only Titles," *Bookseller* 5301 (October 5, 2007): 14.

28. Beth Farrell, "The Lowdown on Audio Downloads," *Library Journal 135* (May 15, 2010), 26–29.

29. Trudi M. Rosenblum, "Audiobooks Online," *Publishers Weekly* 246, no. 23 (June 7, 1999): 48–50; 48; Shannon Maughan, "Sound Bytes: Going Digital Is All the Craze, but Cost Savings Are Not What You'd Think," *Publishers Weekly* 254, no. 6 (February 5, 2007): 29.

30. Rickett, "Talkin' 'bout a Revolution," 18.

31. On Amazon's bookselling, see Miller, *Reluctant Capitalists,* 52–53; Striphas, *The Late Age of Print,* 81–109; Thompson, *Merchants of Culture,* 41–46; Collins, *Bring on the Books for Everybody,* 39–79; and Brad Stone, *The Everything Store: Jeff Bezos and the Age of Amazon* (London: Bantam, 2013), especially 279–318.

32. "Audio Publishers Association 2012 Annual Sales Survey," October 2012, Audio Publishers Association, http://www.audiopub.org/resources-industry -data.asp.

33. Dan Eldridge, "Have You Heard?," *Book Business* 17, no. 2 (April 2014): 20–25; 20.

34. Audible's subscription plans range from $14.95 for one book per month to $229.50 a year for twenty-four books.

35. See Michael Hancher, "Learning from LibriVox," in *Audiobooks, Literature, and Sound Studies,* ed. Matthew Rubery (New York: Routledge, 2011), 199–215.

36. Ryan Joe, "Digital Grows but so Do Units: Downloadable and Hard Formats Co-existing, at Least for Now," *Publishers Weekly* 259, no. 6 (February 6, 2012): 26–27; 26. Production figures taken from the Audio Publishers Association in 2013.

37. Shannon Maughan, "Audible's DIY Audiobook Platform Turns Three," *Publishers Weekly* 261, no. 15 (April 14, 2014): 19.

38. On Amazon's relations with publishers, see George Packer, "Cheap Words," *New Yorker,* February 17, 2014, 66–79. Several aggressive maneuvers have done little to reassure publishers. Audible Authors Services paid an honorarium of one dollar per download (from a fund of $20 million) directly to authors, for example, and librarians felt the pinch in 2012 when Brilliance Audio, an Amazon subsidiary, suspended availability of all audiobook download titles to libraries. See Benedicte Page, "Amazon and Audible Raise Stakes with Publishers," *Bookseller* 5525 (April 20, 2012): 4–5.

39. For example, see Catherine Neilan, "Audible Defends Discounting," *Bookseller* 5342 (July 25, 2008): 6.

40. Nicolas Soames quoted in Tom Tivnan, "Audio Goes Mobile," *Bookseller* 5305 (November 2, 2007): 20.

41. Nicholas Jones, "Audiobooks: Craft or Commodity?," *BookBrunch,* October 25, 2013, http://www.bookbrunch.co.uk/article_free/audiobooks_craft_or _commodity.

42. See, for example, May Wuthrich, "Sustaining the Audiobook as an Art Form," *AudioFile* 23, no. 5 (February/March 2015): 10–11.

43. A-List narrator Dustin Hoffman had not read aloud since participating in a radio broadcast of *War and Peace* made after filming *The Graduate* in the 1960s. Jessica Gelt, "Audiobooks Are Going Hollywood," *Los Angeles Times,* March 14, 2012, http://articles.latimes.com/2012/mar/14/entertainment/la-et-audible -books-20120314.

44. Brian Mitchell, interview with the author, August 27, 2013.

45. Thomas A. Edison, "The Perfected Phonograph," *North American Review* 146, no. 379 (June 1888): 641–50; 646.

46. See Frances A. Koestler, *The Unseen Minority: A Social History of Blindness in the United States* (New York: David McKay, 1976), 153–75.

47. David W. Thompson, "Review: Twentieth Century Poetry in English: Contemporary Recordings of the Poets Reading Their Own Poems," *American Quarterly* 2, no. 1 (Spring 1950): 89–93; 90.

48. Stephen E. Whicher, "Current Long-Playing Records of Literature in English," *College English* 19, no. 3 (December 1957): 111–21; 113.

49. F. R. Leavis, "Reading Out Poetry," in *Reading Out Poetry; and Eugenio Montale: A Tribute* (Belfast: Queen's University of Belfast, 1979), 5–29; 16.

50. Robin F. Whitten and Sandy Bauers, "Golden Voices: Narrators Come into Their Own," *AudioFile* 6, no. 5 (November/December 1997): 15–21; 15.

51. Quoted in Peggy Constantine, "Plugging into the Talking-Book Craze," *Sun-Times* (Chicago), June 30, 1985, 24. Even audiobook naysayer Sven Birkerts admits to being intensely moved by Updike's recording of "Separating" in *The Gutenberg Elegies: The Fate of Reading in an Electronic Age* (New York: Fawcett Columbine, 1994), 147.

52. Digby Diehl, "Words in Your Ear," *Modern Maturity* 32, no. 1 (February–March 1989): 7.

53. Trudi M. Rosenblum, "Audio Sends Strong Signals," *Publishers Weekly* 243, no. 28 (July 8, 1996): 56–57; 56.

54. Joanne Tangora, "Audio Startup Makes Big Debut with Movie Tie-In," *Publishers Weekly* 238, no. 16 (April 5, 1991): 113.

55. Jacques Levy, liner notes to John Steinbeck, *The Grapes of Wrath: Excerpts,* read by Henry Fonda, Caedmon TC1570, 1978, 1 LP record.

56. Whitten and Bauers, "Golden Voices," 17.

57. Quoted in Harmon, "Loud, Proud, and Unabridged."

58. Judith McGuinn quoted in Whitten and Bauers, "Golden Voices," 21.

59. Yuri Rasovsky quoted in Aurelia C. Scott, "An Art Utterly Changed: The Art of Narration, Then and Now," *AudioFile* 20, no. 4 (December 2011/January 2012): 12–15; 12–13.

60. Nate DiMeo, "Read Me a Story, Brad Pitt: When Audiobook Casting Goes Terribly Wrong," *Slate,* September 18, 2008, http://www.slate.com/articles/arts /culturebox/2008/09/read_me_a_story_brad_pitt.html.

61. Advertisement, *AudioFile* 18, no. 3 (October/November 2009): 73.

62. Such lavish productions can be disconcerting. One reviewer complained that the relentless music steered listeners' emotions. S[ue] Z[izza], "The Word of Promise Audio Bible," *AudioFile* 18, no. 4 (December 2009/January 2010): 54.

63. Quoted in Scott, "An Art Utterly Changed," 12. Emphasis in original.

64. Quoted in ibid.

65. Joyce G. Saricks, *Read On . . . Audiobooks: Reading Lists for Every Taste* (Santa Barbara: Libraries Unlimited, 2011), xvi.

66. See Johanna Drucker, "Not Sound," in *The Sound of Poetry/ The Poetry of Sound,* ed. Marjorie Perloff and Craig Dworkin (Chicago: University of Chicago Press, 2009), 237–48.

67. Friedrich A. Kittler, *Discourse Networks 1800/1900,* trans. Michael Metteer, with Chris Cullens (Palo Alto, Calif.: Stanford University Press, 1990), 248.

68. On Sterne's attention to typography, see Peter J. de Voogd, "*Tristram Shandy* as Aesthetic Object," *Word and Image* 4, no. 1 (January–March 1988): 383–92.

69. Laurence Sterne to Jane Fenton, August 3, 1760, in *Letters of Laurence Sterne,* ed. Lewis Perry Curtis (Oxford: Clarendon, 1935), 120–21; 120.

70. "Tristram Shandy: Publisher's Summary," Audible.com (2009), http://www .audible.com/pd/Classics/Tristram-Shandy-Audiobook/B006RHGLX0/ref=a _search_c4_1_1_srTtl?qid=1426762287&sr=1–1#publisher-summary.

71. Quoted in D. T. Max, "The Unfinished: David Foster Wallace's Struggle to Surpass 'Infinite Jest,'" *New Yorker,* March 9, 2009, 48–61. Wallace explains his attachment to endnotes on 56.

72. David Foster Wallace, *Consider the Lobster and Other Essays (Selected Essays),* abridged ed., read by the author (Time Warner AudioBooks, 2005), digital audio file.

73. Andrew Adam Newman, "How Should a Book Sound? And What about Footnotes?," *New York Times,* January 20, 2006, http://www.nytimes.com/2006/01/20/books/20audi.html?pagewanted.

74. "A Note from Hachette Audio," Audible.com (2012), http://www.audible.com/pd/Fiction/Infinite-Jest-Audiobook/B007P00API/ref=a_search_c4_1_1_srTtl?qid=1426681900&sr=1–1#publisher-summary. On fan objections, see Andres Jauregui, "David Foster Wallace's 'Infinite Jest' Is an Audiobook, Minus Endnotes," *Huffington Post,* April 20, 2012, http://www.huffingtonpost.com/2012/04/19/david-foster-wallace-infinite-jest-audiobook_n_1438711.html.

75. Quoted in S. J. Henschel, "Jennifer Egan," *AudioFile* 19, no. 2 (August/September 2010): 26–27. Egan's slideshow is available at http://jenniferegan.com/books/.

76. Henry Jenkins elaborates on transmedia storytelling in *Convergence Culture: Where Old and New Collide* (New York: New York University Press, 2006), 93–130.

77. Zadie Smith, *NW* (London: Hamish Hamilton, 2012), 153; Zadie Smith, *NW,* read by Karen Bryson (New York: Penguin Audio, 2012), digital MP3 audio file.

78. For example, see Rob Reid, *Year Zero: A Novel,* read by John Hodgman (Random House Audio, 2012), digital MP3 download.

79. Smith, *NW,* 211.

80. Aziz Ansari and Eric Klinenberg, *Modern Romance: An Investigation,* narrated by Aziz Ansari (Penguin Audio, 2015), digital audio file. For examples of Aziz's hijinks, see Linda Holmes, " 'Modern Romance,' and the Emerging Audiobook," NPR, June 16, 2015, http://www.npr.org/sections/monkeysee/2015/06/16/414703875/modern-romance-and-the-emerging-audiobook.

81. Amy Poehler, *Yes Please,* read by Amy Poehler, Carol Burnett, Seth Meyers, et al. (New York: HarperAudio, 2014), digital audio file.

82. Quoted in Brian Price, "Neal Stephenson," *AudioFile* 20, no. 4 (December 2011/January 2012): 40–41; 41.

83. Quoted in Sarah Guild, "Adjust Your Headlights: Sarah Guild Looks at Some Unexpected Adaptations to Audiobook Format," *Bookseller* 5012 (February 8, 2002): 10.

84. Quoted in Guild, "Adjust Your Headlights," 10.

85. Ansari and Klinenberg, *Modern Romance.*

86. Sharon Steel, "The Soundtrack of Our Books," *Millions,* January 5, 2012, http://www.themillions.com/2012/01/the-soundtrack-of-our-books.html. Other examples can be found in Justin St. Clair, "Soundtracking the Novel: Willy Vlautin's *Northline* as Filmic Audiobook," in Rubery, *Audiobooks, Literature, and Sound Studies,* 92–106.

87. Michael Sangiacomo, untitled review, *AudioFile* 20, no. 5 (February/March 2012): 50.

88. Mary Burkey, "Audiobooks Alive with the Sound of Music," *Book Links* 18, no. 1 (September 2008): 24–25; 25.

89. Quoted in Ellen Myrick, "Say It with Music: Audiobooks with Pizzazz," *Booklist Online,* November 1, 2008, http://booklistonline.com/Say-It-with-Music-Audiobooks-with-Pizzazz-Ellen-Myrick/pid=3086522.

90. "New Talking Books Announced," *Talking Book Topics* 6, no. 4 (March 1941): 6–11; 7–8.

91. Radio's tradition of dramatizing literature extends all the way from Orson Welles's *The Mercury Theatre on the Air* to BBC Radio 4's *Classic Serial.* LA Theatre Works has been performing literature on air since broadcasting a fourteen-and-a-half-hour reading of Sinclair Lewis's *Babbitt* in 1987. Its Audio Theatre Collection now includes over 400 performances, ranging from a reenactment of the 1858 Lincoln-Douglas debates to an adaptation of Oscar Wilde's *The Picture of Dorian Gray.*

92. Quoted in James Brooke, "Talking Books for Those on the Go," *Des Moines Register,* August 13, 1985, 1.

93. "Go Behind the Scenes: The Making of the Stories from the Golden Age Audiobooks," http://www.galaxypress.com/books/audiobooks/the-making-of/.

94. Sarah Kozloff, "Audio Books in a Visual Culture," *Journal of American Culture* 18, no. 4 (1995): 83–95; 87.

95. Quoted in Stanley Young, "Heard Any Good Books?," *Los Angeles,* September 1986, 53, 57–59; 59.

96. John Goodman quoted in Ben Malczewski, "Multi-Tasker's Dream," *Library Journal* 137, no. 6 (April 1, 2012): 24–28; 26.

97. Advertisement, *AudioFile* 19, no. 2 (August/September 2010): 19.

98. Stefan Rudnicki, "In the Studio," *AudioFile* 22, no. 4 (December 2013/January 2014): 56.

99. On enhanced books and other interactive formats, see Alexis Weedon et al., "Crossing Media Boundaries: Adaptations and New Media Forms of the Book," *Convergence* 20, no. 1 (2014): 108–24.

100. Trudi M. Rosenblum, "First Enhanced CD Audiobook Released," *Publishers Weekly* 248, no. 19 (May 7, 2001): 47.

101. Matthew Thornton, e-mail correspondence with the author, February 24, 2015. Amazon's Whispersync for Voice enables synchronized e-book reading and audiobook listening. Anecdotally, I have noticed that people who use it usually can't recall which parts of the book they read and which parts they heard.

102. Thomas Leitch, *Film Adaptation and Its Discontents: From "Gone with the Wind" to "The Passion of the Christ"* (Baltimore: Johns Hopkins University Press, 2007), 258.

103. Bookless audio can be traced all the way back to the phonograph. While visiting Thomas Edison in 1888, the Reverend Horatio Nelson Powers recorded "The Phonograph's Salutation," a poem that did not yet exist on paper. (It was printed three years later in Horatio Nelson Powers, *Lyrics of the Hudson*

[Boston: Lothrop, 1891]. The verse is reprinted in Oliver Read and Walter L. Welch, *From Tin Foil to Stereo: Evolution of the Phonograph* [Indianapolis: Howard W. Sams, 1976], 413.) The Audio Book Company and other small publishers at midcentury went on to issue series recorded straight from unpublished manuscripts. (AudioGo's recent series of apocalyptic zombie stories written exclusively for audio carried on that tradition.) In 1983, Recorded Books issued Cynthia Carrington's *Astrology Rising* (1983) solely on tape. Tom Wolfe's *Ambush at Fort Bragg* (BDD Audio, 1997) has been described as the first standalone audiobook made by a major author, though it was serialized in *Rolling Stone* and eventually reprinted in the essay collection *Hooking Up* (2000).

104. Alter, "The New Explosion in Audiobooks."
105. Matthew Thornton, e-mail correspondence with the author, February 24, 2015.
106. Brilliance Audio later released the title as an e-book.
107. Quoted in Alexandra Alter, "An Art Form Rises: Audio without the Book," *New York Times,* November 30, 2014, http://www.nytimes.com/2014/12/01/business /media/new-art-form-rises-audio-without-the-book-.html.

Afterword

1. These categories are listed at http://www.gutenberg.org.
2. On speaking automata, see Steven Connor, *Dumbstruck: A Cultural History of Ventriloquism* (Oxford: Oxford University Press, 2000), and Jonathan Sterne, *The Audible Past: Cultural Origins of Sound Reproduction* (Durham, N.C.: Duke University Press, 2003), 73–77.
3. See J. Scott Hauger, "Reading Machines for the Blind: A Study of Federally Supported Technology Development and Innovation" (PhD diss., Virginia Polytechnic Institute and State University, Blacksburg, 1995).
4. See Donald Shankweiler and Carol A. Fowler, "Seeking a Reading Machine for the Blind and Discovering the Speech Code," *History of Psychology* 18, no. 1 (2015): 78–99.
5. On the techniques used by speech-processing technology, see Paul Taylor, *Text-to-Speech Synthesis* (Cambridge: Cambridge University Press, 2009). Audiobooks themselves (especially large repositories like LibriVox) constitute a valuable speech database for text-to-speech systems. See Kishore Prahallad, "Automatic Building of Synthetic Voices from Audio Books" (PhD diss., Carnegie Mellon University, July 26, 2010), available at http://www.cs.cmu.edu /~skishore/ksp_phdthesis.pdf.
6. Felix Burkhardt and Nick Campbell, "Emotional Speech Synthesis," in *The Oxford Handbook of Affective Computing,* ed. Rafael A. Calvo, Sidney K. D'Mello, Jonathan Gratch, and Arvid Kappas (Oxford: Oxford University Press, 2015), 286–95.
7. "IBM Develop 'Most Realistic' Computerised Voice," *Telegraph,* February 1, 2009, http://www.telegraph.co.uk/technology/news/4420798/IBM-develop -most-realistic-computerised-voice.html.

8. Arnie Cooper, "The Voice in the Machine: Is Lifelike Synthetic Speech Finally within Reach?" *Atlantic,* November 2011, http://www.theatlantic.com/magazine /archive/2011/11/the-voice-in-the-machine/308690/.

9. John Philip Sousa, "The Menace of Mechanical Music," *Appleton's Magazine* 8 (September 1906): 278–84; 281.

10. Farhad Manjoo, "Read Me a Story, Mr. Robot: Why Computer Voices Still Don't Sound Human," *Slate,* March 3, 2009, http://www.slate.com/articles /technology/technology/2009/03/read_me_a_story_mr_roboto.html.

11. See Masahiro Mori, "The Uncanny Valley," trans. Karl F. MacDorman and Norri Kageki, *IEEE Robotics and Automation Magazine* 19, no. 2 (June 2012): 98–100. On this concept's relation to text-to-speech, see Jan Romportl, "Speech Synthesis and Uncanny Valley," in *Text, Speech and Dialogue: 17th International Conference, TSD 2014,* ed. Petr Sojka et al. (Cham, Switzerland: Springer, 2014), 595–602.

12. Quoted in James Parker, "The Mind's Ear," *New York Times,* November 25, 2011, http://www.nytimes.com/2011/11/27/books/review/the -minds-ear.html?_r=0.

13. John Hull, e-mail correspondence with the author, May 12, 2014.

14. Heather Cryer and Sarah Home document the gradual acceptance of these voices in *Exploring the Use of Synthetic Speech by Blind and Partially Sighted People* (Birmingham, U.K.: RNIB Centre for Accessible Information, 2008).

15. Roy Blount, Jr., "The Kindle Swindle," *New York Times,* February 24, 2009, http://www.nytimes.com/2009/02/25/opinion/25blount.html.

16. On the influence of speech technologies over the arts, see Norie Neumark, Ross Gibson, and Theo van Leeuwen, eds., *Voice: Vocal Aesthetics in Digital Arts and Media* (Cambridge, Mass.: MIT Press, 2010).

17. Jon Stewart, *America (The Audiobook): A Citizen's Guide to Democracy Inaction,* abridged ed., read by the author (Time Warner AudioBooks, 2004), digital audio file.

18. Aziz Ansari and Eric Klinenberg, *Modern Romance: An Investigation,* narrated by Aziz Ansari (Penguin Audio, 2015), digital audio file.

Credits

Figure 2.7.	Courtesy of the American Foundation for the Blind, Talking Book Archives (ID no. 356).
Figure 2.8.	Courtesy of Samuel P. Hayes Research Library, Perkins School for the Blind Archives, Watertown, Massachusetts.
Figure 2.9.	Courtesy of the American Foundation for the Blind, Talking Book Archives (ID no. 102608).
Figure 3.1.	Courtesy of the American Foundation for the Blind, Talking Book Archives (ID no. 4089).
Figure 5.1.	Photograph by Thomas Keith Aitken (Second Lieutenant). Ministry of Information First World War Official Collection. © Imperial War Museum (Catalogue no. Q 11586).
Figure 5.2.	Blind Veterans UK © Collections and Archives.
Figure 5.3.	© 1921. Wellcome Library, London (ID no. V0048477). Creative Commons Attribution 4.0 International (CC BY 4.0).
Figure 5.4.	© Blind Veterans UK Collections and Archives.
Figure 5.5.	© Blind Veterans UK Collections and Archives, OGA 4796.
Figure 5.6.	© Blind Veterans UK Collections and Archives.
Figure 5.7.	Reprinted with permission. Copyright © Royal National Institute of Blind People (RNIB).
Figure 5.8.	Reprinted with permission. Copyright © Royal National Institute of Blind People (RNIB).
Figure 6.1.	Reprinted with permission. Copyright © Royal National Institute of Blind People (RNIB).
Figure 7.1.	Photograph by Rollie McKenna. © Rosalie Thorne McKenna Foundation. Courtesy of the Center for Creative Photography, The University of Arizona Foundation. CCP Accession no. ag228 _bwp_70_caedmon_1.
Figure 7.2.	Cover of 1952 Caedmon recording from *Dylan Thomas Reading "A Child's Christmas in Wales" by Dylan Thomas*. © 1952 by HarperCollins Publishers. Reprinted by permission of HarperCollins Publishers.
Figure 7.3.	Talking Book Corporation Record Trade Card, "I Am a Dancing Girl" (1919). Image reproduction courtesy of Ryan Barna.
Figure 7.4.	"Talking Book" recording of F. Scott Fitzgerald's *The Great Gatsby*, read by Alexander Scourby. Libraphone, Inc., Long Branch, NJ (Libraphone A-1621). Image reproduced from the collections at the University of California, San Diego Library.
Figure 8.1.	Courtesy of Sigrid Hecht and Duvall Hecht.
Figure 8.2.	Books on Tape, Inc., Los Angeles, California.
Figure 8.3.	Courtesy of Duvall Hecht (founder of Books on Tape, Inc.).
Figure 8.4.	Courtesy of Duvall Hecht.
Figure 8.5.	Courtesy of Duvall Hecht.

Figure 8.6.   Blackstone Audio, Ashland, Oregon. As reprinted in Sarah Kozloff, "Audio Books in a Visual Culture," *Journal of American Culture* 18, no. 4 (Winter 1995): 90. Image reproduction courtesy of Sarah Kozloff.

Figure 8.7.   Published by Random House Audio, 1985.

Figure 9.1.   Courtesy of Matthew Thornton, Audible Inc., an Amazon company.

Figure 9.2.   Courtesy of Carl Amari, Falcon Picture Group, LLC.

Acknowledgments

This project involved listening to people as well as books. My biggest debt is to Garrett Stewart for supporting my research in too many ways to count after we met through a shared admiration for John le Carré's audiobooks. Helen Small likewise deserves special thanks for tirelessly backing this project from the outset. Jay Clayton, Simon Eliot, Francis O'Gorman, and Patricia Meyer Spacks all provided crucial and much appreciated help at early stages too.

This book has benefited immeasurably from the advice of friends, colleagues, and audiobibliophiles. It was begun at the American Academy of Arts and Sciences in the stimulating company of Benjamin Coates, Mary Maples Dunn, Benjamin Fagan, Daniel Geary, Chin Jou, Katherine Lee, Melissa Milewski, Lisa Siraganian, and Matthew Sussman. Subsequent chapter drafts were substantially improved by advice from Jason Camlot, Lisa Gitelman, Chris Hilliard, Annie Janowitz, Jessica Pressman, Sejal Sutaria, Barbara Taylor, Vanessa Warne, and Clair Wills.

Conversations and correspondence with the following people helped shape my thinking: Julie Anderson, Paul Armstrong, Bill Bell, Charles Bernstein, Karen Bourrier, Angus Brown, Rachel Buurma, Roger Chartier, Amanda Claybaugh, Steven Connor, Patricia Crain, Santanu Das, Mike Dicecco, Marcy Dinius, Stephen Donovan, James Emmott, Maria Engberg, James English, Patrick Feaster, Danielle Fuller, Kevin Gilmartin, Ezra Greenspan, Helen Groth, Michael Hancher, Mark B. N. Hansen, Phoebe Harkins, Iben Have, Chris Hilliard, Rachel Hutchinson, Juliet John, Cora Kaplan, Georgina Kleege, Sarah Kozloff, Ross Macfarlane, David Mason, Andrew Maunder, D. A. Miller, Selina Mills, Karla Nielsen, Corrina Norrick-Rühl, Brigitte Ouvry-Vial, Josey Packard, Jussi Parikka, Birgitte Stougaard Pedersen, John Plotz, Martin Regal, Catherine Robson, Jonathan Rose, Vanessa Ryan, Elaine Scarry, Sally Shuttleworth, Lisa Surridge, Joanna Swafford, Hannah Thompson, David Thorburn, Heather Tilley, Shafquat Towheed, Robin Whitten, and Tom Wright.

357

I'm also indebted to the pioneering contributors to *Audiobooks, Literature, and Sound Studies.* To John Hull I owe special thanks for correspondence that has enriched the manuscript. Thanks also to Mara Mills for sharing her expertise and for organizing a conference with me in London entitled "Blindness, Technology, and Multimodal Reading." Colin Blakemore, Laurent Cohen, Ophelia Deroy, Robert Englebretson, and Evelyne Mercure patiently answered my questions about neuroscience. Yannis Agiomyrgiannakis and Hwasung Lee kindly met with me at Google's offices in London to discuss the future of speech synthesis. Thanks also to members of the ARSC, SHARP, and VICTORIA e-mail discussion lists and of Reddit for fielding various queries. Finally, my colleagues at Queen Mary University of London have been steadfast resources and company.

A number of people associated with the audio publishing industry graciously took the time to answer my questions. I want to thank Toni Morrison, Michael Rosen, and Amy Tan for speaking to me about reading aloud their books. Juliet Stephenson and David Thorpe helpfully shared their views on the art of narration. My thanks to Robert Kirkwood for a tour of RNIB's studios during the recording of a racy Jackie Collins novel. I'm grateful to Duvall Hecht, Barbara Holdridge, and Henry Trentman for allowing me to interview them. It was especially generous of Hecht to ship the Books on Tape archive to me (and of my mother to store the boxes in her garage until they found a more secure home at Stanford's libraries). Dan Musselman helpfully provided me with Books on Tape's first recording. I learned a tremendous amount from publishers, too, including Guy Story and Matthew Thornton at Audible; Ana Maria Allessi, David Brawn, and Jo Forshaw at HarperCollins; Nicolas Soames at Naxos; Ravina Bajwa and Roy McMillan at Penguin; Brian Mitchell at Silksoundbooks; and Nicholas Jones at Strathmore.

Presenting my work at conferences and elsewhere inevitably led to smart feedback as well as nominations for my growing list of the audiobook's greatest hits. The "Books and/as New Media" symposia at Harvard and Edinburgh gave me the opportunity to discuss my ideas with Mark Algee-Hewitt, Luisa Calè, Lindsey Eckert, Anthony Grafton, Faye Hammill, Michelle Levy, Deidre Lynch, Tom Mole, Stephen Osadetz, Andrew Piper, Jonathan Sachs, Andrew Stauffer, Kathryn Sutherland, and Richard Taws. I'm grateful for conversations at the following events, too: "Literature, Media, and Sound" at Aarhus University; "Art in Translation" at the University of Iceland; "Victorian Media," held by the Victorian Studies Association of Western Canada; "in:flux 1845–1945: A Century in Motion" at the University of Birmingham; and the London Nineteenth Century Seminar Graduate Conference. Thanks also to Harvard's History of the Book and Victorian Literature and Culture seminars; the University of Pennsylvania's History of Material Texts Workshop; Simon Fraser University's Print Culture series; Birkbeck's Forum for Nineteenth-Century Studies and Material Texts Network; Cardiff's Centre for Editorial and Textual Research; Royal Holloway's Centre for Victorian Studies; and Oxford's Interdisciplinary Nineteenth-Century Culture Forum. My gratitude extends as well to audiences at the Université du Maine, University of Greenwich, University of Hertfordshire, University of Surrey, University of Sussex, Uppsala University, and panels held at MLA, SHARP, and Dickens Society conferences, and also one at the "Blind Creations" conference.

This book's archival research would have been impossible without the guidance and ingenuity of archivists, curators, and librarians. I'd like to thank in particular the American Foundation for the Blind (especially Helen Selsdon); the American Printing House for the Blind (especially Michael Hudson and Anne Rich); Blind Veterans UK (especially Robert Baker); the British Library (especially Stephen Cleary and Jonathan Summers); the EMI Archive Trust (especially Jackie Bishop and Joanna Hughes); Harvard's libraries (especially Christina Davis, Chloe Garcia Roberts, and Don Share at the Woodberry Poetry Room); the Library of Congress; the National Library Service for the Blind and Physically Handicapped (especially Ruth Nussbaum, Steve Prine, Dawn Stitzel, and MaryBeth Wise); the Perkins Library (especially Kim Charlson and Jan Seymour-Ford); the Royal National Institute of Blind People (especially Lesley-Anne Alexander, Pat Beech, Helen Brazier, Clive Gardiner, Sarah Haylett, Philip Jeffs, Robert Saggers, Ian Turner, and Sean Wilcox); and the Thomas Edison National Historic Park (especially Jerry Fabris).

I would like to thank John Kulka and the staff at Harvard University Press for guiding my manuscript through the publication process. I'm equally grateful to its anonymous readers for their thoughtful advice. Chapter 1 appeared as "Canned Literature: The Book after Edison," *Book History* 16 (2013): 216–46. Published by the Johns Hopkins University Press. Copyright © 2013 by the Society for the History of Authorship, Reading & Publishing. Chapter 5 is an updated and slightly expanded rendition of "From Shell Shock to Shellac: The Great War, Blindness, and Britain's Talking Book Library," *Twentieth Century British History* 26, no. 1 (2015): 1–25. Published by Oxford University Press. © 2014 by Matthew Rubery.

Financial support was vital to the completion of this book. I gratefully acknowledge support from the American Academy of Arts and Sciences; Bibliographical Society of America; British Academy; British Library; Chartered Institute for Library and Information Professionals' Library and Information History Group; Leverhulme Trust; National Endowment for the Humanities; and Wellcome Trust. Their generous backing enabled me to carry out a more ambitious research agenda than originally intended and to reach a wider audience.

The comedian Amy Poehler proposes that every book written by parents with children under the age of six should carry a "sleep deprived" sticker. This book certainly warrants one. The past few years of my life have been split between talking books and talking babies. Hence, my final thanks go to my equally sleep-deprived wife, Victoria, and to the culprits of our sleep deprivation, Joseph and Coco. They're now the first to tell me when I'm reading books the wrong way. This one is dedicated to them.

Index